Making Music with

Ableton Live

Dave Hill

PC Publishing

PC Publishing
Export House
130 Vale Road
Tonbridge
Kent TN9 1SP
UK

Tel 01732 770893
Fax 01732 770268
email info@pc-publishing.com
web site http://www.pc-publishing.com

First published 2003

© 2003 Muska & Lipman Publishing, a division of Course Technology

ISBN 1 870775 88 0

British Library Cataloguing in Publication Data
A catalogue record for this book is available from the British Library

Printed in Great Britain by Biddles, Guildford

Introduction

My first experience with Ableton Live dates back to the 2001 Winter NAMM show where Ableton CEO Gerhard Behles and Live conceptualist, Robert Henke (a.k.a. Monolake) demo'd an early beta of Live 1.0. I was there on behalf of Remix magazine, then a fledgling startup zine, begging for cool software to demo. The buzz at the show was that two strikingly tall and savvy German software engineers were showing an out of this world loop software application – something akin to Acid Pro or Sonar, but more fluid and built for live performance, improvisation, and instant loop browsing. This I had to see, and I bee-lined to meet Henke and Behles at their lime-green booth in NAMM's 'software row.' After shaking my hand, Behles smiled confidently and offered me the last chair left in their demo space. Henke was already hunched over his machine readying the next performance, which I assumed was to be the typical pre-constructed software demo, polished up back at the lab for maximum show-floor wow. But a funny thing happened when the demo began, I could without question hear a musician at work. As Henke's slender fingers moved over the mouse and keyboard, I could hear crescendos, fade-outs, filter sweeps, and loops firing. All the while, a musical arrangement was forming. Every so often, Henke's brow would scrunch as he stumbled upon some beta bug or undiscovered method for working within his then infantile – he might say 'his baby' – application. He would stop and note any inconsistencies, and then continue playing, mixing in new combinations of his pre-made loops for the first time, simultaneously discovering and demo'ing the amazing power of his own software, Live. As I stood for the next couple of hours, riveted to each successive demo, light bulb after light bulb began to flash in my mind. Would the years I'd spent editing audio on a computer with paint and play arranging begin to fade? Could it really be possible to perform music from a computer?

Yes, and yes. Since my first launch of Live 1.0, I have become an avid fan, learning to perform, automate, and record in a software application that somehow thinks like I do, as a musician. Currently, I use Live 2 in nearly all of my musical projects, and have also done what I can to evangelize the amazing technology. Why? Because I want Ableton to thrive, continue what they have started, and release many more upgrades for Live. In meeting the Ableton team, I recognized their commitment to greatness, and their willingness to admit how the software could be improved and to openly discuss the dreaded 'b-word' (bugs). Without exception, every single software application has bugs, but few companies want to talk about them. This book continues this self-imposed mission, to spread the power of Live, and my independent hope to see Live 3.0, 4.0, and beyond. I have taken great care to interview other Live power users, glean insider tips from Live's inventors, and document my own examples when performing and recording with Live. Ableton has seen each chapter in this book and has officially approved of this book.

Making Music with Ableton Live is the world's first comprehensive guide to making music with Ableton's revolutionary live performance and studio software, Live. Whether you are a digital audio beginner or a seasoned pro, this book explores each fundamental feature within Live, and provides power-user tips and insider tricks for integrating Live into your home or professional studio. But this is just the beginning. Every last feature, button, fader, and effect in Live was designed for the live performer. *Making Music with Ableton Live* is a book written for musicians by a musician who uses and discusses the software on a daily basis. Whether you use Live for producing, composing, DJing, or film and television, *Making Music with Ableton Live* will help you to put the fun back into music made by computers.

About the author

While I am first and foremost a drummer, I got started toying with samplers at age 16, when I bought producer, composer, and guitarist extraordinaire David Torn's old Emax II sampler. You could say my first few lessons in sampling were days spent sifting through Torn's spine-tinglingly cool sample patches, scratching my head, and then trying to recreate comparable sounds. Since that time, I have become fascinated with drum machines, synthesizers, effects, and finally, the recording process. Through working with a number of inspiring people – most notably Michael Shrieve (ex-Santana drummer); Brad Houser (of Edie Brickell and the New Bohemians and Critters Buggin'), James Rotondi (former sideman with Air and Mr.

Bungle); and Bob Green (a.k.a. The Grassy Knoll) – I began to write music. Nearly a decade after purchasing my first sampler, I discovered the joys of working with audio inside computers, recombining my own drum recordings, and producing several different musical projects. I now live in New York, produce the music for my two projects, jettatura (www.jettatura.com) and brainboxing (www.brainboxing.net), and continue to write for Remix (www.remixmag.com), Mix (www.mixonline.com), Electronic Musician (www.emusician.com), Modern Drummer (www.moderndrummer.com), Guitar World's Bass Guitar (www.guitarworld.com), and whoever else happens to call.

Acknowledgments

Congratulations on your purchase of Ableton Live and *Making Music with Ableton Live*. You have taken a brave and intelligent step toward the future of music – electronic and otherwise – by choosing to make music with Live. It is my sincere hope that this book lives up to the innovation and quality of its subject, Live, an application that I have come to know intimately and rely upon daily. I have put my all into this book to ensure that it is the ultimate learning tool.

I must also credit the incredible innovation of Ableton, and its leaders Gerhard Behles (Ableton CEO), Robert Henke (incredible musician behind Monolake and Ableton Live conceptualist), Bernd Roggendorf, and Jan Bohl for giving me such brilliant subject matter. And thanks to the Ableton marketing team, Vanessa Schmoranzer and Claudia Weidner, who helped my early education on Live. Huge thanks also to Marsha Vdovin, the most knowledgeable press person I know, and Michael Zorn for his help with Ableton's technical edit of this book.

I must also thank my darling Amber for her infinite support, encouragement, love, faith, and loop tolerance, Mr. James Rotondi, my friend, first editor, and co-conspirator in my band Jettatura. Bob Green (a.k.a. The Grassy Knoll), who taught me how to finish what I've started. Bill and Nicky Walters, Steven Cope, Greg Hoy, Erik Rabasca (cuE branE), and Clinton Mainland for being there. Thanks too to Eric Persing for lessons in sound, Jason Donnelly and John Zachman for lending sounds, and my many music teachers, Donald Denegar, Steve Smith, Jeff Hamilton, Matt Chamberlain, David Garibaldi, Freddie Gruber, Garey Williams, Steve Hill, Mike Peterson, and Jerry Garcia. And my eternal thanks and love to Michael Shrieve, who taught me to embrace the future and always be making music – no matter the whims of record labels, management, or other peripheral music biz people.

And finally, I want to send thanks and love to my parents, Jean and Dave, Sr., for putting up with the noise and loving me always. And to my sister Laura, this one is for you, kid. I know you don't do loop-based electronica, but I don't know how many books I'll write.

Thanks for listening; have a lot of fun with Live.
DH

Contents

What you'll find in this book

- Step-by-step instructions on how to create, produce, and remix music in Live.
- Basic definitions of key digital audio concepts such as: What is a sample? What is a loop? and How do my loops and samples become music?
- Loop-making ideas and tips.
- Full explanation of Live's effects and how to use VST plug-ins in Live.
- Audio-interface and MIDI-controller tips and recommendations.
- Simple yet complete explanation of MIDI, as it pertains to Live.
- Recommendations on choosing and using an audio editor for optimizing your loops and samples.
- Step-by-step guide to editing, recording, performing, and paint and play composing with Ableton Live.
- Expert tips, tricks, and interview excerpts with world-famous Live power users and performers.
- Specialized hardware considerations to help musicians feel at home performing with Live.
- How Live, the sequencing instrument, will reinvent your own music and attitude about making music (and not just recording it) on a computer.
- How ReWire makes Live the hub of your software studio, or your new favourite sampler.
- Carefully edited and labelled screen shots give you a first-person view of how experts work in Live.
- Solid web resources throughout the book that will link you to Live-related topics.
- Companion website with templates, updates, and free loops.

Who this book is for

This book is for anyone who wants to make music with audio loops and samples. Ableton Live sews the seams existing between digital audio, live performance, software synchronization, musicality, and fun on a Mac or PC. If you've heard of Live's 'magical' audio and loop dexterity, let this book be your guide to unlocking that power. Or, if you have already discovered Live and want to take your performing and composing skills to the next level, *Making Music with Ableton Live* was written for you.

How this book is organized

Making Music with Ableton Live is divided into 14 chapters and two appendixes. Each chapter contains targeted direction and thoughtful notes about every aspect of Live. The chapters can be read sequentially or used as a reference. This book is not intended to replace the Ableton Live User Manual, but should instead serve as an informed guide to transforming your PC or Mac into a musical instrument, audio workstation, or recording studio. You will also find six 'Who's Using Live?' sections dispersed throughout the book, which show how pros are taking advantage of the many facets of Live.

- **Chapter 1, *Live*** We will begin with a brief introduction to Live, the concept behind its development, and a basic overview of how you might use Live both on stage and in the studio.
- **Chapter 2, *Getting started*** To get you up and running, Chapter 2 provides key PC- and Mac-related recommendations for hardware, choosing an audio interface, installing and running Live, and basic MIDI setup.
- **Chapter 3, *Live interface basics*** This chapter will take you through Live's two main interfaces – Session and Arranger – point out key controls, talk about how to get help and instruct you on how to set up your first song. Chapter 3 teaches you about Clip View and Live's Control (transport) bar, song settings, customization, and general maneuvering in Live. Even experts may pick up tricks in this chapter.
- **Chapter 4, *Digital audio basics*** If you're brand new to the realm of digital audio, this chapter's for you. Sample rate, bit depth, digital glitches and peaks – it's all here. Chapter 4 will also discuss how Live handles (renders and records) digital audio, what makes a sample a sample, and a loop a loop.
- **Chapter 5, *Making music in Live*** Live is used by many different types of people for several different applications. Chapter 5 outlines the four most common ways to make music with Live, unveils key working methods for each group, demystifies the Clip View (warp modes, transients, and sample settings), and dives deep into the Live composition process. Whether you are a DJ, producer, film/television composer, or live musician, this chapter is packed with intermediate level tips and will warm you up for what is to come.
- **Chapter 6, *Playing Live … live*** If you've never seen a musician improvise or perform with a computer, look out. Chapter 6 tells you how to go from count off to cut off without a digital hiccup. You will see how to build a set (or song) in Live, catch some of Live's co-creator Robert Henke's working methods, and garner a huge array of power tips from users all over the globe. You will also learn strategies for mapping MIDI or computer keyboard controllers to harness Live's power in a live setting.
- **Chapter 7, *Editing your performance*** When the gig is done or you've recorded your last take, it is time to edit, overdub, and arrange. Chapter 7 provides some basic music arranging ideas as well as a fat dose of mix and effect automation, rearranging your content, and tips for finalizing your song. This is the book's most focused discussion of rendering and is not to be missed – some say its not how you play, but how you finish.
- **Chapter 8, *Live's effects*** Live's effects are an impressive array of delays, dynamic utilities, and other experimental sonic wizardry. Add to this Live's ability to use VST plug-ins, and the sound processing possibilities are nearly limitless. Chapter 8 attempts to summarize the possibilities.
- **Chapter 9, *Using MIDI*** This chapter takes a deeper look at how to synchronize Live with hardware and software using MIDI Time Code or MIDI Clock. We will also explore MIDI latency, and learn how to optimize Live for use with the most common MIDI controllers and triggers.
- **Chapter 10, *Wave editing tips*** Building on what we started in Chapter 4, Chapter 10 teaches you how to make the most of your samples by using an audio editor. For those who don't have a third-party application, Live's Arranger

View can also be used to optimize loops for live performance, and clean up problematic samples.

- **Chapter 11, *Where to get loops***   The fuel for making music in Live is loops. The better your loops, the better your music. In Chapter 11, I encourage you to go for broke in buying, making, and downloading fresh (and legal) sample material for your future Live projects.
- **Chapter 12, *Recording in Live***   Chapter 12 is the one we've all be waiting for. This chapter will take you through the various ways Live captures audio, how to ensure a clean signal, methods for minimizing input and output latency, and some other inventive tricks for recording success. Live 2's new recording features, such as punch-in and punch-out, and Arranger View recording will be covered in detail here.
- **Chapter 13, *ReWire – synchronizing your software***   ReWire is the key to linking Live with other powerful applications. The good news is you already own it (once you own Live). Now make it swing. Both ReWire master and ReWire slave will be covered.
- **Chapter 14, *Power tips – the magic of Live!***   Chapter 14 is for those looking to take full advantage of Ableton's powerful Warp Marker technology. Other topics include making convincing (or perhaps strange) feels within your loops, how to make breakbeats, and several never before disclosed tips.

Keeping the book's content current

My editors and I have remained in close contact with Ableton throughout the writing of this book to ensure that each instruction, recommendation, and tip works with the most recent version of Live – 2.0.3 at the time of this writing. What's more, Ableton has reviewed and signed off on each chapter during the spring and summer of 2003. However, occasionally ghosts infiltrate the machine. If you should find any errors or have suggestions for future editions, please contact us through the PC Publishing website.

www.pc-publishing.com/downloads

At this site, you can find updates, corrections, and other information related to the content of the book. You should also regularly visit the Ableton website (www.ableton.com) and my personal site www.brainboxing.net/abletonlive for software updates and helpful advice found in Ableton's user forum.

Live

E very so often, a new piece of technology or software application makes an indelible mark on the way things are done. Be it the arrival of the electric guitar, a new kind of synthesizer, or the invention of digital audio recording, the impact on musicians, and the artistic world, can be both major and long lasting. Once conceived, technology can take on a life of its own, inspire a range of other complementary technologies, or even spawn a whole new school of thought. Ableton's Live has instigated a revolution in the audio software world by transforming computers into playable musical instruments, real-time remix stations, and the world's most dexterous audio environment. Live is the culmination of the studio software development of the mid to late 90s and the infusion of DJ and electronic music-making instincts. Live is also a labour of love born out of the desire of a few software-savvy musicians, who wanted to take their elabourate computer-based recording studio on the road.

Like any new idea, the possible uses for Live are only beginning to emerge. From the laptop blip-hop stylings of musicians like Kid606, Monolake, and Akufen, to the more mainstream remix and dance music production of John Tejada, or BT, Live's user base is made up of professionals who demand the most from their tools. Add film scoring and television music to Live's current resume of qualifications, such as Rick Marvin (*U-571* and HBO's *Six Feet Under*) or Klaus Badelt (*Mission Impossible 2, Pearl Harbor*, and *Hannibal*), and Ableton's endorsement list just continues to grow. Recently, former Nine Inch Nails keyboardist and television music composer, Charlie Clouser said this of Live: 'With Nine Inch Nails, it took us two years to finish a record. Today, I finish cues in seven minutes. Without Ableton, it simply couldn't happen. Within eight seconds of downloading the demo, I knew I had to have it at any price'. The ease and skill with which Live can handle audio is a natural for film and TV work.

Live is also a digital DJ performance tool and has begun to replace MP3-based DJ units, CD spinners, and turntables. Also, it is becoming increasingly common to see laptop performing artists employing computers as their primary sound source or record collection. This makes perfect sense when you stop to think that, for the last couple of years, synthesizers, samplers, and their sounds have been purchased en masse via web download or e-mail, instead of as a separate hardware component or sound module. In the next couple of years, more and more musicians, bands, and solo artists will be using Live's technology to realize their artistic vision from the comfort of their own laptop.

What is Live?

In January 2000, Berlin-based Ableton knocked the audio software world on its ear by releasing Live 1.0, the world's first 'Sequencing Instrument'. What is a sequencing instrument, you ask? I too wondered how software might transform a generic PC or Macintosh computer into a musical instrument. Or how it would be possible to access and integrate samples, MIDI, effects, and live audio data quickly and musically enough for a live performance. But after some initial head scratching, much beta testing, and a bit of trial and error, the light bulbs have begun to glow.

A *sequencing instrument*, in Ableton-speak, is one part performance and the other part pre-performance. Similar to a modern software MIDI-sequencer or production sampler, Live (Figure 1.1) relies heavily on your pre-recorded material, and can then be set up to arrange these loops and samples by placing them onto a large, customizable grid. The grid can be thought of as both a loop organizer and sonic palette. Once samples have been dragged into a cell on the grid, you may designate MIDI or computer keyboard triggering options for these sounds, alter the sounds' play functions, and add effects. After you have filled enough cells for the track, it is time for 'the take' or live performance.

This grid/sonic palette makes up the sequencer component of Live, and can be

Figure 1.1
Here is a quick peek at the Session View grid in Live 2.0. The rows make up musical sections called scenes, while the columns function as virtual mixer channels.

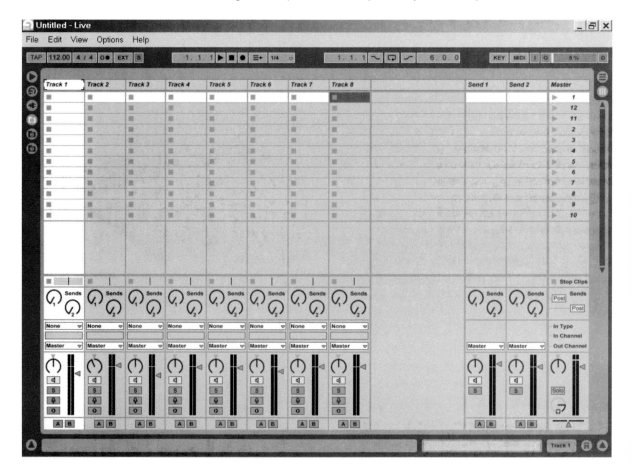

used to trigger groups of loops, like sections of a song. For instance, during a live performance, you might want to progress from the verse to the chorus and then back again. You can do so by triggering a specified row in Live's sample matrix, which in turn directs Live to play the second group of loops (the chorus) and to stop playing the verse loops. To go back you would merely click on the preceding row. This makes it easy to jump around through various sub-sections of the song, break down important song sections, and come up with new possibilities. In addition, any individual samples contained within a grid cell can be played independently, in similar fashion to an 'old school' phrase sampler (like Roland's Dr. Sample). It is quite possible to make altogether new loops and original ideas by playing these one-shot samples, or to overdub a previously made arrangement. Keep in mind that these sounds can be tweaked to oblivion, much like a hardware sampler, only more flexibly with Live.

The 'instrument' housed within Live is the software's ability to play, or play with, sound. Live can be played in a 'jam' situation or simply used as a creative tool to make new loops and samples for your next live set. Live specializes in stretching audio to any desired tempo or pitch. What's more, Live can bend audio within itself so that a sound may start at one tempo or pitch and end up in an entirely different place (all within the same performance). Imagine the editing possibilities. Lucky for us, they have. Ableton has made recording and editing the performance a main function of Live, so that a single software application turns your laptop (or desktop) PC/Mac into a live performance instrument, a multi-track recording studio, a powerful loop and song editor, and a full-blown remix factory. In other words, Live enables you to map the cells of your grid-palette (full of samples) to a MIDI controller or computer keyboard. You can then play your sounds, or rows of sounds, and recombine them with effects, other samples, or overdubs. Then you can record the whole performance for later editing (if needed). In essence, you record a live improvisation for later editing, further arranging, overdubs, and added automation. If the final mix isn't to your liking, you can always take another pass. To get an idea of what I'm talking about, look at Figure 1.2 (see page 4), which features a screenshot of Live's Arranger View.

Musically speaking, Live is a one-two punch whose focus is spread equally between live performance and recording/editing, all in one application. As you learn how to play (jam) in Live, you will also be gradually setting up your song's arrangement and learning new tactics to apply to your live performance. In other words, Live is quite unlike any other software application currently on the market and fills a certain void that has been overlooked by the majority of developers – the needs of the performing and recording musician.

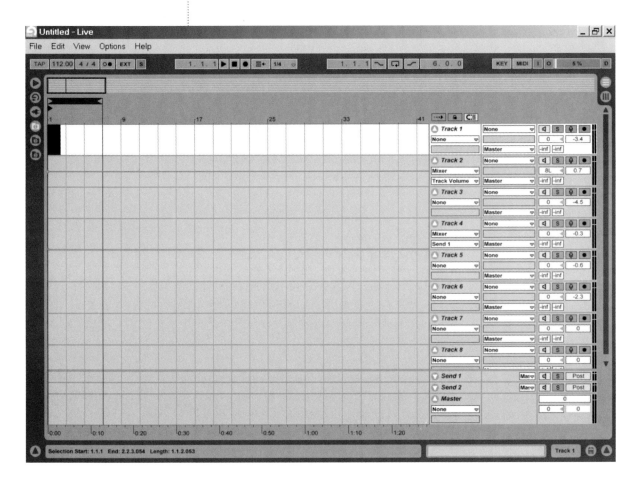

Figure 1.2
If you are familiar with desktop audio, Live's
Arranger View may remind you of many
different programs. However, Live's feature
set is sure to raise a few standards for many
years to come.

Why was Live developed?

One of the greatest advantages for musicians employing Live is that this is a program written for musicians, by musicians. They actually use the very software they
create. And that is a fact we can all take comfort in. Initially, Robert Henke and
Gerhard Behles (paired in the Berlin-based electronica group Monolake) were looking for a better way to create their own music through the use of a computer. Both
were experienced sound designers and had spent time working for Native
Instruments, one of the industry's chief authorities on virtual or 'soft' synthesizers
and sound design software. At the time, the industry lacked a user-friendly software application conducive to creating music as a musician would, intuitively and
spontaneously. There were plenty of 'loop-friendly' applications, and more than a
couple live jamming programs, but most audio software was built for studio use and
lacked the interface necessary to create music the way a musician does: live.

Since the drawing board days in Live's development, Behles, Henke, and the
Ableton team have honed Live's interface and functionality with the performing
artist in mind. While complex, build-your-own software suites, such as Native
Instruments' Reaktor and Cycling '74's MAX/MSP, are powerful sound-generators,
they often prove too complex for the performing musician who may be contending
with any number of distractions, including lighting, sound system woes, fog, etc.

Live, on the other hand, was developed (and has been continually improved) to be the best possible live performance system available on a computer. It contains professional-grade audio tools and software compliance, such as VST effect plug-ins and ReWire software-studio synchronization. These tools will be discussed in greater detail as we progress, but for now, recognize Ableton's commitment to the performing artist and to the end user. And don't just take my word for it, jump on out to Ableton's closely monitored user forum at www.ableton.com, where you can anonymously enter your own wish list of ideas for future development of Live. Don't be too surprised if Ableton CEO Gerhard Behles, Conceptualist Robert Henke, or any of the other Ableton developers chime in to discuss how your idea might better the world of Live.

The world of Live

Over the last several years, the idea of live performance on a PC or Mac has become increasingly attractive. With the ramp-up in processing power and audio storage capacities, even relatively inexpensive computers have become powerful audio editing and recording studios. Producers using audio software have enjoyed exponential improvements in performance and the number and types of tasks performable by a computer. Also, the customization and potential for add-on software/hardware as new technology emerges has made it less intimidating to jump into the fray. For less than £1500, you can acquire a decent laptop, a sound card, and the most powerful and flexible live performance software on the planet, Live. For just a bit more, it is quite possible that your bedroom studio could compete with the pros. Not to mention the fact that an investment in an Ableton Live performance rig is easily cheaper and easier to maintain than a stack of hardware samplers, rack-mounted sound modules, outboard mixers and, well, you get the point.

How does it work?

Live allows you to sort your music into easy-to-define sections, called scenes, while maintaining all the flexible effects and routing options made possible only via PC- or Mac-based software. These scenes, spread horizontally across the screen, look like the rows of a spreadsheet or graph. The columns that are formed correspond with mixer channels. Within each column, only one loop can sound at a time. So to run down your track, you can literally run down the rows, letting each row represent a musical section. Live also enables you to trigger loops and samples, tweak effects, and change mix settings from a MIDI controller, MIDI keyboard, or computer keyboard. You can pre-listen to any loop in real-time at any tempo from within your project. Enhancements in 2.0 empower Live users to handle different kinds of loops specific to their content. For example, a drum beat can be handled differently than a synthesizer or vocal loop. A drum loop typically contains several short sounds, such as hi-hat, snare, and kick drum hits, while a synthesizer or vocal sample (loop) will most often sustain or consist of longer sounds. Since Live is analyzing the loop's contents, it needs to 'look' at each loop in a different way to achieve the best results.

You may also turn off Live's time-correcting Warp feature to make your loops behave more like standard vinyl or samples in a hardware sampler. Live also encourages plenty of loop manipulation, in terms of feel, tempo, and pitch. But how Live really works is up to you. Never before has software been so dependent upon its owner's own proficiency, and never before has software been so intuitive and musical once a few basic principles are understood. Live works with your audio loops, recorded material, and other software applications to make music. You can create new music from scratch, or build a 'remix' from previously recorded material. When it comes to working with audio in Live, the creative possibilities are limitless.

What sets Live apart

If you are an audio software enthusiast, you've certainly heard of powerful digital multi-track studio applications such as Digidesign's Pro Tools, Emagic's Logic Audio, MOTU's Digital Performer, Cakewalk's Sonar, and Steinberg's Cubase (and Nuendo). These programs, and their hardware counterparts, are often referred to as DAWs, or *Digital Audio Workstations*. Their main task is to ensure that audio is recorded and played back properly in a studio situation. Other, more loop-oriented, products such as Propellerhead's Reason, Arturia's Storm, Sonic Foundry's Acid Pro, Cakewalk's Project5, or Sonic Syndicate's Orion Pro are also touted in the media for their originality, and have become popular along with the self-contained studio paradigm. Each of these programs allows for using the computer as a stand-alone music composition center and loop factory. Like the aforementioned products, Live can operate by itself, record multiple audio sources, integrate loops, and handle other basic studio functions. But Live also introduces the idea of performing with software and editing your improvisation afterwards. And automating has never had a better platform.

To fully understand why Live is such an innovative program, it helps to take a look at its feature-set.

- First of all, Live works on both Mac (OS 9.1, 9.2, X.1.5 and up) and PC (Windows 98, ME, 2000, XP) platforms and takes advantage of all current industry standards such as ASIO drivers, VST effect plug-ins, and ReWire synchronization software.
- Live is among the first programs for the Mac that allow loops to be previewed at the project tempo independently from pitch. Other programs have tried, but none have succeeded in bringing the Mac this kind of efficiency. As for PCs, Acid Pro and Sonar do a nice job of time stretching, and as long as you have Rex files, ReCycle can also help out too. But Ableton could definitely make a case that Live 'sounds' better, provides more types of stretching algorithms, and can recalibrate tempos in an instant, which is important if you consider that some time-stretching may need to be done in front of an audience.
- In addition to generating word and MIDI clock, Live can also be synched to another program's MIDI clock.
- As mentioned above, MIDI-note information can be used to trigger sounds or MIDI-controller info for knobs and sliders. Even your laptop computer keyboard can trigger samples. Better still, all MIDI-controller and keyboard triggering information can be assigned while Live is in playback mode, so the music doesn't have to stop.
- In terms of routing, Live is only constrained by the limitations of your sound card. You can route input and outputs pre or post Live's mixer. And as I've alluded to, ReWire software applications (such as Reason, Cubase, Sonar, MAX/MSP

and ReBirth) can be directed through Live's mixer in a variety of ways. You can record audio from an outside source straight into Live or render (record) Live's own output to a fresh track (for later use) while you play.

- And while all of these elements make Live sound attractive, Ableton's not-so-secret weapon, 'elastic audio' is the feature that has caused many a jaw to drop. Aside from being able to quickly quantize an audio loop's start and end points at the current project tempo, Live uses what's called 'Elastic Audio' to wrestle WAV (or AIFF) files into submission. How is this done? Live has the ability to elasticize audio to any degree the composer would like. We will dive into this in great detail in subsequent chapters, but for now, be aware that Live makes a living out of dividing samples into sections, much in the way Propellerhead's ReCycle would. The difference with Live is that you are able to move slices (called warp markers), thereby stretching (or compressing) the loop's contents. This may seem minor, but for a moment consider that in Live, any sound within a given sample can be played at any time within itself.

    Confused? Here is an example: Live can speed up a 25-second sample so that it will play in 5 seconds or vice versa (slowing down the 5-second sample to take up more time). Taking it a step further, you could chop up this sample and resize select portions of the sound, thereby radically changing the duration of certain segments within the original sound. Amazingly enough, Live can do this with just a couple of mouse clicks, while you monitor the results. More common examples include matching up bass and drum loops, using select portions of a long performance, correcting sloppy takes, fixing near perfect ones, humanizing a drum machine part, the list goes on. For more on the power of elastic audio, see the section on Clip View in Chapter 5, 'Making Music in Live'. You can also truncate the loop's end points, move the loop reference (starting point) anywhere you like, and fine tune the pitch in either half-step or cent increments.

- Another distinguishing feature of Live is the DJ-style crossfader built right into the performance mixer (new in version 2.0). Just like the DJ mixer pictured in Figure 1.3, you can assign mixer channels to A, B, or both channels and mix between the two with a MIDI or mouse controllable crossfader. This subtle tool enables gradual song and loop transitions, along with more flexible performance options, not to mention DJ-style fader-flipping and cross jags.

Figure 1.3
DJ mixers have evolved over the years to the point at which software counterparts can barely keep up. With this in mind, Ableton Live's DJ mixer is an excellent tool for crossfading your mix. Cueing, EQing, and other DJ functions are still best handled from a pro DJ mixer.

Because Live's design has been engineered for live performance, Ableton has created a powerful studio ally, almost by accident. Producers are already beginning to see the advantage of mocking up song sections in pre-production, remixing stale arrangements, or auditioning fresh material by using Live. Placing television and movie cues is a natural fit for Live. Let's face it, even the best-equipped recording studio would be doing itself a disservice by not integrating at least one computer running Live to handle some of these tasks. While most applications are focused on a specific task, such as sound design or the recording process, Ableton has zeroed in on the concept of making music, while still catering to the studio all the way.

Possible applications

Before we jump in and start making music with Live, let's consider for a moment why this software was developed. Perhaps you have been lucky enough to spend some time in a recording studio using analog tape, or a digital medium (such as ADAT or Pro Tools). If not, you have most likely seen pictures of a decent-sized studio, and can imagine a fairly large mixer console (desk), accompanied by several pairs of different-sized speaker monitors, power amplifiers, racks of outboard effects, and the inevitable patch bay full of cables. Now imagine the last concert you attended. You may have seen a band (complete with cocky lead guitarist sporting all his/her shiny effects pedals), a keyboardist with bigger and shinier effects gear, or even a DJ with his/her two-plus turntables, DJ mixer, and crate upon crate of back-breaking vinyl. Can you see where I'm going with this? Live eliminates the messy patch bay, the nightly set-up and teardown of elaborate effects and amplifiers, and the need to carry your vinyl. Live can even save your entire performance for later editing. To say Live is a replacement for tried-and-true analog studios (or a substitute for your obnoxious guitar player) is to miss the point entirely. What is certain is that Live can not only survive in today's music making environment, but thrive. What's more, Live is only beginning to realize its full potential.

Figure 1.4
Pat Mastelotto incorporates a laptop running Ableton Live and Propellerhead's Reason by triggering the software to produce sound via electronic drum pads. This is but one imaginative way to use Live 2.0.

Artists such as Ex-Nine Inch Nails producer Charlie Clouser are using Live daily for scoring television and film music. Super-drummer Pat Mastelotto, pictured in Figure 1.4, (King Crimson, Sugarcubes, XTC) has taken to using Live both onstage and in the studio as a way of creating music in ways he had only dreamed of previously. Electronic music is a natural beneficiary of a program such as Live, as sample- or loop-based dance music has proven to drive the audio software world in some fascinating ways.

Here are some other possible Live scenarios:

- **Stage** If your band plays with a sequencer, and your drummer is used to playing with a click track, you could easily incorporate live loops into your music. Some bands use phrase samplers to add in a layer of percussion, noise or effects loops, or even backup vocals.
- **Studio** We have already mentioned why Ableton Live would be a perfect addition to any studio. It can function as a high-power drum machine, a flexible loop remixer, or versatile audio sketchpad. While some may use Live as their only studio application, bigger Pro Tools studios may simply enjoy Live for its ability to take bits of a project and let artists, producers, and engineers hear some different arrangements quickly and easily.
- **Club** The Laptop DJ trend has been building steam for several years now. The benefits included less wear and tear on your vinyl, lightweight transport, the many possible software tricks for enhancing the sound, and more. To be fair, there are a few compromises to recognize, such as the time it takes to digitize

vinyl and the look and feel of the performance. While paradigm shifts are always tricky, one thing is for sure: My vinyl weighs a ton.

Goals of this book

Like Live, *Making Music with Ableton Live* was written by a musician – a drummer in fact, but don't let that scare you. I've spent plenty of time performing with Live and have been recording and remixing in Live since it was first released. Live is built to be musical and this book will aspire to be the same. It is my hope that you have many long hours of enjoyment using Live while creating some interesting new music. Though this book is designed to be a 'power user' book, don't be deterred if you are new to Live, new to music, or new to computer-based audio. This book will serve as a basic guide to interfacing with Live and an advanced tip and tricks collection for taking advantage of Ableton's industry rocking technology.

Many sections in this book are not specific to Live, but are included as a reference for novice and intermediate digital audio studio owners. Topics such as wave editing, loop making, and sample manipulation are broken down so that you won't have to seek out this information somewhere else. General audio computing tips, such as configuring your PC for audio, will help you make the most of any audio application you currently use and will only bolster your basic working knowledge of computer-based (digital) audio as musicians should understand it.

If you are already familiar with Live, this book should feel like a souped up reference manual with some powerful tips and musical ideas for you to incorporate into your Live vocabulary. This book should help you optimize Live's settings for speed and sound, which should translate into maximum musical output. *Making Music with Ableton Live* covers some sticky but rewarding topics, such as Live's new *elastic-audio* loop-handling method, editing Live's mix automation, and using virtual EQs and compressors for professional audio results.

For downloadable starter loops and templates, visit this book's website at www.brainboxing.net/abletonlive.

Getting started

If you are accustomed to buying studio gear (hardware), you are probably like me get the sucker home, tear open the box, and start making noise. Manuals are for other people after all and, well, who's got the time? When it comes to software, however, there is one fundamental difference. It is almost always up to you, the end user, to set up and configure the hardware properly, install the software the way it was designed, and set up the preferences so that the new application won't interfere with any legacy applications, cause strange hardware issues, or impair general functionality. In short, you become the final manufacturer. It is this sort of engineering control that is both the advantage and disadvantage of personally transfiguring your computer into a recording studio, a performance sampler, or a Live sequencing instrument.

Before we dive in and start producing hits, it is important to take a moment to verify that your computer system is up to speed and then to install Live properly so as to ensure maximum performance potential. This chapter will provide more than a few recommendations to help you through the lonely installation process and a few rarely mentioned tips for fine-tuning your Ableton Live instrument. We will cover both Mac and PC setup and talk about several methods for optimizing your system. Also, remember that Ableton's technical support is an excellent way to get to the bottom of anything not covered in this book, as is Ableton's online user forum (www.ableton.com > forum), which is usually rich with tips, tricks, and advice (see Figure 2.1).

System requirements

Listed below are Ableton's posted system requirements, dependent upon system make, and followed by my recommendations. For the record, I've tested and composed music using Live on several different makes of Windows PCs and Macs running both OS 9.2 and OS X.2.3. Still, as mentioned above, every computer is customizable and this can lead to unforeseen problems. If Live is acting strange for example, if the audio is stuttering or if each edit is taking a very long time, try running Live completely by itself. Make sure you are not running any other applications in the background, such as MP3 players, office suites, or (as we will cover in Chapter 8, 'Live's Effects') third-party VST effects, which can cause CPU performance problems.

Keep in mind that the vast difference in Requirements versus Recommendations

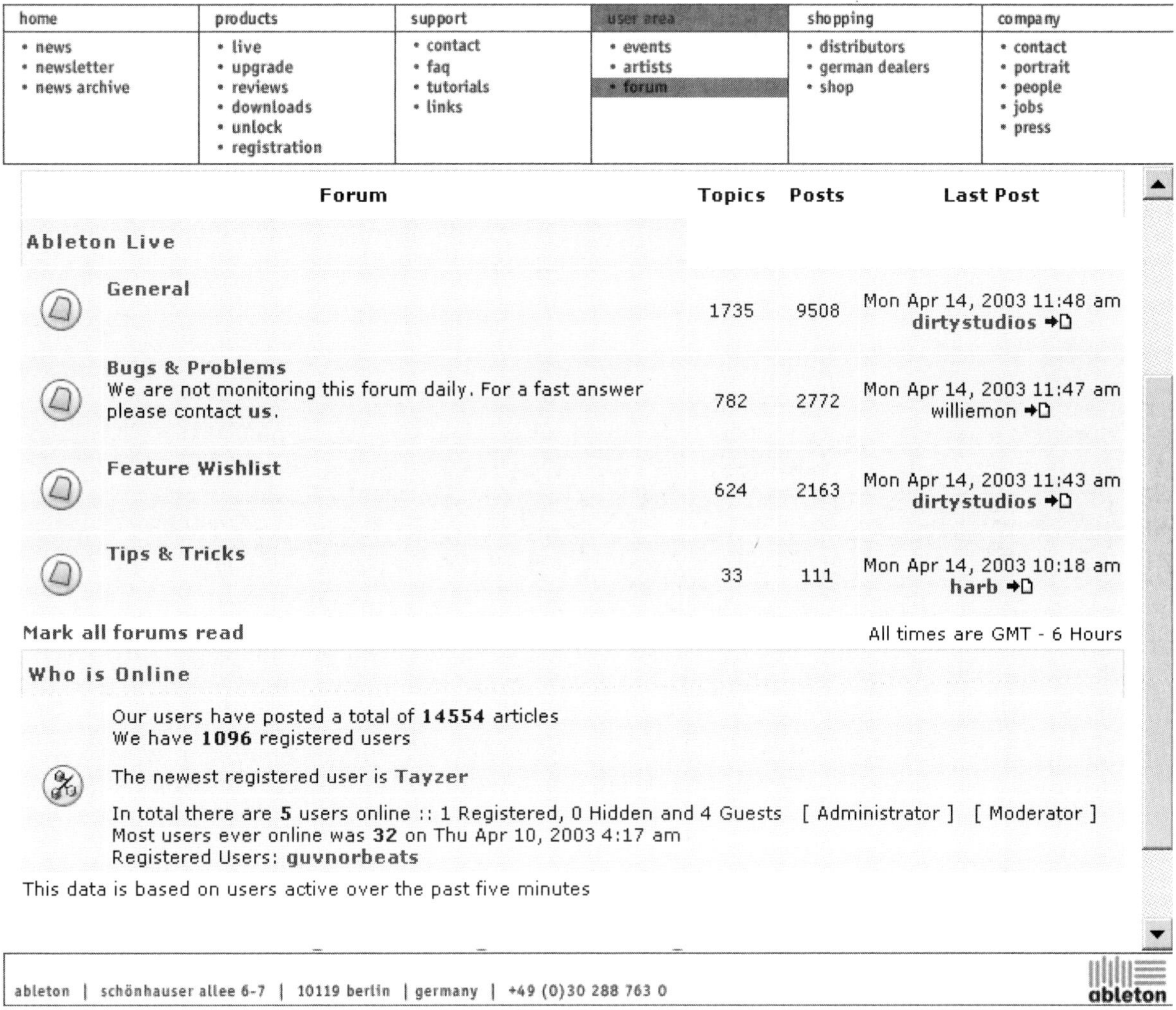

home	products	support	user area	shopping	company
• news • newsletter • news archive	• live • upgrade • reviews • downloads • unlock • registration	• contact • faq • tutorials • links	• events • artists • forum	• distributors • german dealers • shop	• contact • portrait • people • jobs • press

Forum	Topics	Posts	Last Post
Ableton Live			
General	1735	9508	Mon Apr 14, 2003 11:48 am **dirtystudios** ➔◘
Bugs & Problems We are not monitoring this forum daily. For a fast answer please contact **us**.	782	2772	Mon Apr 14, 2003 11:47 am **williemon** ➔◘
Feature Wishlist	624	2163	Mon Apr 14, 2003 11:43 am **dirtystudios** ➔◘
Tips & Tricks	33	111	Mon Apr 14, 2003 10:18 am **harb** ➔◘

Mark all forums read   All times are GMT - 6 Hours

Who is Online

Our users have posted a total of **14554** articles
We have **1096** registered users

The newest registered user is **Tayzer**

In total there are **5** users online :: 1 Registered, 0 Hidden and 4 Guests   [Administrator]   [Moderator]
Most users ever online was **32** on Thu Apr 10, 2003 4:17 am
Registered Users: **guvnorbeats**

This data is based on users active over the past five minutes

ableton | schönhauser allee 6-7 | 10119 berlin | germany | +49 (0)30 288 763 0   ableton

could well mean the enviable difference between functioning and flourishing with your Ableton product.

Ableton Live system requirements for Macintosh
- Any G3 or faster
- 256 MB RAM
- Mac OS 9.1 or later
- Mac OS X.1.5 or later

My Mac recommendations
- G4 or faster
- 512 MB RAM
- Internal SCSI, ATA/IDE, or External 7200 RPM FireWire Drives only (USB hard drives tend to be slower and less reliable)
- Mac OS X.2.5 or later
- ASIO compliant sound card w/ MIDI interface

Figure 2.1
Ableton's user forum is packed with good information. Make sure you take full advantage by logging on (selecting a user name and password), so that you can receive private messages, converse with other members, and be notified when any of your posts have been responded to. Also, by using the forum's search window, you can usually find some reference to the problem you are facing, and eliminate needless inquires to commonly asked questions.

Ableton Live system requirements for PC
- 400 Megahertz CPU or faster
- 128 MB RAM
- Windows 98/2000/XP
- Windows compatible soundcard (preferably with a DirectX or ASIO driver)

My PC recommendations
- 1 Gigahertz CPU or faster
- 512 MB RAM
- Windows 98SE/ME/2000/XP
- No USB hard drives
- ASIO compliant soundcard w/ MIDI interface

Installing, running, and updating Live

If you are brand new to Live and haven't yet picked up your copy, or have never installed audio software before, then this section is for you. Sometimes a little background information helps make for a more rewarding software experience. Here are a few general tips for installing, running, and updating Live:

- Live can be purchased by ordering the packaged version through an Ableton distributor (M-Audio, www.maudio.co.uk) or retail outlet. No matter where you get it, Live can run on Mac OS 9.1 and up, OS X.1.5 and up, as well as PCs running Windows 98, 2000, ME, and XP. Note: If you have downloaded the Ableton Live 2.0 Demo, you will still need to order the full version to purchase Live. The demo version is limited to 30-minute sessions and cannot be upgraded (for anti-piracy reasons).
- To begin making music in Live, you will need samples, recorded music, or an audio interface that will enable you to record into your computer. The original Live CD contains a decent-size dose of about 400 MB of loops and samples from industry leading production houses, including Big Fish Audio and Power FX. If you are anxious to get your hands on some fresh rights-free loops, please see Chapter 11, 'Where to Get Loops'. Also, there are literally hundreds of Web sites and other sources of free and inexpensive loops, as well as a couple hundred professional-grade companies that make high-end sounds, such as Ilio Entertainment, E-Lab, QupArts, etc.
- At the time of this writing, 2.5–3 GHz PCs are outperforming Mac G4 1.0 GHz processors (at least when it comes to running Ableton Live). Like most good rivalries, expect the processor battle to rage on as Mac will presumably release G5 chips and beyond, and Intel, Celeron, and other processor chipmakers will continue to innovate. Ableton may also help matters by integrating Altivec code, which will enable Live to take advantage of Apple G4's latest processor efficiency. Rest assured that Live can run well on both kinds of machines and that as time goes on Live's performance will only improve.
- In terms of audio, Live supports DirectX for PCs and Soundmanager for Macs if you don't have an ASIO- or WDM-compatible sound card. However, be prepared to hear some audio latency when recording and playing back recordings made in Live when using DirectX and Soundmanager. For a more detailed expla-

nation of audio and MIDI latency, and a discussion of all their trappings, see Chapter 12, 'Recording in Live'.

- Also, aside from the infallible book you hold in your hand, it won't hurt to take a look at Ableton's manual. The packaged version of Live contains an HTML manual that can be viewed in a browser such as Netscape Navigator or Internet Explorer. To locate this same HTML script online, jump out to www.ableton.com, click on live, and then click on online manual. The box version of Live includes an analog (printed) owner's manual, which is still worth referring to even though you have wisely purchased this book. It is worth noting that Ableton frequently updates Live, and when they do, Live's virtual manual will also be updated.

Live installation tips (Mac OS 9.1 and beyond)

Though installing Live 2.0 in OS 9.1-9.2 is as easy as point and click, it can be advantageous to spend just a little time configuring OS 9's memory allotment. Live 2.0 tends to be more processor-intensive than RAM-intensive, due to the number crunching involved when warping audio files or applying dense effects, such as reverbs. A clean installation and proper RAM allocation setting can help smooth out Live's operation in Mac's OS 9.1 to OS 9.2. If you are new to Macs or new to setting memory allocations, here's how to do it:

1 Once you have installed Live, locate the Live app (or application) on your hard drive. Note: this is not the shortcut (or alias) on your desktop! The best way to locate the app, if you don't know where it is, is to click on (highlight) the shortcut and select File > Show Original (CMND + R). Next, click one time gently on the application file and select File > Get File Info > Memory Settings.
2 You will then have the choice of constraining the minimum and maximum memory settings for your Mac. For standard use, I recommend about 100 MB of RAM for Live.
3 To check how much RAM your Mac is actually using, start up Live and begin playing the demo song (or one of your own compositions). Next, click on your desktop or the Mac finder window, and click on the apple in the uppermost left. Choose 'About this computer' and a small box will pop up telling you how much RAM is being used and by which programs. Depending upon your system setup, there is a small degree of trial and error involved in determining exactly how much RAM you want to allocate to Live. Some actions will pull on the RAM a bit more than others, so you will want to leave some headroom. You will also want to save some RAM for running other applications, such as Reason, in ReWire mode. I recommend trying a few different configurations depending upon your setup. Figure 2.2 shows the screen of my G4 titanium Powerbook (often called a TiBook) running Reason and Live and their relative memory allocations.

In the following screenshot you will see the memory allocations for my G4 laptop running Reason 2.0 and Live 2.0.

Live installationtips (Mac OS X.2.3 and up)

Due to Ableton's foresight, and Live's minimal dependency upon an operating system, Live was the first audio multi-track application on the planet available for OS X. As you might expect, installing Live on OS X is a breeze. Insert the Live installation disc, open the disc dialog, and drag the Live folder to your hard disk. Follow

Figure 2.2
In this screenshot you will see the memory allocations for my G4 laptop running Reason and Live.

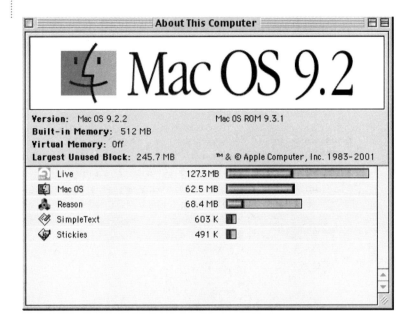

the onscreen directions, and the installer will create an Ableton Live Folder on your hard drive. All pertinent files, including Live's manual will be contained here. For quicker access to Live, you may want to install a shortcut onto the OS X dock (if you are using it). This makes Live easier to open and a little more fun you can watch the bouncing Live icon as the program comes up. To do this, simply open your applications folder, or the location on your drive where you decided to install Live, and drag the program icon to the dock. An instant shortcut is made. To remove the item from the dock, drag it to the trash or to the desktop and watch it go 'poof'.

Windows 98, ME, 2000, XP

Installing Live onto a Windows machine is much like installing any other Windows-based application. Once you click on Setup and follow the instructions, Live's installer will ask you where you would like to place the Ableton folder and its files. I recommend keeping Live in your program files, under Ableton, which is the default setting. You will want to pay special attention to where your VST plug-in folder exists. If you have any other programs that use VST effects, you will want to centralize your files into a single folder where all audio applications can look for VST plug-ins. For instance, Live can just as easily look into your Cubase SX/VST Plug-ins folder as it can in any other. After the installation, you will want to customize your preferences (see the 'Setting Preferences in Live' section later in this chapter).

Updating Live

To check what version of Live you are currently running, click on Live > About or on a PC, Help > About Live. Both the version and serial number will be displayed (see Figure 2.3). Click anywhere on the popup screen to close this window. To see if there is an update for Live, you will need your serial number. This added level of piracy protection is new to version 2.0. Visit www.ableton.com and click on downloads, then simply follow the instructions for downloading and installing the latest version. I recommend checking for updates as often as your time and interest allow. Updates seem to be posted approximately once a quarter. Ableton remains ambitious about tracking down even the smallest bugs in Live and posting software updates. Their user forum (click on forum) is also of value and is a great place to pick up new tips, suggest ideas to Ableton, trade songs, and just plain network with other Live users. (See Figure 2.1.)

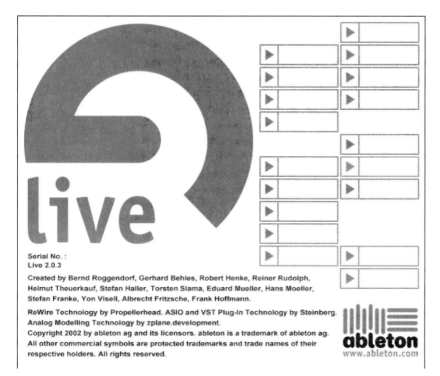

Figure 2.3
This screen will confirm which version of Live you are currently working in. After you update your copy of Live, follow the steps described in Updating Live to make sure that the new version is running properly. You may need to swap out old desktop or dock shortcut icons because they will continue to point to (launch) the old version of the product.

Copy protection

Ableton uses a challenge-response authentication system to protect Live from the ills of software piracy. Many companies are employing this concept now because of both its effectiveness in deterring illegal copying and its ease for the customer. I like it because you really don't even need to rely on the original system disk, which can become scratched or broken. With this system, you could be in the middle of a tour, notice a new update online, click on Live's About menu and jot down your serial number. Live keeps track of all challenge and response codes internally, as does Ableton's database, although it is a good idea to save and print a .txt file with your software serial, challenge, and response numbers.

Here's how it works. After installing and launching Live you will be asked to enter a serial number. Live will then generate a unique (to your machine) number that coincides with your serial number. This new number is your challenge number. Then, simply click on Authenticate and Live will handle all of the challenging and responding invisibly behind the scenes. This can also be done via email. In fact, you have ten days to complete this authentication procedure before Live will not operate. If for some reason you don't have access to the Internet (if, for example, the computer with Live on it does not have a modem), you can obtain this information via fax or phone. You can then manually plug Ableton's response number into Live when the authentication dialog box emerges. Note: Live will only ask for this information immediately after the first installation, after major software upgrades, or until the information is provided within the first ten days.

Basic computer specs

When buying a computer, you're often faced with a dilemma centred around brand, timing, processor speed, and a ridiculous number of options. You can spend your entire life chasing processor speeds, and faster CD-R drives. My feeling is that it is more important to get a functional machine rather than bending-edge technology that may or may not be 100 percent stable. Here is a list of the most important considerations when buying a PC, Mac, or laptop for using Ableton's Live software.

Processor speed

It is in our very nature to want the fastest and most efficient processor available. Business folks want to spend less time waiting for massive data crunching, and musicians want to hear fewer digital 'hiccups' in their music. Two or three years ago, a case could be made that Pentium III may have completely out-clocked a Pentium II, or now that the 1.25 GHz Titanium G4 Laptops (called Tibooks) have arrived, they should be light years ahead of last year's 500 MHz. This is not always the case, however, and although faster may be better, don't spend all of your time chasing processor speeds. Trust me, it can be an expensive proposition. Instead, set your sights just below the industry top dogs. For example, at the time of this writing, the 3 GHz PC chips and dual 1.25 GHz are the PC and Mac (respectively) top performers. Ableton Live doesn't necessarily require this kind of processor speed to perform basic functions. Sure there are limitations, and contrary to popular belief, there always will be. So instead of spending £2500 (or more) on your next industry champion, take a step back, save several hundred pounds, and invest in a quality sound card and a pair of professional speakers. Your music will be better for it.

Hard drives

Fast hard drives, on the other hand, are essential. Say what you want about processor speeds, when recording audio, your hard drive spin and data throughput are terrifically important. Most drives run at 7200 RPM these days, but be wary of buying one of those 5400 RPM internal or USB hard drives. As for seek time, 9 milliseconds or less is the maximum I would tolerate. Super fast SCSI hard drives are the best option if money is no object, but I find that 7200 FireWire drives or internal ATA/IDE drives are plenty fast for most single and double (stereo) recording and overdubbing.

RAM

In Live, most of your short samples (less than 5 MB) will sit in RAM, as opposed to on the hard disk. 512 Megabytes should be plenty for any serious computer musician. Though of course more is always better if you've got the cash. You can make it with 256 MB for a while, but more RAM will help to ensure stability during live performances as well as help if you have other applications running in the background or in complement with Live.

Cache

Cache is generally thought of as ultra-fast RAM that handles mission-critical data even closer to the hardware level of a computer. The amount of cache and speed of the motherboard can enhance overall system performance. Laptop users want to be particularly careful not to get jilted out of their cache. Since it is pricey, many resellers will diminish its importance. Most of Macintosh's Titanium G4 Powerbooks now ship with Level 3 cache, When talking about cache, you will also hear talk of bus speed, which refers to the speed limits of your CPU's circuitry. Most motherboards these days are clocking in at around 100 to 133 mHz, which is plenty fast enough for Ableton Live.

Your sound card (audio interface)

No piece of hardware is more important in determining the audio quality of your work than your audio interface choice. Almost invariably, the audio card that comes with your PC or Mac is lacking. Depending upon your needs and budget, you will want to either replace it or add a second card to your system. Sound cards can connect in several different ways. PCI cards and laptop cards are thought of as internal sound cards, while USB, FireWire (IEEE 1394), USB 2.0, and, eventually, FireWire 2 connectable sound cards can be thought of as external cards. Pro Tools TDM interfaces, in which the hardware and software are integrated, can be thought of as a combination of the two. Here are some items to consider:

How many outputs do you need?

The advantage to multiple outputs is an increased amount of control over your project. With Live, you may want to send drum and percussion tracks to outputs 1 and 2, while sending the vocals to output 3. These outputs are often routed through a hardware mixer (separate and apart from the computer). All sound cards that I am aware of provide at least two outputs, a stereo pair. Other common specs include 4, 6, and 8 outputs, and many provide outputs in other kinds of formats, such as S/PDIF (digital), Light Pipe (digital), XLR, RCA, and others.

How many inputs do you need?

Like outputs, the number of inputs you need will narrow the list of cards to consider. Generally sound cards have a minimum of two input channels, a right and left input summing in stereo. These can either be RCA, XLR, Digital (SPDF or Lightpipe) or other (such as ADAT). Keep in mind that for more than two channels of input, FireWire or internal PCI and card slot cards will be a more efficient means than USB in delivering the large amount of multi-track audio data to your hard drive.

Choosing a MIDI interface

Even if you are new to MIDI, mapping a MIDI-controller to Live is a breeze and can be extremely gratifying, or even essential when performing with your computer. Many soundcards boast at least one MIDI-in and one MIDI-out. More high-end or MIDI-only cards can feature up to four or more MIDI ins and outs. In the near future, touch-screen technology should eventually replace at least some of this MIDI interfacing, and artists will be lucky enough to use their fingers on the virtual faders. For specific examples, see the MIDI-controller interface section later in this chapter.

What kind of sound card interface should I get?

External sound cards are portable and efficient, but many feel that USB is just plain not fast enough. This is due to the fact that USB can transmit only up to 12 MB per second (Mbps) while FireWire cards push up to 30 or more Megabytes per second (called throughput). Playback is usually decent on USB cards because you are often just listening to a stereo mix (two channels), but when recording multiple tracks (more than three or four), USB can have some problems keeping up. You should consider carefully which applications (besides Ableton Live) you plan to use and then decide upon the best hardware platform. USB is plenty fast enough for typical Ableton Live use, where typical is one or two inputs and a stereo output mix. Power-users will want to take advantage of Live's multiple ins and outs (routing) to employ hardware mixers and outboard effects, and will therefore need a card to support it.

Selecting the right sound card

Road-worthy components, great sounding analog-to-digital converters, and responsive tech-support are the three most important qualities to consider when selecting your most vital piece of hardware outside of your computer: the sound card. Here is a short list of tried and true sound cards with quality, precision, and portability in mind.

M-Audio (www.maudio.co.uk)

M-Audio's Delta series has proven that professional specs can also be affordable. (See Figures 2.4 and 2.5.) Nearly all of M-Audio's Delta series cards connect via PCI, and support the leanest audio drivers (ASIO and WDM). However, M-Audio's latest (2003) Audiophile card, and many of their planned cards, are USB only. My advice is to remain careful about USB cards in general because of the smaller throughput (bandwidth) that the large audio data needs to traverse. As mentioned above, USB can prove to be a shaky solution for large multi-tracked projects; however, M-Audio is a company committed to Live like no other; they are Live's number one UK distributor.

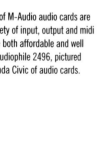

Figure 2.4

The Delta series of M-Audio audio cards are made with a variety of input, output and midi options. They are both affordable and well supported. The Audiophile 2496, pictured above, is the Honda Civic of audio cards.

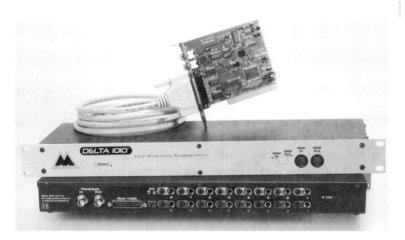

Figure 2.5 (left)
The delta 1010 pictured here is a powerful professional audio card that can handle eight analog inputs and outputs and an additional two stereo inputs via S/PDIF. The pictured front and back rack-space portion of the unit, like many breakout boxes of this type, connects to the additional PCI card inside your computer (seen on top of rack unit).

Figure 2.6
Echo Audio's Indigo audio card provides consumer level audio support that is both inconspicuous and simple. No Audio inputs, MIDI, or digital transfer is supported, but what do you want for a hundred bucks?

Echo Audio www.echoaudio.com

With their newly revamped product line, Echo has its eye on the pro-audio crowd. With 24-bit/96 kHz sampling, the Layla line of laptop sound cards has garnered some excellent reviews. Echo's Layla24 and Gina24 are similar in design to M-Audio's Delta 1010 (seen in Figure 2.5), with professional hardware drivers and plenty of input/output options. If these boxes are too expensive for your budget, you might want to take a peek at their newest product, Indigo, which is an inexpensive ($99), high-end consumer level audio card that could easily support small clubs or informal editing sessions. Indigo has two $1/8$ mirrored stereo outputs, but no audio inputs and no ASIO drivers. (See Figure 2.6.)

RME Hammerfall www.rme-audio.com

As I prepped to write this book, Hammerfall's Multiface (Figure 2.7a front and 2.7b back) turned up again and again as the sound card most preferred by laptop aficionados. It has too many capabilities to list here, but if you are looking for a solid, professional solution, you will not be disappointed. The Digiface and Multiface breakout boxes (external audio interfaces with multiple inputs and outputs) add an exceptional level of professional audio support and flexibility to laptop producers, and connect via the RME's card slot connection. For standalone PCs and Macintosh, RME offers a PCI interface, so that you can transfer either of the above two breakout boxes to laptop or your home/studio computer. RME has done a commendable job of making sure all possible digital formats are covered.

Figure 2.7b (below)
The back of the multi-face. There are connections for eight inputs and outputs, SPDIF, ADAT, word clock synchronization and more. Multiface is your top-of-the-line studio on the go.

Figure 2.7a
RME makes the most flexible, and possibly the most professional, laptop audio card on the market.

Digigram (www.digigram.com)

The 'Pocket' series by Digigram is a family of pro-level cards that, as the name says, are small enough to fit in your pocket, though you really should just put them in your laptop card slot. Newer Digigram units feature on-board processing, which can really take the load off of a strained processor and free up headroom for more audio content. One other advantage to Digigram's products is that the card slot design (pictured in Figure 2.8), like Echo Audio's hobbyist-oriented Indigo (see Figure 2.6) is contained inside the laptop. There is nothing else to carry, power-up, or break as the case may be. Digigram's less expensive 'pocket' series cards are known to sound great and are simple enough to use.

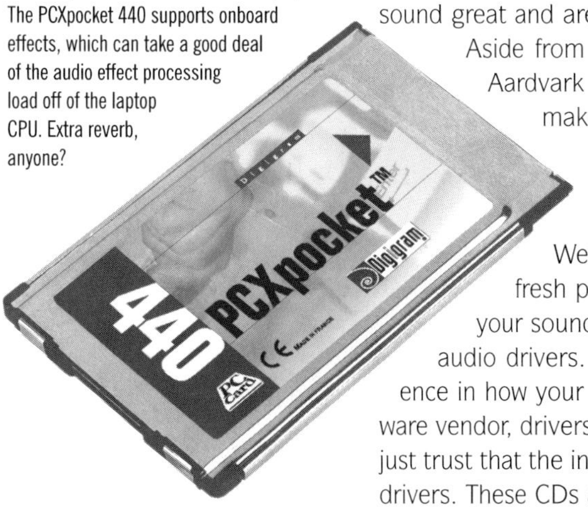

Aside from the above-mentioned sound cards, Emagic (www.emagic.de), Aardvark (www.aardvarkaudio.com), and Edirol (www.edirol.com) all make professional-level sound card products. It almost goes without saying that times change quickly and new technology emerges. So keep your eye on the latest reviews in magazines such as Computer Music, Remix, Mix, Keyboard, EQ, and non-biased Web sites such as Harmony Central (www.harmonycentral.com) for fresh product info. Also, it is extremely important to continually check your sound card's manufacturer's Web site to be sure you have the latest audio drivers. Current and correct audio drivers can make a world of difference in how your software performs in your system. Depending upon your hardware vendor, drivers may be updated as frequently as once a month or more. Don't just trust that the included CD (that ships with your soundcard) has the most recent drivers. These CDs are usually packaged well before the final tweaks to driver software are finished, and well in advance of software innovations.

Figure 2.8

Digigram makes several similar-looking cardslot pro-audio soundcards for laptops. The PCXpocket 440 supports onboard effects, which can take a good deal of the audio effect processing load off of the laptop CPU. Extra reverb, anyone?

What do you need to know about ASIO drivers?

ASIO (Audio Stream Input/Output) was first invented by German software-slinger Steinberg (www.steinberg.de or www.cubase.net). Originally, ASIO drivers were created to help musicians and producers using Cubase to digitally record with minimal amount of time lag within their digital system. This time lag can be a real buzz kill and is called latency. Latency occurs when the sound you are recording is forced to travel through extraneous instructions in your operating system, your system bus, and host application to end up on your hard drive. Like bad plumbing, the signal may be coming down the pipe, but there are unnecessary clogs and corners that must be navigated. The gist is that sound can't escape or enter the host application fast enough, and is thus latent.

Live supports ASIO on both Mac and PCs, and you'll be happy to know that most popular consumer and professional-grade audio cards do too. It has become an industry standard thanks to the fact that it works cross-platform (both Macs and PCs) and can cut latency down to barely detectable levels. Properly installed, ASIO drivers will make Live as responsive as a hardware instrument, with less then four milliseconds of audio delay. ASIO helps Live users hear the instantaneous results of MIDI commands, Audio input/output, mouse moves, and keyboard commands. Someday we'll all look back and laugh that latency was ever an issue, but for now, count your blessings that there is ASIO. See the 'Setting Preferences in Live' section later in this chapter for more on the infamous 'L-word'.

Choosing a MIDI interface

Nothing makes playing Live more rewarding than cranking real knobs and watching virtual faders move (or perhaps I should say hearing them move). You can move virtual faders, adjust the amount of effects and their settings, modify the tempo, and do just about anything else you can imagine, all by using a MIDI interface. In the next section, we will take a look at several portable, affordable, yet full-featured MIDI controllers a product category that has grown exponentially over the last couple of years.

One of the most envied of recent MIDI-controllers is M-Audio's Surface One (www.m-audio.com). The future of digital audio will almost certainly include touch-screen controllers, but Surface One (Figure 2.9) is the logical link in the chain with fiber optic enhanced ribbon controls that feel like smooth fabric or vinyl, yet control MIDI information similar to faders. Surface One is the largest of the pure MIDI-controllers mentioned here. Still, its ergonomic design, and M-audio's reputation for releasing innovative products, make it worthy of a second look.

Figure 2.9
Surface One may be the most sci-fi looking musical instrument interface around. You can slide your fingers on velocity (touch & pressure) sensitive ribbons to control any MIDI parameter mapped to the unit. If you prefer to use your wrists, knobs are also provided.

Encore Electronics, www.encorelectronics.com, makes several basic MIDI-Controllers. The two shown here, Knobby Control in Figure 2.10 and Slidemate in Figure 2.11, are perfect for small stage setups, tight budgets, and minimizing programming hassle. Both the Knobby and the Slidemate can be programmed via a computer and can also send SysEX (system exclusive) messages a great asset for those hard to reach MIDI parameters.

Figure 2.10
Knobby Control features what else? Knobs! Eight to be exact. These come in handy with a program like Live and just like Live, Knobby can be updated on the fly.

Slidemate's eight live-programmable sliders will comfort those missing their old analog desks (mixers). Slidemate programming is nearly identical to Knobby above, though some Live tweakers may want both.

German-based Doepfer,

Figure 2.11
Slidemate's eight live-programmable sliders will comfort those missing their old analog desks (mixers). Slidemate programming is nearly identical to Knobby above, though some Live tweakers may want both.

www.doepfer.de, makes a mean blend of quality controllers with customizable parameters and a small footprint for inconspicuous fader-flippin'. The Pocket Dial's (Figure 2.12) endless rotary knobs make tweaking Live a blast. You can grab or turn a knob and not have to worry about its previous placement. 1-10 or 0-10 knobs can limit the creative possibilities in a program such as Live by causing unwanted spikes in whatever parameter you are adjusting. Endless rotary allows you to pick up wherever the value is at a given time, and modify it from that point. Of course, endless faders are not really an option, but Pocket Fader, pictured in Figure 2.13, helps to migrate software-based remixes to your desktop.

Figure 2.12

My personal experience with Pocket Dial has been nothing short of a joy. Its small footprint and 16 knobs times 4 banks for 64 accessible presets make Pocket Dial one of the best all around options where inexpensive MIDI-controllers are concerned.

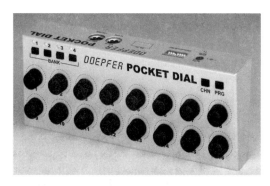

The above MIDI-controllers begin to give you an idea of what is available for just a couple hundred bucks (or less) with the exception of M-Audio's Surface One ($799). Virtually any MIDI controller, including MIDI-based Mixers, can work with Live. You can assign sliders, knobs, or faders in an infinite amount of creatively rewarding ways. In Chapter 6, 'Playing Live… live', we will explore specific ways of making a MIDI map. There are literally millions of possibilities. Imagine mapping these controllers to adjust panning, effects, tempo, crossfader, frequency filters, EQ settings, and on and on.

Figure 2.13

Fade outs and volume swells never really feel that great on a mouse, not to mention that it is hard to control multiple tracks (unless you are creating an aux bus). Pocket Fader is specifically designed to handle these kinds of tasks.

MIDI connectivity

MIDI Controllers usually connect in one of two ways either via USB or through your Audio Sound Card (if MIDI input is supported). Earlier, when we discussed USB for audio, I suggested steering clear of USB and recommended going FireWire, PCI, or card slot (on a laptop) when looking for a reliable audio card. With MIDI, however, USB is a safer route because MIDI information is much less cumbersome than digital audio when traveling over your system bus. MIDI information is so small that it can even be transmitted over serial port, but in recent times, we have become accustomed to pairing MIDI-controller information and digital audio through the same card. If your sound card does not support MIDI, USB is an efficient means to interface. Several companies, including Edirol and Midiman (the same company as M-Audio) make simple little single-input MIDI connectors, such as the UM-1S and Midisport (pictured in Figures 2.14 and 2.15, respectively).

One of the most popular combination MIDI-keyboard/controllers to hit the market was M-Audio's Oxygen8 (Figure 2.16). The original unit was cheaply made,

Figure 2.14
The design and release of Oxygen 8 created quite a splash among laptop studio owners and other MIDI-happy musicians concerned with overall space.

Figure 2.15
Midiman has been making MIDI connectivity devices for as long as I can remember. Well, at least since around the time MIDI was invented in 1984.

with less than optimal controller knobs, but it represents the merging of two similar worlds (keyboard and MIDI controller), and has inspired competitors like Edirol to release their own knob-and-fader keyboard conglomerates, the PCR-30 (Figure 2.17) and the PCR-50. In response, M-Audio has attempted to outdo itself by releasing an improved version of the Oxygen8, called Ozone, which also features a preamp and soundcard. As you can see, the only thing certain about the future is change.

Figure 2.16
The design and release of Oxygen 8 created quite a splash among laptop studio owners and other MIDI-happy musicians concerned with overall space.

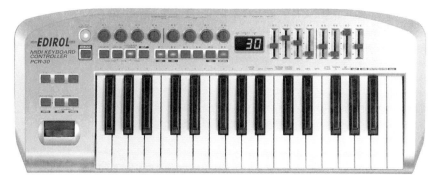

Figure 2.17
Edirol's hybrid PCR-30 sports keys, faders, and knobs, and is really made for musicians who think small, at least in terms of their desk (studio) size.

Setting preferences in Live

Optimizing Live's preferences is essential for smooth operation. You see, preferences are more than merely your personal whims about how you would like Live's interface to be colored, or where your files are automatically saved. Preferences are your primary control centre for fine-tuning Live's ability to actually work in your customized computer/audio environment. From the Preferences menu, you will be able to control default loop traits, audio and MIDI interface settings, and audio/MIDI latency settings. Sound like too much to manage? Read on, and let's

Figure 2.18
Let's begin with customizing the Misc preferences in Live. This is the best place to adjust Live's initial treatment of audio loops and samples.

Figure 2.19 (right)
The Behavior section is for specifying Live's treatment of audio files.

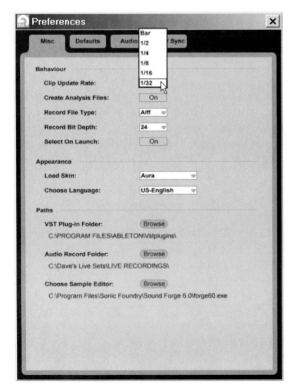

Figure 2.20
By adjusting the clip update rate, Live can change loops (per your direction) more quickly. An excellent advantage for the live laptop loopist.

tame this beast. To call up the Preferences dialog box on a PC, select Options > Preferences; on a Mac select Live > Preferences. The emerging dialog box contains four abs: Misc, Defaults, Audio, and MIDI / Sync. We will discuss them in order, so click on the Misc tab if you are not already there. (See Figure 2.18.)

The Misc Tab

Just because this tab is titled Misc, don't assume these parameters are extraneous. Each of the three sub-sections; Behaviour, Appearance, and Paths are important in creating a smooth Live environment.

Behaviour

The first section, 'Behaviour', (Figure 2.19) determines how Live handles loops once they are loaded (dragged or recorded) into Live.

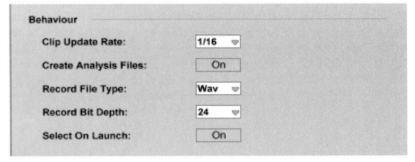

Clip Update Rate is the frequency with which Live re-calculates changes to the clip. For instance, if you transpose a clip in Live, while the Clip Update Rate is set to 1/32 note, you will hear nearly instant changes to the pitch of the loop in the clip. Conversely, choosing a Clip Update Rate of 1/4 note, or the even slower rate of 'Bar' (meaning one update per measure), will result in changes occurring more slowly. This is meaningful during a live performance, in which changes may need to be heard as they happen instead of after the fact. For example, if you are working in the studio with Live, or if you're editing and noticing slow performance, turn down the Clip Update Rate to 1/4 note (its default setting), as seen in Figure 2.20. When performing, go for broke at 1/16 or 1/32 note settings.

Another performance option is to have the Select On Launch feature turned off. When on, as in Figure 2.19, this feature makes the loaded clip viewable in Live's clip view screen at the instant it is loaded. When off, you will retain your original view and need to double click the new clip to see clip view. As I mentioned, many users turn this off when performing because their loops (clips) are pre-configured and they want to access effects or mix settings rather than the clip's properties. In fact, the Create Analysis File option allows Live to make a small ASD file to correspond with each loaded clip. This ASD file stores tempo and graphic clues for Live so the file will load quicker the next time it is selected. The ASD will be stored in the same directory as the loop, so don't be alarmed when you discover two files in the same folder, with nearly identical names for every file that has been loaded into Live. For instance, you will see the file 'drum loop.wav' or 'drum loop.aif' and then a second 'drum loop.asd' By the way, ASD files are extremely small and will not be visible from Live's browser (only from Mac's Finder or Windows Explorer.

Other Behaviour settings are more self-explanatory, but it is worth noting that a PC's native format is WAV, and a Mac's is AIFF. You can invert these settings, but if you want to have these files available in native applications you may run into problems. I also recommend setting the bit depth to 24 when recording (the Record Bit Depth option), so long as your sound card supports it. This ensures the maximum detail for newly recorded sounds. You can always render a file downward (to 16-bit), but cannot really go up, to add detail that is not there. Think of it this way: a colour photo can easily be degraded to black and white, but the reverse is much more difficult, and requires some special technology.

Appearance

The Appearance section (seen in Figure 2.21) allows you to choose the skin for Live. About 20 skins are provided with Live and artists such as Monolake (www.monolake.de) are developing new ones all the time. To test out which scheme you like best, simply click on the Load Skin window in the Preferences dialog box, and use the up and down arrows on your keyboard to scroll though the options. If you download a new skin or two, place these inside the Skins folder. For PCs, the skins are located in the Resources folder in the Live directory. For Macs, skins can be found in the Ableton Content/Skins folder. To add skins to OS X, control-click the Live 2 application icon, select 'show Package Contents' and then open the folder Contents > App-Resource > Skins. Then place the newly downloaded skins here.

Figure 2.21
Live's Appearance section. These two menus allow for customization of Live's Skin and Language settings.

Info

The skin I'm in

Many GUI (Graphic User Interfaces) have customizable color schemes called skins. Just as Windows and Mac screens can be altered via preferences, Live can be given a face-lift by loading a new skin. This feature will have no bearing on the performance or sound of Live, but can make for an inspiring change of scenery.

Also, it may be of interest to point out that Live's internal language settings, which affect its internal help menus, interface text, and informational messages, can be set to read in French, Japanese, and German as well as English. If you do not see one of these languages, you can visit the Ableton Web site and click on Download to find the Ableton Live application file with the languages you need.

Paths

Pictured below in Figure 2.22, is the Paths settings section of the Misc tab. Here you can map out Live's VST plug-in folder, Audio Record(ed) Folder, and Choose Sample Editor.

Figure 2.22
By pointing Live in the right direction, you will be able to access compatible VST effects and launch your wave editor in the blink of an eye. Also, the Audio Record Folder will help you keep track of your Live session files.

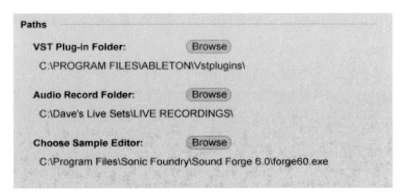

The VST plug-in folder can be set to any folder on your machine that holds VST effects compatible with Live. The only sure way to know if Live is compatible with a VST effect is to try it out. To do this, place the effect in the folder and re-start Live. If you can see the effect in the VST folder by pressing the VST plug-in section of Live's Browser, then chances are Live will at least be able to load the effect. Live will occasionally not work with the VST plug-in. Or the effect may be incompletely developed. If this occurs, please do everyone a favour and send in a quick bug report to both Ableton and the third party VST effect developer. Some will function in some diminished way, but this functionality is not yet supported by Ableton (as of version 2.0.1). Each time Live is started, the program scans your system for new VST effect plug-ins and audio files in the designated sound location folders. If you notice an unusually long startup time (an extended view of Live's splash screen), you may have added a large number of new VST effects or sound files, or unintentionally added an incompatible VST effect that is having trouble 'talking' to live. Note: At the time of this writing VSTi (virtual software instruments) are not officially supported in Live.

The Audio Record Folder is the folder into which Live places all WAV and AIFF audio files once recorded. You will find that once you save a file (song), you can choose to place all corresponding audio into a designated (a.k.a. less confusing) location. So think of this folder as a temporary scrap heap that you can retrieve old files from, browse for hidden gems, or just flush periodically.

The Choose Sample Editor setting is for defining the shortcut that will direct Live to choose your favourite wave editor, such as Sonic Foundry's Sound Forge, Steinberg's Wavelab, Bias Audio's Peak, Syntrillium's Cool Edit Pro, and the list goes on. For a more involved look at wave editors, please refer to Chapter 10, 'Wave Editing Tips'.

The Default tab

Preference's Defaults tab (seen below in Figure 2.23) will likely be a place you visit as you discover your own preferences for working in Live. Save Template is really the default setting for Live. Any Live song saved with this button will become Live's default, or start up, set. This can be helpful for pre-configuring commonly used settings such as MIDI assignments, input and output routing, and common effect patchwork (such as EQs on every channel). But note that you can save only one template in this Preferences tab.

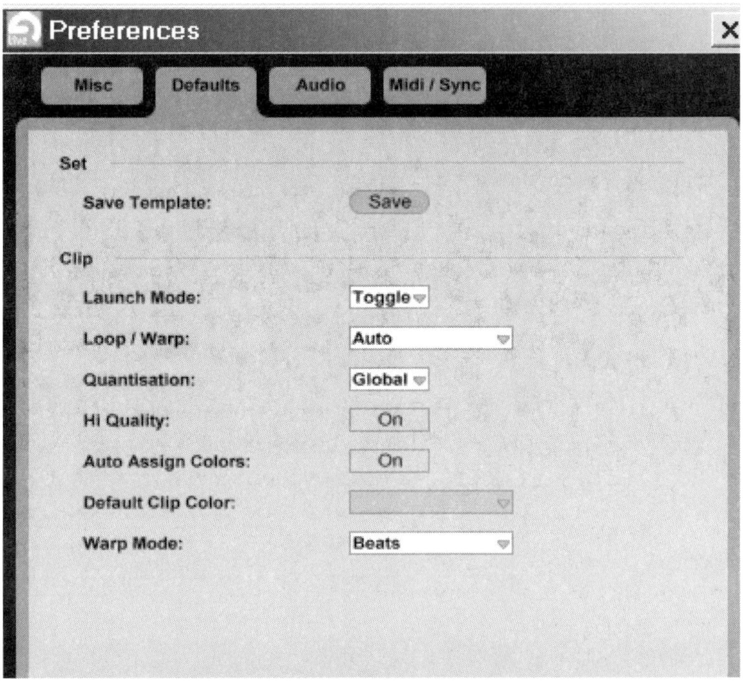

Figure 2.23
Live will automatically open loops the way you like once you tame the Default tab in Live's Preferences. Your settings in this tab will likely change as you experiment with how you most often use Live.

The remainder of the Default screen determines Live's clip settings. As you begin performing with Live and build a few practice sets, take note of how you tend to configure your clips. You can choose between any of Live's four clip launch modes Trigger, Gate, Toggle, Repeat and pick from four different Loop/Warp settings: Unwarped One Shot, Warped One Shot, Warped Loop, and Auto, which lets Live recommend the best method. These terms may sound strange if you are new to Live or new to loop-based audio software. A Warped One Shot is a single playing of a sample in the tempo of your piece, while an Unwarped One Shot is a direct playback of the sound (without any of Live's magical time-stretching applied). Most of the time, I rely on Live's intuition (using Auto mode). The important distinction here is between loops and one-shots. A loop, as we will see in the very next chapter, is a repeating sample. One-shots are just like they sound, a single playback of a sample. In Chapter 4, 'Digital Audio Basics', we will cover some of the fundamentals of digital audio as applied to loops, samples, and Live.

Quantization

The idea of quanitization is to force your performance to fit into the groove of the current piece. Any time you launch a sample in live (called a Clip), you have the option of launching it on the 'one' of the next bar, or every second bar, every fourth bar, every eighth bar, or by picking a note quantifier to begin playback on the very next 1/32, 1/16, 1/8, 1/4, or 1/2 note after you trigger the sample. Of course this is a grand selection of choices and the right selection can depend upon the type of sound you are launching. For instance, an orchestral or ambient guitar sound might not need as strict a quantization as a conga or cowbell loop. You can also opt to turn Quantization off by default by selecting None from this dropdown dialog box, or the safest bet for novice and/or careful Live musicians is to select Global, which will assume the same quantization setting as the project a good way to keep every sound in line.

Hi Quality

You will also want to pay attention to the Hi Quality default toggle button, which (when activated) will make Live use a more complicated algorithm when calculating Live's loop warping attributes. The reason to not use Hi Quality is simple; it demands a bit more system resources and, when applied to all of your loops, can really create a noticeable CPU spike. You can also opt to leave Hi Quality off as a default setting, yet still use it on select loops by double clicking on a clip and adjusting its clip settings more on this in Chapter 5's 'Clip View' section.

Colours

Next up in Live's Defaults tab are the Auto-Assign Colours toggle switch and the Default Clip Colour selector. With Auto-Assign Colours on, Live will randomly choose a colour for each new clip or recording. These colours can be changed at any time in a screen called Clip View, which will be covered later in the book. If Auto-Assign Colours is off, the Default Clip Colour comes into play by determining which colour Live will default to for all new audio. Of course, colour will not affect the sound and is strictly a matter of preference.

Warp Mode

Warp Mode, the next and last item on the Defaults tab list, is another story entirely. New in Live 2.0 are three loop modes. The original product, Live 1.5, treated every loop as a beat, which can be problematic when treating melodies, basses, drones, ambient textures, and, well, just about anything without a well-defined percussive texture. Here is a DJ style breakdown of the four warp modes in Live. This is a topic central to understanding how Live works and will be revisited in chapters to follow. Remember, these are merely the defaults; all can be changed once the

- Beats Mode: Beats mode is the original Live warp mode. The program automatically breaks up the loop into sections determined by the Transients settings. For instance, Live can divide a loop into 1/32 notes, 1/16 notes, 1/8 notes, 1/4 notes, 1/2 notes, and full measures. As long as the sound is rhythmic and fairly short in duration, Live does an impeccable job of making the loop sound as though it were recorded at your project tempo. Drum loops, dance grooves, and percussive instrument loops (bass, short synth, turntables, or funk guitars), can all be convincingly stretched in beat mode.

- Tones Mode: This is the mode for bass and keyboard lines, melodies, pitched sounds that are not necessarily grooving in perfect time with a metronome, such as a legato horn line or harmonic chord progression or even vocals.
- Texture Mode: For sounds more complex than melodies and rhythms, Ableton has brought us Texture Mode. This is the mode to use for ambient effects, atonal pads, and indefinable sounds. Texture Mode bears the distinction of further tweaking possibilities with Grain Size and Flux (fluctuation) controls. These two new parameters determine the intensity, severity, and randomness of Live's slicing. This can be an excellent sonic deconstructing tool for any kind of loop in addition to the ones mentioned.
- RePitch Mode: For loops that just can't be sliced, or for samples that offer the right attitude only when they are sounding their fattest, Ableton's RePitch Mode removes all pitch correction, yet still corrects the loop's tempo to fit into the piece at hand. Some loops may sound funny at their new pitch, but this is a sure-fire way of eliminating strange artifacts that can sometimes appear when retiming and repitching a loop simultaneously.

Also, Live now allows you to turn any of the above four modes off entirely. This means that the sample/loop is played back exactly as is, at its original tempo and pitch. This no-warping mode can be achieved by deselecting the warp button at the bottom of the clip view, and is the preferred mode (non-mode) to use when setting up your tracks for a DJ set. For more on DJing with Live see Chapter 6.

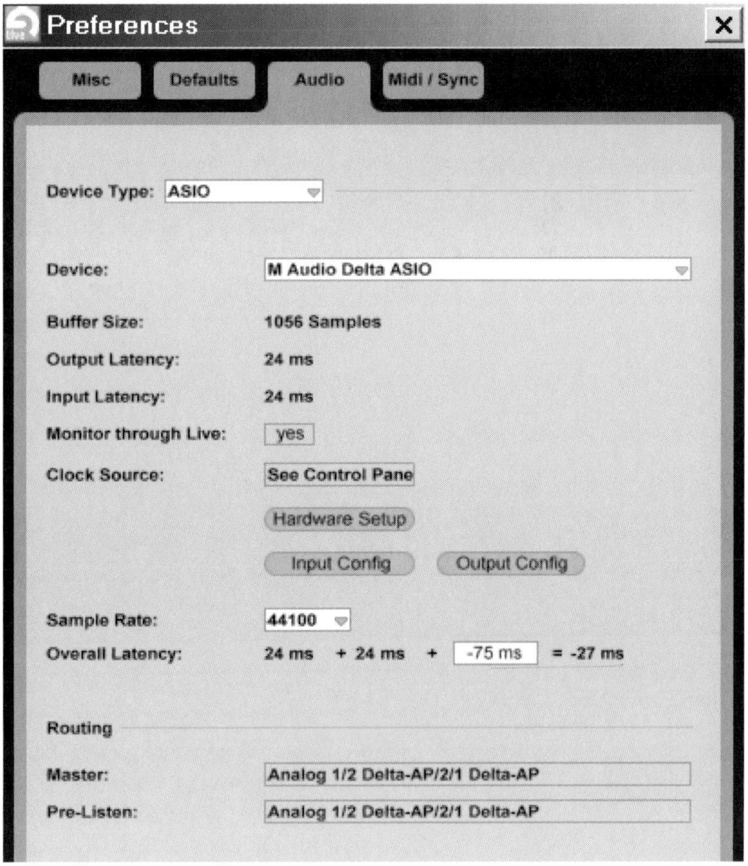

Figure 2.24
Audio preferences will be revisited often as you seek out the perfect audio latency settings, audio interface routing, and monitoring (pre-listening) set up.

The Audio tab

The first section you will likely get to know is the Audio tab in Preferences seen in Figure 2.24. This tab's pull down menus will depend largely on what kind of sound card you have, and whether it is correctly installed. In Figure 2.24, you will see that I am using an M-Audio card (an Audiophile 2496 PCI card to be exact), with ASIO drivers. It says 'M Audio Delta ASIO ' because Delta is the series of card.

Device and device type

Please note that your device (audio interface) may differ from mine, and that Live will always seek out the audio interface last saved in Preferences each time the program launches. If Live cannot find the sound card, for instance, if you have unplugged or swapped out your sound card, Live will still launch, but with no audio enabled. In this instance, you will see a small warning message mentioning that Live cannot find the audio card and that audio will be 'disabled' upon startup. You will also notice a second warning on Live's actual interface (after the program launches) that says 'The audio engine is off. Please choose an audio device from the Audio Preferences'. After you do this, you will again be ready to set up Live for audio.

Buffer size

You may or may not be able to adjust your sound card's Buffer Size from this Preferences menu. Most ASIO and other sound cards need to be accessed directly through their own driver interface this can often be referred to as the ASIO setup dialog. If you are using a standard or consumer-level audio interface, such as Apple core audio, you will see a buffer slider here. The lower your Buffer Size setting is (in milliseconds), the less latency and more potential problems you may face. In other words, too much Buffer will increase the amount of undesirable latency, yet too little latency will most often result in your system choking and wheezing in the form of digital pops, audio dropouts, and the like. In the next section we will take this latency discussion up a level and give you a couple ideas for possible workarounds.

Latency settings

Latency. There is that dirty word again. Here is how to approach optimizing your Live software to work with your computer and soundcard to achieve the least amount of audio latency. First, recognize that there is output latency, input latency, and MIDI latency. Each type of latency imposes a different kind of problem, and while there are some ways to combat these timing issues, zero-latency is still not really a viable option for applications reliant upon an operating system (such as Windows or Mac OS 9, X). Realize also that latency is designed to be a buffer for when you put extra strain on your system and your CPU is having trouble keeping up with all of the demanded processes.

Output latency is the amount of time lag from when you trigger a sound to when you hear it. Or if you add an effect, such as distortion or reverb, the extra time that it takes to actually hear that sound is output latency. Do not confuse this output latency with Clip Update Rate, described above. For instance, if your Clip Update Rate is set for 1/4 note, you may hear a small (1/4 note or less) pause before hearing many of Live's clip effects. This can be remedied in the ways we discussed earlier.

You can stress test your system for latency and alleviate the above-mentioned confusion. Here are the steps for the stress test:

1 Click on the Misc tab, and turn your clip update rate to 1/32 (32 note timing).
2 Load a decent size audio clip, preferably a stark drum loop, into the session view.
3 Load several Live effects, until your CPU meter in the upper right hand corner reaches about 70 percent of capacity. For my system, a couple reverbs, a couple EQs, and a chorus on a single track do the trick.
4 Then, while slowly reducing the Output Buffer Size, listen for pops or clicks in the audio. Adjust your final setting to a comfortable level above the popping

level. Note, this buffer size may need to be adjusted from your soundcard's settings, or if it is not greyed out can be set in the Preferences' Audio tab.

Don't be surprised if you can go extremely low and detect no discernable latency. It is there all the time, but often miniscule when using ASIO or WDM drivers.

Input Latency is usually a bit trickier, and will be discussed in greater detail in Chapter 12, 'Recording in Live'. In the meantime, take note that input latency is the delay that exists between playing a sound into your sound card from an outside source, such as a synth or guitar, and actually hearing and recording the sound. You can imagine the difficulty you would have if you are monitoring your take and hearing it just five milliseconds behind your finger striking the key or string. This was the reality of many digital workstations in the 1990s and to some degree still lingers in nearly all audio applications running on standard PCs. If you are looking for a remedy, now would be a good time to skip to Chapter 12 where we will discuss how to optimize your Overall Latency box, and handle other recording related issues.

MIDI latency can be divided into two camps, synchronization problems and MIDI triggering delays. The latter has nearly disappeared with wide adaptation of Steinberg's ASIO technology, and the recent integration of Windows WDM drivers in Windows 2000 and XP. But trying to create a reliable solution for MIDI sync has proven tougher than trying to catch the proverbial chicken. Like input latency, this issue will be handled later in the book in a more advanced chapter. If you are experiencing MIDI sync problems, or timing issues here and now, please do skip ahead to Chapter 9, 'Using MIDI'.

Monitoring through Live

If you are using ReWire or wanting to monitor your recording source through Live's session mixer, this button should be turned on otherwise leave it off for smoother running. Also, many combat the ills of input/output audio latency by monitoring their source through the mixer instead of through Live. We talk more about how to record and specifically discuss monitoring options in greater detail in Chapter 12, 'Recording in Live'.

Sample Rate

The Sample Rate setting in the Audio preferences tab will determine the recording quality of both Live's output and recorded input. A good basic sample rate to start out with is 44100, or 44.1kHz. As you learn more about digital audio, or if you are pro already, the Sample Rate dropdown box will give you a multitude of friendly choices. I never recommend using anything lower than 44100, but if you are long on system resources (including hard drive space), you might experiment with 96000 so long as your audio interface can handle it.

Routing

When you make music in Live, you have to send it to the outside world somehow. For simple audio interfaces, Live will automatically set this up for you by sending a stereo master output to your audio interfaces master output. However, if you have the good fortune to have an audio interface that supports multiple outputs, then you can take advantage of that here. In Chapter 6, 'Playing Live...live', we will talk about how to capitalize on Live's pre-listening (cueing) ability via sound cards with multiple outputs. Also, if you have the option of digital or analog output, this is place to set up that output.

The MIDI/Sync tab

This brings us to the final Preferences tab, shown in Figure 2.25, the MIDI/Sync tab. If you are not planning on synchronizing Live to work with a hardware or software MIDI sequencer, then many of the MIDI/Sync parameters will not be of much interest. The tab is divided into three sub-sections, MIDI Control, MIDI Synchronization, and MIDI Timecode. Beginners will want to step right up and tackle the MIDI control box, which is the place to assign any of the toys discussed in the 'Choosing a MIDI Interface' section earlier in this chapter.

MIDI control

Live 2.0 allows for two MIDI control devices and one MIDI output (acting as a thru for note and control data). To select your input device, simply use the drop down menu, and then close out of Preferences. To be sure MIDI is working, move a knob or key on your controller and note the blue (usually blue in most skins) 'I' light up in the upper right-hand corner of your screen. 'I' stands for input, as in MIDI input. The 'O' right next to it signifies MIDI output and will only illuminate when you have selected an output path in preferences' MIDI Control section.

You will also notice a bar reading 'Send Control Updates Now' beneath the device menus. This bar/button is handy for resetting Live's automatic MIDI detection that happens at Startup. For instance, you may have added or removed a MIDI interface after Live has started up and the device will therefore not present in any of the necessary drop down menus. Rather than get frustrated, or restart Live, simply press this bar once or twice and see if your MIDI item doesn't show up on its own.

Figure 2.25
The MIDI/Sync tab found in Live's Preferences box. This is the logical place to handle how Live works with MIDI and syncs to the outside world, and to resolve MIDI timing issues.

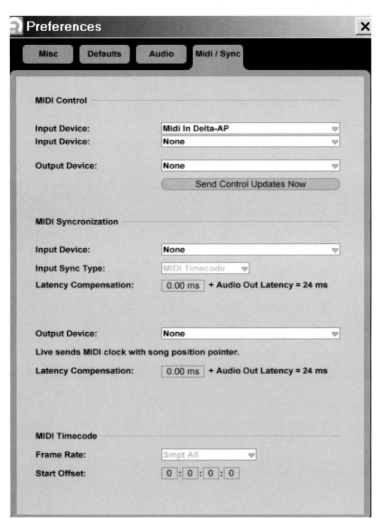

MIDI synchronization and timecode

MIDI synchronization is a two-way street. Live can either drive or be driven. To drive Live, you will want to either send MIDI timecode or MIDI clock. The difference between MIDI timecode and MIDI clock is simple. MIDI timecode is time information, given in minutes, seconds, milliseconds, etc., and is more useful in scoring music along with images, such as movies or television. MIDI Clock, on the other hand, is tempo, measure, and note information, such as beat 1 of measure 5, moving at 120 beats per minute. MIDI Clock is usually best when implementing MIDI sequencers because of their sensitivity to the tempo of the piece. There have been some reports of Live having MIDI synchronization problems, especially in version 1.5.1. Version 2.0.3 has made some improvements in this nature but will require some degree of trial and error on your part, depending upon your system. Again see Chapter 9 for more on this.

Most often, MIDI synchronization is used when playing with an external hardware (or occasionally software) sequencer. Video synchronization is also very popular, and while Live can do this type of work, it may be best used when run in tandem with any one of a number of programs adept at video work. In other words, I would recommend syncing Live to that application, also called running Live in slave mode. This is not to be confused with running Live in ReWire mode which is a form of MIDI synchronization that runs transparently between two ReWire enhanced software applications. For more info on this, see Chapter 13, 'ReWire synchronizing your software'.

Similar to input and MIDI sync latency issues, MIDI synchronization is an advanced concept and will be dealt with in Chapter 9. For now, notice that Live provides you with two more dropdown boxes with choices such as MIDI In (Delta-AP on my card), or MIDI-out (Delta-AP if you have a Delta series audio card). Here you will see whatever input and output devices are located on your system. From here, you can also fine tune Live's handling of the sync, choose your method (timecode or MIDI Clock), and adjust for latency.

For the best results, synchronize one machine at a time, using a process of elimination to figure out the hardware or software (usually the problem) culprit. Also, don't forget to try swapping out MIDI cables. They can easily go bad and will make you crazy if you don't check on them.

The final section of Live's preferences is perhaps the least relevant to most Ableton Live users: The Frame Rate and Start Offset for MIDI Timecode. This menu is for those synchronizing Ableton Live with MIDI timecode who want to choose their SMPTE (pronounced 'simptee') flavor. The Start offset is for correcting latency within SMPTE. In later chapters, I've provided step-by-step examples for how to synchronize Live with other software and hardware. Don't be concerned if all this talk of MIDI and SMPTE seems to be more than you bargained for. The goal of Chapter 2 is to be up and running with Live and to have a general idea about how the Preferences settings will affect your workflow. As we move throughout the book, I will again and again direct you to Live's Preferences. In Chapter 3 Live Interface Basics, we will proceed with the rest of your introduction to Live's two primary views. More importantly, we will see how to bring your loops into Live.

Live interface basics

One of Ableton's software development team's crowning achievements is the creation of Live's simple but elegant interface. Only two views are needed to accomplish everything in Live: Session View and Arranger View. Session View is geared for live performance and loop experimentation, while Arranger View better facilitates studio editing, song arranging, and multi-track recording. Each subsection of Live's paired-down interfaces is intuitive, easy to maneuver, and contains built-in help to remind you of any onscreen buttons or features that might be unclear in the heat of a mix. Ableton's Zen-like approach to audio software provides solid relief in a world full of gargantuan multi-track applications with gaggles of resizable popup windows, and confusing setup and routing schemes. Instead, Live is a breath of fresh air, boasting streamlined controls with easy-to-read menus, and discernable mixer and effect settings. Even with the fog machine blowing and lights down low, Live lets you get into the mix, rather than trying your patience with unnecessary system customization.

In the next few sections, we will break down each section of Live's two primary landscapes, as well as point out some timesaving ways to maneuver in Live. Later in the chapter, we will look at some of Live's more customizable viewing features, a few pertinent file saving schemes, and the permanent parts of Live's screen real estate. Feel free to skip around if you need help in a particular area, and if you are a Live user but are new to version 2.0, you will want to pay extra attention to the new crossfader and improved bus management.

Session View

Live's Session View (Figure 3.1) is where you will spend the greater part of your performing and composing time. With some practice, Session View can take on a musical life of its own, and may well be the software world's first 'jamming' software. Even better is that after the jam, Live permits an infinite amount of additional recording, editing, and arranging, which we will get to later in this chapter. There are four main sections contained within the Session View:

- The Clip Slot grid
- The Scene launcher
- The Session Mixer
- The Input Channel Routing strip

The grid-like screen in the upper-right corner of your monitor is the actual Session View, while the side and bottom retractable-rectangle views (such as Browser Info, and Track/Clip View) are present in any view when you want them to be. Session View is where most people experience the creative spark in Live, so if you should create something worth saving while you are working through this chapter, go to File > Save Live Set As, and name your new sketch of a song. I also want to point out that while we will cover each element in the interface, the Browser and Info View will be explained later in the chapter, while Track and Clip view will be saved for Chapter 5, 'Making Music in Live'.

Figure 3.1

Pictured here is Live's Session view. This is the window used for live performance. Each clip slot, located in the grid beneath the Track Title Bar (with the default Track 1, Track 2, etc.) is a placeholder for samples or loops.

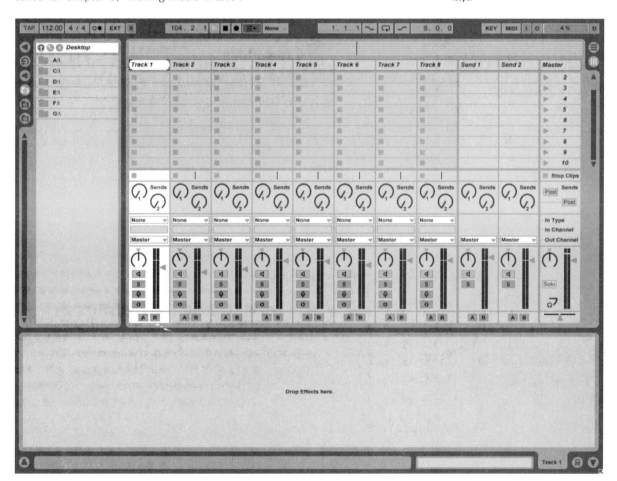

This ordinary looking grid will be the launch pad for many a Live jam. Each cell (Live calls them clip slots), can be triggered via the mouse, computer keyboard, or MIDI-controller, depending upon your settings. Each clip can be played in similar fashion to an Akai MPC 2000/3000 drum machine or similar phrase sampler. For example, artists such as DJ Shadow may lay out several sampled drum hits across the 16 pads of an MPC 2000, and then play them with the MPC's comfy rubber pads. Live's Clip Slot grid, which we will explore in detail below, is similar in design and can house an unlimited number of loops and samples. You will need to supply your own triggering, as we suggested in Chapter 2, 'Getting Started'.

Clip slot grid

Session View's clip slot grid (Figure 3.2) is actually the first tool you will use to organize your loops and samples into a song. Live uses rows and columns, referred to as 'scenes' and 'tracks' to differentiate between different kinds of audio uses. Scenes (or horizontal rows) can be triggered all at once, meaning that several samples can be played at one time, while Tracks (vertical columns), can play only one audio sample at a time (similar to the way a channel on a hardware mixer will play one audio signal at a time). Any clip slot containing a sample can be triggered independently, or within a given scene (row). Musical arrangements in Live often work best if you think of your music as starting in scene '1' (the top row), and then progress downward, scene by scene (row by row). In other words, scene '1' may be an intro section, scene '2' may be a verse, scene '3' may be a chorus, and so on. As you read on about the rest of the interface, this concept will begin to make sense.

Figure 3.2
A clip slot grid view. Any clip slot (or cell) can house a loop. You can add as many scenes and tracks (rows and columns) as you like.

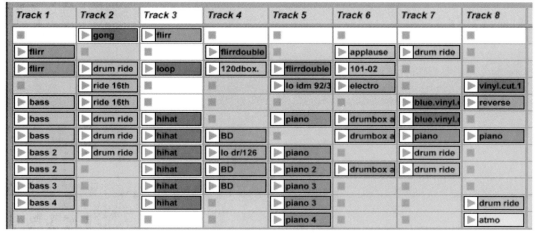

Track 1	Track 2	Track 3	Track 4	Track 5	Track 6	Track 7	Track 8
	gong	flirr					
flirr			flirrdouble		applause	drum ride	
flirr	drum ride	loop	120dbox.	flirrdouble	101-02		
	ride 16th			lo idm 92/3	electro		vinyl.cut.1
bass	ride 16th					blue.vinyl.	reverse
bass	drum ride	hihat		piano	drumbox a	blue.vinyl.	
bass	drum ride	hihat	BD		drumbox a	piano	piano
bass 2	drum ride	hihat	lo dr/126	piano		drum ride	
bass 2		hihat	BD	piano 2	drumbox a	drum ride	
bass 3		hihat	BD	piano 3			
bass 4		hihat		piano 3			drum ride
				piano 4			atmo

Any clip slot (or cell) can hold exactly one clip (an audio sample, or loop), which can be placed there by dragging it with the mouse, or by being cut, copied, and pasted into place. You can also record audio directly into a clip slot via Live's audio 'Input Type' routing or software ReWire channel. In the Session View example in Figure 3.3, note that loops and samples can be dragged from the Browser (on the left, and which we'll cover in detail later) to the right Clip Slot grid. You can drag loops to any clip slot (or cell) one at a time, or several at once.

Notice that in Live's Session View, the Scene Launcher is located just to the right of the Clip Slot grid. By pressing the sideways triangles in the scene launch strip (under the Master track column), called a 'fire button' in Live, you can launch simultaneous playback for all loops in the given scene (row). Fire Buttons prove useful when composing live, 'on the fly' arrangements, during which you may want to jump from one song section to the next, and then back again. In Chapter 5 we will see more examples of how to best take advantage of the scenes and clip slots, as well as how you can maximize your song arrangement ideas.

What's important is that you begin to think of Live's clip slot grid as a palette upon which to place your sonic colours (in this case loops or samples) for later audio 'painting' and further colour exploration (sound combining).

By loading clips into the clip slot grid, you are arming Live with loop ammo. Next steps range from firing off sounds in a live performance to creating new sample combinations (songs) to switching to the Arranger View for more editing. Figure 3.4 shows a single scene (row) in Live's Session View.

Different Live-users will explore their own creative ways to use Live's interface. For the laptop DJ, scenes may represent complete songs or pieces of music (as opposed to short loops), in which one clip slot could contain a clip that is really an entire song. In this instance, a 'scene' change is more like swapping vinyl than moving to a new part of the song. Back in Figure 3.4, you can see eight clip slots in a single row, all playing a separate loop at the same time. We will take this concept further in Chapter 5 Making Music in Live',

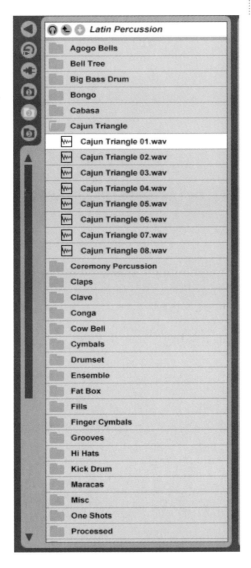

Info

Two scenes are better than one

One of my favourite shortcuts is the one for duplicating scenes. This command will insert a new scene directly below the scene you are working in, and copy all present loops—a huge time saver! To do this, press CNTL (CMND) + SHIFT + D. By using this technique, it is easy to build basic song progressions for a more varied sounding musical composition. Incidentally, you can duplicate the contents of a single clip slot by pressing CNTL (CMND) + D.

but for now concentrate on the fundamental difference between columns and rows. Each has a function and will help to shape your song.

It is worth repeating that any sample played within a given clip slot will halt the playback of any other clip on that track. You'll be able to play any number of sounds (samples) without affecting anything except your CPU load, as long as they are not aligned vertically (on the same track). The more sounds you play, the larger the strain on your computer's processing and memory, and the slower Live will operate. Figure 3.5a shows an example of two samples in a column, while Figure 3.5b shows two samples in a row. Note: in Figure 3.5a, you can play only one of the samples at a time, while in Figure 3.5b you can play all eight at once.

Figure 3.4
Scenes can be used as song-sections, such as the verse, chorus, or bridge of a song.

Figure 3.5a
Two samples in a column. Each Column is a channel in Live's virtual mixer.

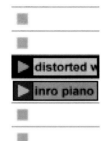

Each row can house whole musical sections, new song directions, or merely a slight modification in the piece currently playing. Many Live users think of their songs from top to bottom, advancing their song as they move down the grid, one row at a time.

The fact that a track can play only one sound at a time, rather than being a limitation, is actually a tool that can be used to your advantage in a couple of different ways. For instance, by using variations of the same drum loop–each in its own clip slot, stacked in the same track–you can make more realistic-sounding, or at least very interesting, drum fills, 'breakbeats', and rhythmic turnarounds. This is also a great method for organizing other instrument tracks that change parts when

Figure 3.5b
Each row can house whole musical sections, new song directions, or merely a slight modification in the piece currently playing. Many Live users think of their songs from top to bottom, advancing their song as they move down the grid, one row at a time.

moving from scene to scene (such as two bass guitar samples differing in chords, one for the verse, the other for the chorus). By dedicating a single track for variant clips of one particular instrument (one track for drums, one for bass, one for piano, etc.), you will create a more common mixer setup, one that will feel more like an actual recording studio.

Tip

Channel strip

Live's session mixer approximates its analog cousin in a couple of important ways. For starters, any mix, panning, or effect settings on a given channel will be applied to any loop/sample on that channel. If you plan carefully, you can take advantage of this fact by keeping similar instruments on the same track. For instance, if you apply an EQ to track 1 and boost the highs, all highs on all loops/samples on this channel will be boosted. As you move from scene to scene, verse to chorus, the settings remain the same. We will see in later chapters that Live's arranger view allows us to automate effects, toggle them on and off in the middle of a song, etc.

Info

Ram tough

All of these copied loops will not strain your CPU more than the one instance of the loop playing. Live 'knows' to allocate your computer's resources exclusively to audio playback.

In other words, Live's session mixer resembles an analog studio mixer. Track 1 = kick drum, Track 2 = snare drum, etc. The difference is that you will have several kick drum clips vertically aligned on the same track in each scene. Here is a more complete song (Figure 3.6). Notice how the same loop is copied multiple times on each track (in multiple scenes).

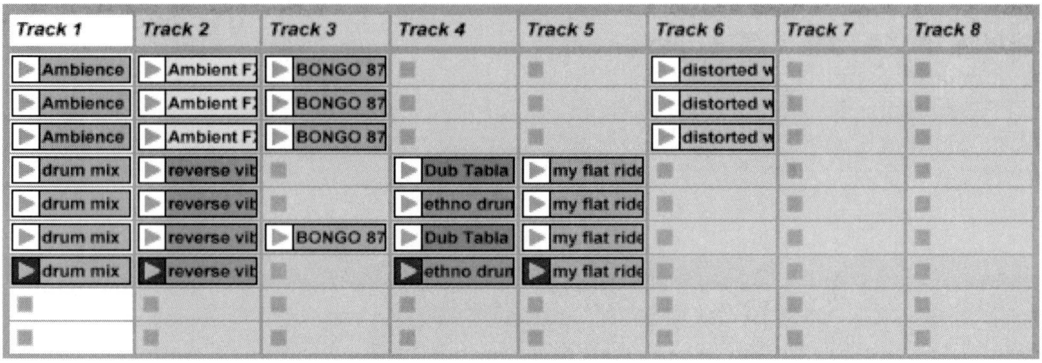

Figure 3.6
This more complete looking clip slot grid shows how a more developed song might work. You will move through the song sections scene by scene (row by row).

Track 1	Track 2	Track 3	Track 4	Track 5	Track 6	Track 7	Track 8
Ambience	Ambient F	BONGO 87			distorted w		
Ambience	Ambient F	BONGO 87			distorted w		
Ambience	Ambient F	BONGO 87			distorted w		
drum mix	reverse vib		Dub Tabla	my flat ride			
drum mix	reverse vib		ethno drun	my flat ride			
drum mix	reverse vib	BONGO 87	Dub Tabla	my flat ride			
drum mix	reverse vib		ethno drun	my flat ride			

Scene Launch

In order to move downward scene by scene, row by row, you must make use of the Scene Launcher in the Session View. Scenes can be triggered only by pressing the Scene Launch vertical strip (with cursor, computer keyboard, or MIDI keyboard) on the right-most side of Live's clip view grid (Figure 3.7). You can also trigger a scene by pressing the Enter (Return) key so long as the scene number/name is highlighted. Changing the highlighted scenes can be done with the arrow keys, and then triggered again with the Enter (PC) or Return (Mac) key. Note: if you select another clip slot or parameter on the mixer, you will need to highlight the scene again to begin triggering with the Enter/Return key.

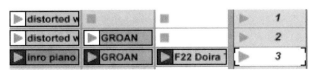

Figure 3.7
Live's Scene Launch strip (titled Master) appears to be just another column in the grid, yet these are the triggers for firing multiple loops at once. Here, Scene Launch 3 is triggering 3 loops.

Any loop within a given scene can be played (triggered) by clicking on the right facing triangle (called Fire Buttons) next to the scene name or number.

Scenes can be named and renamed as you like (the default name is simply a number). Many Live users label their scenes by song section, such as 'verse', 'chorus', 'bridge', and/or 'breakdown', in order to remind them of what scene they are triggering. To rename a scene, click on its current name or number, press CNTL (CMND) + E, and then type what you like in the clip slot, or choose Edit > Rename. Press Enter, or the Return key, to accept the new name or ESC (escape) to leave it as it was.

If all this talk of scenes vs. clips vs. tracks is beginning to confuse you, stay with me. Session View's music organizing tactics are fairly original and take a little getting used to. Once you get the hang of organizing your musical thoughts into Live's clip slot grid, you will be adding to or modifying new song sections without ever pausing your track's playback. Remember that Live favours creative working strategies; it encourages customization and is ripe for your own original configurations.

As we implied earlier, you may want to skip using scenes entirely and instead focus on triggering each clip slot individually. Many artists find that they can build a song quite naturally by adding one loop at a time, and by not pre-determining their scenes or set-list, they are keeping their options open.

Some Live users prefer to build their entire song in Live by using several small yet simple loops, and then using Live's Session View to organize, improvise, or compose. Other artists may show up to the gig with a blank slate, along with a stash of well-organized loops, and practice building their mix from the ground up in more gradual, yet still improvisational way.

Tip

Space out

The Spacebar starts and stops audio in Live 2.0 and in almost every other audio software application.

Info

Knobby digital

To adjust any of the virtual knobs found in Live 2.0, click on the knob and move the mouse forward and backward for right to left movement. In other words sideways mouse moves are a waste of time. Don't feel silly practicing how this feels; after all, it's your 'Sequencing Instrument.'

Tip

Moving scenes

To move a scene, simply grab the 'track name' with the mouse and drag it up or down to the preferred location. All loops (clips) in the scene will be included in the move.

Tip

Insert scene

To insert an additional scene (row) in Session View, or to insert a scene at a given point, select the scene above the desired location where you would like the new scene to appear, and press CNTL (CMND) + I.

Additional scenes can also be added by choosing Edit > Insert Scene. If you create a new scene in the wrong place, see the 'Moving Scenes' Tip.

The session mixer

Live's session mixer, seen in Figure 3.8, approximates a hardware mixer in both concept and design, but since it's a software mixer, it is also completely automatable, MIDI-mappable, and expandable. Similar to its hardware cousin, Live's session mixer comprises a set of individual track controls and a master section.

Individual track controls

Input, Output, Channel, and Aux Sends can be configured via Live's channel routing strip. Each vertical audio mixer channel coincides with the clip slot grid's columns (commonly referred to as tracks) described above. Like hardware mixers, each channel sports a vertical Track Volume slider, round left-to-right panning knobs, up to four Aux Send buttons, and four monitoring source select buttons. These four control buttons, Track Activator (mute), Solo/Pre Listening (solo), Monitoring (for input monitoring), and the all important Arm Session Recording, make Live's session mixer capable of professional recording, monitoring, and routing schemes. You can route Live's outputs and inputs to as many different possibilities as exist on your computer. One other important distinction is that unlike most hardware mixers, and many other software mixers, Live's mixer channels do not include EQs. You will have to add those using Live's effects.

Live's virtual 'session' mixer is similar to its hardware cousin. Each control knob, slider, or button can be mapped to a MIDI controller of your choice. Also of interest is each channel's flexible, and sometimes hidden, input/output channel routing strip. These two sub-sections of Live's Session View may be Live's most inconspicuous features. If you don't see them, press CNTL (CMND) + ALT (Option) + I or select View > In/Out.

Figure 3.8
Live's session mixer looks similar to most other virtual mixers. Each vertical strip will represent a channel with individual values for volume, panning, and routing.

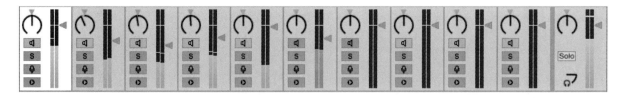

Master controls

To the right of the individual track controls, you will see Live's master mixer settings, complete with Master Volume, Stereo Positioning, and the Pre-Listening Volume. Note: the master solo volume and the Pre-Listening Volume are the exact same control, which makes perfect sense, since soloing an instrument is akin to pre-listening or cueing. If you have the crossfader view activated, you will also see a horizontal slider below the master volume and pre-listening controls.

Figure 3.9 is a close-up of session mixer's master settings and two auxiliary send channels.

DJ style crossfader

New to Live 2.0 is a weapon like none I have ever seen in audio software – the MIDI-mappable DJ-style crossfader (Live calls it just a plain old crossfader). For over 20 years now, analog crossfaders have been making magicians out of DJs by enabling them to mix two or more tracks together, juggle those mixes, and break up monotonous loops by fader flipping. Scratch DJs have also taken crossfader technique to incredible levels. The Live adaptation of the analog crossfader (seen in Figure 3.10) is the humble-looking horizontal slider just below the Master Volume section described in the preceding section.

Figure 3.9
Controls for Live's Session View mixer as well as two auxiliary bus send controls.

To use the fader, you will have to assign session mix channels to either A or B sides of the crossfader mixer. If you are new to crossfaders, think of it as the double-edged sword of volume faders. As you move to B (to increase the volume of all channels set to B), you decrease the volume of all channels set to A. The reverse holds true when you come back to A–A channels get louder, while B channels get quieter.

Here are a few tips for jumping into Live's new crossfader feature:

- Assign a couple of channels to A or B sides of the crossfader. When selecting your session mixer channels to A or B, you don't have to designate all of your active tracks (to A or B). By not assigning a channel to A or B, you have, by omission, selected both. This means that you will hear any non-specified channels all of the time. DJs often like to bring in a different groove under the same

Figure 3.10
Live's crossfader adds a whole new set of performance (and mix) tools to Live's Session View.

Tip

Hideaway

Live can feel a little constrictive, with its profusion of virtual controls. Here is a quick tip for hiding (and retrieving) some of the session mixer's key sub-sections. To hide or view the mixer, press the toggling shortcut CNTL (CMND) + ALT (OPTION) + M. To hide or view the input and output routing, press CNTL (CMND) + ALT (OPTION) + I. And to hide or view the DJ-style crossfader, press CNTL (CMND) + ALT (OPTION) + F. You can also activate or hide any of these views in Live's View > Mixer, View > In/Out, View > Cross Fader menus.

music bed and vice-versa. Simply leave all of your tracks as they are and make one drum groove A and the other B. Now gradually flip back and forth on the crossfader.

- Get your MIDI on. By assigning a MIDI-controller to control Live's crossfader, you can add a whole new performance element to Live. To do this, you will need a MIDI-controller or MIDI keyboard set up for your computer (see Chapter 2). Then all you need to do is press the MIDI button on the upper right hand side of Live's screen. Click once on the crossfader, and then move a knob or keyboard wheel (I like to use the modulation wheel).
- Dry up the mix trick. You can quickly 'dry' up your mix (remove all audible effects) by routing each of your effects sends to one side of the crossfader. To do so, simply route all effects sends to B, and leave all other crossfader assigns alone (no assignment). Assuming you have effects on your Aux sends (we will describe how to do this in the following sections), by moving the crossfader to position A you will hear no effects, while the B position will be fully effected.

Channel routing

Live's session mixer is even more flexible, once you get under the hood. The Input/Output Channel Routing is capable of routing any input imaginable into Live, by merely selecting the tab (see Figure 3.11), and picking your source. Any multi-channel input such as an eight channel sound card or multiple outputting software such as Propellerhead's Reason can have inputs routed to correspond with any given channel. If, for example, you want microphone input number one to be recorded on session mixer channel one (or any other), the drop down menus will accomplish this.

Figure 3.11
A session mixer input/output tab. In Live, you have the choice of configuring Input Type, Input Channel, and Output Channel.

Any ReWire applications currently existing on your computer will be seen in the Input dropdown menu. (ReWire is a software linking technology invented by Steinberg that allows Live to run, control, or be controlled by programs such as Reason, Sonar, Cubase, Project5, Storm, and many others.) By routing a Rewire application through Live's inputs, you will be able to monitor and record that application's audio output as you would another audio source. You will also, curiously, see Live's own 'Master Out' in the inputs section. This is available in case you want to send Live's own output to itself, for instance, when you have finished a track and want to render your song in real-time, or if you want to make a quick submix of more than one track. Sub-mixes will be covered more in context in Chapter 6, 'Playing Live...live'. Also, in the next chapter we will discuss 'audio rendering', and after studying Chapter 12, 'Recording in Live', and Chapter 13, 'ReWire–Synchronizing Your Software', all will be clear.

Auxiliary bus sends

You can add up to four auxiliary sends in Live's Session and Arranger view windows. The default setting is two (out of the box), but you can change these in Live's Preferences default tab–and then you can reset your Live Template once you have the desired number of aux sends. To do this, press the Save button as shown in Chapter 2. Aux Send channels cannot carry (hold) audio, so there is no need for recording or monitoring buttons, although you do have panning, solo, mute, and volume settings so that any effects or audio routed through these channels can be acted upon as they would be in the analog world. Add Aux Send channels by selecting Edit > Insert Send Track or via the key command: Alt + Cntl (Cmnd)+ T.

If you are new to audio, mixers, or aux sends, the concept of an Auxiliary Bus is a fairly simple one. Sends save you time and trouble by allowing you to route several channels to one. In Live's channel routing section, you can route any mixer channel into the sends only. Why would you do such a thing? Well, you may want to adjust the volume of 2 or more tracks with just one volume slider. To do this, simply route all audio you would like to control (at the same time) to an open aux bus, making sure to change the sending channels' output to Sends Only. Now all tracks will be controllable via the single Aux Send channel that they are routed to by cranking the corresponding aux send knob on that channel. For example, if you want to route track 1 to aux send 1, change the output to Sends Only and then turn the virtual aux send knob accurately titled 1 clockwise until you hear the audio coming through on the send.

Even more common is to use aux sends as a means to alleviate the need for placing multiple instances of an effect on each channel. The following is an extremely common and helpful method for conserving computer resources and achieving professional results.

1 Place a loop in any one of Live's clip slots.
2 Turn up the track's 'contribution' level to Send 1.
3 Drag Live's Reverb effect precisely to the aux channel label on Send 1. Note, so long as the send is highlighted, you may also double-click to add the effect.
4 Make sure the Reverb's Dry/Wet is set all the way to wet, and the size is set to about 3 o'clock (you can use Live's Large Factory reverb setting by pressing on the effect's dropdown menu).
5 Now play the scene, and hear the effect.
6 Turn up the Send 1 level on other tracks (that you would like to send to that same reverb). You can send as many tracks as you like.
7 For a different effect, hit the Post button on the Master Channel so that it reads Pre (these buttons toggle Pre/Post). Then turn the volume down on the original track and listen to the effect. When Pre is depressed, the channel volume for that channel no longer determines the level going to the send. This routing is great when you are trying to eliminate the dry signal from the mix, creating a swimming-in-reverb effect.

Pre or Post Fader

In the Sends section of the master strip, you will see buttons that say Post. mentioned earlier, these buttons toggle between Pre and Post and will change the position of your Aux Sends to pre- or post-fader (respectively). In the pre-fader position, your sounds on that channel will go straight to the send regardless of what the channel's fader position is. Conversely, if you select 'post' (for post-fader), you will hear loops sent to this auxiliary send only if their respective volume sliders are up and there is signal coming though.

As you might imagine, there are creative advantages to both settings. Pre-fader is an excellent way to ensure your sound gets whatever effect is placed on that channel, or to quickly create a multiple channel bus as described above. Post-fader is better for keeping control of your mix, keeping your effect level proportionate to your channel volume level.

Arranger View

Beginners may think of it as merely Live's 'other' window, but Arranger View (seen in Figure 3.12), is the place for recording and editing your Live Session View jams, performing overdubs, automating additional effects, and rendering your final track. If Session View is the spontaneous right-brain-tickling creative screen, Arranger View is the analytic, left-brain-stimulating, 'finishing touches' side of Live. You may notice that Live's Arranger View closely resembles many other multi-track applications' 'Arranger' screens. Programs such as Acid Pro, Sonar, Cubase, Logic, ProTools and many others seem to be committed to horizontal, left-to-right–based audio. If you like this trend, you will be right at home making music in Live, Arranger style.

Figure 3.12
Live's Arranger View will contain the output of your Session View songs. Each horizontal line in Arranger View represents a Session View Track (mixer channel) that will correspond to a horizontal channel in Arranger.

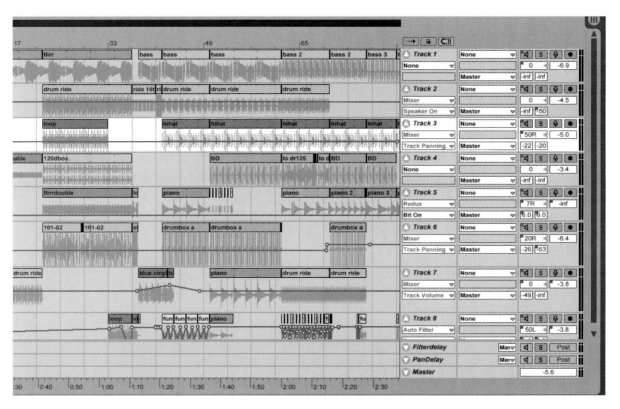

For those who didn't read the figure caption, I'll say it again: Each track in Session View corresponds precisely with its track counterpart in Arranger View. If you have eight tracks in Session View, you will have eight tracks in Arranger View. You can add a track in either view, and it will behave as if you are working on the same project.

There is, however, a very important difference between Session View and Arranger View. Once you record one of your Session View jams (compositions) in Live, the mix settings of each view, Session and Arranger, will operate separately, and sometimes (when mix automation has been recorded) independently from one another. This is an extremely important concept to grasp, so let's look at it a bit more closely by loading up the Live Demo song 'Live 2 Demo Arrangement'. After you have loaded the file found in your original Ableton Live folder in the subfolder entitled Content, follow the steps below.

1   When you load 'Live 2 Demo Arrangement' you will be looking at a completed song in Live's Arranger View. Press Tab to switch to Session View.
2   Take a look at the session mixer and notice all the red markings. These markings mean that the knob, fader, and/or button contains automation data. (Automation data consists of the recorded movements of every fader, knob, or button you moved when you did your Live recording.) We will cover this in great detail throughout the book, but most notably in Chapter 7, 'Editing Your Performance'.
3   Now move the volume slider on Track 5. Notice that the red blip goes away, and the red light on the Back to Arrangement button (on the control bar) lights up. You have now told Live to ignore that specific fader's automation.
4   To reinstate the automation–so you can listen to the song's original recording settings–simply press the red Back to Arrangement button on the control bar to the right of the record button. Notice how Track 5's fader level will jump back up to its original position.
5   Press Tab to go back to the Arranger View.
6   Press Play or your Spacebar and hear/watch Live's settings move with the music. You will see panning and volume settings change on the right. Double-click on the name Track 8, and start the arrangement around measure 42 to see a filter in action.

In any given project, you will be able to hear the mix settings for Arranger View only when the Back to Arrangement button is dark (Figure 3.13). And I'll repeat, because I have been frustrated many times, that you should always double check exactly which mix you are hearing when making adjustments.

Figure 3.13
Whether you are in Arranger View or Session View, you can always revert to the Arranger View's mix settings, which usually contain automation.

This view-dependent mixer settings concept is a drastic difference from other applications you may be used to. The reasoning is simple: You will want to hear entirely different settings on your improvised remix or jam than you will on a finished piece of music. It can be handy to remove the automation, or, if you are in Session View, to hear the automation at a moment's notice. For this reason, and others we will delve into later, remember that Arranger and Session View track settings are not always the same mix—hence they will not necessarily sound the same.

Track settings

Figure 3.14
Each track in Arranger has the same controls as the tracks in Session View.

The Arranger View's track settings are located on the right side of the screen and take up about one-third of the working portion of the Arranger View, as seen in Figure 3.14. To maximize (view) a track, click the downward-pointing triangle. Any sample on that track will reveal its waveform, and several hidden track settings will now appear.

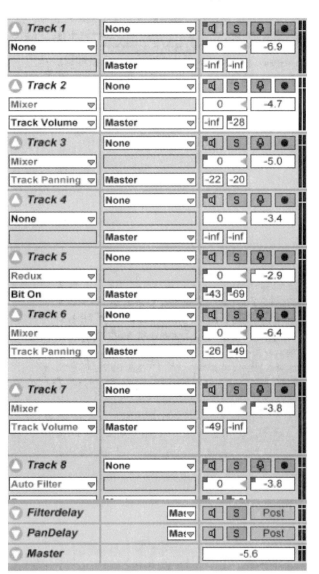

All of the usual suspects are here. Volume, Panning, FX sends, Solo, Mute, Monitor, Arm for Recording, and all of the same track routing features found in Session are in Arranger. The difference is visual: The controls have been turned on their sides. Another visual difference is that adjustments to each parameter will produce a red, editable envelope line on the track (as seen in Figure 3.15).

Master settings

The mixer's Master Settings are located on the bottom line of Live's Arranger View. You can edit (automate) Mix Volume, Mix Panning, Speaker On (Mute), Tempo, and Crossfader master controls via envelopes on this track (see Figure 3.16). Note: Envelopes (referred to as Breakpoint Envelopes in Live) are small editable lines that direct the parameter to which they are assigned.

Device and control choosers

Before we step into the world of mix-automation in Live 2.0, it is important to locate and understand the Device Chooser and Control Chooser drop down menus found on all tracks (including Master and Aux Sends) in Arranger View, as seen in Figure 3.17. The contents of Device Chooser will depend upon what devices (effects) are on the track. Any Ableton or VST effect will show up here as will Mixer to tell you that you are working with the mix settings such as Track Volume, Track Panning, Send Levels (Send 1, Send 2, etc.), Mute (Speaker On) and X-Fade Assignment. Note: the None value tells you that no device has been chosen.

Each track, master channel, and aux send will also contain a Control Chooser (located just below the Device Chooser) with any number of selectable effect and mix parameters in its drop down menu. When we begin to work with and apply automation later in this chapter, Control Chooser will enable you to see which mix parameter, in the form of a Breakpoint Envelope (see

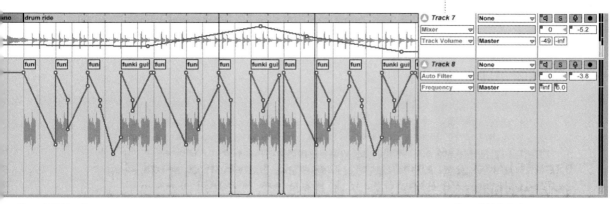

Figure 3.15 (above)
Each control in Live's Arranger View can be
automated, or drawn via envelope.

Figure 3.16 (below)
Live 2.0 has added tempo change and
crossfader automation to Arranger View's
master track.

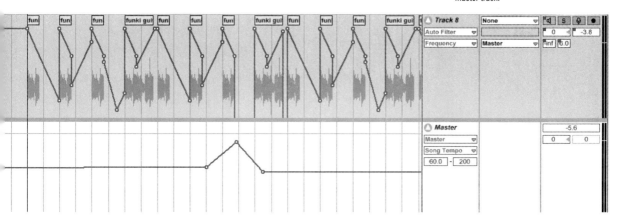

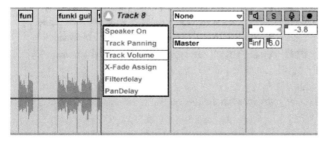

Figure 3.17
The Device and Control Choosers help
decipher which mix-parameters you are
working with. You can change your device or
working parameter by using their drop down
menus, or by physically clicking on the
device (and device control) that you would
like to work with.

next section) you are seeing. For any effect that has been chosen in the Device
Chooser's menu, the Control Chooser menu will house the list of controls for that
device. You might have also noticed that by clicking on any mix setting or effects
knob/slider, you can change the Device/Control menus to that knob/slider–or it will
appear that the menus follow your mouse clicks. For example, if you have an EQ
Four (Live's parametric equalizer plug-in) loaded on a track, clicking on the EQ
Four on/off switch will immediately switch to read EQ Four in the Device Chooser,
and Device On in the Control Chooser. For more practice, try clicking on any other
control in the effect and watch the Device and Control Chooser Menus change.

Breakpoint envelopes

Live's Breakpoint envelopes (in Figure 3.18) control the mixer settings in Arranger View. Like a line-graph, you can draw in multiple plot points (called Breakpoints) to direct a track's volume, panning, aux send level, or any effect parameter. Nearly everything in Live can be controlled by the breakpoint envelope, and, as we will see in later chapters, Breakpoint Envelopes are the key to unlocking Live's automation. To select an envelope, locate the Device Chooser on the track or master section that you are looking to edit, and then pick which parameter you want to manipulate via the Control Chooser dropdown box. Once the line appears, double-click on any portion of the line to create a Breakpoint; double-click again on that Breakpoint to delete it. Drag any Breakpoint up or down to gradually slope your parameter over time. The most common Breakpoint edits are surely volume fade-ins and fade-outs. As you may imagine, a clean, evenly sloping line is ever so much smoother than your shaky fader hand.

Figure 3.18

Sloped Breakpoint Envelopes represent movement within the track. You may add and delete Breakpoints as you like to create either radical or simple moves in mix and effects parameters.

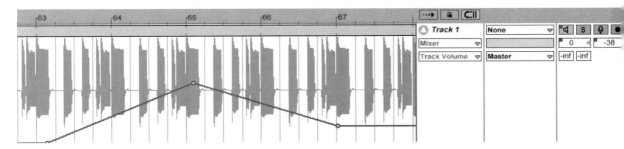

The end result of using Breakpoint envelopes is to create an automatic (or pre-programmed) increase, decrease, or change in a given value. This change, performed for you by Live, is called Automation. Effects automation (or Mix Automation) can also be done by using your hand (mouse) in real-time – rather than drawing it; either way Live promises countless hours of fun and excitement. The premise is simple enough. You can record your mix settings, such as volume, panning, effects parameters, etc., and they will be forever reproduced (until you change them). Arranger View is the place to actually see your automation envelopes, while Session View is the screen to actually watch your faders move as if a ghost is moving them.

If you have never tried mix automation, take a moment to do so, and be forever inspired.

1 Load a clip or two into Live's Session View.
2 Press the Stop button twice to be sure you are reset to the top of the track.
3 Press the Automation Record Button in Live's top-of-the-screen control bar.
4 Press Play on your loop.
5 Now while you are recording, move the Session Mixer volume control up and down, and move the panning a bit.
6 Hit Stop (or Spacebar), to stop recording.
7 Hit Play to hear your results.
8 Watch the 'ghost in the machine'. The Volume Fader and Panning Control knob will move on their own.

Info

Transport basics

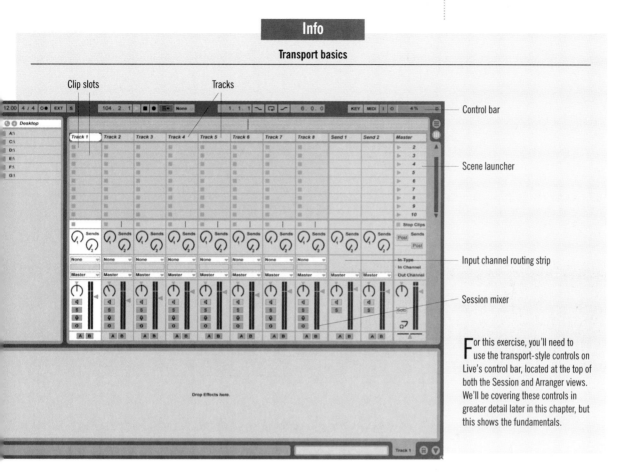

Clip slots

Tracks

Control bar

Scene launcher

Input channel routing strip

Session mixer

For this exercise, you'll need to use the transport-style controls on Live's control bar, located at the top of both the Session and Arranger views. We'll be covering these controls in greater detail later in this chapter, but this shows the fundamentals.

After you have watched your newly made automation in Session View, hit Tab (the toggle control for view switching) to call up Arranger View. Now maximize the track with the loop content on it by pressing the Track Fold-in downward pointing triangle-shaped icon next to the track label. Next, click on the Device Chooser drop down menu. Select Mixer (which should be red because it contains automation information), and then Track Volume in the Control Chooser drop down box. You will see a red line with several small circular points on it. Each point (called a Breakpoint in Live) represents a small directional change in the value automation. You can move these as you like to change the sound, or double-click on the line to add or delete them. You can add (or delete) edit-points at will by double-clicking anywhere on the line.

As we discussed earlier (with the Back to Arrangement button feature), any further adjustments made during playback mode will cause the Back to Arrangement button to light up, signaling that you are no longer hearing all of your automation or Arranger View mix settings. Any altered automated controls will cease to move as recorded until this Back to Arrangement button is deactivated. To hear the mix effects of your original recording, press this red button. This is the same distinction we discussed above in Arranger View.

In later chapters, we will discuss some tips for creating livelier mixes by using envelopes.

Overview

Figure 3.19
Live's Overview is quite literally the view from above the track.

Standing tall above Live's Arranger/Session Views and just below the control bar is the Overview (of your Live song). The Overview, which resembles a musical staff, is there purely for navigation and reference to show you where you are in your song. So long as you have audio recorded into Live's Arranger view, **it offers** a bird's eye view of your entire track. You will see tiny coloured lines representing your loops and recorded audio, in the Arranger View. The Overview (Figure 3.19) can be seen in Session View but is a permanent fixture in Arranger View. You can hide the Overview (in Session View) by pressing Cntl (Cmnd) + Shift + O. line.

To use Overview to move to a new location, hover the mouse over the portion of the Overview bar you want to move to; the magnifying glass icon will appear; click once and you will be moved to the corresponding location in the arranger. To zoom in and out, hover over the Overview bar; depress the mouse button (left on PC), and move the mouse forward and backward to zoom in and out (respectively). You can quickly skip from the beginning to the end with one click of the mouse – though I should point out that you will still need to place your cursor in the desired location and then hit your Spacebar to start playback. Try this a couple of times; it takes some getting used to.

Control bar

Figure 3.20
Live's control bar remains constant at the top of both of Live's main views. Here you will find standard symbols for Stop, Play, and Record, as well as time/tempo information.

Headlining each one of Live's two different working views (Session and Arranger) is Live's own version of a transport bar. Typically, transport bars function as the start/stop mechanism and track position finder all in one. Although transport bars are often free-floating in many applications, in Live the Control Bar is fixed to the top of your screen. Still, most 'power-users' default to keyboard shortcuts such as the Spacebar for starting and stopping playback. Also, many Live aficionados map Live's control bar functions to MIDI or computer keyboard controls. We will cover this in detail in Chapter 6, 'Playing Live...live' and Chapter 9, 'Using MIDI'.

In the control bar, you will find pertinent song information such as time-signature, tempo, and processor load (a vital stat for the computer-based musician). Control bar will also help you pinpoint your exact location within the track and determine Live's master quantize settings. New to version 2.0 are Live's punch-in/punch-out buttons for recording. And, a Tap Tempo and metronome make recording your Live projects from scratch just a tad more manageable.

Time, tempo, and song settings

On the left side of the control bar you will find Live's tempo, time signature, and song settings subsection (Figure 3.21). The buttons are from left to right, Tap Tempo, Tempo, Signature Numerator, Signature Denominator, Metronome, External Sync Switch, and External Sync Indicator.

The Tap Tempo button is a handy new song-starting feature in Live. For a quick test-drive of one of Tap Tempo's features, click on the button four times, and your project will begin at that tempo. This is a handy feature if you need to sneak in while another DJ is playing, synch up with your drummer, or match another device such as a turntable or CD player. You can also use Tap Tempo to help map out songs and better align groove clips. Sound confusing? Chapters 5 and 6 will clear it up.

Figure 3.21
This subsection of the control bar is devoted to time, including MIDI sync, tempo, time-signature, and song settings.

Next up are Live's project Tempo and Time signature settings, which are found just to the right of the Tap Tempo button. Live can handle tempos ranging from 20 to 999 BPM (beats per minute), and time signatures with numerators ranging from 1-99 and denominator choices of 1, 2, 4, 8, and 16 – a huge range of possibilities.

Moving to the right of time signature, you will come upon Live's Metronome button. This feature/function works complementary to the Tap Tempo. When engaged, you will hear a customizable click track (metronome) that can serve as a guide for new recordings and help with loop editing.

Lastly, the External Sync Switch engage button, and the External Sync monitoring light show how Live is handling the job of synchronizing to an external device. Provided that Live's preferences have been set up correctly (to synchronize playback with another MIDI source), the External Synch Switch engages or disengages Live's MIDI-synchronization to an outside source, while the S monitoring light announces that the MIDI sync signal is being received.

Start, stop, and quantization

Most starting and stopping in Live is best handled with the Spacebar (tap it once to start, tap it again to stop); however, the second area of Live's control bar section (Figure 3.22) sports official Start and Stop buttons. You will also find the Automation Record Button and the Back to Arrangement button (discussed above in the Breakpoint Envelopes section), which you will use during the track-editing process.

Figure 3.22
Here is the second element of Live's control bar. Keep your eye on the Quantization Menu. This is the key to sounding like a pro when you fire off your loops.

Other points of interest include the Arrangement Position box, and the global Quantization Menu, which bookend the second segment of the control bar. The Arrangement Position box provides a continuous readout, in measures, beats, and subdivisions, of where you are in the song, whether you're listening or recording.

The global Quantization Menu, to the right of the Record button, sets the default triggering timing for Live's Session View. You have the option of selecting 1/32, 1/16, 1/8, 1/4, 1/2, and the full measure (called bar). What this means is that each loop triggered in the session view will 'fire' at the very next subdivision you have selected. For instance, at the Bar setting, your 'fired' loop will not begin to play until the first beat of the very next measure. If your setting is 1/16, your loop will begin playing at the next 1/16 note. You can imagine how this quantitative correction tool will clean up your performance. This can be a huge help and very cool trick for guiding rapid-fire sample sections, or just ensuring that your next scene launches right on the first beat.

If quantization sounds sterile to you, and you want your music to breathe more, you can also set this menu to None or no quantization of any sort. Any loop you fire while None is selected will sound the instant the sample is triggered.

In Arranger View, the Quantization Menu helps to guide the 'snap to' editing for loop and sample placement. If 'snap-to' is off, and the Quantization Menu is set to 1/4, you will only be able to drag your sounds to begin at a given quarter note. The above setting options all still apply.

Punch in, punch out recording

Live provides several new features that are built for both the (self-engineering) recording musician and the mad loop concocter. Punch In and Punch Out is just such a tool. Using it, you will be able to record a select length of audio or create a sub-mix of Live's output. Recording in small segments like this can be an excellent way to make original loops for your collection or add in just the right bit of music to your track. We will cover recording in detail in later chapters, so don't worry if this description seems a little overwhelming. The third set of tools in Live's Control bar section, seen below in Figure 3.23, includes controls for two loop points, the start and the end. If the Loop button is depressed, then Live's playback will loop (the defined start/stop length) continuously, as opposed to playing though to the end of the song. If the two punch points are activated, Live can be set to record in typical multi-tracking get in/get out fashion. This tool is meant to provide a quick way of recording for a specified amount of time.

Figure 3.23

Live 2.0's new Punch In and Punch Out functionality makes recording Live's output or tracking some additional input a breeze.

System monitoring

The fourth segment of the control bar (Figure 3.24) is the system-monitoring and Key/MIDI set-up area. We will cover the many ways to configure MIDI and computer keyboard triggering and controls in Chapters 5 and 6. However, I want to point out that the Key (Key Map Mode Switch) and MIDI (MIDI Map Mode Switch) buttons are your entrance point to controlling Live with an outside hardware controller. Ableton was ingenious enough to make sure that all MIDI and Keyboard mapping can be done on the fly, without ever stopping playback – no small feat.

Knowing how much gas is left in the tank – or whether you're running on fumes – is important in the laptop world. Here to help, Live's CPU Load Meter continuously shows the amount of strain on your system for a given set of audio processing or loop playback. If for any reason, this bar is beginning to approach 100%, the D (Hard-Disk Overload Indicator) button just to the right of the CPU meter, will begin to flicker red.

Live's custom views

Live also hosts several concealable windows accessible in both Session and Arranger Views. These secondary windows enable you to explore your loops, Live's effects, VST effects, and Live's integrated Info menu. Unlike most configurable software applications, these windows pop up or close with the click of a single triangle shaped icon (see Figure 3.25a and 3.25b). For instance, if you are working on the song arrangement, you will likely not need to have the loop browser open.

Figure 3.24
Pictured above is the fourth segment of Live's control bar and song settings section. From here, you can monitor your hardware (CPU load and MIDI input/output action) and set-up your Key and MIDI controls.

Info

MIDI prognosis

The I and O buttons, just left of the CPU Load Meter, represent MIDI Input and MIDI Output signal presence by lighting up (turning colors) when Live is sending or receiving MIDI signal.

Figure 3.25a
Live's Session View with the Browser, Info, and Clip View (Chapter 5) maximized (open).

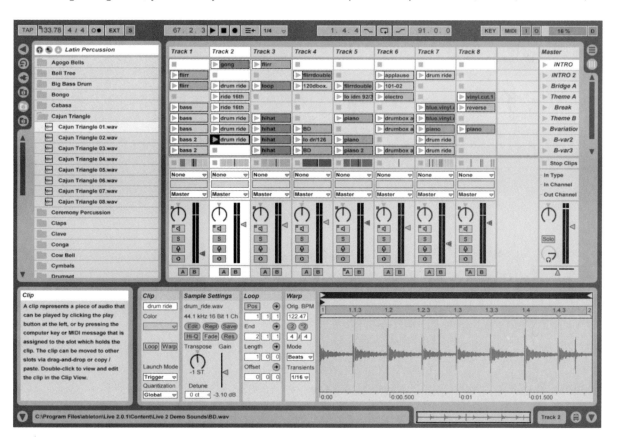

Figure 3.25b
With Browser, Info, and Clip View closed,
Live's screen is wide open for you to strike
up the band.

Or, if you are finished recording, you might want to close any extra inputs or ReWire channels. After some experimentation, you will discover your favourite working views in Session or Arranger Views. The idea is that you may want to hide collapsible windows in order to maximize screen real estate.

The Browser

The Browser window (Figure 3.26) is the means to access all of your audio files (samples) and audio effects – both plug-in effects (VST plug-ins) and Ableton's own effects. The Browser is retractable and located in the upper left section of either the Session or Arranger View. By clicking the leftward-pointing triangle-shaped arrow, you can hide this window. Conversely, if the arrow is pointing to the right, simply click once to view the Browser.

Loop previewing

Warning! Do not underestimate the power of Live's browser. With it, Live boasts the unique distinction of being the only Mac-based application in which loops can be previewed in real-time at the project tempo. Cakewalk's Sonar and Sonic Foundry's Acid Pro both do this for the PC, but all other programs require some pre-formatting before this can be achieved. Auto-previewing, or as Ableton calls it, 'pre-listening', can be toggled off and on by clicking on the miniature set of headphones to the uppermost left of the loop browser.

Drag and drop

If you happen to like the sounds you are hearing when previewing loops, simply drag and drop the loop(s) into either the Session or Arranger Views. You can place it in a clip slot in Session View, or onto a track (at any point you like) in Arranger View. The sound file can then be accessed immediately in Live's Clip View. In Chapter 5, 'Making Music in Live', we'll discuss Clip View in detail).

Navigating the browser

The default position of Live's loop browser will be the exact same position that you were searching when you last closed Live. To facilitate faster manual searches, Live enables you to set up shortcuts within three different File Browser placeholders (seen in Figure 3.27). These will save you time as well as aid in the time-consuming process of organizing your loops for a live show.

At the top of the browser, and just below the tap, tempo, and time signature information, are three key icons. They will be just to the left of the name of your current folder (Figure 3.28). You will see a set of headphones (Live's Pre-Listening button), and two separate arrow markers – one hooking up (the Move Up button), the other pointing down (the Root button). The Move Up and Root buttons help you to locate the file you are looking for, and then designate the browser position, to save you time.

Three browser shortcuts (or bookmarks) will help you to skip between your three favourite folders

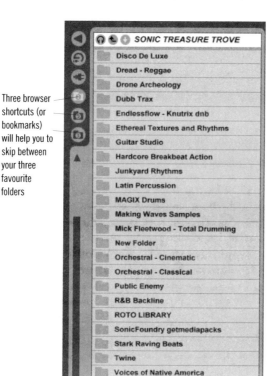

Figure 3.26
Located on the far and upper left hand side is Live's hide-able effects, VST plug-in effects, and sound File browser.

Figure 3.27
The File Browser place holders. They may be tiny, but they are a mighty big time saver.

Figure 3.28
The Pre-Listening, Move Up, and Root (place-setter) buttons.

In the above sections, we touched on the importance of pre-listening to your sounds in the browser before bringing them into your project. The Pre-listening (headphone-shaped) icon will engage or disengage Live's loop pre-view function. I generally leave this on while I'm home and composing and experimenting, and then turn it off when it is time to go to the gig. The logic is simple, in that I don't want to accidentally pre-view (hear) the wrong loop during a performance unless I am routing my pre-listening output through a separate sound card. Generally, when prepping for a live performance, my loops and samples will be organized and named descriptively enough that I will not have to hear them before importing them into my project.

The next two icons, Move Up and Root, will help you by place-setting or book-marking your location in Live's browser so that each time you open Live you can begin looking in the same folder. Since you have three separate File Browser Choosers, you can set three different bookmarked locations. Here's how to do it:

1 Open Live's Browser and click on one of the File Browser Choosers (the file folder icons numbered 1, 2, and 3).

2 Next, click into the folder you would like to browse sounds from by cycling down the file folder tree. You may need to click through several folders to get to the one you are after.

3 Now click once on the folder you would like Live to default to (your new desired bookmarked location for this file browser).

4 Press Root (the downward-pointing arrow-shaped icon in the browser). Once you click Root, the browser will move that folder to the top (starting position) for all future browsing. If you change your mind, or want to go back to a folder that you cannot see, click on the Move Up button (the upward-pointing arrow-shaped icon). The Move Up button simply moves your browser's view up one folder level at a time.

Organizing your sounds

New to Live 2.0, you can rename your loops inside the browser. This can be an enormous time saver and creative tool when composing in Live. To rename a loop, simply highlight the loop in the browser (shown in Figure 3.29) and then press key-board shortcut keys Cntl (Cmnd) + E. You may also do this via the menu, by highlighting the loop and selecting Edit > Rename.

Figure 3.29
By highlighting a sound or loop in Live's browser, you can rename the file. Simply press Cntl (Cmnd) + E, and begin typing the new file name. If you change your mind at any point while typing, press ESC (escape).

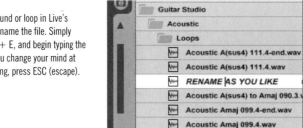

Develop a system of organizing your loop/sample collection that works for you. It is important that your naming scheme is informative and promotes creativity. For instance, if you name every drum loop sequentially, drumloop1, drumloop2, drumloop3, etc., this may be definitive, but ultimately not inspiring to work with. I try to come up with short titles that give me a brief idea of what I was thinking when I first made a given group of loops. For instance, bigloudDR1 and bigloudDR2, would be a couple of big loud drum loops. This brief but apt description can limit long searches through your mounds of loops and help you to better find the sonic character you are seeking. Also, if you stumble across a sound you are particularly fond of, you can take a look at some others in that same batch.

Effects View

Live's Concealable Audio Effect window (see Figure 3.30) contains both Ableton Live's own effects and any VST effects you might have. Each effect has its own tab or section, where the Ableton Effect Call-Up button resembles the Ableton Live logo and the Plug-In Effects tab looks like the male end of an AC adapter plug.

We will explore each of Live's wonderful effect plug-ins and learn how to incorporate VST effects in Chapter 8, 'Live's Effects'. For now, it's enough to know that when you double-click on one of Live's effects, you instantly add (or plug-in) an instance of the selected effect into the channel you have highlighted. For instance, if you have selected Track 1, and then double-click on Live's Auto Filter effect, you will automatically insert this effect into Track 1. To add an additional effect after this one, double-click another effect. To change the routing order or signal path of your audio, simply drag and drop the effect within the channel in the Track View (appearing in the bottom half of your screen when an effect is added). This double-click move can also add effects for sends and master channels. The only limit to the number of effects you can insert in a given channel is your own CPU. By keeping your eye on the CPU load meter on the far right side of Live's Control Bar, you can know when your machine has had enough.

In Figure 3.31, I created one instance each of Live's Filter Delay and Chorus effects. To delete an effect, click once on the effect in the Track View screen, and press your Delete (Mac) or Backspace (PC) key.

Figure 3.30
Live's Effect menu. To add an effect, highlight the track you want to receive the effect, and then double-click the effect.

Figure 3.31
To create this figure, I double-clicked on two separate effects.

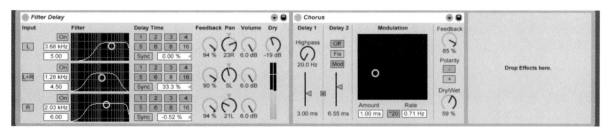

Tip

Preset effects

To audition a different effect preset, double-click on the downward pointing arrow (the Recall Preset button) on any of Live's effects. Simply click on any setting appearing in the drop down menu, under the Factory Settings tab and you will see the effect snap to the corresponding parameters. To save your own effects settings, click once on the picture of the disc (just to the right of the downward pointing arrow) and enter a preset name. Your new preset will be visible in the drop down window from now on when opening that same effect.

Live's built-in effects

The good and bad news is that Ableton's effects are only available in Live. This means you will not be able to use them in Cubase, Logic, or ProTools, or any other program other than Live. These plug-ins are designed specifically for optimized use in Live. They are extremely stable, and are of a design similar to that of Live 2.0. In short, they look good, feel good, and sound great. There were originally ten effects in Live 1.0. A deep and interesting reverb was added in 1.5.1 and now, new to 2.0, are two new effects, Gate and Redux, (bringing the total to 13).

Another thing you should know if you are a previous Live 1.5 user is that all of Live's effects now support saveable, a.k.a. customizable, settings. You will now be able to recall your favourite effects presets, as well as audition any of several Ableton presets. These factory presets are especially handy for helping to familiarize you with the capabilities of each effect. More on this in Chapter 8, but for now here is a quick tip.

VST plug-in effects

VST Plug-ins have become wildly popular in the last few years as a result of the efficiency that VST plug-ins are capable of delivering (in terms of system performance) over DirectX and Soundmanager Plug-ins. One reason VST development is so rampant is that the code remains free to download from the Steinberg Web site. While this open-source philosophy sounds fantastically carefree, be forewarned. Free code can spell danger. There are some incredibly smart, well-intentioned, software developers who are building innovative and interesting audio software (even for free), but with only the smallest of beta test pools. That means you should be wary of any plug-in, regardless of how expensive it is until you have tried it on your system, with your sound card and your music, in several different situations/combinations. We will recommend some safe plug-ins in Chapter 8, but for now recognize that Ableton's 'house' plug-ins are capable of handling most common audio situations (and do an excellent job at it). Unless you are absolutely certain there is a plug-in available that you 'need' or have thoroughly tested, don't assume all VST plug-ins are trouble-free.

Figure 3.32 demonstrates one of my favourite (and more stable) VST plug-ins from PSP's Mix Pack.

All of your VST plug-ins need to be in the VST folder Live searches at each start-up. If you've been following along, we set this folder up during Preferences. If not, I recommend giving Live its own VST folder and simply copying all VST plug-ins you would like to run in Live into that folder. The reason I don't just use my Cubase, Fruityloops, or other VST folder is that since Live does not yet support VSTi (virtual instruments), and there are some spotty VST effects out there, Live will start up quicker and run more efficiently with less VST 'garbage' to look through. Any Live-compatible plug-ins in this folder will be visible by clicking on the small AC adapter in the browser window. To add the plug-in to your project, you either drag and drop to the channel you like or simply double-click on it while the channel/aux send is highlighted. Here is a tip for more effective VST plug-in use.

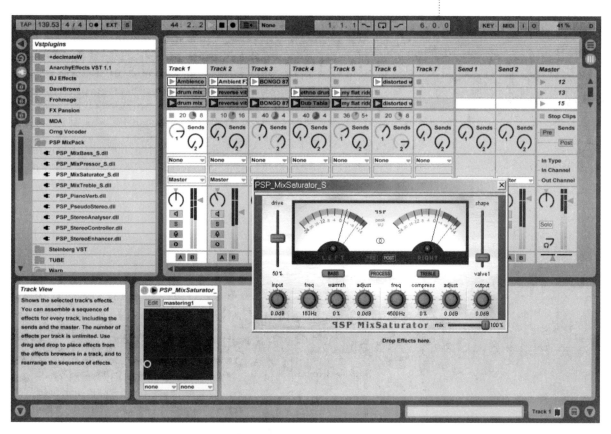

Figure 3.32
A VST effect added into the mix. For more immediate, detailed information, you may want to skip ahead to Chapter 8, 'Live's Effects'.

Tip

I want my VST

Any VST plug-in that cannot be seen via Live's browser cannot be used in Live – even if it is located in the correct directory on your PC or Mac. Be sure to move (delete) these plug-ins out of the VST folder that Live searches each time the program launches. Remember, this is the folder that we told Live to look in when we set up Live's initial preferences (See Preferences > Misc > Paths > VST Plug-in Folder). As a result, Live will start up faster. Also, if you notice a plug-in not working properly in Live, you should also take these out of the plug-in directory, write down the settings or combination of events that created the error, and send Ableton and the third party plug-in manufacturer the feedback. By doing so, you may just help some small software developer zero in on a problem that would otherwise take months to figure out.

Info

Note – no VST presets

The Save and Recall preset functions are not available for VST plug-ins at the time of this writing.

Tip

Auxiliary power

To maximize efficiency in Live, use Live's Aux Sends (Auxiliary Sends). Live usually has two Aux Sends open in any default project (if you can't see them, select View > Sends or Cntl (Cmnd) + Alt + S). By placing effects in these auxiliary channels and turning up the associated send on any audio track, you will route your audio partially through the effect. For instance, if you want reverb on two tracks, you can load one reverb into the Aux Send and then turn up the sends on two (or more tracks) to use that same reverb. Of course they will be restricted to utilizing the same effect setting.

Info

Saving grace

When saving in Live with the simple Save command, it is important to realize what you have and have not done. You have told Live to save a file with all song information (such as arrangement, mix settings, effects, etc.). You have also told Live to remember where all the sound files, samples, and loops reside on the hard drive(s). What you have *not* done is saved these audio files (necessary for your song). These files will remain wherever they were until you use the Save Set Self-Contained command. At this point Live will create a copy of all audio files and place them in a folder labeled *Your Song Name* Sounds. I recommend saving Set Self-Contained each time you add an audio file to your mix, as well as habitually using the Save command as you are working[md]CNTL (CMND) + S [md]as a safeguard against unexpected system crashes.

Info

Saving face – keeping your files intact

When saving as self-contained, Live saves the song file in the designated folder and then creates a corresponding Sounds folder just beneath it (one folder level down). For instance, if your song is called 'Eye of the Tiger', you will notice that Live will create a folder with all of the sounds for your song and automatically title it Eye of the Tiger Sounds.

Saving files and songs

If you are new to audio software, that is a good thing. This means you come without preconceived notions of how difficult it can be just to organize all the files necessary for a given audio project. If you are a Pro Tools or Logic veteran, you know that calling up last week's session from a CD you burned that night might not be so simple. New to Live 2.0 is an enhanced file-saving scheme sure to reduce at least some of the frustrating missing file searches and 'which version am I working in?' blues.

Live offers four ways to save project files: Save Live Set, Save Live Set As, Save a Copy, and Save Set Self-Contained. If you are familiar with common computer documents, such as word processor applications, Save and Save As work in exactly the same way. Save, which can be done by pressing Cntl (Cmnd) + S, saves the document (in this case a Live song file) in its present state, under its present file name. This is the most common way you will save while you are working on new tracks (sets), especially when you like the results.

Save Live Set As, done via Cntl (Cmnd) + Shift key + S, is the command for saving the current song file in its current state under a *different* name, and is usually done only when you want to begin a new song or modify an existing song without changing the original version. To do this, select File > Save Live Set As, select the location where you would like to place the file, and type the song's newest name.

If you are modifying a song but would like to preserve the original, or if you would like to make a backup just for safety's sake, File > Save Copy will automatically add the word copy to the end of your file name.

Saving set self-contained

The greatest save method is undoubtedly Save Set Self-Contained. If the very idea of a self-contained file makes you smile, you are no stranger to computers. It is a terrible inconvenience (to put it mildly) to lose a file. Save Set Self-Contained eliminates this problem by guaranteeing that all related audio files, as well as Live's proprietary analysis files (recognizable by the file extension .ASD), are stored in a single folder (called sounds) as a brand spanking new copy of the original. Note: Saving Set Self Contained will *not* make your song into a single file (such as a Word document or text file), but will create a single folder for all of your sound and sound-analysis files. To play/load your song you will need this folder (automatically labelled *Song Name* Sounds by Live) *and* the Ableton Live Set (.ALS) song file that contains all of your song-specific information.

Sounds great, doesn't it? I mean, imagine never ever having a problem again locating a file, opening a song on a different computer, emailing a track to a buddy, or just coming back two days later and not having any trouble recalling your song just as you had left it.

To save your Live set as self-contained, select File > Save Set Self-Contained, and then navigate to the folder where you would like to place the song (and all of its related audio files).

Even though saving as self-contained sounds all-encompassing, and it does wonders for keeping all of your audio files in the same easy-to-locate folder, there are still some items to keep in mind.

- **VST effects.** While Save Self-Contained can be an effective way of keeping all of your audio files together, any VST plug-ins (used in a given song) will not be saved inside your file. This means that if you transport your song to a different computer or uninstall any VST effect plug-in that is present on the song you are saving, the plug-in will be missing. If this is a free plug-in this isn't too big of a problem; simply download a new version from the site where you originally got it. However a shareware or store-bought plug-in is an entirely different matter. I'll recommend again that beginners should stick with the Ableton-included effects.

- **Multiple copies.** Long (large) audio files will eat up a lot of hard drive space so be conscious of how many copies you make when saving as self-contained. This can be a real problem on smaller laptop hard drives, or if you are planning on sending a song over the Internet or even setting up FTP downloads for collaboration. I recommend burning any song worth saving to a CD or DVD once you have saved all pertinent files via Save Set Self-Contained.

- **Don't forget the Song file.** When you are making a backup of your song, you will need to save both the song file and its associated folder full of sounds. This fact is critically important when transporting, backing up, or otherwise relocating your Ableton Live song files. Remember: the song file will never be placed into the Sounds folder (created by the Save Set Self-Contained feature), only the sounds, samples, loops and recordings go into the Sounds folder. I repeat, you must have the Live song file and the folder full of sounds to open up your complete song.

One other nice thing about Live's Save Set Self-Contained feature is that upon subsequent saves, Live will make sure that all files in the Sounds folder are being used. For instance, if you delete a sound and are no longer using it in the project, Live will notice this and, the next time you save, will ask,

'Remove unreferenced sample' x, y, and z (whatever your files are called).wav or .aif? This sample is contained in the Sounds folder 'C:\your directory\your folder\song name Sounds\' but the Set doesn't use it anymore. Please consider the sample might be accessed from other Sets'.

I rarely delete them unless they are alternate takes or large, unused, recorded Wav/Aiff files that are taking up too much space. I figure that any loops or samples that were there in the first place are in line with the composition's original intent. But this is just my personal preference.

Saving as self-contained is the best method for saving any Live song. You can try just saving the file and keeping your audio where it is, but my experience and that of many expert audio users is that if you do, you will inevitably be referring to the section that follows.

Finding lost files

It's going to happen. You can count on it. No I'm not psychic, but if you work in Live over an appreciable length of time, you will lose a beloved audio file, loop, and/or sample. This usually happens when files are moved, saved quickly (using the standard quick save, CNTL (CMND) + S), or after adding audio from a sample CD or temporary hard drive (and then ejecting/detaching the disc).

Here is what to do (if you are unsure of where you moved the file):

1   Click on your Mac or PC desktop.
2   For Mac OS X, Press CMND + F. For OS 9, activate the Sherlock Search tool. For Windows select Start > Search > For Files or Folders....
3   Type the file name you are looking for and make sure you are looking on all possible hard drives.
4   If the file is located, jot down its location so you will be able to direct Live to the correct folder.
5   If you cannot find the file, I will pray that you have backed up your sounds to CD/DVD and will find it there. If not, well...back to the old drawing board.

Saving multiple versions

By now you can guess that I'm going to heartily recommend that you save multiple versions of every song, creation, loop, or other chunk of digital data that is near and dear to your heart. Every time I do this, I feel just a little bit of reassurance that my creative work is safely documented and will not be lost by some idiotic press of a button, or some random Bill Gatesian infection, etc.

To do this in the most effective and least confusing manner, I typically set up a folder entitled Backup. I then copy my files exactly as they are named into my Backup folder. Sounds simple enough doesn't it? It is, but many people create elaborate backup file names that can be hard to remember.

If you have a multiple-partition hard drive, make sure to put your Backup folder and files on a different partition (a different drive letter) than the original song and sounds files. Or you may wish to back up to a different hard drive altogether. This will ensure their safety if your original partition gets corrupted.

Getting help

The software world is big on searchable help menus, online help files, and gazillion-page PDF manuals. Between Google.com and online forums (such as Ableton's), the challenge is in the sifting.

Activating/deactivating info view

Are you having trouble locating what you need quickly enough? Once again, Ableton has anticipated the needs of their end user – this time in the form of many methods to seek out help in Live. Built into the very interface of Live is the 'Info View' – a retractable and informative window that will discuss whatever topic correlates with the button your mouse is hovering over. See Figure 3.33. This won't always provide enough information to satisfy the power user you are becoming, but in a pinch or sudden memory lapse, it is the perfect thing to remind you of, 'oh yeah, that's what this button is for'.

Feel free to pop this baby open any time you are unsure about a specific element of Live. You can easily hide it again, to protect your reputation, when your friend looks over your shoulder.

Getting help on-line

We all know the Internet holds an amazing amount of random and erroneous content. Finding precisely what you are after can be more elusive than Elvis's ghost. Thankfully, Ableton knows this better than most and remains faithful to their customers by providing the Live 2.0 user forum, and reliable technical support. You can also feel free to drop corporate headquarters a note and tell them what a great job they've done.

All you need to do is click on Live's Help menu and you will see these options:

Info View

Provides a brief description of the user-interface element the mouse is currently over. To save screen space, fold-in the Info View by clicking the triangle-shaped button in the lower left corner.

Figure 3.33
The info view can be hidden or expanded to give you quick bits of pertinent Live 2.0 wisdom.

- Read the Live Manual. The Live 2.0 manual is greatly improved over 1.5's, so if you have given up on that earlier version, give it another whirl. The new manual is in linked HTML format and only takes up about two and a half megabytes of hard drive space. Most of the information is expanded upon in this book, but sometimes a point in the right direction may do the trick.

- Visit Ableton.com. Ableton's Web site is easy on the eyes and full of neatly organized goodies. If you are looking for some helpful distraction, the Artist page hosts scores of interviews, loops to download, and insightful hardware and setup tips. You'll also notice that Ableton prides themselves on acknowledging bugs as they are reported instead of denying their existence. After all, bugs are a part of software and Ableton's admissions and frequently provided workarounds, will tell you that you are not alone with your problem.

- Join the User Forum. Ableton Live users are some of the more savvy audio software heads on the planet. Try posting your question and set the option for email notification (you'll get an email message when someone responds to your post). Nearly all sensible inquiries are answered, even if they are repeats, or misnomers. In fact, once in awhile, real live Ableton employees will jump in on the discussion. Now that's team spirit.

- Talk To Ableton. This link is really more about general inquiries, ideas, and feedback. If you're looking for information, try the 'Get Support' option (see next bulleted item). However, if you just want to put in your two cents or share an idea or a complaint, then drop a line here.

- Get Support. Every so often, the user board isn't fast enough, or a problem is just plain weird enough that you really need a direct line to the author. Realize that Ableton, like most specialized software houses, is small – only 25 employees – and they may need a couple of days to get back to you.

- Get Downloads. In the realm of leading edge software, Downloads can be your lifeline. Check back on this link every month or so to see what's cooking, what's the latest update, and to be sure you have the latest version number. There is nothing more embarrassing than hounding your soundcard or computer manufacturer about some strange conflict only to realize you have yet to download Ableton's latest patch. Trust me, somehow I know.

Updates via the web

Because I do make music with this software, I have developed a few different template ideas that help inspire me to get creative in Live. I have arranged a small loft in cyberspace for the express purpose of sharing some of these ideas with you. And since there is a good chance Ableton will make some small changes or upgrades to the software that may affect this book, and not to mention any additional information I think of (the day after the final edit is sent), I will be using the site to post corrections and changes. New artist tips and Live working strategies will also end up on this site.

The site will also be updated with templates, loops, and feedback about the book and future versions of Live. I will place news, corrections, and any suggestions you might offer (should they be sharable). To check in on what's going on in the world of Live, check out www.brainboxing.net/abletonlive.

WHO'S USING LIVE?

Charlie Clouser – Musician/Producer/Remix Artist

Charlie Clouser got his start in a Manhattan music store around the dawn of MIDI. By making it his business to know the ins and outs of each new keyboard, synth, and piece of electronic gadgetry, Clouser became the 'call-guy' for anyone playing New York and looking for a synth. A short time later, Clouser went on to play keyboards and design sounds for the seminal industrial act Nine Inch Nails. He has become one of the world's most inventive and sought-after remix artists and composers. His recent projects include a Rob Zombie remix for *Enter The Matrix* and scoring the high-impact television show *Fastlane*.

A self-proclaimed 'Mac guy', Charlie likes to multi-track several different Macs running various software into his Pro-Tools and Logic rigs. Because of the sheer size of his sample/loop library, Clouser relies heavily upon Ableton Live's instant loop synchronization and preview features. In an interview hosted by Ableton, Charlie explains, 'I use two dual processor 1GHz Macintoshes side by side; one running Pro Tools, the other Ableton Live and Reason. The Ableton computer has an RME Hammerfall card in it with Lightpipe over to the big

guy and a Midiman 4 port MIDI interface, slaved by a beat clock tied to a master sequencer. There's no analog inputs or outputs on my Ableton rig at all, it's strapped to 24 channels of ADAT bridges on the Pro Tools system. When I'm working in Ableton, I break

out to 12 stereo pairs, which come up on Pro Tools' screen faders. Basically, I think of Ableton as a drum machine. It's as simple to operate as a can of soda. It works all day long and it will not crash. I'm old school – I still have stacks of drum machines. You hit the spacebar on Pro Tools and everybody lights up and runs – old style. I treat Ableton in that same manner. Certainly I do complete performances on it, but I am always recording its output as though it were a performance instrument, which I then record on my multi-track, which just happens to be another computer.

'Quite literally Ableton is the holy grail of software. I've been waiting for 15 years for a method to preview my loops, one at a time, in sync to my song. One mouse click, one button. I even had a cash bounty on the problem. Several of us were going to chip in $5000 to get someone to write it! Then Ableton came out – I drove 60 miles to go pick up the first copy the day it hit the streets in America. Just the ability to choose loops and hear what they will sound like in context to my song has revolutionized the way I work.'

Digital audio basics

The sonic differences between digital and analog recording studios will be debated for years. Even experts disagree on the best recording methods in terms of sound, reliability, and stability. Regardless, both analog and digital formats are widely used and supported. Just as the invention of the compact disc did not alleviate the need for vinyl, digital recording could never replace the wonderful sounds attainable only in the world of analog. Engineers and musicians alike frequently swear by the sound of analog (referring to the punchy quality produced from sound 'hitting' tape), or the human-inspired character and warmth produced by carefully crafted tube and ribbon microphones (which can still be used in the digital arena, but perhaps not as effectively). There is also the indisputable evidence of some the world's greatest recordings, which have been produced by analog recording studios.

Since Live is a digitally based product, and that is my area of expertise, the best I can do is to point out that digital audio studios can save musicians thousands of dollars, provide unbelievable audio editing capabilities, and be transported from session to session inside a briefcase. My point is not to sway you from one to the other, but rather to celebrate the fact that with all the fascinating technology around, there really hasn't been a better time to make music.

As we mentioned in Chapter 1, 'Live 2', a couple thousand dollars can secure a small, but powerful, project recording studio. In Chapter 2, 'Getting Started', we made a few suggestions on how to spend that hard-earned cash by picking up a pro-level sound card and MIDI-interface, and Ableton Live 2 software of course. Chapter 3, 'Live Interface Basics', should have gotten your feet wet in how to maneuver around in Live, given you a couple of power tips, and a brief overview of what's in store.

Now…we're going to take a step back. I know you're thinking. C'mon, give me the good stuff, I wanna rock, get my groove on, and all that…but sometimes a little homework helps make the test go more smoothly. So instead of pressing on to discover the bountiful treasures of Live, as we will in Chapter 5, 'Making Music in Live', let's take a few minutes to look at some of the particulars of digital audio. Live is, after all, a digital master-manipulator of the first order, and I have found that a little background in the ways of digital audio can do wonders.

Info

Too cool for school

If you're yawning already, or feel you've got a good handle on digital waveforms, sampling, and how to put it all together, you may want to flip to Chapter 5. However, I promise to be brief and only provide pertinent information, so as to keep us moving to our end goal: making music in Live.

What do I need to know to make music?

Out of the immeasurable amount of music that has been created, only one truth holds certain: There is no single 'right' way to do it. I believe Music is a natural phenomenon, and that anyone can do it. No rules need apply. No minimum level of talent, know-how, or experience will be required of a musician simply trying to express himself or herself. I'm not saying that it's all blind luck either, but rather there are no barriers to entry. Want to make music? Go for it. It's your Live.

Some have suggested that audio software, and loop-based software in particular, has taken all the fun (and some may suggest talent) out of the equation. However, just as sampling artists like DJ Shadow, Amon Tobin, and Public Enemy, have proven their ability to create new music out of previously recorded sample snippets, software applications like Live are proposing we reexamine old ways of working, and create completely new musical possibilities. It is reasonable to think that just as a talented percussionist can play a plain old paint bucket or a folk singer a ratty guitar, a laptop performer can create a whole new piece of original music out of the smallest twig of sound.

Throughout this book, we will discuss ways to work with samples, how to apply virtual studio effects, and talk about how to record your own audio into the computer. But don't for a moment lose sight that after all it is music we are talking about and that in the end what is pleasing to your ears may not be pleasing to mine (and vice versa). In the next few sections, we will leave the philosophy behind and move on to more of the practical matters at hand. Still, in such a technical book, and a digital world, it is important to take a moment and think about what it is we are accomplishing. Keep in mind, that because of the possibilities, we should all strive to explore and create, while analyzing just enough to get the job done.

The digital process

It is important to understand some basic digital-specific ideas to succeed as a composer in a digital medium such as Live. Digital audio differs drastically from analog in that it is a finite and dissectible batch of data packets made up of 1s and 0s (ones and zeroes). This data typically resides on a hard drive or other digital medium (such as a compact disc) as opposed to a linear stream of audio on a tape reel. Each time you make a digital recording, you are essentially converting analog sound to digital by use of digital audio converters – commonly referred to as analog-to-digital converters for recording and digital-to-analog for playback. These converters are located in nearly any computer sound card but can vary drastically in terms of quality and flexibility. Professional quality converters will capture a more precise digital audio image of the source sound. Both the detail and audio frequency range can be affected or lost by using sub-par or hobbyist level digital audio converters.

Once captured (sampled), digital audio can be viewed as a waveform – since the audio is now in the form of numerical data, it can be plotted out in similar fashion to a stock chart or numerical graph. These waveforms can at first seem mechanical, even overly analytical for the digital audio novice. But I assure you that with a little more familiarity, waveforms will come to represent your music in a sensible and helpful way. You will learn to work with waveforms in an unimaginable number of ways in Live.

Digital audio is everywhere. Every CD you buy is 100 percent digital audio. There is no such thing as an analog CD. The same can be said for all audio on your computer's hard drive. Every MP3, RealAudio clip, or QuickTime Move is 100 percent digital information. Mini-discs, DATs, and ADATs are also pure digital information. The reason this is important is that if it's digital, you can import it into your computer, and you can then use it in Live.

Bit depth

At the time of this writing, Live uses only 16- or 24-bit digital audio data recorded in either a WAV or AIFF file format. WAV (Waveform Audio) is the general standard for Microsoft Windows PCs. AIFF stands for Audio Interchange File Format and is more commonly found in use with Mac-based software applications. In the last couple of years, PCs and Macs have become more accepting of one another. You should encounter few problems swapping AIFFs or WAVs on either a Mac or PC. At some point in the future, it is quite possible that Live will support other file types, such as MP3s, but at the time of this writing, WAV and AIFF are both excellent-sounding professional audio standards that should hold for the foreseeable future.

I often think of deeper bit depths as longer and more descriptive sentences. Because the file is also longer, this analogy helps me to decide if I want less or more 'description' to the sound. To give you an example, a short drum loop recorded at 16-bit might be 454 KB, while the same loop at 24-bit would be 680 KB. Smaller bit depths also have a purpose, and make for crunchier, harsher sounds (reminiscent of antique samplers that could only sample at 8 or 12 bits). To handle this, Live 2 has a new Redux effect expressly for that purpose that can lower both bit depths and sample rates.

Sample rate

The other common statistic that categorizes digital audio is its sample rate. A sample rate indicates the numbers of audio snapshots taken by your digital audio recording equipment in a given second. For instance, a sample rate of 44.1 kHz means that the source sound is being sampled (recorded) more than 44 thousand times every second. Think of a higher sample rate as having greater sonic detail as a result of more frames being shot on the initial capture. Like increased bit rate, higher sample rates also use more system resources, such as RAM and hard drive space. Consumer-grade compact discs are almost always produced at 44.1 kHz, 16-bit. That is 44.1 thousand samples at 16 bits deep. Many professional recording studios record at 48K or 96K, and can crank the bit rate up to 24, 32, and the trend suggests eventually more. This higher degree of detail is done to ensure the best sonic accuracy possible (given the equipment), by recording the full spectrum of audio frequencies. Though not all of these frequencies may end up in the final product, the additional audio clarity can benefit both mix-down and mastering, which ensures the when the final project is burned to an audio CD (at 44.1 kHz and 16 bit), only the best remains.

What does all this mean? Quite simply that you will want to experiment a bit with different sample rates and bit depths to see what strikes your fancy. I recommend sticking with 44.1K rate and 24-bit for most studio projects and only using lower rates for live performance sets if you are short on hard drive space.

Info

A little bit

Bit depth refers to the number of bits included in the encoding of digital audio. Bits are like layers of the file, the more, the deeper. A 24-bit sample is larger than 16-bit and therefore can retain a higher degree of sonic detail (particularly in the high and low frequency registers). This detail will eat up more hard drive space. But what do you expect? Nothing's free, baby.

The nature of digital audio

While digital audio comes in lots of shapes and sizes (i.e. hard drives, compact discs, minidisks, ADATs (Alesis Digital Audio Tapes), and DATs (Digital Audio Tapes), the information contained on these mediums, is essentially the same. The very same binary code (ones and zeros) we discussed in 'The Digital Process' section, is actually quite easy for computers to work with. To do this, a computer or computer chip must be instructed (via audio software) to know how to disassemble, analyze, and then reassemble this binary audio information. In recent times, software has advanced to very sophisticated levels, enabling us to do more than play and record digital audio – computers can now synthesize new waveforms, support digital signal processing (DSP), and ultimately help us make the most of WAV or AIFF audio material.

Occasionally, the two worlds, analog and digital, will collide. You can record to tape that is synchronized to digital, which is usually done by recording a SMPTE (digital encoded) stripe on analog tape and then running both formats in tandem. Also, since digital editing options are so powerful, many analog recordings are imported into ProTools or other digital audio applications for post-session edits.

Digital is transferable without loss

Digital data, unless corrupt, will always sound the same on each playback, while analog tends to deteriorate. For instance, a vinyl record or analog cassette tape will eventually produce audible crackles, sound dulled out, lose high frequencies, and can even wear out completely. In contrast, a digital recording such as a compact disc will sound exactly the same each time it is played so long as the disc is not scratched or otherwise defective. This consistency, along with digital data's flexibility, is the key distinction for musicians, and one of the many benefits of working with audio in the digital realm. Digital audio can be transferred from machine to machine, retaining the same sample rate/bit depth, without losing any information.

Occasionally you may encounter a problem such as a digital pop or wrinkle in a transfer, but this is a problem in the transfer, such as a spiked (strained) CPU. We will discuss these issues both later in this chapter, and in Chapter 10, 'Wave Editing Tips'.

Digital is a fragile medium

You should also be aware of the fragility of digital media. It is important to back up both your music and your song files after each session. Hard drives, compact discs, ADATs, DATs, and minidisks are all easily corruptible. I have personally witnessed data corruption on all five of the above storage media, as well as several other data storage devices, such as Zip, Orb, and FireWire drives. Crashes, scratches, drops, cracks, and moisture can be catastrophic if you do not have a backup. Let's hope that someday a permanent, or even near-permanent, storage medium will be invented. But, for now, be skeptical about the safety of all recordings, samples, and irreplaceable digital material (such as Live song files).

Visual audio: enter the waveform

The very fact that we can see audio is amazing. We can't hear visuals, or touch a scent. The power of this duality is not to be underestimated and is central to the revolution, and future evolution, of digital audio. The following descriptions and working tools for waveforms can be extremely valuable as you begin to get comfortable with Live. Be sure to reread the following sections a couple of times so that the information becomes second nature. I've kept it generic so that you can apply this information to Live or any other wave editor you might use to complement your files in Live.

Let's *see* what we can accomplish with digital audio. Enter the basic Waveform (Figure 4.1).

At first, all waveforms may look the same, but after a short while, you will begin to notice subtle differences, and eventually be wholly amazed at the vast contrast between one squiggly line to the next. For instance a stereo waveform will have a pair of waves, the top line usually being the left speaker, the bottom waveform representing the right speaker (see Figure 4.2).

Let's contrast a couple of different waves. Pictured below are a drum loop (Figure 4.3) and an orchestral melody (Figure 4.4). Note their visual differences.

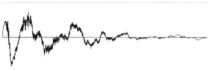

Figure 4.1 (far left)
Here is a simple mono waveform.

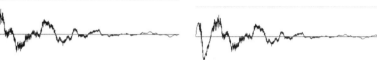

Figure 4.2 (below)
Here is a simple stereo waveform.

Figure 4.3 (left)
A drum loop in waveform format. Each of the spikes represents a different strike of the stick. In other words, each peak is a sound and each valley is the timeline of that sound decaying, or fading away.

Figure 4.4
In this figure, a violinist is playing a simple melody over the rest of the orchestra's simple roll.

Once you get the hang of how waves look, you will be able to tell the difference visually between long, short, loud, quiet, and other kinds of recordings. Note: the height of the waveform generally represents volume or dB (decibel) level. Remember though, that since you can zoom in and out, the size can change relative to your viewing option. This may make a quiet loop look much louder than it actually is.

In later chapters, we will discuss how to record, edit, and work with your own waveforms, or samples, but first, let's take a look at a couple of problem waves to get an idea of what you want to avoid.

The peak

Pictured in Figure 4.5 is a digital peak. Like screaming into a microphone, at some point the target device can only take so much. This point of overdoing is called a *clipped peak*. If you hear the peak (distortion), but can't see it, you are overloading your speakers or your soundcard's output.

Figure 4.5 (right)
Clipped peaks make problems. They are tough to repair and almost never sound 'cool.' If you notice a clipped peak while you are recording, you will want to rerecord or resample your source. Turn down the input to the computer/soundcard. If you can see the problem in the waveform, it is not in your output.

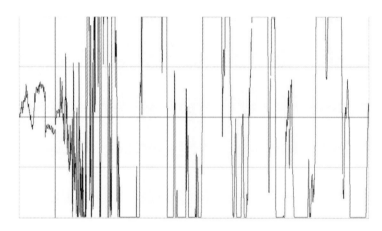

The glitch

How glitches (or pops) get created is a long and not so interesting tale. If you are brand new to digital audio, digital pops like the one pictured in Figure 4.6 are as annoying as household rodents. They don't eat much, but the fact that they are there is intolerable. Ableton Live 2 has a couple of built-in safeguards or features to help stave off the obnoxious little guys, but first let's see what we're after.

Most glitches are at the beginnings and endings of loops. The popping sound happens when the gain is suddenly redirected, lopped off, or redrawn. This often happens at the very beginning or absolute ending of a given loop or sample. Here is a quick remedy to exterminate this annoyance.

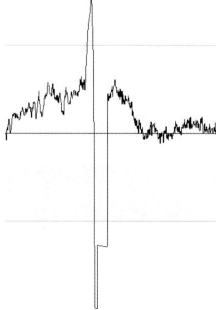

Figure 4.6
Luckily, there are ways to remedy the detested glitch. The glitch above is the redirection of the wave line that creates a nasty looking jag.

1 Find the glitch. This is not as easy as it sounds. You can try 'scrubbing' the audio if your wave editor supports it, or simply zero in on the wave until you see that inconsistency in the waveform line.

2 Fade the glitch. If you are at the beginning of the loop, fade in. If you are at the end of the loop, fade out. If the glitch is in the middle of the loop or sample, roll up your sleeves; this is going to take a little surgery.

3 Redraw the glitch. Most wave editors have a pencil or drawing tool that can be used to shape the waveform.

The notion of redrawing sound is indeed a crazy one. I recommend redrawing waves only if you cannot solve the problem via fade in/out or some other method. Several manufacturers make 'declicking' or 'depopping' effects plug-ins. Though these were originally made for declicking vinyl, they tend to work with digital glitches as well. No matter which method you choose, there will be a noticeable difference in the sound. But if you are forced to redraw, I've made you a couple more pictures to better explain what to do. See Figure 4.7 with a nasty glitch in the centre of the image. Who knows how it got there? Maybe an out of phase drum microphone, a sound that has been cut in half, or a maxed out hard drive struggling to keep up with the recording of the audio. Figure 4.8 is the fixed version, achieved by using Sonic Foundry Sound Forge's redrawing feature, which enables you to hand-draw any waveform that may be misbehaving. If you do not have access to a professional grade sample/waveform editor, you may have to delete the glitch and permanently alter (omit) part of your recording.

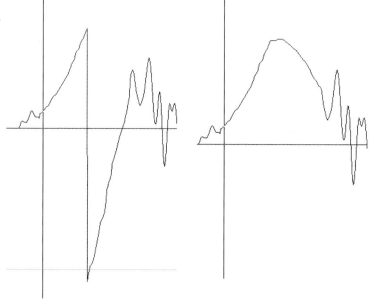

Figure 4.7
Here is the before screen shot, with a nasty glitch front and centre.

Figure 4.8
Here is the remedied waveform.

Notice the smoother roll to the graphic wave. By visually smoothing out a wave, you will often iron out the sound, eliminating the offending pop. This smoothing is not to be billed as standard procedure however. Undesirable side effects that can emerge from too much tinkering with the frequency redraw. And you will not always

Tip

Don't do it ... undo it

Undo is the most important shortcut to learn. Cntl (Cmnd) + Z. Live 2 has about 999 levels of Undo. Each time you save, you have cleared your Undo memory and will not be able to wipe out changes.

Info

Sample vs. loop

Sample
A sample is a recording. No more, no less. Samples can be any size. If the sample does not repeat, it may be referred to as a 'one-shot'.

Loop
A repeating sample.

be successful. Some glitches (pops) are exceptionally difficult to remove, and your attempt to fix them may only make things worse. Once again, use your ears, and remember the power of the almighty Undo command present in Live and nearly all decent wave editing applications.

In later chapters, we will talk about Live's optimized loop playback (the Hi-Q setting in Clip View), and cover some more creative ways to work with and capture waveforms. The basic digital audio concepts we have discussed so far, and our introduction to the waveform, are the cornerstones for beginners with digital audio, and will only help your looping endeavors.

Intro to sampling

A sample is a recording, no more, no less. The act of sampling, however, is an art form that can take years to master – especially with those clunky old hardware samplers and their tiny LCD screens. Ableton is well aware of this challenge, and have made working with samples in Live as easy as possible. Now don't get confused, Live is not merely a sampler, which is traditionally used for creating instruments or sound FX, or for re-pitching a given piece of audio. Instead, Live is more of a sample arranger and playback interface, with some sampler-like tendencies. Like an automobile running on gasoline, Live uses loops, a.k.a. samples, to do its thing. Live facilitates the creation of larger pieces of music enabling you to construct sample collages, remix loops, and redefine raw samples. In Live, you may use a small snippet of a sampled melody, or a single hit of a drum. Then again, you might use a long sampled performance on top of some looped drum recordings. Samples can be as short or as long as you need them to be. Live can work with virtually any size chunk of audio. But before we discuss the particulars of Live, let's run through the basics of sampling in order to clear up any misconceptions.

Any time you are working with a piece of audio, you are working with a sample. As far as legality is concerned, unless the sample (recording) is completely unrecognizable by the original artist, it had better be yours. Any recording made by anyone in the world other than you is not your property. If the sound comes from a CD with a copyright, you can be sure that every sound on that CD is unusable without the proper clearance. Artists who use samples of other artists' work in their own creations need to take the proper legal steps to clear the permissions for that sample if they are going to claim the resulting work as their own. What a buzz kill. Well, not entirely. We will see that DJs all around the world are using Live 2 to play and perform with their personal record collection. This is not illegal. If you buy a record and make a recording for personal use (a waveform on your hard drive for instance), you can use it in your DJ set. If, though, you then record a DJ set and want to sell it, you must go back to the top of this paragraph and decide if the music is in fact yours to sell.

What is a loop?

If you have bought a copy of Ableton Live and this book and do not have any idea what a loop is, that is beautiful. The music industry, and especially the electronic music-making world, needs a fresh perspective, such as your own, to continue the innovation that has begun.

A *loop* is merely a repeating sample. A loop can be simple or complex, loud or soft, frenetic or static, or whatever else you can imagine – so long as it repeats. In Live, you will use loops as the building blocks for your musical compositions. Since each piece of audio can take on an infinite number of permutations and characteristics in Live, your loops and recordings will help to give your music legs, motion, and consistency. Since nearly all dance music is based on rhythmic consistency and repetition, loops are a natural fit. For instance, you might take a repetitive techno beat or funk drum groove and then begin layering complementary bass, guitar, and synthesizer loops on top. You might want to use a single occurrence (called a *one-shot*) of a crash cymbal for punctuation, or mix in a small drum fill at the end of a song section. But don't for a minute think that Live can be used only for dance music. Live is the ultimate tool on the market for creating your own music based solely on combinations and rearrangements of your looped and sampled recordings. Your choices, and your skill at realizing your sonic ideas, become the **artistry**.

As we have discussed above, digital audio is incredibly flexible, and therefore, so are loops (and samples). In Live, you will be able to work with loops in an infinite number of ways. Any sonic event, drum hit, note, blip, guitar pluck, vocal sound, noise, etc. can be either pushed or pulled to create new rhythmic permutations. You can start a loop at any point within itself and truncate the start and end points to any point in the larger recording. Live can also change the pitch or tuning of a loop, as well as raise and lower the gain (volume level). And then there are all the amazing things possible with Ableton Live's built-in effects plug-ins, as well as a growing number of third-party effects plug-ins.

Perhaps one of the most impressive features of Live is its ability to stretch a loop's tempo (speed) independently of pitch. This means that any loop can be played at any other loop's tempo. In later chapters we will learn ways to fine-tune how Live 'sees' a sample, but for now it is important to understand how drastic the idea of changing a loop's speed or pitch is, and exactly what that entails. Similar to waveforms, there are some special circumstances to consider when altering the pitch or tempo of your looped samples. Artifacts, for instance, can be a real problem.

Info

Artifact Jack

If your looped samples sound out of sync or lack the power and punch or the original sound file you may be hearing artifacts. Artifacts are an undesirable side effect (most of the time) heard when a sample is stretched beyond its reasonable tempo constraints. Most artifacts are caused when slowing a sample down while preserving its pitch. However, speeding up samples can also cause nasally, high-pitched, buzzing sounds commonly referred to as artifacts.

Warp Markers

Lucky for us, Ableton has assumed that most samples you use in Live will be looped continuously. Ableton's infamous Warp Marker technology can help shape loops rhythmically, as well as make loops behave at the tempo and pitch of your choice in an extremely flexible manner. For many, this feature alone is the best selling point of Live; it allows users to create movable Warp Markers, or footholds on the waveform, that can be adjusted independently of one another (see Figure 4.9). In later chapters we will explain how to make the most of refining a loop's Warp Marker settings. If you are looking for quick information on this topic, please see Chapter 10, 'Wave editing tips', and Chapter 14, 'Power tips – the magic of Live'!

Figure 4.9
In the above example, each beat of the measure has been made into a Warp Marker (by double-clicking on the numbered warp definition, 1.2, 1.3, etc.). Now beat 'two' can be moved to be closer to beat 'one' or 'three.' Want to fix your bass player's mistake? Or are you just looking for a little bit of float in your drum machine track?

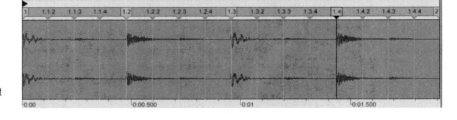

Warp Markers allow you to massage the playback timing of audio loops or samples in unbelievable ways. To activate them in Live, simply double-click on a grid marker in Live's Clip View. You can then drag the marker left or right to make the loop slow down or speed up relative to the other markers. Naturally, Ableton describes it best when they say Live sees loops like audio rubber bands that can be stretched in any way you can imagine. Warp Markers are like movable thumbtacks for anchoring the rubber bands in place. The possibilities are endless – really, they are.

Warp modes

New to Live 2 are four enhanced warp modes, or loop recognition modes, which further augment the power of Live's time-stretching and tempo-aligning tactics. Why did Ableton create these new warp modes? For this reason: Any loop that does not have clearly defined audio events, such as a droning didgeridoo, a legato saxophone line, or even the human voice, will cause problems for a program such as ReCycle or even Acid Pro – for the reasons we discussed above: glitches and peaks. Remember, we learned that if you were to dissect a waveform while sound is playing at a consistent volume level, you would create a glitch. In contrast, Live's variable warp modes give you the option of how a given loop is analyzed, and how it will then be stretched – thus often eliminating artifacts and avoiding digital glitches. By choosing different warp methods (modes), Live is directed to analyze loops with varying degrees of detail as if Live can 'look' through different kinds of lenses. While each mode's name hints at its strengths, the following overview should help get your head around this concept that is unique to Ableton Live. In the next section, we will define each of Live's warp modes.

Any clip's warp mode is selected manually via the Mode drop down box in the Warp section of Clip View. You can choose from Beats, Tones, Textures, and Re-Pitch modes, as well as turning off the Warp Mode entirely. To bypass all warp modes (the warp off option), click (disengage) the Warp button in the Clip section (far left) of Clip View. Each of the above modes (including warp off) provides powerful flexibility for Live users trying to eliminate artifacts or to uncover new creative possibilities within a given loop. Beats Mode is the same (and only) warp engine used in previous versions of Live. Tones, Textures, and Re-Pitch Modes were added in version 2.0 to give even more flexibility with loops lacking percussion, drums, or clear rhythmic distinction. In both Tones and Textures Modes, Live can ease the intensity with which it scrubs for transients, thereby creating a smoother and purer sounding result – by pure I mean loops will more closely resemble the original timbre, clarity, and intent of the original. If this isn't clear yet, it will be once we dive in deeper to the power and versatility of each of the new modes, as well as the tried and true Beats mode, in subsequent chapters.

Since most modern styles of music, such as Electronica, drum 'n bass, Hip Hop, Trip Hop, Big Beat, Jungle, Techno, House, Reggae, Rock, Blues, and even Jazz rely on repetition, you will need to get to know your Warp Modes. What follows is a brief introduction to Live's Warp (loop handling) Modes and what they have in store for your sample collection.

How Live sees loops

Live can see loops, or one-shot samples (if they're non-repeating samples), in several different ways. The differences are so distinct that you may completely change a song's feel by changing a single warp mode (of a sample). To take full advantage of Live's versatility, it is helpful for you to begin to categorize your samples in terms of what type of sound they are (pad, texture, beat, sound FX, vocal, etc.). Decide whether you want to hear the sample in its original groove and timbre or want to make some drastic changes. You can always change your mind later, but for the sake of the loop, and the track you are working on, this sort of categorization will help you to use your time more productively. As we saw in Chapter 2's 'Preferences' section, you can configure Live to default to any of the four Warp Modes (or RePitch) the first time it sees any sample. Generally speaking, Beats Mode is a good place to begin. But since each mode is configurable, make sure to experiment so you can discover your own preferences and favourite warp settings.

Beats Mode

In Beats Mode, Live analyzes a loop by seeking out transients (the immediate, opening attack of a sound) according to each loop/clip's current transient setting (which can be configured independently for each clip). Increasing the number of transients in Live's Beats Mode will make Live seek out more sonic events in the sample – and therefore create a more strict tempo alignment in the loop's playback. Decreasing the transient setting for a given clip will limit the number of transients Live detects. This looser detection method will allow the sample to breathe a bit more, which can often lead to a slightly sloppier, if more human feeling track.

The result of this analysis is that Live can then play the sample at the song's tempo (whatever that may be), yet retain the pitch of the original sample. The smaller the quantization setting, the more finely Live will comb the sample for transients. For instance, the 1/8-note transient setting is smaller (and therefore more detailed) than the 1/4-note setting – a 1/32-note transient detection setting will align nearly all sonic events, as opposed to a much more coarse 1/2-note setting.

A simple 4/4 drum beat with a kick on 1 and 3 and a snare on 2 and 4 (and 1/8-note hihat groove) would be a simple task for Live's Beats Mode.

Tones Mode

Tones are not beats, and for that reason they suffer when minced by programs such as ReCycle. Specifically, it is the lack of definitive sonic events/transients that renders the default Beats mode ineffective with tones. In other words, a tone-oriented loop (such as a guitar, bass, or piano sample) without an obvious beat confuses programs specifically designed to look for drum and percussion patterns. To solve this problem, Live's Tones Mode allows you to use a softer approach to analyzing a waveform, and allows you to further refine your loop's time-stretched playback by adjusting the Grain size. Small to moderate grain size is usually best for loops with a clear pitch contour. Larger grain sizes will eliminate pesky artifacts in loops with less clear direction in regard to pitch. While Beats Mode can tend to sound choppy with samples/loops that contain more than drum and percussion parts, Tones Mode can be a little more forgiving, smoothly adjusting the sample and thus preserving the sound's tonal (as opposed to percussive) quality. Basses, vocals, monophonic (or simple) synthesizers or keyboards all work decently in the Tones Mode setting. But that's not to say you should never try using Beats Mode on a tone type of loop for a special effect.

Texture Mode

Sometimes life is complicated, and well, sometimes so are your sounds. Thick, rhythmic or harmonic, samples require a little more specialized treatment than either Beats or Tones Mode can provide. If you have one of these sounds and it is sounding choppy in Beats Mode and still not quite right in Tones Mode, Texture Mode's softer transient detection may be just the tool you need. Texture Mode can also be Live's most creative warp mode and is perfect for handling orchestral samples, field recordings, thick keyboard pads, or similarly dense audio files. Similar to Tones Mode, Texture Mode provides even more allowance for long fuzzy, or otherwise rhythmically void sounds by allowing you to adjust the Grain Size, and an additional randomness control called Flux (larger values create more randomized results).

Re-Pitch

To judge by its name, Re-Pitch sounds as though it may be the most radical of the four selectable modes in Clip View; however, Re-Pitch for Live simply means *relax*, don't automatically change the pitch from the original. Re-Pitch mode actually turns off Live's warping mechanism in favor of playing the sample/loop in time with the piece at hand. The pitch will *not* be adjusted, but will instead change based on the tempo of the sample. In other words, Live will not warp the loop, correct the pitch, or add artifacts. Re-pitch dictates that a sample playing back at double time will be one octave higher in pitch. The above three modes would all leave the pitch intact, which means Live is calculating the adjustment between original tempo and the new tempo and compensating for the difference in pitch. Re-Pitch is a great option if you know the loop you are working with was recorded at the exact same tempo as the project you are working in. This is also a good option for tracks you record or overdub into Live.

Tweaking the modes

Each of the above modes, except for Re-Pitch, has additional fine-tuning adjustments. In Beats mode you can adjust the note value of the transient markers. For a simple rhythm, such as a housey, four-on-the-floor kick drum part, you may only need to set this to 1/4 note value. However, if you have a more syncopated drum part, such as a Cuban hand drum groove, you may need to ratchet the transients up to 1/32 note sensitivity. Fine tuning in both Tone and Texture Modes has to do with the shape and error potential of the transients in Live.

In Tones Mode, you can adjust the Grain size or the measurement in Warp Marker sensitivity. Low grain size implies the sample is a simple audio event that can be easily picked out at a low grade measuring setting. For more complex (a.k.a. thick) loops, an increase in grain size will help to alleviate loop artifacts.

In Textures Mode, you have the additional control of Live's Flux setting, which, as the name implies, serves as a randomizing feature. Flux makes Live guess a little more at how to apply grain size and transient information. Both Grain and Flux adjustments can seem a little vague, but with a little experimentation, you can really smooth out the kinks in your waves.

Digital recording

There are several ways to get sound into your computer. We will cover this in more detail in Chapter 11, 'Where to Get Loops', but to introduce this concept, here are a few places to start.

- Download sounds from the Internet. You can do a Google search (www.google.com) or go to a pay-for-download site such as Sonomic (www.sonomic.com) or PrimeSounds (www.primesounds.com).
- Rip audio from CD. Programs such as iTunes (Mac), Musicmatch (PC), and Winamp (PC) are able to import your audio CDs as WAV or AIFF files. You may want to build your DJ set one track at a time, or just grab a piece of sonic inspiration for later reworking.
- Digitize your vinyl. Many DJs today are turning their vinyl collections into MP3 files. Because Live can't read MP3s, you will need to digitize your vinyl to WAV or AIFF.
- Convert your MP3 collection to WAV files. Most decent wave editors can make waves out of MP3 files. More on this in Chapter 10, 'Wave Editing Tips'.

As noted earlier in this chapter, there may be legal ramifications to sampling copyrighted works. Other recording methods include plugging instruments into your microphone jack on your computer, recording into an A/D converter, or transferring digitally made recordings through lightpipe, SPDIF, or FireWire. As you can see, there are lots and lots of ways to get sound.

All digital recordings make use of what are called A/D (analog-to-digital) converters. Every computer with a microphone input has some kind of A/D converter and, like most audio components, they come in varying levels of quality, and most professional audio engineers have their favourites. If you're thinking 'Sure, analog to digital conversion, like a sample...hmm, I wonder what sample rate and bit depth I should use', congratulations. You've been paying attention. This is how

---

Tip

Realize your drum potential

Because acoustic drum sounds (and many electronic drum sounds) are made up of so many frequencies, they are often the most sonically depleted when time stretched. A fast groove slowed down can begin to break up and sound 'out of phase' or just plain thin. To make your drums sound better, use a loop that is as close to your current project tempo as possible and then set the loop's setting to Re-Pitch. The drums will usually sound de-tuned (assuming you slowed them down), but the tonality will be fuller and more realistic.

audio engineers think all the time. The rate and depth that your audio card is capable of, and the quality of the overall transfer has everything in the world to do with what kind of sound quality you will achieve. A/D (and digital to analog, D/A) can define a recording as much as a type of microphone or guitar. They help to determine the raw quality of the sound. Many studios purchase separate A/D converters made by companies such as Apogee (www.apogeedigital.com) or Universal Audio (www.uaudio.com).

But what should you do if you've spent your last penny on a brand new laptop and sound card to run Live? Don't worry, your sound card will have at least audiophile-grade A/D and D/A converters. You can also get creative with your sample collection, make new sounds out of old sounds, and perform a few other tricks we'll get into in Chapter 11.

Rendering

Rendering is the process of recording your completed mix once you have finished recording, mixing, tweaking, overdubbing, and otherwise manipulating it in a given software application. I like to think of rendering as the process of recording my computer's output to itself. Rendering is usually the last step in the process before sending the track out to the mastering engineer. However, unlike mastering, there are no glamorous options or frilly excess gear to buy when rendering. It is usually a simple process, but must still be done with much care.

Live 2 can render to 16- or 24-bit files at sample rates ranging from 22 to 96 kHz. Rendering can be done in a single step (from the File Menu) or in real-time to an empty stereo track by routing your entire mix to two separate channels (outputs) and recording the results. We will cover this again and include even more detail in subsequent chapters, but for now, here are general rendering guidelines for any program you meet during the rest of your audio software life.

- **Don't clip your peaks when you render.** If you render your audio too loudly, you will know it by either hearing horrible digital glitches (like the sound of ripping metal sandpaper), or you will see it in the waveform, if it appears more like Figure 4.10a than Figure 4.10b.
- **Close all other applications when you render**. Rendering audio demands a large amount of system resources. If you push your computer, while it is gasping for air you may create small digital pops (glitches) or creases (a sound similar to the crackle of a bad instrument cable). Also, your computer may not be able to keep up with a massive project with lots of audio tracks and DSP (digital signal processing). That brings us to the next step.
- **Render extremely large projects in sections**. If you are chaining several of your coolest new plug-in effects only to find that when you render, your computer crashes or produces errors, try rendering a couple of the larger, more processed tracks by themselves. You can mute the other tracks, or delete them all and save the project as a new project with only the problem tracks in place. After these tracks are rendered, import the freshly rendered tracks into your original project in place of their processor-hogging counterparts, and try the whole song again.
- **Don't render**. What? But I'm so good at it now! Seriously though – many engi-

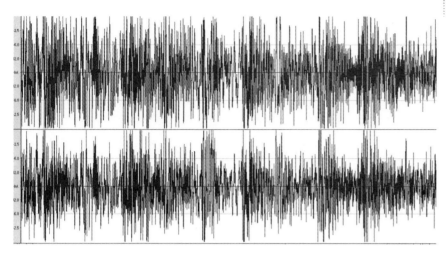

Figure 4.10a
A clipped peaked waveform. If your finished, rendered track resembles this, lower the master volume of your mixer and try again. These levels will be impossible to work with.

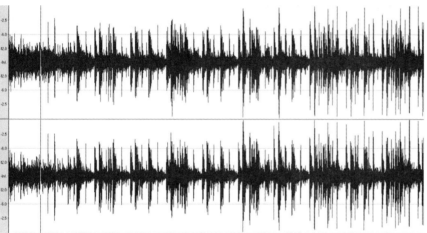

Figure 4.10b
A more normal-looking waveform. In fact, it is so normal you may want to 'normalize' it to boost the overall level to a more acceptable level. However, if you are going to have your music mastered professionally, let the mastering engineer handle the normalizing and stop here.

neers find that the best way to 'render' audio is to merely play it back in real-time and record the results on two fresh tracks. Other engineers simply route their computer output to an outside digital recorder (such as a DAT tape). By rerecording the entire song into two fresh tracks (right and left stereo, the only tracks you monitor while doing so), you can check the mix as it is laid down for the last time.

Where does Live come in?

If you have made it this far, you have earned your reward. Things are going to get rather interesting in just one or two more pages. First, take a minute and be thankful for how lucky you are to be living in an age in which audio can be sculpted, re-sampled, and then again scrutinized from 32,000 feet above the earth. Your studio can be packed up in 12 minutes and then set up again in 25 (or less). You can make field recording samples of the neighbour's dog barking or a motorcycle screeching around a tight corner and import these sounds into your music. When all is said and done, you can bring any sound you like with you to a stage nearby and begin to combine, remix, and reuse.

Artists such as Charlie Clouser (see page 64), of Nine Inch Nails fame, calls Live, 'the holy grail of audio software', and while his words are strong, think how long we have waited to make music by instantaneously synchronizing any sound in our library the instant we grab the sample. Charlie Clouser relies on Live's ability to synchronize his loops (in the Browser) for maximum previewing power – an invaluable tool for a time-crunched producer scoring music for the television show Fastlane.

As we continue to explore Live, it becomes increasingly obvious that the music being made today is less and less about who can afford studio time, and more a matter of taste. DJs, who have traditionally been tastemakers, may have been the first to point this out (almost inadvertently) by playing venues previously reserved for bands. At times, it can feel as though we are in a land of software engineers rather than musicians in the traditional sense. This chapter was intended to help level the playing field and demystify a few engineer-type concepts (such as digital audio, samples, loops, and waveforms). Once you begin to consistently make music in Live, these digital concepts, and the methods you'll learn in coming chapters, should become instinctual. As with any other instrument, whether it be a turntable or electric guitar, mastering sample-based music-making takes practice.

Berlin-based DJ Highfish (Figure 4.11) has this to say about his transition to Live from traditional turntables, 'Originally people called themselves DJs because they could synchronize two records, but since it is such a normal thing now, what makes a DJ good is the music, their track choice, and the mix itself...with Live I'm able to concentrate on the music and the mix, and not just synchronizing the records. It's not about making it easier, its about making it better'.

Live has radically redefined the landscape of digital audio and making music with a computer. Your choice to purchase Live and this book demonstrates that you are an innovator in your own right and have chosen to take your music and live performance skills to the next level. By this point in the book, you have gained an appreciation for the limitless world of digital audio. The musical (and digital) possibilities available within Live could barely be imagined only a few years ago. While future versions of Live are already being developed, and other similar applications may eventually follow, Live 2 is here now – and it is a viable, reliable, and fun means of realizing your musical dream. As we move on to Chapters 5 and 6 and start to learn how to make and perform music with Live, remember that ways and methods for using Live are still being uncovered. I encourage you to explore and develop your own methods and ideas for working in Live, and above all, follow Ableton's credo 'have a lot of fun with Live'.

Figure 4.11
Berlin-based DJ Highfish uses Live to realize his creative vision. Though he is a Live power-user, he most enjoys the fact that Live lets him focus on making music.

Making music in Live

A t last, the time has come to begin making music in Live. In this chapter, we'll cover how to analyze and prepare files for use in Live. We will explore the depths of Clip View and, through practical examples, discover some of the most common ways music is made in Live. We'll also take a look at software configuration and general working methods for the Live musician. After the stage is set, Chapter 6, 'Playing Live...live', will help you get ready for your first gig with Live.

Whether you are playing in a trendy nightclub or in the privacy of your own home, the basic Live configuration and performance concept is the same. Before writing this book, I spent a good amount of time interviewing Live 'Power-users', the Ableton Live team, and conceptualists Robert Henke and Gerhard Behles. Through these discussions, and my own practice, I have discovered that nearly everybody is using Live just a little bit differently, depending upon their musical style and live performance needs. DJs demand different things out of Live than do producers creating remixes. Film and television composers may be looking for different kinds of sounds than a musician playing Live in a band. As you read this chapter, think about how you want to use Live, and focus on the areas that make sense for your situation. After all, there is no reason a DJ can't borrow from a film composer and vice versa. As we proceed through the various ways to work in Live, take a minute to try some of the provided examples. As with learning any musical instrument, discovery will lead to inspiration, additional detail will bring delight, and a little practice never hurt either.

Working methods

One of the remarkable things about Live is that no two people use it the same way. Some musicians come to use Live as a quick and flexible multi-track recorder that allows them to explore their own music in deep and original ways. Other artists use Live as a way to quickly integrate their samples and loops into a performance or group environment. Recent television and movie music composers such as Charlie Clouser (Ex-Nine Inch Nails keyboardist, currently scoring the television program *Fastlane*), Klaus Badelt (*Gladiator*, *The Thin Red Line*, *Mission Impossible 2*, *Hannibal*, *Pearl Harbor*, and other big budget films) as well as Rick Marvin (*U-571*, *Six Feet Under*, and many more) have been using Live's time-stretching capabilities to enable them to synchronize their music to video images. DJs are using Live to play their favourite tracks, as well as to integrate their own material and pre-produced loops. In other words, DJs are producing and remixing full-length tracks on the fly, while producers are acting more and more like DJs all the time by mixing unusual textures, rhythms, and styles into a single track. On that note, one of the most popular uses for Live will be from remix and dance music producers, who take a pre-produced track, break it down, and rebuild it in another musical style. Let's take a closer look at each of these methods, to better understand each one's perspective and see why Live is the perfect application for each approach.

The producers

Since the beginnings of computer-based music, remix and dance music producers have been the driving force behind many of the industry's most impressive innovations. Of course, 'producer' is a loose term that usually refers to any remix artists, producers working with bands or vocalists, or musicians with a penchant for hard disc recording and editing. Whether they are set up in a fancy studio, or holed up in their college dorm room, producers using Live may be the largest and most feature-savvy group of them all. Many producers have already tapped into the exciting prospect of remixing another artist's work, as well as creating new music, when using Live's instant time-stretching and unprecedented sample manipulation ability. Producers want to compose, make music, put together unusual elements, find the 'right' hook, etc. Live allows them the creative freedom to stick to the task at hand while keeping the process simple enough to remain focused on the music.

Live DJs using Live

Today, DJs make music using CDs, minidisk players, MP3 players, turntables, and computers. Their artistry involves selecting their own mix of music or musical components (beats, samples, etc) to entertain, explore, or make something altogether new. Live fits into the DJ world perfectly, as it allows for WAV or AIFF files to be synchronized to other tracks and other playback devices. Many of the DJs I've talked with use Live in conjunction with turntables, CD players, and other computers. Often they will spend a good deal of time configuring their songs for use in Live. This can involve editing tracks in a wave editor, mapping each necessary warp marker for the entire tune in Live's Clip View (more on this later), or merely cropping their favourite portion of a larger track (to be used as a loop). The bottom line is that DJs are benefiting from the flexibility and choices Live offers. DJs can use different parts of the same song looped against one another at the same time, or take advantage of multiple tracks (as opposed to being limited to a finite number of turntables, CD players, or mixer channels). Not to mention the fact that a digital DJ doesn't ever have to worry about wearing out precious vinyl and irreplaceable acetates or scratching a CD surface.

Bands playing with Live

The organic nature of bands may seem like an unfit environment for computers. But today, many bands are used to playing along with sequences, click tracks, and, yes, computers. Live can synchronize with an existing MIDI sequencer or even send a click track out (usually in the form of a headphone mix). The amount of flexibility provided in this arena is incredible. Live musicians using Live can actually create live remixes as well as drop in samples, work with loops, and record to disc.

Multi-track Jack (or Jill)

Crafting songs by multi-tracking can be one of the most rewarding and creative outlets a songwriter can take part in. Whether you are a solitary artist or a band with limited input channels, multi-track recordings can allow you to add many layers of music to the same piece of audio without erasing a previous track. In today's age of unlimited audio tracks we take for granted the power of layering ideas on top of one another, auditioning different digital arrangements. Live can be a perfect composition tool or arrangement auditioning tool. I have shown several songwriters Live's ability to easily and musically rearrange a song (whether it was recorded to a click or not). Often their eyes are wide with disbelief. While Pro Tools, Logic, Cubase, and other multi-track studio applications are powerful, their audio flexibility cannot match Live's instant audio warp ability. In the next few years, watch for your favourite songwriters to be employing Live instead of their ratty old tape decks.

Scoring video with Live

They say timing is everything. Nowhere is this more evident than in scoring music for the moving image. Whether you are attempting to add sound effects or mood music or creating a complete soundtrack, Live's ability to stretch audio is the perfect tool for the job. As we begin to discuss Live's unique 'elastic audio' ability in the next few sections (Warp Marker Magic, Warp Markers, and Prepping Audio), you will see how Live is built to make sound behave in ways that were simply not possible before. Film and television music composers often run into problems when trying to synchronize audio and video. For instance, the audio track may need to speed up and then slow down. The music then must reflect this. Movie and TV music also need to be done quickly, and Live's ability to be played, rather than only programmed, is a huge advantage.

While we have pointed out some of the typical ways creative people like you are making use of Live, we have by no means covered it all. New uses for Live continue to emerge. In fact, you may well invent a few of your own. As an example, check out this brief excerpt from an interview with Film Composer Klaus Badelt (taken from the Ableton website). In the 'Who's Using Live' section at the end of this chapter, we will gain even more perspective on how Badelt is employing Ableton Live in his motion picture soundtrack work.

In the next section, we are going to take a brief but important sidestep to explore the more practical side of Live's interface, Clip View and Track View, as well as several tips for working with loops and samples. Later in the chapter we will return to the idea of working methods, and different approaches for using Live. The combination of both practical knowledge (clip/track view) and tried and true examples should put you well on your way to discovering your own particular way of harnessing the power of Live.

Clip View

In Chapter 4, 'Digital Audio Basics', we discussed Live's primary interface components. I intentionally saved both Clip View and Track View for the moment you are ready to start composing, for these sub-interfaces are, for me, where the music begins. Both Clip and Track Views are found on the lower half of the screen in either Session or Arranger Views. To see a clip in Clip View, double-click on a given sample (as seen in Figure 5.1). Note: you can toggle between Clip and Track Views by clicking on the Track View Chooser tab or Clip View Zoomer. Clip View is Live's sub-interface for editing all samples/loops (clips) that are either in a clip-slot (Session View) or a track (Arranger View). Track View, which will be the place to edit, add, and delete all effects (both Live and VST), will be examined closer in its very own 'Track View' section below.

Figure 5.1

Clip View, pictured above, is similar to a sample or wave edit window.

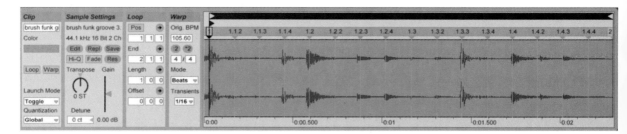

All audio samples, or loops, loaded into your Live project, can be examined, tweaked, and completely reworked in Clip View. Whether you are in Session or Arranger View, you need only double-click on a clip or track to instantly open that sample in the Clip View. I like to think of Clip View as the house that WAV and AIFF samples live in, or more aptly, the slide awaiting examination on Ableton Live's sample microscope. From here, you can establish how loops will sound, to include where a loop or sample will start and end, how the loop will be triggered (more on choosing Warp Modes later), and at what volume. Understanding Clip View is the best way to increase your skill at the 'art' of sampling, or in this case, the 'art' of sample playback. Any given sound can be played back thousands of different ways. Live allows settings for each clip to be set independently. In other words, you can have the same sample or loop copied to several different places within a Live song or set and have as many separate configurations. Live is limitless in its ability to keep track of different settings of duplicated loops/clips. All audio adjustments, or fine-tuning, for each Clip must be edited in their own clip view. To get started, simply double-click on a clip slot or sample in arrange and you will see the corresponding clip in the lower half of the screen.

Four different sub-sections are always present in Live's Clip View. These are clearly labelled Clip, Sample Settings, Loop, and Warp. In addition, the waveform can be seen clearly in the Sample Display section pictured in Figure 5.2.

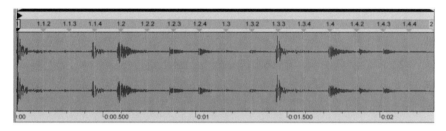

Figure 5.2
The jagged waveform introduced in Chapter 4 is back in Clip View.

Once you have a waveform in Clip View, take a minute to zoom in and out of the Sample Display area by hovering the mouse cursor on the waveform and click-dragging down (zoom in) and up (zoom out). Note you can also click-drag the waveform left and right to locate the area of the sample you are working with. This can take some practice.

As we saw in Chapter 4, a waveform's peaks and valleys correspond to the relative amplitude of portions of the sample. Located above the waveform are numbered 'Grid Markers', (which can also be instantly transformed into a Warp Marker by double-clicking on them). The numerical values represent measure, beat, and subdivision callouts, for instance, 2.1 is measure two, beat one (usually thought of as beat one of bar two). If three numbers are visible, which usually happens as you zoom in on the waveform, the third digit is a beat subdivision, such as an 1/8, 1/16, or 1/32 note. You will see subdivisions to 3 decimal numbers in the next screen shot, Figure 5.3. Note: measure one, beat one (1.1) is highlighted in all loaded clips.

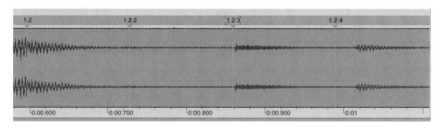

Figure 5.3
Each number can be thought of as a subdivision counter. Thus 1.2.3 is measure one, beat two, and the third sixteenth note.

Warp Marker magic

You may have already guessed that Clip View is where you will tap in to Live's 'elastic audio' tweaking properties. The way Live accomplishes this is through the use of Warp Markers (the 'green' or highlighted Grid Markers we saw above). Ableton explains, 'a Warp Marker ties a meter grid position to a sample position'. What this means is that once you have created a Warp Marker, you have created a sort of anchor in time for your loop. As you move a Warp Marker, you will gently affect the loop's timing or 'feel'. Of course, you can also radically shift a loop's timing in some crazy ways, but the tool will more often than not be used for slight, rhythmic fine-tuning, rather than major shifts. I will leave the creative decision-making up to you, but take some time out to practice how Warp Markers will affect your loops. Now let's see how work.

Each time a loop or sample is dragged into Live, Live examines the loop's transients (sonic events), and creates a sample-associated ASD file. In doing so, Live makes a drawing of the sample (a waveform) and then places Grid Markers for each beat and subdivision across the visual waveform as a guide. Once the waveform has been drawn, Grid Markers will inform you about the loop's timing in comparison to the perfect, more mathematical, grid. As we have pointed out, each of these numbered 'Grid Markers' (like 1.2.3 above) in Live can be turned into a Warp Marker by double-clicking on the numbered subdivision. In Figure 5.5 below, I have clicked on four separate Grid Markers, thereby turning them into time stretchable Warp Markers. Take a minute to practice double-clicking on these various digit-sets (Grid Markers). Notice that you can release the Warp Marker by again double-clicking on it.

Figure 5.4
Each highlighted Grid Marker in Live has been transformed into a Warp Marker. Warp Markers enable Live to time-stretch audio. The non-highlighted Grid Markers are merely informational until double-clicked, providing a visual reference point.

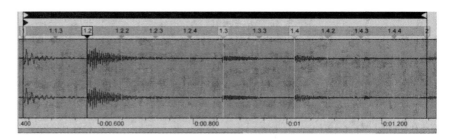

Warp Markers can then be moved left or right inside the clip. When a Warp Marker is moved, the rest of the waveform's audio will move with it. This is the essence of Live's power because it allows you to gently move the entire loop's contents rather than drastically shifting a single audio event. Now, I will demonstrate how to manipulate the timing of the loop. To do this, I will first add several warp markers (see Figure 5.5a), and then I will drag the second Warp Marker towards the first, and the third towards the fourth (See Figure 5.5b).

You can move the beat and beat subdivisions by dragging the Warp Markers to a different place in the clip. Yet, time will still move at the same speed. Your sample will be reinterpreted along the way. As we've already alluded to, Warp Markers can help you to assure your sample is firing right on the one, or correct a certain portion of the sample that is not lining up with other loops in the song. You may also try some creative effects, such as creating several Warp Markers and then moving each event in the sample to a specific place – perhaps a different place than was originally intended.

In the next example, I will take a one-measure drum groove, and zoom in on the snare hit on beat two of the bar. This is a common editing procedure for ensuring that grooves line up with the track. Even the best drummers will occasionally 'shave the beat', meaning that they hit a little ahead or behind the actual two (and four) of a typical drum groove. In Figure 5.6a you will notice that the peak of the waveform happens just after beat two's Grid/Warp Marker, while in Figure 5.6b I have corrected it to line up smack on the two.

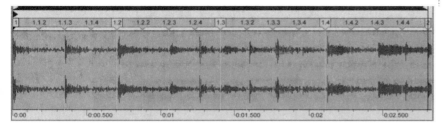

Figure 5.5a
In the Clip View above, I have double-clicked on several Grid Markers to transform them into Warp Markers. These Warp Markers will enable me to perform precision editing of the Clip's timing.

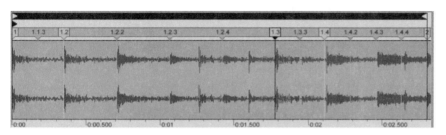

Figure 5.5b
I have moved the second and fourth Warp Markers to change the sound of the loop's timing.

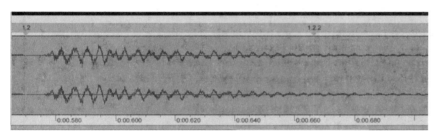

Figure 5.6a
This snare drum hit is a little late. You see beat 1.2 (measure one, beat two), and then you see the waveform (representing the snare drum sound).

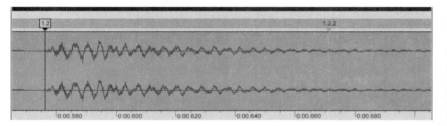

Figure 5.6b
Warp Marker 1.2 (measure one, beat two) has been moved to occur at the same instant as the snare drum hit. You can think of it the other way around if it helps you (that the drum hit was moved), but the actual audio component of the sample has not changed. You have just altered the way Live is interpreting the file.

Since Warp Markers are temporary, they do not permanently alter the sample and can always be moved again later if you wish. The above screenshot may make it seem as though Live has moved the audio. However this is a graphical illusion that Live creates to clue you in on the approximate sound of the edit. All editing in Clip View (and Session and Arranger View too, for that matter) is non-destructive. This means that the actual WAV or AIFF file remains intact. Only Live's interpretation has changed.

When positioning Warp Markers in Live, the results can at first be a little confusing. When a Warp Marker is moved closer to another Warp Marker, your instincts may tell you that you will be speeding up the groove. However, the reverse is actually true. Think of it like this: a Warp Marker that is moved closer to another Warp Marker directs Live to play a smaller portion of the clip in the same period of time (number of beats). Conversely, a Warp Marker moved farther away from another Warp Marker will force Live to play more of the clip in less time (thus sounding faster).

What follows are descriptions of each of Clip View's parameter adjustments sections. For more on the joys of manipulating warp markers and the 'art' of sample-tweaking, turn to the discussion of warp markers in Chapter 14, 'Power Tips'.

Clip Loop/Region

The size of the actual sample, versus the size of the portion that you choose to use, can be vastly different. In other words you may have a 20-second sample, but decide to use only a $^1/_2$-second of the sound. Clip Loop/Region defines the length of the sound that is played. This is the tool to use for specifying your loop points, but it can also be used to simply set the beginning and ending of a one-shot sample. In the example below (Figure 5.7), I am using only a portion of a larger sample. To do this I constrained the length of the loop by adjusting the Clip Loop/Region brackets to the location I wanted. Note: you can make these adjustments while you are listening, and even recording, in Live.

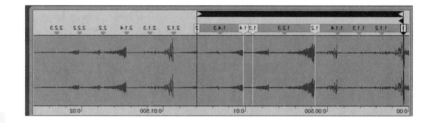

Loop Offset

Like a sentence, the point from which you start a musical phrase can make a huge impact on getting your meaning across (or so my editor tells me). Live's clip view has been expressly designed for this sort of audio rewording. To quickly see what I mean, load a drum loop in one of Live's clip slots. Double-click on the clip to launch Clip View and then direct your attention to the Sample Display. Next, grab and drag the small black triangle just above the graphic wave file (just above the Sample Display window) circled in Figure 5.8. Now, drag this triangle (called Loop Offset) right and then left again. By changing the Loop Offset, you are telling Live to begin that clip's playback at that point. Sample-heads will know this trick as changing a sample's starting point. This can be done during playback or while editing. You can also change a sample's playback when editing your arrangement (while viewing Arranger and Clip View at the same time), but I will save that for Chapter 7, 'Editing Your Performance'. Regardless of how stunning your first couple of attempts may be, keep trying. This is one of my favourite sample tweaks, because of the incredible amount of variety it can create.

To quickly turn the beat around, all we need to do is to move the Loop Offset to the 2 of the bar (position 1.2). Check out Figure 5.9 to see this simple yet powerful trick.

The groove will now begin here and play though the bar back to beat two again, centreing the loop at this new starting location. If you try this example with one of your drum loops you may think that the loop sounds exactly the same. It does. The only difference is the starting point, so you will need to hear it in context in order

---

Figure 5.7
You can adjust the endpoints of the loop or sample by moving the brackets, or shift the entire region by grabbing the top region marker.

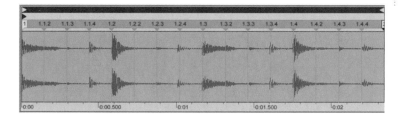

Figure 5.8
Here is a basic drum loop with the loop offset squarely placed on the *one*, along with the first kick drum.

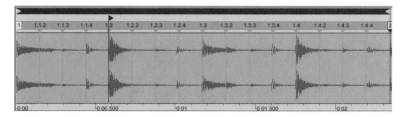

Figure 5.9
In this Figure, I have moved the loop's start point to 2. In Live this is called adjusting the loop offset.

to determine the impact of shifting your sample start point. Here are a few of the most common ways to creatively use Loop Offset:

- Drum Fill. Drummers (and drum programmers) typically rearrange their main drum part or pattern to add variety or signal the song is changing, building, etc. By changing the starting point of a loop, you can make it seem as though the drummer or drum machine is making a musical statement.
- Limit Loop. Sometimes you may not want to use the whole portion of a loop. When changing a clip/loop's region, I often find that I will adjust the Loop Offset as well. For instance if I am using the last half of a sample, the loop offset gets automatically moved (when you adjust the region) to beat 3.
- Instrument Turnaround. Like the drum fill idea above, adding variety to a sample's playback parameters (such as loop offset), can alleviate the monotony in repetitive loops. Also, you may create some interesting section transitions or 'turnarounds'.

Clip settings (in Clip View)
The first of the four small settings boxes in Clip View is called, simply, Clip. It contains the following functions.

Clip name
The first light-coloured box is the title of the loop, which can be changed by clicking on the box and typing in a new title. Once you have typed the new clip name, click Enter, and you will see the change in the clip slot above in Session View, as well as in the clip view. In Arranger View, you will see the clip name updated in the track as well. If you change your mind in the middle of the renaming process, press Escape (ESC) to keep the old name.

Clip colour
Each clip's colour can be changed here. You can choose between 16 different colours, or let Live choose a new colour as each loop is loaded or dragged onto the Session or Arranger interface. It can be helpful to devise your own personal colour-coding system based on the type of instrument used in the clip or the section of

the song in which the clip will most likely be placed. For instance, you may assign one of the three shades of green to all drum loops, while red could be for guitars. This may help you remember what a loop sounds like or give you a basic idea of what kind of sound you are about to trigger. Remember in Chapter 2, 'Getting Started', we discussed how to choose a default clip colour. You can also activate or deactivate Live's clip automatic colouring by going to Preferences > Defaults (Tab) > and clicking the On/Off - Auto Assign Colours.

Loop switch

This toggle switch makes Live loop or simply play a sample. When activated, the sample will loop infinitely. When deactivated, the sample becomes a one-shot and will then play only one time when triggered. When you turn on Loop, you will always turn on the Warping functionality. However, you will only warp a sound once you have activated warp markers in the Clip View's Sample Display.

Warping (on/off button)

With the Loop switch in the off position, you can toggle Live's Warping on or off. When off, the sample is merely played directly as it is from the hard drive of your computer. None of Live's warping magic will be applied. This can be a good solution if you are working with a sound that is at the right tempo, at a complementary tempo (such as half or double time), or devoid of tempo. I often use string and horn samples with warping in the off position.

When on, you can change the playback of the sound (using Live's Warp Markers), whether or not the clip is looping. This can be helpful when correcting a vocal take to line up in a track, as done in remixing vocal music.

Launch modes

Each clip can be triggered in one of four different modes. The mode in which the clip is triggered will affect the way you perform, via mouse, keyboard, or MIDI-keyboard. If you find a mode you are particularly fond of, make it your default setting in Live's Preferences. To adjust the trigger mode, click in to the dropdown box seen in Figure 5.10.

Figure 5.10
The dropdown box lets you select independent launch settings for each clip.

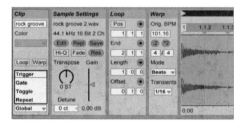

Trigger   The most common launch mode for use in most performance situations is Live's Trigger-mode. Each time you fire the clip, it will launch. Once a clip is launched and playing, you will be able to stop its playback only by pressing the Clip Stop button located in Session View's Clip Status Field. This mode ignores the up-tick off the mouse (letting go), computer keyboard key, or MIDI-keyboard. Each clip can be fired as rapidly as the Quantization will allow (more on this in the 'Launch Quantization' section that follows).

Gate   When triggering a sample in Gate mode, you will only hear the sound for as long as your mouse or keyboard key is depressed. This is an excellent setting for dropping in snippets of samples without sounding the entire clip. In short, holding your left mouse button (or MIDI/computer-keyboard key) down will continuously play the clip until released.

Toggle   With Toggle mode engaged, Live makes each clip start or stop (the opposite of what the clip is presently doing) when the Clip Launch button is depressed. If you 'launch' a clip that is playing, it will stop. Launch the stopped clip, and it will begin playing. This also works at the scene level if you trigger a scene with clips set in Toggle mode. Each time you trigger the scene, loops that are playing will stop, stopped loops will start. It is this functionality that makes Toggle mode my personal favourite. Each Clip Launch button can now have two functions: Start *and* Stop.

Repeat   Repeat mode is a way of re-triggering a sample by holding down the mouse. This can be a creative setting if you like this effect. But this is not recommended as a default because Repeat mode is best applied to one or two loops at a time for special drum and instrument fills, stutters, and loop-variances. My suggestion would be to use Repeat sparingly, as a special effect.

Launch Quantization

Quantization at the Clip level will allow you to create a separate quantization launch setting for any clip. We will discuss Quantization in detail in Chapter 6, 'Playing Live…live'. However, this key setting will affect when a loop starts to play, once it is triggered. Tight quantization, such as 1/4-note or even bar, corrects your clip triggering so that the loop/sample plays exactly on 'the one' or within the desired rhythmic framework of your piece. This can be a huge help during a live performance, or Session View recording. Note: the Clip View Launch Quantization works in conjunction with the global Quantization Menu in Live's transport bar section (unless you specify otherwise). The settings for each clip can be independent of the larger Session/Arranger settings but can also be specified to act in whatever way the global Quantization Method is set to by selecting Global within the Clip as shown below in Figure 5.11.

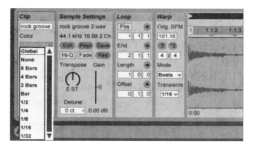

Figure 5.11
By setting the clip to Global, Live will force the clip to trigger at *the same* setting as the overall project. This should be the default setting for beginners and performers who use Live live.

Other possible settings in Clip View's Launch Quantization include 1/32, 1/16, 1/8, 1/4, and 1/2 notes. And new to Live 2 are measure aligning Quantization settings of Bar, 2 Bars, 4 Bars, and 8 Bars.

Info

Warning

The setting of None can be misleading! None means absolutely no quantization of any kind. You will instantly trigger the loop when you hit the Clip Launch button. This is recommended only for occasions when you need to be sure that the clip starts playing the instant you launch it.

Tip

Timing is evereything

If you are going to be playing in a club, theater, or other live performance situation, check to be sure the Quantization Menu (in Session View) is set to something complimentary to the music you will be playing in your live set (Bar or 1/4-note settings are generally preferable).

Then, make sure that all of the clips you are triggering have been set to Global in Clip View's Launch Quantization setting (to use the same setting you registered above in Session View). You may have to click into each loop to verify this. I also recommend that Global be your default setting.

Figure 5.12
Both Transpose and Detune alter a given sample's pitch. This can be a powerful and musical-sounding effect. Note ST is short for Steps, which is really half-steps. The above loop has been transposed down three half-steps (a minor third).

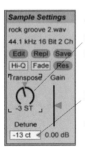

Transpose the sample in half-steps.

Define the loop +/– in terms of cents

Sample settings

Each clip's settings can be controlled using the submenus in the Clip View screen. As you begin working in Live you will quickly discover that each instance of a clip can have completely unique settings. For instance, you may have the same eight-bar drum loop loaded into several scenes, yet have completely different sample settings in each instance of the sample. One may be truncated using the Clip Loop/Region setting we learned about earlier. Another may be pitched down to add drama to a certain musical section. Still another may contain a different Loop Offset (explained earlier in the Loop Offset section) so that the listener hears a new portion of the loop first, giving the aural illusion that the drummer did something different.

In the next sections, we are going to add to your arsenal of sample and loop tweaking tricks. Take a minute to experiment with each subsection so that you fully grasp the possibilities and to get in a little practice while you are at it.

Transpose and detune

One of my favourite methods of sonic exploration is to radically re-pitch a loop. In Clip View, this can be done in one of two ways: Transpose or Detune. Transpose is a literal semitone, or half-step, in the traditional chromatic scale. Live allows for +/-32 half-steps for any sample, which translates to about two and a half octaves in either direction. You can easily create harmonies by playing two of the same or similar loops, and tuning one up 4, 5, or 7 half-steps – to deliver the major third, perfect fourth, and perfect fifth harmonies. I also love to radically re-pitch drum, percussion, and FX loops to create interesting textures and sounds.

The Detune option in Clip View pictured in Figure 5.12 is geared more for fine-tuning a pitched instrument or voice in cents. Think of cents as microtones lying between the notes defined by a Western chromatic scale. Live allows for +/–50 cents on any given clip.

Info

Warp speed ahead

If Live's warp feature is engaged, transposing or detuning a clip will not result in a tempo change. For instance, if you are playing a warped clip and you adjust the tuning in any way, you will hear the clip pitch change, but not the tempo. With warp disengaged, your clips will act more like a DJ turntable when you increase or decrease the RPMs. Since there are times when either option is desirable, take a moment to glance at the Warp box in the Clip box, just to the left of the Sample Settings box (where the tuning options are located).

Gain (and the dangers thereof)

Live's Clip view does a fairly accurate job of displaying the waveform's volume in terms of the size of the graphic. Large waveforms almost invariably sound louder (unless there is some frequency-cutting effect applied, see Chapter 8, 'Live's Effects'). In short, size correlates with volume.

There are at least two ways to raise a sample's level. In the Clip View Sample Settings box, the vertical gain fader can pump up the volume of your sound +/-24 dB. Most of the time, +24 dB is going amplify the wave to outlandish proportions

and will almost inevitably cause a level peak in the track. This is undesirable nearly all of the time. I would say all the time, but some experimentalist, sonic extrem-
ist out there will say, 'Hey I love digital distortion!' The rest of the world, it is safe
to say, does not. Here are a couple examples of waveforms at various volume/gain
levels (See Figures 5.13a and 5.13b).

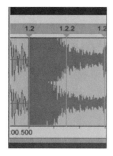 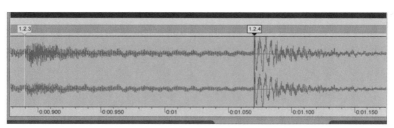

Figure 5.13a (left)
This waveform has
peaked and will sound
distorted.

Figure 5.13b (right)
This waveform is at a
more normal level.

We will talk more about volume and level throughout the book. For now,
remember that Clip View has one say in the matter. In Chapter 10, 'Wave Editing
Tips', we will look at some steps you can take to prepare your loops for stage using
methods like normalization and compression.

Sample settings buttons

Above the Transpose and Gain controls, are six very helpful buttons (Figure 5.14).

Figure 5.14
These six buttons can
be handy time savers
when working in Clip
View.

Edit   The 'Edit' button simply launches your preferred third-party wave-editing
application (we will talk more about this in Chapter 10), such as Sound Forge or
Wavelab. You specify which wave editor to associate with the 'Edit' button in Live's
Preference/Misc. tab. Press Browse next to the Choose Sample Editor: path.

Replace   *Repl*, short for replace, is a shortcut for swapping samples (and loops). The
Replace (Repl) button can help you reinsert a sample that didn't load correctly or
was lost, which can sometimes happen when you are moving your files from
machine to machine. You can also use Repl for creative means. Try replacing a
drum or music loop with something altogether different. To use this button, you will
need to know the current location of the sample you want to import into your Clip.
Two important things to remember about Replace is that this action cannot be
undone, and that all Clips using the same sample will be affected (exchanged for
the replacement clip). If you accidentally replace a sound, simply close your project without saving (assuming the project had been recently saved prior to the acci-
dental replacement), and then reopen it.

Save   The Save button tells Live you are happy with the current Clip View settings
for a given sound. By pressing this button, Live will update the corresponding .ASD
file. From this point forward, Live will always load that particular sample with the
current Clip View specs. If you move the sound out of the folder or erase the ASD
file, Live will default back to the original settings.

Hi-Q   Hi-Q, short for High Quality Sample Readout, uses a more sophisticated inter-
polation algorithm so that samples that have been pitch-shifted sound cleaner. The
catch is that Hi-Q absorbs more of your CPU's processing power. I recommend

using this setting for any major sound, such as a bass or drum track, that has been pitch-shifted. This is different from Warp settings, which we will cover later in this chapter.

Fade   Live's Fade button in Clip View creates a very short (about 10 milliseconds) fade-in and fade-out for the clip to which it is assigned. This feature will eliminate the most common pops or clicks heard when the sample starts or stops. You can do this manually in your wave editor of choice, but this button will save you time. The only regrettable side effect is that by fading samples in and out, you can lose some of the attack, also described as presence, of the sound. We will talk more about this technique in Chapter 10, 'Wave Editing Tips', and give you a couple of different options for eliminating pops.

Res   When all else fails, hit the Res button. Res, or Restore Default Settings, will make Live see the loop as it did the first time. Note: if you don't like the way Live initially loads the loop, see the defaults tab in the 'Preferences' section of Chapter 2.

Loop settings

Figure 5.15
Each of these loop settings can be specified by clicking on the square and moving the mouse up and down or by typing into the boxes, where the digits correspond to measures, beats, and subdivisions.

Loop Settings (in the Clip View), seen in Figure 5.15, often proves to be a more informational than practical way to change a loop's start, end, length, and offset. Still it is worth noting its features and considering how you may jump to certain parameters by making use of each parameter's three boxes.

Pay special attention to the Start/Position Toggle button (usually in the Start position). When Pos (Position) is selected, by pressing Start, you can move the entire Clip Loop/Region to a new position within the track by scrolling within the boxes via mouse.

Also, the arrows beside each locator are a shortcut for zooming to that exact position in the Sample Display. For instance, you may be working on a specific portion of the loop, such as the beginning or the end, and then want to quickly view the entire length of the loop. To do this, press the Show Loop right-facing arrow beside the Length button. Similarly, you may wish to jump to the end or beginning of the loop. Simply press the Show Loop Start or Show Loop End arrow buttons to make this happen.

Warp settings

Figure 5.16
The Warp Settings box in Live's Clip View. The original tempo of the loop will be calculated by Live. It can then be modified as long as the loop's length is not altered.

Warp settings may be the winner of version 2's greatest improvement award. There are three additional loop modes new to Live 2, with the added option of foregoing Live's warp engine entirely. This brings the combined total to five different ways to warp a loop (or sample). If you are still unclear about warping and Live's warp modes, refer to Chapter 4, 'Digital Audio Basics'. You can see the Warp Settings for Clip View in Figure 5.16.

Original tempo (BPM)

Live's calculation of the original tempo is done by measuring the length of the loop. However since Live cannot tell if you are in 'double-time' or 'half-time', Live also considers the quantity of audio events. Because it is an educated guess done by a computer, Live will occasionally guess wrong. Usually the guess will be twice or half as fast as the loop actually needs to be. This brings us to the next buttons in Warp settings.

Half/double original tempo

If a loop is cut correctly, Live usually will be able to guess the tempo. When Live guesses incorrectly, the loop is often twice as fast (double Live's original tempo), or half as fast (half Live's original tempo).

Original time signature

Live also assumes all songs and samples are in 4/4 (common) time. Of course, this may not always be the case, or you may, for creative reasons, want to make Live see the file differently. Strangely, Live does not change the speed of files when you change the time signature. It makes sense that 5/4 and 4/4 are heard at the same tempo, but Live makes no distinction between 'cut-time' and regular time or denominator shifts (that could be used for some form of metric modulation), such as from 6/8 to 3/4. Numerators can range from 1 to 99. Denominators are logically allowed to be set to 1, 2, 4, 8, and 16.

Warp Mode

As we mentioned earlier, Live 2's three new Warp Modes make for cleaner, more musical warping. What's warping, you ask? Well, in this instance (remember this is different from Warp Markers), warping is when Live automatically corrects the pitch and tempo of a loop. Warp Mode affects the way in which Live approaches Warping. Four different Warp Modes are possible in Clip View's Warp Settings section: Beats, Tones, Texture, and Re-Pitch. Each mode also features a special set of controls that will appear below it in the form of a Transients dropdown menu, grain size box/knob, and flux box. We will cover these in each subsection below. Also, don't forget that you can simply turn off Live's Warp engine altogether, and just play the sample at its default speed and pitch. Since we touched on these in Chapter 4, here is a brief reminder of what kinds of different sounds you can expect when switching between these four Warp Modes.

Beats Mode   Beats Mode is the same warping mode that was used in Live 1.5. This is a great mode for rhythmic loops, percussive samples, and even entire songs. You will usually want to use Beats mode with percussion, drums, drum machines, and sounds characteristically containing minimal decay (sustain). When importing songs (or long wave files), the same rules apply. Occasionally, if the sound is too textured, or lacks rhythmic definition, you may hear artifacts. Artifacts happen when Live tries to warp a non-percussive file, such as a drone or flute melody. Live's transient detection settings, just below the Warp mode settings, allow you to zero in on busier patterns or to relax the warp engine for more sparse-sounding loops.

The typical transient setting in Beats mode is 1/16-note and in extreme cases 1/32-note. If you hear artifacts or stuttering effect in your sample, try a 'looser' setting (1/8-note or 1/4-note) or even another mode. How about Tones Mode?

Tones Mode   Tones such as bass guitars, synthesizers, vocals, keyboards, or other long-sustaining instruments can sound much less affected when playing in Live's Tones Mode. You can roughly adjust Live's Grain Size to help reduce undesirable

Info

Definition of transient

Transient detection is a critical element of Live's warping functionality. A transient is the short, sharp attack portion of the sound. The steeper and less frequent the waveforms, the easier it is for Live to detect transients. This is why drum, percussion, and similar kinds of samples are the easiest to time-stretch. Tones and noise samples look more like a solid wave and therefore lack the sharp (detectable) attack needed to correct the sample's timing and pitch.

artifacts on less-defined samples. Ableton advises, 'For signals with a clear pitch contour, small grain sizes work best. Larger values help avoid artifacts that can occur when the pitch contour is unclear, but can result in audible repetitions'.

Texture Mode   Texture Mode is built for using orchestral samples, field recordings, thick keyboard pads, and similarly dense audio textures. Like Tones Mode, Texture Mode is a hybrid and more relaxed version of Beats mode, in which Live's analysis of the sound file (using a mathematical algorithm) is less strict. You can further loosen the settings by adjusting Grain Size and Flux (randomness).

Re-Pitch   Re-Pitch mode is more like true vinyl DJing – Live will alter the pitch of the sample depending upon the playback speed. This mode will produce few to no artifacts, especially if the warped, looped, re-pitched sample is played close to its original tempo. Thus Re-Pitch differs greatly from Beats, Tones, and Textures modes, all of which preserve the sample's original pitch.

Setting the scene

Until this point in the chapter, we have been talking about Clip View and the various parameters that can be adjusted for each particular sample/loop (called a clip) in Live. In the next few sections, we are going to shift the focus back to Session View, since this is the view you will use for setting up your live performance and arranging the clips we just learned about. Remember, by double-clicking on any clip-slot, you will open up the corresponding Clip View (beneath the session grid). Ingeniously, this happens without closing either Session View or Arranger View, so that you never lose sight of the song.

As we delve into what it takes to create a song in Live, keep in mind that every artist has his or her own way of working. That said, the remainder of this chapter is devoted to making music in Live, as well as learning how to organize and manipulate Live's scenes into actual music.

Set up

Each time you begin to work in Live, take a minute to consider some of your Live song settings, such as tempo, time signature, and MIDI/Keyboard configuration. If you set up a template, as we did in Preferences, you will begin to rely on the same settings for each of your Live songs. The power of consistency should not to be overlooked.

Tempo

Many Live newbies often forget to consider their song's tempo and will then compose each and every song at the default tempo of 130BPM. Make sure you give tempo the same kind of thought as you would key signature and sample selection. After all, tempo can really determine the mood of a song.

New to Live 2, you can automate tempo changes within your Live composition. We will explore the many levels of automation in greater detail in Chapter 6, but for now, let us look at how you might create a tempo change in your Live song. In Arranger View, maximize the Master Track as shown below in Figure 5.17.

Track Fold-In

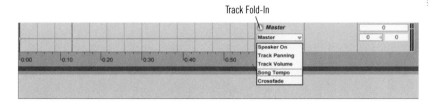

Figure 5.17
Maximize the Master Track in the Arranger
View so you can prepare to automate tempo.

Next, select 'Master' in the Choose Device automation window, and select Song Tempo in the Choose Control dropdown window (Figure 5.18).

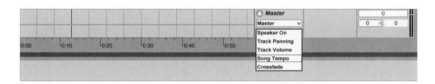

Figure 5.18
When you select Song Tempo in the Choose
Control dropdown box, Live displays a thin
horizontal red line in the master track
symbolizing the track's tempo.

To manually add the tempo change, double-click on the red line (breakpoint envelope) to create a breakpoint (edit point) for the change. You can now drag this or any other breakpoint you create up or down (vertically) to make your Live song faster or slower (respectively). To adjust the timing of the speed up, for changing the point in the song at which the tempo change occurs, drag the tempo change breakpoint laterally across the song. If you change your mind or inadvertently create too many breakpoints, simply double-click on them to delete. Figure 5.19 is an example of a gradual increase and then decrease in tempo with several applied breakpoints. This is a powerful tool for film or television music as well as ambient or electronic music effects.

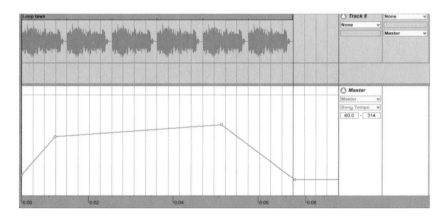

Figure 5.19
Here is a basic tempo change mapped
manually through the creation of breakpoints
in Live.

There is also another powerful way to achieve the above results (automation) within Live. Simply hit Record and Play, and then mouse-drag Live's Tempo Control box in the transport bar above as shown in Figure 5.20.

In Figure 5.21, you will see the large number of breakpoints created via real-time automation recording. We will delve deeper into the joys of automation soon enough, but this example should provide an inkling of the awesome potential that lies ahead.

Figure 5.20
You can automate nearly anything in Live by the above method. However, with each breakpoint, Live will require more precious CPU power, so use this technique as sparingly as your computer may insist.

Mouse-drag tempo
while in record mode

Record mode
is active

Figure 5.21
Look at all those breakpoints! While this tempo change will prove ultimately very complex, Live will demand a lot of work from your CPU.

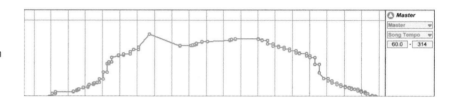

Time signature

Giving some thought to your time signature can alleviate frustration, or on a positive note, add new dimensions to your music. You may find it advantageous to work in a time signature that is double or half of your actual tempo, depending upon what kind of feel you are going for. In fact, odd time signatures are often a source of new musical phrasing ideas and original combinations. However, I want to point out that adjusting the tempo in Live is really only cosmetic. The grid will move, but the song tempo/feel will not. Though you can adjust the song tempo from the tempo menu, or the feel from manipulating Warp Markers, time signature is really just an organizational tool. At the time of this writing, you cannot create time signature changes within a single song.

MIDI/Keyboard mapping

I find it helpful to control Live the same way for nearly every song. This basic working strategy helps to keep Live behaving in the manner I am used to and therefore saves time and boosts creativity in the process. For example, it may be helpful to assign your MIDI controller's faders and knobs to the same parameters in each Live song by default. If you do not have a MIDI controller or interface, skip to the next section.

Here is how to map a MIDI control in Live.

1 Click on Live's 'MIDI Map Mode Switch' on the Transport bar.
2 Mouse-click on the parameter you would like to control via MIDI.
3 Move the hardware controller knob, fader, or key that you would like to associate with the above parameter. Live will then 'learn the assignment'.
4 Repeat for as many controls as you would like to set.
5 Finish editing your MIDI map by again pressing (deactivating) the MIDI Map Mode Switch.

Each of Live's user interface elements will behave differently when receiving MIDI information. For instance, switches or session view slots will toggle on or off, while a continuous control (such as a fader) or radio button (such as a pan knob) will receive a gradual stream of information in a specified direction. In Chapter 9, 'Using MIDI', we will discuss different types of MIDI controllers, and how to maximize your MIDI potential.

Occasionally you may need to create a different MIDI-map for a specific effect. When doing so, save the new set up and give it a descriptive name. Also, I usually delete any audio files or mix settings so that this file can be later used as a template.

Creating and working with scenes

Live's default set loads with 10 blank scenes. This may be many more than some DJs need, since they will load and delete clips as they go through their set. Figure 5.22 is a sample DJ style setup in Live's session view.

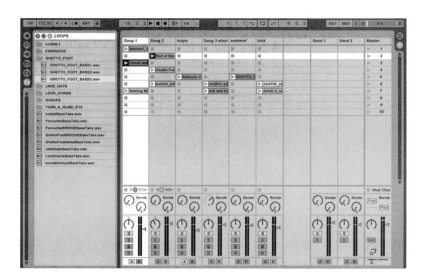

Figure 5.22
Here are the beginnings of a typical DJ Session View in Live.

While it may not look very organized, this is entirely the point. Each clip will be loaded as the DJ is interpreting the direction he or she would like the set to go. This can be done spontaneously, on the fly, while the DJ cues in another sound location. The DJ may play all or part of each track depending upon his or her need. The entire track will be pre-configured ahead of time – with the DJ inserting as many Warp Markers as the piece of music needs.

At the same time, 10 scenes may not be nearly enough for a film composer, who may want to have lots of similar scenes with only subtle differences between them. In Figure 5.23, I have mocked up a potential Session for someone needing several scenes, with subtle to dramatic differences.

Some bands or musicians will find that they need multiple songs to keep track of different tempos, effects, and routing schemes, but again, experimentation is key. I have found that I

Figure 5.23
There is no limit to the number of scenes you can create. Theoretically, you could score an entire show with one Live song and a multitude of scenes.

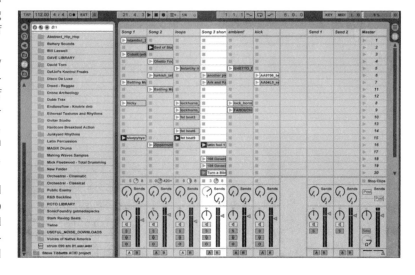

like to develop one large set per live performance, so that I do not have to open and close files during a show. Typically, my set will contain several songs, where each song is made up of several scenes. I also routinely develop specific scenes for transitional purposes (such as from song to song). In Figure 5.24, Ableton Live co-inventor and Monolake mastermind Robert Henke outlined his standard approach to a gig.

Figure 5.24
The creative palette-style approach of Monolake is actually quite pragmatic. Most clip-slots seen above are filled with an entirely pre-produced song (as a DJ might set it up). Other smaller loops are also sprinkled throughout Robert's scenes to be used as transitions.

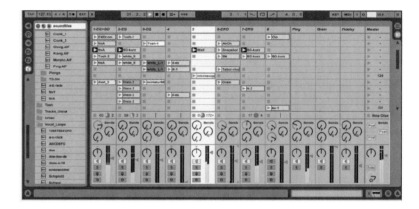

Robert's sets usually progress logically downward scene by scene. However, he leaves plenty of room for improvisation between songs. Often he will layer texture-producing audio effects such as reverb and delay to add a little cover between songs. Or, he may rely upon a small single loop to help provide a backbone.

Prepping the clip

Performing with Live requires a little planning. Depending upon what you are trying to accomplish, most clips, tracks, samples, and loops need to be prepared ahead of time. In theory, this is no different than a band or combo rehearsing before a gig, or a songwriter working up a new arrangement. You will want to hone your song as much as possible, getting your music ready for the ultimate test, a live crowd!

As we mentioned early on in this chapter, each Live artist will develop his or her own working strategy. In a few paragraphs (starting with The Producers) I have detailed some effective working strategies gleaned from known Live artists and endorsees on how they prepare their samples for use in a Live set. No matter which group you may fall into, take a minute to read them all. We can all learn from each other.

Fine-tuning the scene

Now that you are beginning to see how music is formed in Live, and you're learning that different applications may demand different configurations, here are a few more pointers on how to maximize the sonic potential of your scene layouts.

Clip matching

Occasionally, loops that you want to use together will be timed differently or played with a slightly different feel. For instance, a drum loop in 6/8 time may feel as though it is swinging compared to your straight eighth-note Cuban cowbell loop. To align the loops, you will have to use your ears. Try soloing one, two, or several loops to hear them more cleanly. Then add warp markers to help synchronize their performances. In Figure 5.25, I have taken a jazz drummer's ride groove and straightened it out (he's probably turning in his grave as we speak!). Still, this sort of modification can make all the difference when mixed into the final track. Notice how I have made Warp Markers for each and every beat because of the severity of the feel change. Often, only one or two Warp Markers will do the trick.

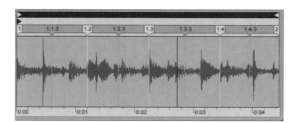

Figure 5.25
In the figure above, I have 'fixed' the performance to line up better inside my Kraftwerk remix. This drummer's beautiful jazz swing feel was messing up my track, ha!

Loop soup

A word of warning. Be careful not to overindulge in Live's loop-mixing tactics. Since it is so easy to add several busy or complex-sounding loops at once, make sure each track really needs to be there.

The producers

If you are new to music production and the art of remixing, you may want to skip to Chapter 11, 'Where to Get Loops', immediately after reading this subsection. After all, without any samples, loops, sounds, or instrument recordings to tweak, you are going to get pretty sick and tired of playing with Live's demo song.

If you are feeling impulsive, jump on out to www.sonicfoundry.com, www.big-fishaudio.com, or www.soundsonline.com, and pick yourself up a couple of loop CDs. For less than £30, you can score a basic 500 to 600 MB sample collection (usually classified in a specified genre such as techno, drum 'n bass, rock and roll, blues, etc.). If you can't wait for the mail, you can always do a Google Search for free loops or loops for download, which at the time of this writing yielded about two million results pages. Keep in mind that, as with most things, you get what you pay for. Most free loops are usually just some fun found sounds that are great for getting your feet wet.

Info

Loop-based mush

When composing loop-based music, I find that subtraction is as important as addition if you want to make your music speak. When problem scenes stick out from the rest of the track, you might try eliminating a loop or two from that scene to see if it sounds less jumbled. Panning and EQ filtering are also two common tricks to help make a mix sound more balanced. By eliminating the bass frequencies in your guitar part (by applying a high pass filter using EQ Four), you may actually be able to hear the bass and guitar more clearly. We will explore more sonic alternatives in Chapter 8, 'Live's Effects.'

Tip

Mounds of sounds

Keeping track of your samples and loops usually requires some kind of personalized system. I typically keep one hard drive (or drive partition) dedicated for samples only. This way, you can bookmark your sample folder in Live's Browser and then cherry-pick the best samples for the track by using Live's pre-listening feature. We will revisit this topic in detail in Chapter 11, 'Where to Get Loops.'

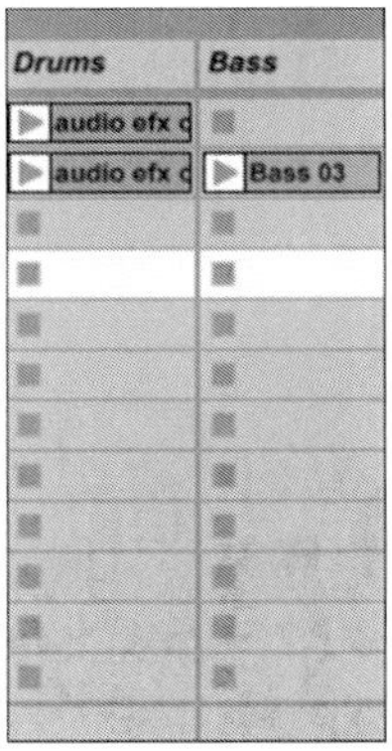

Figure 5.26
By starting from the upper left and moving down and to the right, you will be able to easily see the way your song is progressing. If you change your mind midway, you can always alter the track order by dragging the track name to the insert point.

Drums	Bass
▶ audio efx c	▦
▶ audio efx c	▶ Bass 03
▦	▦
▦	▦
▦	▦
▦	▦
▦	▦
▦	▦
▦	▦
▦	▦
▦	▦

After you have set your song's tempo, drag your favourite drum loop to an empty clip slot. To keep things simple, let's drag it to scene one, track one (see Figure 5.26). Launch the clip and take a minute or so to work with the loop. Does the loop need correcting? What Loop Mode is best? Do you need to fix or change the beat by adding Warp Markers? Try to do this sort of work at the moment the first instance of the loop is loaded. That way each copy of the edited loop will contain all of the necessary settings, making for quicker, more inspired arranging.

Rhythm section tracks, such as drums, percussion, and basses are often a good place to start when creating a remix. You will want to begin to get an idea about chord progression, and song structure from the beginning, so that all extra parts, samples, or sections move toward that goal. If you are concerned that this feels too rigid for your creative process, don't worry. In Live, there are plenty of ways to create those 'happy accidents'. This organization will only bolster your creativity.

For the sake of this exercise, we are going to pretend the song starts with the drum loop (so scene one is complete). For scene two, we are going to want to have the same drum loop from above, plus one more loop, which we'll place in scene two, track two. How about a bass? To quickly duplicate your drum loop into the next scene, click on the clip and press Ctrl (Cmnd) + D. This is one of my favourite time-saving commands – get to know it well! Next, drag a bass loop or something thereabouts into the clip slot position, scene two, track two (Figure 5.27).

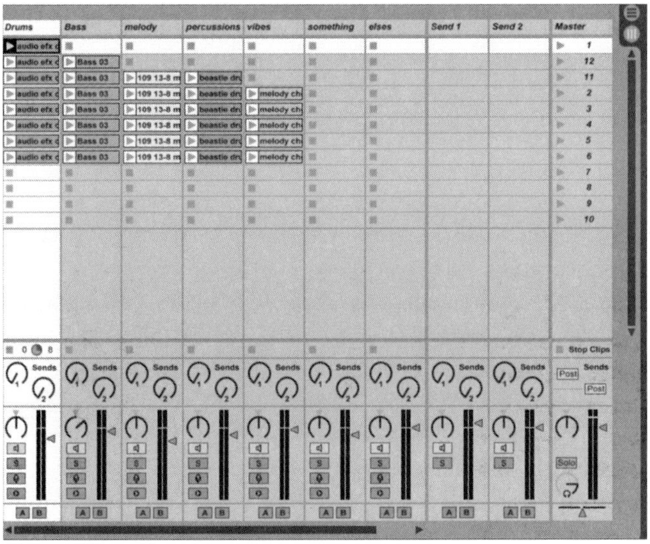

Figure 5.27
Already the song is starting to take shape. For now, keep it simple. Each time you add a loop, duplicate the loops from the previous scene down using the shortcut above.

Or for an even cooler shortcut, click on scene two's launch button (on the far right) and click Ctrl (Cmnd) + SHIFT + D. You will notice that Live has now inserted scene number 11 in between scenes 2 and 3. But the real time saver is that Live has also copied both of the above loops. This is an extremely effective live performance shortcut, but it also works well when organizing a dance remix or other loop-based track.

By following our example for the first two loops, continue to add one or two loops per scene until your Session View grid looks something like Figure 5.28.

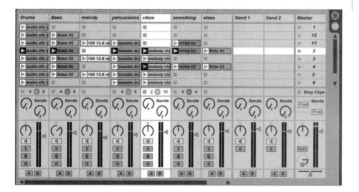

Figure 5.28
We have added one new loop per scene in a sort of stair step layering method. Gradually adding (and subtracting) musical parts is a common trick in any kind of dance music.

By grouping your loops in this way, it is easy to play one scene at a time to verify that the tune is going in the right direction. As you run the track down, I recommend keeping your Quantization Menu set to Bar or 1/4 note so that each scene is triggered in time. Listen to make sure that each scene flows into the next. You will need to adjust each track's volume, panning, and effects settings (just as you would in a hardware studio). Keep in mind that Session Mode is not the recording or final arrangement, but a mock-up of potential song ideas, which can be used live or in the writing process. In Chapter 6, we will record the actual track in a single performance by playing these scenes and clips in a live sequence. We will also look at how to edit your final performance in Arranger View. But before we jump ahead of ourselves, let's take a look at how some other artists are using Live, to see what we can learn.

The Digital DJ

The difference between a live DJ and a remix producer is that DJs are commonly working with long pre-produced tracks or completed songs, rather than short studio-ready loops (source material). Most of the DJs I spoke with are using Live to run WAV (or AIFF) file versions of their vinyl and CD collections, which have been transferred to disk using another software application. The process of transferring vinyl to audio is commonly referred to as *digitizing* vinyl. Each track must be converted to WAV or AIFF so that Live can read the files. CDs can be ripped with software such as iTunes, Mac's OS 9/X MP3 player, and music library organizer, or PC users can use **Winamp (www.winamp.com) or MusicMatch** (www.musicmatch.com). If you are fortunate enough to have a wave editor such as Steinberg's Wavelab, Sonic Foundry's Sound Forge, or Bias's Peak, you will find some key tips in Chapter 10, 'Wave Editing Tips'. If not, save your pennies. A professional wave editor will take your sound to the next level in and of itself.

Once your files are converted, it is time to make sure Live will load them correctly at the gig. This involves setting the warp markers and original tempo and then pressing save in Clip View as discussed above.

After your track or song has been digitized, you should prepare the music (track) for use in a Live 2 performance (or session). To do so, you will import the song/track, correct it for any tempo fluctuation, and save the ASD file. Here is a screenshot of a freshly imported track (see Figure 5.29). Notice that there are no Warp Markers (except for measure 1, beat 1), only Grid Markers. The goal by the end of step #10 is to have Live's Grid and Warp Markers map out the correct

Info

Saving grace

Once your Clip's properties (such as Trigger mode, Pitch, Warp Marker settings) are set, you should create an ASD (analysis) file, by pressing the small Save button in Clip View's Sample Settings section. By doing so, future Live sets will be able to instantly recognize and recall the previously saved settings for this sample. If you are using the same loop file in two (or more) projects, it is a good idea to save the song as Self-Contained to create separate copies of each sample[md]one for each project. Note: All ASD analysis files are stored within the 'Sounds' folder when you Save as Self-contained. Incidentally, ASD files are tiny compared to the size of your wave files. The information they contain however, can be a huge help.

tempo. You will then create an ASD file for each one of your tracks. After doing so, each time you mix a Live set, you can flexibly integrate your songs at your set's tempo.

Figure 5.29
Here is what a freshly imported song looks like in Live's Clip View. Notice that in the Sample Display for this four-minute waveform there are no Grid or Warp Markers. This song has not been looped yet.

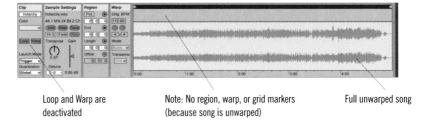

Loop and Warp are
deactivated

Note: No region, warp, or grid markers
(because song is unwarped)

Full unwarped song

1 Rip the track that you would like to incorporate into your DJ set. For more ideas on how to rip a track, check out the Rip Van Vinyl note later in this chapter.

2 Next, import the tune into Live (by click-dragging the file from Live's browser or by selecting File > Open and selecting the track).

3 Play the track (by pressing the Launch Clip File triangle).

4 Press Live's tap tempo button several times in rhythm along with the track. Notice the BPM Live suggests.

5 Once you feel that you have zeroed in on the target tempo, press Loop in Clip View. Instantly the Original Tempo readout in the Clip View will match the project BPM. Hint, since most music is produced in conjunction with a sequencer or click track, you will find that many of the songs that you are working with will be at a rounded and consistent tempo (such as 100, 110, 120 BPM, and so on).

6 Make sure Warp is also depressed.

7 Here is where it gets interesting. Drag the Warp Marker labelled '1' to the right until it is just before the first part of the waveform. You will now add as many Warp Markers as you need to make your track follow the tempo (as best you can). Depending upon how correct or quantized the original track is, you may not have to add any Warp Markers at all. Occasionally though, you will have to manually add many clip-correcting warp markers. One trick I also use (related to the hint in step 5) is to try rounding the Original Tempo box up or down within the nearest beat or half beat. For example, if your manually tapped tempo generates a value of 122.09 BPM, I will select the box, type '122' and then press Enter. I find that most of the time (particularly with electronic oriented music), that the song will be at a more rounded number.

8 To test the tempo, you may want to engage Live's Metronome and begin listening for inconsistencies, or make your own test loop (such as a standard techno or trance drum loop) to check against.

9 The new track may deviate from the click in certain places, but not others. Take note of these 'problem spots', and polish the track as you go.

10 For each inconsistency, you will want to make and drag a Warp Marker in the right direction. This takes a little practice.

In extreme cases, say for an ambient or orchestral piece of music, DJs will need to place a Warp Marker for each and every beat (or even in-between beats). Most of the time, however, you will use only two or three for the whole song. I generally place a marker every four to eight bars if I am working with a less rhythmically defined piece of music (ambient), and depending upon what effect I am trying to achieve. If I am looking for precision, I will put in more markers. Most of my Warp Marker moves are aligning downbeats with the grid. Below are two screen shots to compare. Figure 5.30a is a basic dance groove in which the beats are not lining up with the metronome and Grid Markers. In Figure 5.30b I have corrected the beat by adding and moving only one Warp Marker. You do not always need to place a marker on each groove. This is the beauty of elastic audio and Live's interpretive nature. By moving one Warp Marker, you are shifting the entire file.

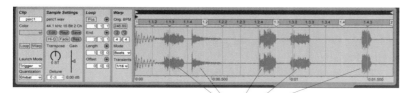

Figure 5.30a
At the sound of the above song, everyone on the dance floor is standing, staring at the DJ, mouths agape, wondering how they are supposed to party.

Notice how the drum hits are
not landing on the beats

Figure 5.30b
Order has been restored, the beats are back where they need to be, and the dance floor is again moving as it should.

One other factor to consider, when you are warping and adjusting the clip, is the clip's transient marker setting. Depending upon what kind of musical content is happening in the clip, you may want to lessen (relax) the clip's transient detection. I generally shoot for 1/8 note for most dance-oriented music. Some DJs shoot for 1/4 or 1/2, but these can be tough to correctly line up, meaning they will take an excess of Warp Markers (and time) to make them solid at these lower detection settings. 1/16 and 1/32 are fine if the music is choppy Techno or House trax, but remember that Live will be working very hard to keep up (using more CPU).

Ripping CDs is fairly easy. Mac users merely need to change their import settings for iTunes to WAV or AIFF and then pick the folder they would like to drop the new tracks into. If you're on a PC, simply download Winamp, MusicMatch (my two favourites), or your favourite MP3/CD-playing application and follow the instructions for ripping. If you have the option, make sure to import at 16-bit/44.1 KHz – the standard for consumer audio CDs. 24-bit won't help you here.

'Live' band – the laptop musician

In many ways, performing as a laptop musician (a DJ using Live) with a band or group of musicians is similar to creating a live DJ set. Like DJs, laptop musicians need to be able to react to their musical environment, bandmates, or audience. But unlike musicians, a DJ's preparation ahead of the gig involves selecting samples and recordings ahead of time. In other words, laptop musicians need to organize their sample libraries and be spontaneous at the same time – not an easy task.

Info

Rip van Vinyl

Digitizing vinyl can be as involved a process as you can imagine. All of the elements we touched on in Chapters 2 and 4 come into play. Pre Amps, A/D converters, Soundcards, and even your cabling will have an impact on the sound quality of your vinyl transfer. To get you started, be sure to tune up your turntable and replace your stylus/needle if need be. Take time to clean the vinyl if you can, so that you will experience minimal pops and dust crackle.

Figure 5.31
Live's input dropdown menu. You can record Live's own output, your sound card's input, and any Rewire software application's output, such as Reason.

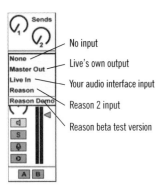

Just as other performers need their instruments, laptop musicians need instant access to loops and samples, or pre-configured scenes; organization is key. Since nearly all of the samples a laptop musician uses will be made ahead of time, file management (organization) is only one piece of the puzzle. The real challenge is in creating scenes and audio routing schemes that make sense within the context of the live performance. For instance, most musicians playing with software such as Live will need a click track or monitor out from Live. You may also need to set up a MIDI synchronizing link between Live and another sequencer. Also, you will often want to create loops on the fly by recording loop sub-mixes from within Live during your actual performance. That way if you want to revisit a particularly powerful segment or section of music, you can do so without replaying the original scene. It is also possible to re-route certain instrument signals (from your band) through Live's session mixer, for yet another way to create within the creation.

Multi-track tactics

In looking at the ways and methods for using Live, it is safe to say that the lines are often blurred. While DJs and remix producers may use similar or differing approaches, these next two groups of users, Multi-Trackers and TV and Film Music producers may use any of the above methods, plus a few of their own. As we talk about how each group sets up their scenes, imagine how you might mix and match these different techniques.

New to Live 2 is the ability to record in Arranger View. You can record a whole track or designate a punch-in and punch-out point to record a small section or overdub. In Live 1.x, all recording was done in Session mode, which is still a valuable feature in 2.0. Recordings can be as long as your hard drive can handle at a rate of about 10 megabytes per stereo minute of audio. In the steps below, we will set up Live for recording as you would in any other DAW or even analog studio.

1 Make sure you can see Live's Input Type selection dropdown box. If you cannot, select View > In/Out.
2 Select Live Input as your desired source from the choices present in the drop-down box. Live Input will coincide with whatever input source you have specified in Live's preferences; the choices are limited by the number of inputs present on your sound card. If you select Master Out, you will be able to record Live's own output onto a track. If you have installed any Rewire applications, you will also see these here (in Figure 5.31 you see an option for Propellerhead's Reason).
3 To ready the track, or column of clips, for recording, press the Arm Session Recording button at the bottom of the channel in Session Mixer. You will notice that each empty clip-slot will contain a small red circle with a triangle shape in the middle. These are each clip's Record Launch buttons.
4 You can now record to any clip you like. To stop recording, press the Spacebar, the Clip Stop Button, or launch another clip.

You can also continue your recording session by pressing another clip's Record button. I often do this to be sure that I have captured a clean take of the desired input. For instance, I may let a guitar player or keyboardist keep playing and continually capture different segments of the performance on different clips. This way you can keep your clip size to a minimum.

The other option is to record for a long time and use select portions of the file (defined by the length of your Clip Loop/Region and the placement of your Warp Markers). This method often results in large files that can bog down your laptop. Depending upon whether you are producing remixes or cutting your band's next demo, you will discover different ways to use Live for your own benefit.

TV and film music

The timing issues involved in creating TV and film music make combinations of the above three methods necessary when using Live. For starters, a composer may want to use a pre-existing piece of music along with smaller loops and samples. In this instance, the tempo and timing of the piece will be critical and so will Live's time-stretching ability. He or she may also want to create smaller sub-recordings of the master mix (a sample of the samples) for sections that need to be recalled or repeated.

Since this chapter's focus is on setting up Live, I will conclude the practical examples above by saying that while Live's setup may depend on your working method, your organization of scenes will increase the quality and quantity of your results. Like a guitar or piano, your scenes in Live need to be finely tuned in order to run effectively.

Wrap up

As you move on to Chapter 6, 'Playing Live...live', we will cover some of the same ground, but from a different angle. The fact is that playing Live on stage demands strategies similar to those employed in the studio or other creative environments. The key is to not be intimidated by Live's unique approach to organizing audio, and to dive headlong into using scenes to make song sections. Think of it as an experiment in organizing your audio material, or a new approach to composing.

Once mastered, scenes are an awesome organizational tool. For me, there is nothing quite like the feeling of creating a fresh, new tight-sounding scene. Each good scene will help inspire another. New scenes will give you perspective, or provide direction to the track at hand – or point out a glaring weakness.

As with most musical composition, one thing often leads to another, and Live's scenes do just that. In Chapter 6, we will explore many ideas specific to the live Live performers, such as improvisation, cueing new tracks, applying Live's crossfader, and much more.

Info

Score lord

When scoring for TV, Charlie Clouser uses a slightly unusual approach, playing one computer (running Live, Reason, and other performance-oriented software) into another computer (running Pro Tools) dedicated for recording. The idea makes sense when you consider that Live is really an instrument.

Klaus Badelt – Film Producer

Klaus Badelt got his start in film music by working with the prolific soundtrack and score creator Hans Zimmer. Since that time, Badelt's grand scale soundtracks include Gladiator, Mission Impossible 2, Pearl Harbor, Hannibal, and many more. When using Live in a film setting, Badelt uses his main sequencer on one computer to trigger Live (running in sync with Propellerhead's Reason) on a separate computer[md]for more on Reason Live sync, which is called ReWire, see Chapter 13, 'ReWire[md]Synchronizing Your Software.'

'I then drag in the loops I'm using (into Live) and trigger them from the keyboard,' says Badelt in an interview conducted by keyboard magazine's Greg Rule (and found in its entirety on the Ableton website). 'I use the effects in (Live), but basically sub-mix and then send to the mixer. I basically use it (Live) as a synthesizer. I have to be able to use Reason and Live at the same time. They're always integrated.'

Explains Badelt, 'Reason turned out to be fantastic because it's basically a rack of synthesizers. I can plug in, load samples into, create sounds, store

them, and recall them immediately. I use a lot of these built-in synthesizers in Reason, especially the new Malström, which has fantastic, weird sounds.' Klaus also spoke of his affection for Live, 'I have to say that ever since Live came out, it changed my life. It enabled me to use our whole library of percussive loops. I'm not talking about loops in the sense of just electronic loops, but all kinds of orchestral or ethnic percussion loops. I'm finally

able to use them all very quick and try them out in tempo. It makes it possible to work much faster, especially when you only have a few days to write a whole score.'

Badelt goes on to explain that computerized music technology has eliminated the need for racks of samplers, synths, and outboard gear. 'I don't have a single sampler anymore,' says Badelt, 'I used to have 28 EMUs, 21 Rolands, and four Kurzweils. We needed all these samplers to hold the orchestral library. But now we have switched more or less completely from the hardware samplers into software. I still have a few hardware synthesizers, especially old analog ones, but I'm probably not going to buy hardware synthesizers any more because software synthesizers are much more flexible. In our world, we have to be very fast. We have to change from one musical style to another within the minute. So the total recall is very important.' This total recall is a natural part of Live. In later chapters, we will see exactly how you can link Reason to Live, and stream huge amounts of samples from your hard disk.

Playing Live…live

If you've been following along, as opposed to skipping around, Chapters 1 to 5 have prepared you for the reward found here in Chapter 6. After all, playing Live is what you set out to do and you should by now have a good enough foundation to jump into the deep end of the pool (if you haven't already). After Chapter 6, you will have no trouble believing that musicians, DJs, and sonic experimentalists throughout the world are using Ableton Live to realize their sonic ideas. As we will soon see, the resulting musical expression and improvisation made possible by Live is astonishing. The time you've spent familiarizing yourself with Live's interface and preferences will pay big dividends when working up a Live performance set. This chapter will assume that you have a basic working knowledge of Live's Session View interface, what a sample or loop is, and how to add those loops, samples, and songs to Session View's Clip Slots in a Live Song.

Performing with Live

Since playing in front of an audience will create an altogether different kind of pressure, Chapter 6 will provide several general strategies for working speedily and efficiently when performing with Live. I will also provide you with a few specific tips from Live power users such as Charlie Clouser and Robert Henke (Monolake). The goal here is for you to be making music with Live quickly and relatively easily. Feel free to experiment, go your own way, or get distracted, if one of the following sections inspires you. Fun should be the means and the end.

In some sense using Live in a performance situation is similar to using a sampler or other sequencer-driven instruments such as keyboards or sound modules – of course you won't be staring into a tiny LCD screen any more. In fact, here is a quick tip for expanding Live's interface.

Set up

In the next few sections, we are going to cover some important concepts for making the most of your Live set and software configuration. When performing with Ableton Live, you will need to pay special attention to how you configure both your hardware and software instrument, as well as how you choose to organize your songs (and audio files). Here are a few keys to succeeding when preparing your Live set for a gig.

Tip

Power save

There are several ways to minimize CPU strain within Live, but nothing is more direct than bypassing a CPU-intensive reverb or filter delay. Also, effects such as EQ 4 allow for individual bands to be shut off (bypassed) by clicking on their corresponding number. Do this to avoid maxing out your CPU.

Because many clubs' sound systems will be less precise than your home audio environment, don't be afraid to make use of the Aux Sends and route more tracks through one or two effects as opposed to having effects on each channel (track).

Note: Any effect can be bypassed by pressing the green power button on the upper left side of the effect's interface. Bypass does mean that you will no longer hear the effects of the effect on the sound, so eliminate your most superfluous effects first.

- Stability is key. Push your musical expression or ideas to the next level, not your CPU. Keep Live's processor demands in check (under 75 percent) at all times – especially during a performance. If the 'CPU Load Meter' indicates you are regularly pushing 75 percent or higher, try bypassing (turning off) some effects, or sub-mixing tracks with heavy effects – see tip below for more on this.
- Organization is also key. Keep all of your files in the same folder with their respective audio files saved as a self-contained set. Since gigs or performances usually evoke some degree of urgency, looking for lost or moved loops or VST plug-ins during your performance is not the kind of pressure you need. Make sure all song files load quickly and are ready to go before you do so at the gig.
- Data integrity is like a skeleton key. Make sure your data is safe by creating CD-R backup copies of your Live songs and loop files, as well as Live's latest software update. This way, you can run Live for 10 days without authorization in case of an emergency. Once you have made CD-R, write down your unique serial number on the top of your CD. This sort of paranoia ensures that you are covered in the event of a hard drive crash. After all, CD-Rs are the cheapest form of disaster prevention I know.

Starting out

Because computers and software are so flexible, your user preferences and working habits in Live will eventually become quite personalized. DJs may opt to set-up Live's Pre-Listening feature to cue up the next track or loop during a performance. Or, if they are fortunate enough to have a sound card with multiple outputs, many find it beneficial to send different Ableton Live Session Mixer tracks to separate outputs patched to a hardware or DJ-style mixer for hands-on control during your set. Of course you can also have a great time running your set from a standard stereo audio interface, and you can still make a number of customizable settings in Live's software configuration.

As we move through this chapter, you will see that how you choose to set up your software and audio content can greatly affect your performance and music. Some Live musicians like to load a single Live Song (one song per set) with all of their fully produced tracks set up and ready to play. Others will want to improvise using a preset template (made by the performer) and import loops and songs 'on-the-fly'. You may also choose to load specific Live song files for each song, though if you do this, you will want to make sure that you have enough time between songs to load the new piece. As with most skills, experience is an excellent teacher. However, trial and error can be painful when learned on stage in front of an audience. In the next section, we'll step through some possible gig setup schemes.

Basics (organization)

Up to now, I've led you to believe that all music in Live results from organizing and sequentially playing a group of 'scenes' (or song sections), to build your complete song. This method is simply one way to work in Live. Another common strategy is to load one instance of each loop (or song) that you would like to use in your set and then trigger (or stop) clips individually as you would like to hear them. For instance, you might start with a drum loop, then add a bass loop, and then a guitar. After a couple of measures, you may want to play a different guitar part or stop the bass loop, and so on. Of course, the number of possible combinations is infinite. The point is that this is very different from leading your song along from scene to scene (or loop group to loop group). Let's take a look at how one might begin making music in Live in this manner. This may seem basic, but follow along anyway to see if it is helpful.

1 To start your Live practice/performance, launch Live and make sure you are in Session View.

2 Open Live's Browser and locate the folder where you have saved your loops and songs. With the Pre-listening (headphone shaped) icon depressed, you can get some idea of how any given sample will sound once it's dragged into the project. Of course you can alter the sound later by using Live's effects and clip parameters – so don't be discouraged by the initial sound of the loop.

3 Drag the desired loops, samples, or songs into empty Clip Slots.

4 Now launch a loop via the Clip Slot's triangular Clip Launch button.

5 To stop any clip's playback, click on any of the square-shaped Stop buttons located on the same track (either above or below the loop playing back. Or you can stop all clips via the Stop button on the Clip Status Field.

6 Practice playing and stopping loops in different combinations.

7 You may want to adjust the volume and panning settings on the mixer to vary the feel of the music.

8 Once you have the basic palette of sounds for your piece, save the song (File > Save Live Set As).

A DJ may want to load up several songs or loops at once in order to 'prep' his or her set. In Figure 6.1 (see page 4), I have loaded more samples than could ever fit in my computer's 256MB of RAM to give you an example of how Live reads the samples straight from your hard drive. The only potential limit you will face is the number of loops, samples, or songs that are playing at the same time – which is determined by your computer's power.

Each Clip Slot contains a different sample, or longer song file, which I have dragged over to Session View's Clip Slots en masse from the browser. To import clips in this manner, open a sound folder in Live's browser that has more than one loop or sample. Click on one sample you would like to import. Next, press and hold down Ctrl (Cmnd), and then hand select (highlight) as many loops as you would like to import. If you want to grab the whole folder or several consecutive loops, press and hold Shift and then select a loop further down the list in the Browser. You will see all of the loops in between the original and the new Shift-clicked loop become highlighted. To import either of the above two selections into Live, release the Shift or Ctrl (Cmnd) keys and drag them to the desired track. Live will immediately begin creating analysis (.ASD) files for each of the new clips.

To keep your set organized, try classifying or categorizing each track according to the type of sound or loop that track contains. For instance, you might designate track 1 for bass loops and/or samples with low frequencies only, while track 2 will be reserved for loops or samples with mid to high frequencies. In Figure 6.2, I have labelled the mixer channels and named the loops to ensure that I trigger the sounds I am looking for when the performance begins. You can organize Songs in a similar fashion. Percussion-heavy songs could be designated to one channel, while ambient pieces of music are relegated to another. Some Live musicians set up distinguishing EQs and compressors to ensure that certain channels will produce only

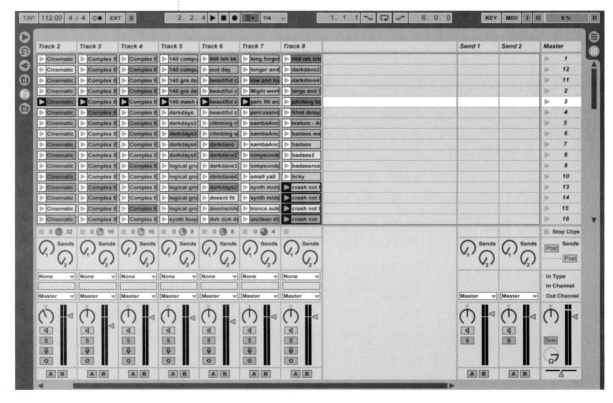

Figure 6.1
Each Clip Slot contains a different sample and would be triggered individually as opposed to as a scene. This is yet another method of working in Live.

select frequencies. I recommend that you spend some time experimenting to discover the method that works best for your unique mixing style and your batch of samples, loops, and songs.

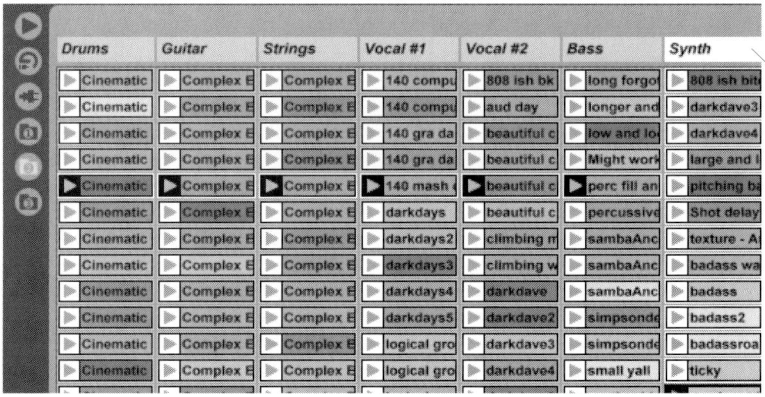

Figure 6.2
Taking a moment to label your Live session mixer channels and clip shot loops can add a bit of clarity to your live set.

Label your channels to help organize your files

Scenes as song sections

If you haven't checked out either of the Ableton Live demo songs, now would be as good a time as any to do so. Regardless of what build (version) of Live you have, Live 2 ships with two different demo songs, located in your Ableton Live/Demo Songs folder. For our purposes in this chapter, load the file called 'Live 2 Demo

Session' into Live. Live's other demo song, 'Live 2 Demo Arrangement' will come in handy in Chapter 7, Editing Your Performance', when we will investigate Live's arranging and editing faculties.

After you have loaded the demo song, take a good look at the scene's labelling scheme used by Ableton. You will see the following titles: Live !, Intro 2, Bridge A, Theme A, Break, Theme B, Bvariation, B-var2, B-var3, B-var4, B-low, END, Start, Playing, and ! (as pictured in Figure 6.3). Even if you are new to making music, these titles will begin to give you some idea of how you can organize scenes in Live. As indicated in scenes such as Theme A, and Theme B, each scene can represent a section of your song in your set. Typically, you will start, stop, and play with the loops in each scene (row), and then progress through your set, scene to scene – and in this case section to section – of a larger song.

Figure 6.3
Live 2 Demo Arrangement's Session View. Check out the Scene names on the right-hand vertical column.

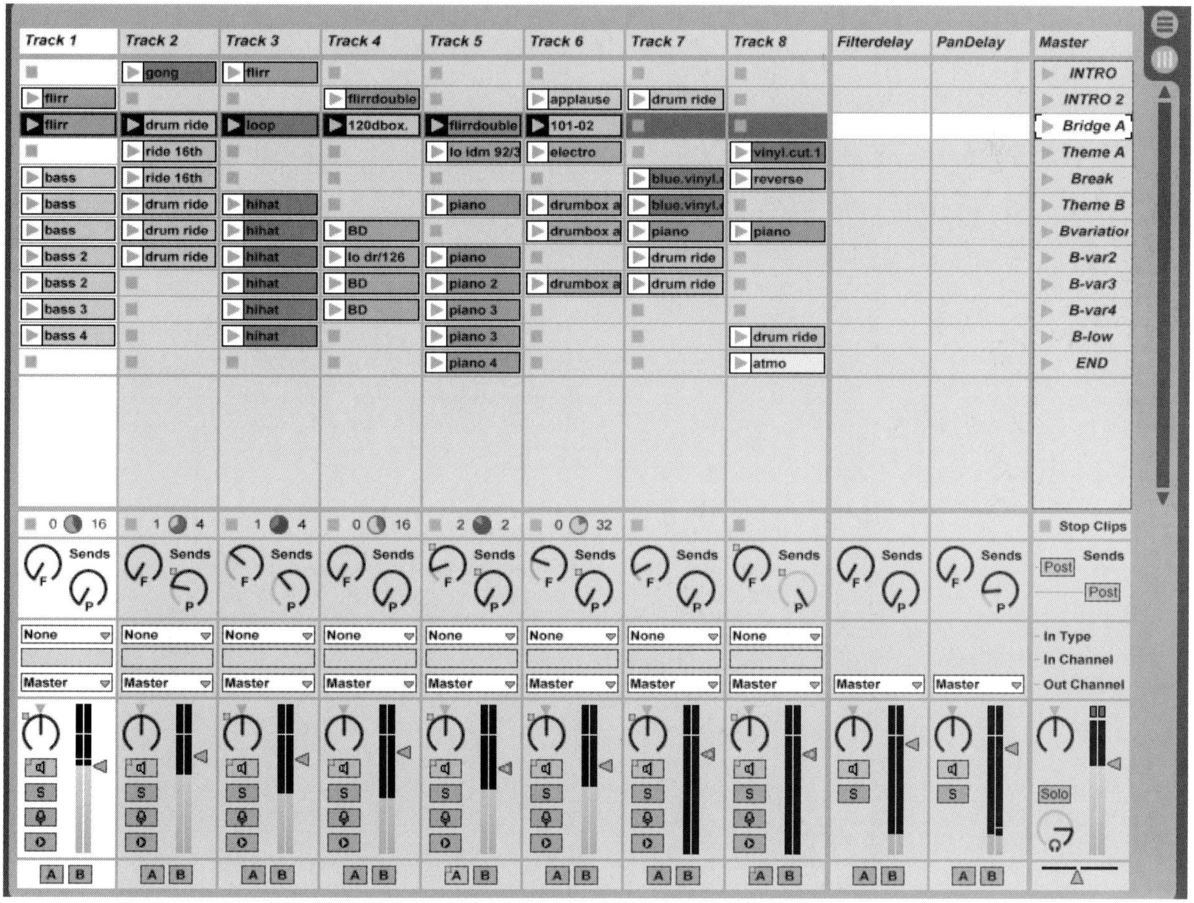

Track 1	Track 2	Track 3	Track 4	Track 5	Track 6	Track 7	Track 8	Filterdelay	PanDelay	Master
	gong	flirr								INTRO
flirr			flirrdouble		applause	drum ride				INTRO 2
flirr	drum ride	loop	120dbox,	flirrdouble	101-02					Bridge A
	ride 16th			lo idm 92/3	electro		vinyl.cut.1			Theme A
bass	ride 16th					blue.vinyl	reverse			Break
bass	drum ride	hihat		piano	drumbox a	blue.vinyl				Theme B
bass	drum ride	hihat	BD		drumbox a	piano	piano			Bvariation
bass 2	drum ride	hihat	lo dr/126	piano		drum ride				B-var2
bass 2		hihat	BD	piano 2	drumbox a	drum ride				B-var3
bass 3		hihat	BD	piano 3						B-var4
bass 4		hihat		piano 3			drum ride			B-low
				piano 4			atmo			END

| 0   16 | 1   4 | 1   4 | 0   16 | 2   2 | 0   32 | | | | | Stop Clips |

Sends	Sends	Sends	Sends	Sends	Sends	Sends	Sends	Sends	Sends	Post Sends
None	None	None	None	None	None	None	None			In Type
										In Channel
Master	Master	Master	Master	Master	Master	Master	Master	Master	Master	Out Channel

Some Live performers will use each scene as a complete song, in which case an Ableton live set file (ALS) will contain many songs aligned vertically on one or two tracks. To play songs in this manner, you might employ the crossfader or manually crossfade the old and new tracks. Also, many DJs like to loop sections within a song, as opposed to simply playing a song in its entirety. We will cover this, and several other live performance strategies in greater detail in the following sections.

Cueing songs

Some DJs/musicians map out their entire set prior to their arrival at the gig. In these instances, cueing the mix (while performing) may not be as imperative as it would be to the improvising DJ. If you are going to attempt to improvise or 'read the crowd', you will want to engage Live's Pre-Listening feature. By doing so, you will be able to hear the next track or loop before it is in the house mains, which can improve the smoothness of your set, or in some cases, skirt disastrous volume peaks or valleys, or buzz-killing tempo mismatches. To do this properly, you will need a sound card (audio interface) with more than two outputs, or two stereo sound cards on the same machine.

Here is how to set up pre-listening (DJs call it cueing) in Live 2.

1   Open Live's Preferences dialog (Options > Preferences (PC and OS9)).
2   Select the Audio tab.
3   In the Audio tab's Routing section, select your sound card's Master and Pre-Listen outputs.
4   After closing out of Preferences, make sure that Live's browser is open.
5   Activate the Pre-Listening (headphone shaped) icon by clicking on it. Now all loops or samples that you click on will be heard through the sound card outputs designated in your Preferences in Step 3.

In Figure 6.4, I have selected outputs 3/4 for my Master Output on my Emagic EMI 2/6 card, and outputs 1/2 for Pre-Listening – 1/2 happen to double as the headphone output on my card. By directing the master output to the mains, and pre-listening via headphones, it is easy to select the next track.

For those with one sound card (with only a stereo pair of outputs), you may want to go mono. That way you can monitor on one channel, while cueing on a Session Mixer Track (as opposed to the Browser). Here's how:

Figure 6.4
Here, I have split Live's main output and pre-listening (cue) outputs. For both DJs and group efforts, cueing the next track can be a great help during a live performance.

1 Send a mono mix to the house system – one idea is to bring a Y-adapter/splitter and send one channel over two plugs. For instance, take the left output from Live's Main Output and route it through a Y-adapter (splitter) to give the house sound system a parallel signal (two times mono).

2 Next, pan Live's main output all the way to the side you sent to the house.

3 Then route the other output to your headphones (using a mono-to-stereo headphone adapter).

4 Designate one of your tracks in Live as a Cue track and pan it to the opposite side of your main output – in this case to the right. In your headphones you will now hear both the master and cue mixes on opposite sides.

If you are thinking that sending your Main Output in mono is a poor option, keep in mind that many club sound systems are still mono, or virtually mono, since speakers are pointed in a multitude of directions and only part of the audience will be positioned in the middle of the room. Also mono signals can sound very tight and present.

Two power tips

Remember that Live will automatically synchronize your song and loop tempos (called beat matching), but you will decide which beat gets the one. Many DJs using Live will load multiple instances of the same loop or song, or create copies within the Session View Clip Slot grid. They will then toy with the different clips' properties to create an altogether new version of the sound. There are many different ways to do this, and we will explore more methods in subsequent chapters. For now, here are a couple of power user tips.

Tip

No panic if you practice

Since Live 2 makes the jump from 'audio software' to 'sequencing instrument,' home practice is the key to success. In other words, I recommend running through each of the above cueing techniques under less intense circumstances than your actual gig. Just as a band rehearses its material, or a singer runs through her song, you should spend time at home simulating a live gig using Live so that you can enjoy the performance when it happens.

Tip

Charlie Clouser tip

Ex-Nine Inch Nails keyboardist and programmer Charlie Clouser is one of the world's most highly regarded remix artists. Talking studio tips with Charlie is like talking treasure with Blackbeard. Here is a gem that slipped out of his pocket.

Load a drum loop into the clip slot located at scene 1, track 1, and set the Clip's Launch Mode to Repeat. Now duplicate the sample at least four times (by pressing Ctrl (Cmnd) + D. Next, click into each clip and change the loop offset (triangle above the waveform) to a different position within each clip. Charlie suggests that you experiment with alternating the placement of the offset markers from on the beat to between beats (off beats). Also, make sure that each clip can be triggered via your computer's keypad (he recommends letters a, s, d, and f to keep it simple). Next, adjust the Quantization of each clip to various settings (keep at least one set to Bar). Charlie also likes to set at least one clip to 1/32 for a Squarepusher-style buzz roll effect. When you are playing, keep the Global quantization set to 1/4 or 1/8 note setting.

Playing with loop start points and triggering new instances of the same loop can also be great with bass, keyboard, or almost any other kind of sound. There are an infinite number of permutations for any one sound, and methods for working with loops. While this next tip is similar to the last one, it is worth mentioning because of the human quality it can add to electronic music and the popularity of Breakbeat rhythms.

DJ Fischer-P tip

In the LA club scene, DJ Fischer P is an innovator and well known Hip Hop party DJ. When he has time, he helps spread the word about Live and Reason for M-Audio (www.m-audio.com). He had this golden nugget to pass on to you.

As above, load a drum loop into the clip slot located at scene 1, track 1, and set the Clip's Launch Mode to Repeat. Now duplicate the sample at least four times (by pressing Ctrl (Cmnd) + D. Next, click into each clip and change the loop offset to a different position within the clip. Again, make sure that each clip can be triggered via your computer's keypad (he recommends letters a, s, d, and f to keep it simple). Here is the difference: click in to each clip and change the

transient settings to progressively looser settings. Scene 1's loop should remain 1/16 note, set scene 2 at 1/8 note, scene 3 at 1/4 note, and if your original loop is pretty exact, you can try setting Transients to Bar. Now play the different loops and notice how the groove will float a bit. In some cases you may get some sloppy sounding results, but often you can create some interesting variety in the performance. If you are playing a fast loop at a slow tempo, the lower transient setting will make the loop sound rushed. Conversely, slow loops at faster tempos will drag for an instant. This can be a great way to create laid-back melodies or rhythm section parts.

Sound check

Like bands, Ableton Live performers can benefit from a sound check. And just as a guitar player or keyboardist may tweak his amp to best fit the room, you will want to internally adjust Live's master output. Each club's PA and room will provide its own particular acoustical characteristics, and will therefore affect the sound of your music. Also, since most Live musicians compose using studio speakers or head-phones, we are bound to hear things differently in different rooms.

We will be covering Live's effects in greater detail in Chapter 8, 'Live's Effects', but this next section will serve as a general guide. To prepare your Live set for a sound check, add an EQ Four (and possibly a Compressor) plug-in to your Master output of Live by clicking once on your master output and then once on EQ Four (and then Compressor) as shown in Figure 6.5. Some musicians will not want to compress their audio output, a decision which results in a fuller dynamic range. Others will want to add a compressor before the EQ Four, to really squeeze the mix. Typically, a subtle amount of compression activated at the last link in the chain can help reign in wild volume inconsistencies over club sound system.

Figure 6.5
An EQ can be a powerful ally when tuning your computer up for the room.

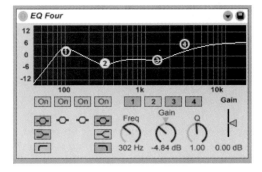

Typically you will want to watch the extreme lows and highs that many club sound systems are incapable of reproducing. Then, after alleviating any rogue sub bass or hissing highs, gently pull back various amounts of mid-range frequencies as desired. In Figure 6.6, I have mocked up one possible EQ Four/Compressor scenario. Each room will certainly demand different results.

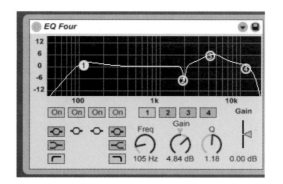

Figure 6.6
In this example, I have reduced the lows and highs to eliminate excess strain on the house system. I have also adjusted the mids to accentuate the room I am playing.

Typically, frequencies above 18 kHz and below 40 Hz cannot be correctly reproduced. If these extreme frequencies are pumped through a standard sound system, they will actually draw away power and consistency from the other frequencies, resulting in a sort of sonic mud or shrill nasal sound. I should add that whenever you use an EQ, try to reduce unwanted or undesirable frequencies rather than boost favourable ones. Any boosted frequency will increase the volume of the clip and edge closer to peaking. You can reduce the gain, but doing so may affect the 'presence' of the sound.

Muting channels

Running loops and muting channels can be an effective performance tool, and lucky for us, Ableton thought so too. Each of the first eight keyboard Function keys doubles as a channel mute, where track 1 corresponds to F1, track 2 to F2, and so on. To hear the power of 'playing' Live's channel mutes, load a loop into each of the eight tracks and launch the corresponding scene. Then practice depressing and pressing the various channel's mutes at musical intervals (every four, eight, or sixteen bars). Usually mutes are applied or released on the beat, or in rhythm with the piece of music at hand. Note for Laptops, you often need to hold the Function key (fn on my Tibook), along with the function key. Many artists use this as one of their main performance tactics. I'm keeping this paragraph short in an effort to inspire you to investigate how musical (and fun) this can be. Don't just sit there, go give it try.

Hiding slot buttons

Located in each empty clip slot in Live's Session View is a small grey square Stop Button. The Stop Button's function is to halt playback on any loop or sample playing back on that same track. The reason they exist is simple: if you are moving through your song from scene to scene, you not only want to play the new loops in the next scene, but also want to stop all loops in the previous one. However, sometimes you will want to launch a scene (full of samples) without stopping the loops in the previous or next scene. In this instance, Ableton Live's Hide Slot Button command is the perfect tool. Here is how it works.

Imagine that you have a scene full of loops that are playing and you want to trigger the next scene. For some reason, you don't want to stop all of the loops that are currently playing. For an example, see Figure 6.7, in which scene 1 is playing and you want to trigger scene 2. For the sake of the exercise, imagine that you want channels 1 and 2 to continue playing in scene 1 and not be stopped, as they normally would.

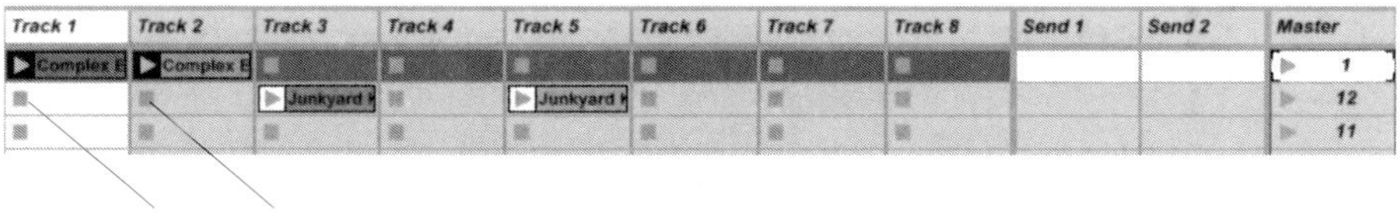

Figure 6.7
Scene 1 is playing and you want to trigger scene 2.

Track 1	Track 2	Track 3	Track 4	Track 5	Track 6	Track 7	Track 8	Send 1	Send 2	Master	
▶ Complex E	▶ Complex E									▶	1
		▶ Junkyard F		▶ Junkyard F						▶	12
										▶	11

Clip Slot stop buttons – when scene 2 is fired, they will stop scene 1's loops

To fix channels 1 and 2 so that their Clip Slot's Start button does not stop the loops currently running, you will want to highlight the Clip Slots in track 1 and 2, scene 2 and hide the Slot button, as shown below in Figure 6.8.

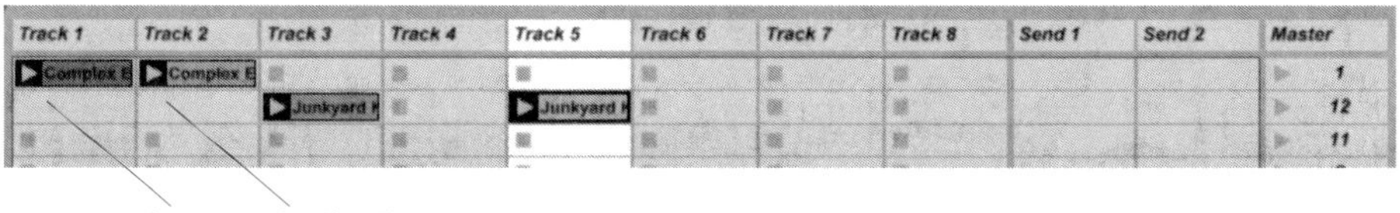

Figure 6.8
To hide the Slot button, click on the cells and press Ctrl (Cmnd) + E.

Track 1	Track 2	Track 3	Track 4	Track 5	Track 6	Track 7	Track 8	Send 1	Send 2	Master	
▶ Complex E	▶ Complex E									▶	1
		▶ Junkyard F		▶ Junkyard F						▶	12
										▶	11

By pressing Ctrl (Cmnd) + E, you eliminate the slot buttons

To hide a Slot button in any given Clip Slot, click directly on the cell in Session View and press Ctrl (Cmnd) + E. If you forget the shortcut, you can always hide slots by clicking Edit > Remove Slot Button. You can remove multiple slots (in multiple cells) at a time, or any one cell. Note: the Hide Slot Button feature could go entirely unnoticed and you can still make great music in Live. However hiding slots can be a real space saver and make for some interesting musical transitions.

Creating scenes on-the-fly

When you are in the creative 'zone' or the middle of a mix set, you need to move quickly. In Live, handling basic tasks, such as duplicating scenes or loops, moving, copying, and/or pasting samples, may be done without ever stopping audio. In the next few sections, we will consider ways to keep the creativity flowing, while building a workable arrangement for repeating (or how about an encore?) performances. We will also talk about how to grab audio samples/loops on-the-fly so they can be used later (and even take less processing power).

Duplicating clips

My favourite shortcut in Live has to be Duplicate. It's devilishly simple, but can tremendously expedite your workflow. There are actually two different ways to duplicate in Session View: duplicate clips, and duplicate scenes. You can also use Duplicate in Arranger View as a quick means of copying and pasting any given loop or audio in your song. Duplicating in Session View is also a quick way of copying and pasting, which can be a fast tool for building arrangements. To do it, click on any clip (sample) and then use the keyboard shortcut Ctrl (Cmnd) + D to create a duplicate clip in the Clip Slot directly below.

Here is how you might use this on the job.

1 Load Live's demo song (Live 2 Demo Session).

2 Start playback by launching the scene called Intro 2.

3 Next click on the clip entitled drum ride in track 7 and duplicate it by selecting Edit > Duplicate or using the keyboard shortcut Ctrl (Cmnd) + D. You will then see the loop copied to the scene below. If there is already a loop below the loop you are duplicating, it will be deleted / replaced by the new duplicated loop.

To see how this will look, see Figure 6.9a (before) and Figure 6.9b (after) below. Duplicating loops is an excellent tool for creating similar or related sections within a song. Also, you will find it easy to cast 'breakdown-sections' or restatements of a theme. For instance, you may decide to create several versions of the same scene, tune some of the loops to different pitches, or even change a sample's Warp Marker settings. Often I find it is helpful to have one scene that is simply one or two loops for use as an intro, outro, or song transition. I will then duplicate the scene (see the following 'Duplicating Scenes' section) and build it up from there.

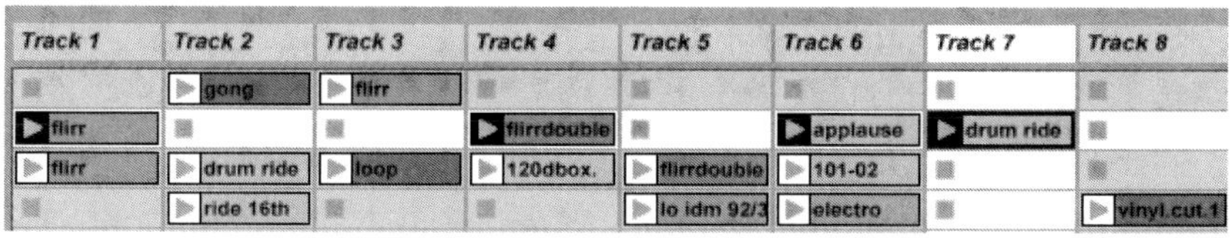

Figure 6.9a
The original Demo Song Session.

Figure 6.9b
In this Scene, I have duplicated the drum ride loop.

Duplicating scenes

Even more impressive than duplicating clips is the shortcut for duplicating scenes. The key difference here is that when a scene is duplicated, Live generates a copy of all the clips in the scene, and inserts these clips into a brand new scene directly below. Remember, duplicating a clip will not create a new scene, only a copy of the clip. You may duplicate an entire scene by clicking once on the scene and pressing Ctrl (Cmnd) + SHIFT + D, or by clicking once on the scene and selecting Edit > Duplicate Scene.

Live also ingeniously names the newly inserted scene with a sensible variation of the original. For instance, duplicating Scene 2 will result in Scene 3. Try this a couple times to be sure you have the shortcut memorized. Remember, multiple duplications of scenes contained within the same song will require *no* additional system resources. Your song file can be 900 lines long or just 2. It makes no difference to Live. This is a vast improvement over hardware (and most software) samplers.

Track bouncing (sub-mixing part 1)

The idea of sub-mixing was born from analog tape operators needing to increase the number of available audio tracks. For instance, when recording on an 8- or 16-track reel-to-reel tape machine, an engineer may run out of tracks on large or complicated projects. To remedy the situation (and provide more tracks), engineers did what is called track-bouncing. *Track-bouncing* is the act of recording the output of several tracks onto two empty tracks (a stereo pair) or a single stereo track. The result is a two-track sum of the whole, which is most often bounced to another mix reel (in the analog world). For instance, an eight-track recording might end up with tracks 7 and 8 being the sub-mix of drum tracks 1, 2, 3, 4, 5, and 6. By bouncing these tracks, you will have new-found room (tracks 1–6) for recording bass, guitar, piano, and so on. Similarly, you can bounce the guitar, bass, and keys to make room for more vocal tracks or percussion.

Since Live can handle a nearly unlimited number of audio tracks (depending upon your CPU), bouncing-tracks in Live is not really necessary. Sub-mixing, on the other hand, can be a valuable tool.

Aux sends (sub-mixing part 2)

Similar to bouncing tracks is the routing of a sub-mix on a live mixing board (or Ableton Live's Session Mixer). Creating a sub-mix is the act of re-routing several audio channels to a stereo auxiliary bus or unused mixer channel. By doing this, you are able to control the level, EQ, and effects of the audio on several channels in one or two stereo mixer strips (channels). In short, a sub-mix is really just a way to control several channels at one time (on a single stereo track). You will be able to apply one effect to several different tracks at the same time (minimizing CPU strain), or to control the volume, panning, and mix settings via one channel. By creating one or more sub-mixes within a Live song, you can achieve a more musical approach to your overall mix. Here's how to do it:

1 Make sure you are in Session View. Load the Live 2 Demo Session song.
2 Determine if you can see the In/Out section of Live's Session Mixer. Press Ctrl (Cmnd) + Alt + I to toggle this view off and on.
3 Once you can see the Outputs, change all tracks except for track 4's output to 'Sends Only'.
4 Next turn up each of the tracks' (that you have routed to the sends) contribution to the send channel (Send 2, which is labelled 'P' for PanDelay). For this exercise, turn the virtual send knob all the way to the right.
5 For the sake of the exercise, delete the PanDelay effect by double-clicking on the PanDelay track title bar and then clicking once on the Ping Pong Delay effect and pressing Backspace (PC) Delete (Mac).
6 Now launch the scene entitled Bvariation and listen for a couple of seconds. To hear the effects of your new Aux Sends routing scheme, gradually decrease the Track Volume of both Sends by moving the virtual fader in Live's Session Mixer on the Send tracks labelled FilterDelay and PanDelay. You will hear all but the lone kick drum of track 4 disappear. To bring back in your mix, raise the fader on the PanDelay Send. You can adjust the relative volumes of each track by moving either the track's volume fader or send level. The master volume for the group will be the corresponding Send Track.

Rendering on-the-fly (sub-mixing part 3)

Similar to Rendering (discussed in Chapter 4, 'Digital Audio Basics'), sub-mixing can also be done on-the-fly (during a performance) by using a hybrid of the above sub-mix strategies. Rendering on-the-fly is done by recording any of the currently playing clips into a brand new Clip Slot (on an empty track). Why would you want to do this? The most common reason is that by recording several tracks onto one, you will have more flexibility over the new recording (sample). In other words, by bouncing several complex Clip (or entire scene) combinations to a single sub-mix sample, you can simplify working with that audio snapshot. Also, since effects can sometimes hog large amounts of your processor load, you can render the original sample with effects, and then turn off the effect once you have a rendered recording.

To record WAV or AIF audio output from Live on-the-fly from Live's very own Session Mixer, you will need to set the destination track's input to Master Out. If Live is in Playback mode, and you are hearing audio, you will see the meters indicate that a signal is present. Next, simply press Record and then Record or Clip Launch to stop the recording. Your newly rendered clip will be ready for action the instant the recording is complete. Note: When you decide to use it, you will want to turn off (stop) all of the original clips, to prevent phasing. In Figure 6.10, I have set up an example of how I might render a scene to a single clip by simply clicking on the corresponding scene's Launch button. To do this, the target clip's track must be armed for recording, and the meter should be displaying a signal.

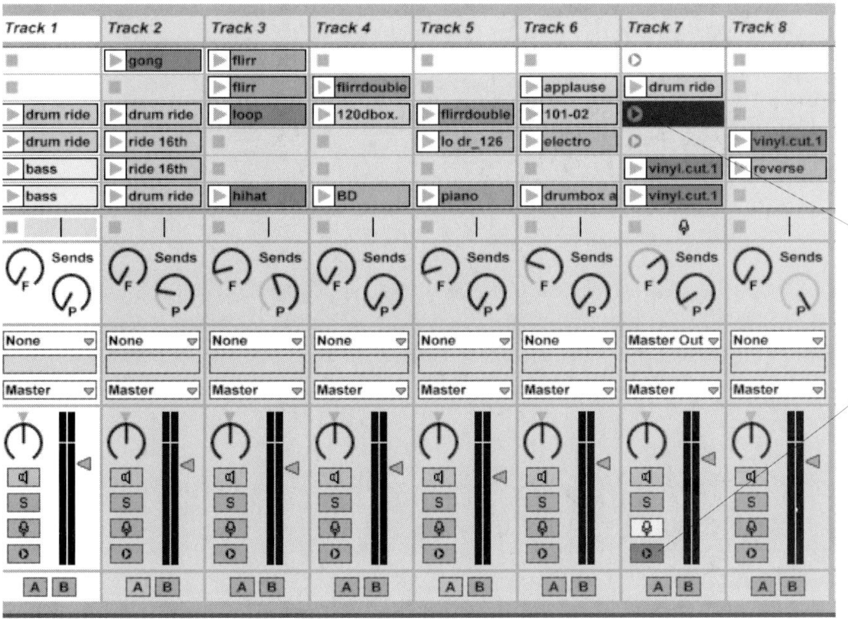

Figure 6.10
Tracks 1–6 are playing clips that will be recorded as a stereo pair to track 7. After making the recording, I will usually move the clip down into the song and away from the original tracks.

Set to record tracks 1–6 here

Arm session recording

Other advantages to rendering are that you will have to work with only one clip instead of many, which makes it easier to trigger, add effects, pitch-shift, and otherwise manipulate the entirety of the sampled sub-mix. Also, you will be free of running all the other tracks, minimizing CPU load, and often simplifying your song's arrangement. Keep in mind, though, that your newly rendered clip (sub-mix) will be set and impossible to adjust in terms of relative levels, separation, and effects. You will not retain the flexibility of re-mixing even a single loop (inside the rendered clip), so it is a good idea to keep your original scene around in case you change your mind.

Phrase sampling

When incorporating live musicians into the mix, you may want to attempt to capture small phrases during the actual performance for later recall (re-triggering) or to record the idea as it happens. To do this, you will want to designate at least one track for recording (with the channel's inputs set to Live In). I recommend recording in mono most of the time, for a couple of reasons. First of all, you will consume half the drive space, processing power, and memory (buffer) on your machine, which is often a noticeable difference. Second, a mono signal will sound more present (strong) in the mix – an important factor when competing for volume on stage.

Here are the steps for grabbing a quick (or long if you like) piece of audio in the middle of a performance:

1 Create a track for the new audio by pressing Ctrl (Cmnd) + T.
2 Route the source to Live by selecting Live In as the new track's input type.
3 Set the global Quantization Menu to Bar, 1/2 note, or 1/4 note to ensure an even recording time.
4 Depress the track's Arm Session Recording button, but be forewarned that you may hear any audio coming through your Live input and may potentially cause microphone feedback. For live recording situations, I recommend monitoring only the track's input meter levels. To do this, mute the track by deactivating the Track Activator speaker-shaped icon on the session mixer channel strip.
5 Click on any Clip Slot's Record button (small right facing red triangle) to record audio.
6 Click on the same Clip Launch (red triangle) to stop the recording and launch the clip in time. If you just want to stop the clip, press the Clip Stop button in the middle of the channel strip.

After recording a loop (of any length), it is then advisable to double-click on the newly created clip-slot to open up Live's Clip View. You will want to make sure that the loop is the desired length and has not been truncated in the recording process due to latency or your mouse-trigger-finger timing. You also may need to configure a loop's start and end points, move a warp marker or two, or adjust the loops level.

Of course, the loop you just recorded could look like anything, but here is a fresh example of what a normal looking, symmetrical loop looks like (Figure 6.11). We will explore recording in Live more thoroughly in Chapter 12, 'Recording in Live'.

Triggering possibilities

One of the chief characteristics of Live that make it 'feel' like a musical instrument is that you can play it like a musical instrument. In Live, there are two quick ways to trigger any loaded clip: via a MIDI-controller or via the computer (or QWERTY) keyboard. Remarkably, both setup schemes are identical (once your MIDI prefer-

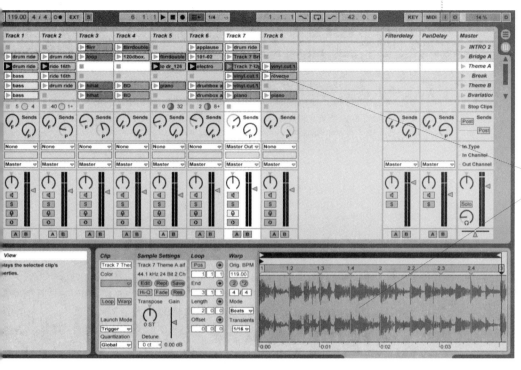

Figure 6.11
Notice that this loop looks symmetrical and will be ready to fire when you are.

This clip is a recording of the other clips currently playing

ences are configured, as we did back in Chapter 2, Getting Started'), and can be done without stopping audio playback. Here is how to do it:

Computer keyboard

There are only a couple of programs on the market today that can take advantage of computer keyboard triggering. Lucky for us, Live 2 is one of them. Triggering by computer keyboard can be a huge time saver, and a whole lot of fun. Here is how to take advantage of this option.

1 To trigger a clip (sample), press the Key Map Mode Switch (pictured in Figure 6.12) in the upper right corner of either of the Live views (Session or Arranger). Immediately, you will see many of the cells and mappable parameters sport a shaded highlight colour. Note: Clips cannot be triggered yet by mouse, key, or MIDI (until the Key Map Mode Switch has been turned off).
2 Next, select a cell with a clip loaded into it either by mousing to the box, or by using your computer keyboard's arrow/direction keys.
3 Then press a lettered key on your computer keyboard that you want to assign to trigger that sound.
4 Set up more cells in this same way if you so desire.
5 To finish designating Live key commands, again click on the Key Map Mode Switch.

Figure 6.12
The Key Map Mode Switch.

Tip

Keyboard trigger finger

Here is a tip for doubling the possible number of assignable QWERTY keys. Since you can only use the letter keys on your keyboard to trigger Live clips and settings, why not double your options? By pressing on the Shift (or Caps Lock) key, you can assign twice as many keys to a given Live setup. For instance, a lower case *a* can trigger a completely different element than a capital *A* will.

Tip

Single sound bliss

Not all clips need to be long or complicated audio samples in order to be effective. One favorite method among Live aficionados is to grab just a single kick drum sample and set the loop length for 1/4 note. By doing so, you can create a single four-on-the-floor techno/house kick drum groove independent to its own track. This can also work with short bass, percussion, or hi-hat one-shot samples as well.

MIDI controller

As we have discussed, all of the triggering customization described above can be set up while Live is in motion (playing a song or loop, or even while recording). Also, the same methods used above work for MIDI, and MIDI-controller knobs, such as those found on an Oxygen8 keyboard or Doepfer Pocket Dial (seen in Chapter 2). Here are the steps to set up Live's MIDI triggering:

- Depress the MIDI Map Mode Switch in the upper right-hand corner of either Session or Arranger Views in Live. You will then see several cells, virtual knobs, and sliders become highlighted, signaling you that they are ready to receive MIDI-note information.
- As with QWERTY Keyboard settings, clips cannot be triggered (sounded) until the MIDI Map Mode Switch has been turned off.
- Next, select a cell with a clip loaded into it, or a fader, or knob that you want to tweak. Note you can map VST effects and Live's effects to MIDI just as any other control in Session or Arranger Views.
- Press the MIDI keyboard key, or turn the MIDI-controller knob that you would like to use to trigger (or control)the sound (or parameter). The knob or key will then automatically correspond to the chosen Live parameter.
- Repeat these steps as many times as desired.
- Finish editing by clicking the MIDI Map Mode Switch to turn off editing mode.

Which faders and knobs you decide to control is entirely up to you. It is often a good idea to map track volumes and effect parameters for Live performances, since these will be the hardest controls to reach in a hurry via mouse.

MIDI keyboard

By now, you have a good feel for how to set up MIDI-control parameters in Live. Since Live is not a traditional sampler, you may be wondering why you would want to use a MIDI keyboard. Here are a couple of fun and inspiring methods for triggering loops from a MIDI keyboard.

- **Triggering**. Triggering Loops via the keyboard can help make a performance more musical. To set this up, simply map each key on the keyboard to a Clip Launch icon by pressing Ctrl (Cmnd) + M, clicking on the Clip Slot, and then depressing the MIDI key on your keyboard. When you have finished mapping all of the desired keys, press Ctrl (Cmnd) + M to close the MIDI control setup.
- **Toggle launch mode**. If you set your Clip's Launch Mode to toggle, you can easily play most of your set from your keyboard by starting and stopping loops. Many small two-octave keyboards (such as the M-Audio's popular Oxygen8) also feature a quick octave jump button so that you can easily set up multiple scenes or 8 octaves worth of mapping. One additional tip is to place small pieces of masking tape or coloured electrical tape to cue you in on what loops you are triggering.

DJing with Live

One of the reasons DJs love using Live is because of Live's ability to work with, and reestablish, a song's tempo. You will also be able to loop sections of songs, add effects, and change the pitch and key of a given track. Each song that you plan to use in Live, will need to be 'prepped' in advance of the gig to make sure that the warp markers are correctly lined up with the beats of the music, and that the track's beginning is clearly established. As we saw in Chapter 5's 'The Digital DJ' section, this can take just a few seconds or a few minutes. Once tracks are mapped with the correct tempo, it is time to take advantage of all Live has to offer, and begin creating your first Ableton enabled mix set.

Once your songs and loops are ready to go, you may want to simply store the songs in the same folder or organize by tempo range. This way you can bring in songs using Live's browser as you wish and properly cue the track using Live's Pre-Listening feature. Otherwise, you can drag in several songs that you know work well together, pre-determine a few loops within a song (making several copies of each song), and start mixing and matching.

Looping within songs

Making smaller loops within a larger song can really add a new dimension to your mix set. Not only can you extend your favourite sections, but you can remix on-the-fly. Because Live allows for multiple instances of any clip, you can run loops of the same song against itself, or use elements from other songs, loops, or samples to spice up a simpler section of the track. There are at least two ways to work with looped sections of a larger song in Live 2's Clip View. The first method will require only one instance of the clip, while the second may require many more copies of the same clip.

Method 1: Single loop Once you have a large (a.k.a. long) WAV or AIFF file loaded into clip view, find a portion of the song that would sound good looped. Of course this is subjective, but I find that you generally want a fairly sparse piece of music that is longer than two measures long.

Figure 6.13 shows how I typically create a loop within a song. This is done in Clip View by restraining the Clip Loop Region sample ends to the desired length. Try to make things easy on yourself when you're first learning to loop by making your loop an even length (2, 4, 8, or 16 bars). If you can get away with a longer loop, it is usually better for a variety of reasons, but most importantly, your loop will sound more musical.

> **Tip**
>
> **Simple pleasures**
>
> Usually simple loops are best. Find an area of the song where there is not a lot of busy percussion or soloing going on. Grab endpoints that seem to make clean breaks with a rhythmic pulse as opposed to cutting off a long sound or reverb decay. You should also try to loop as long an area as possible because short loops become stagnant more easily.

Figure 6.13
Here I have truncated the Clip View's Loop Regions to a specific point within a larger song. You may loop song segments to create an effect or to build a section of the music.

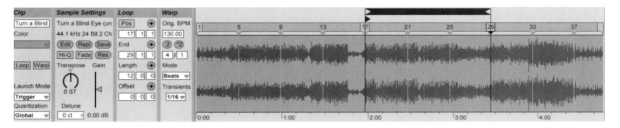

One clever way to work with these loops (once you have a smooth one) is to then play with adjusting the loop's Loop Offset or its numeric counterpart Loop Start in Clip View. You can start by adjusting the bars to jump to a later portion of the song. Adjusting the Beat of the loop's beginning can also yield some cool-sounding results. For instance, you may want to start your loop on beat 2 (1.2) and end your loop on beat 2 (5.2) to make an even four-bar loop. Why would you do this? Perhaps there is a crash cymbal on one that you don't want to hear. Or maybe a delay or reverb is still decaying over into your loop, in which case you may want to make allowances. Also, strange and wonderful syncopations can arise when realigning loops to begin in unusual places.

Method 2: Multiple loops

The second method of working with loops made from longer songs is to create several copies of the same main song clip and then several subsequent duplicated clips so that you may quickly jump around to different segments of the song. Or you may even create a remix of a song by using different portions at different times. Here is an example for mapping out multiple loops from within a single song.

1 Make an eight-bar (or other length) loop of a song that you have loaded into Live using the instructions described in Method 1.

2 Then duplicate the Clip several times (using one of our favourite shortcut keys Ctrl (Cmnd) + D. Note: Each duplicated clip will retain the properties of the original. While this is obvious, try to use this to your advantage and get Clip 1 set up to your liking.

3 Next you will want to choose other segments within your song to loop. These can be any length you like. There are no rules in terms of what is best, but you will want to find sections that sound musical and that will be good canvases upon which to place other audio or apply effects.

4 Take a minute to label each scene (unless you are doing this on-the-fly). I usually do something obvious like Verse1, Verse2, Chrous1, Chorus2, CoolMix, and DrumBrk. Use terminology that works for you. The shortcut to renaming a scene is to click on the scene and press Ctrl + E.

5 Once you have a group of loops, save your Live song file.

Depending upon what you are trying to achieve, you may decide that you want to do this just with certain songs or with all of them. If you are performing Live, it may be a good idea to treat many songs as described above and then mute the tracks. For instance, you may have a single song per track and have all but one track muted. Or you may be doing a remix of a song and need only the one song. Regardless of your goal, being able to loop sections of a song can add stability to a live DJ set. Don't be discouraged if this takes some practice.

DJing with Live's crossfader

Live 2's new crossfader is one of my favourite Live performance tools. If you are unfamiliar with how a crossfader works, simply imagine your favourite DJ seamlessly mixing two different pieces of music. As one new piece of music is slowly added to the mix, you will hear less and less of the original (other) track as the crossfade occurs. The simultaneous fade-in and fade-out that you hear is called the crossfade. Smooth crossfades allow for musical-sounding transitions and trick our ear into believing each new audio element is part of the original track. With turntables or even MP3 mix software, seamless crossfading can take a great deal of practice and preparation. With Ableton Live, crossfading is an adventure. Here's how to get started.

1 Load the Live Demo Session song.
2 Activate (View) the crossfader. Ctrl (Cmnd) + Alt + F toggles it into view.
3 Assign half of the tracks to channel A, and the rest to channel B.
4 Now play a scene and then move the crossfader (located at the bottom of the Master Fader in Session View only) from side to side. You will hear the loops on the B channel fade-out as you move the fader to the left (towards 'A'), and vice versa as you move towards channel B. If you do not see the crossfader, press shortcut keys Ctrl (Cmnd) + Alt (Option) + F.

If you have a MIDI-controller, or MIDI keyboard with knobs or faders, try mapping it to control Live's crossfader. Future versions of Live will likely contain enhancements to the crossfader to include the ability to select the type of curves (that will determine the speed of the fade-in/out), and perhaps most importantly, DJ-style cueing controls for pre-listening to either channel. Most modern DJ-mixers allow a variety of cueing methods to enable DJs to plan their sets more effectively and match up songs as they go. This is not to say that Live is incapable of cueing, but just not from within a given song (only from the browser).

Pre-listening to loops/songs

Before you begin firing off new loops, or songs, you may want to cue up the track first by using Live's Pre-Listening feature. This is usually done via Live's browser by clicking once on the WAV or AIF that you are considering launching. Make sure that the Pre-Listening button is activated. You will know if it is activated when it is coloured in rather than transparent.

You can also cue loops via the session mixer by routing the main outputs as a mono signal to one side and the preview track to the other. This option will depend on your audio sound card and wiring choices. For more information see the 'Cueing Songs' section earlier in this chapter.

Tip

Too short

No sound is too short to loop. For a quick techno/house style kick drum loop, load a single one-shot kick (bass drum) hit and set the Clip/Loop region for a full beat (from 1 to 1.2 in the sample display), as shown in Figure 6.14. This can also be a great way of adding hi-hats, snare rolls, and other sonic effects.

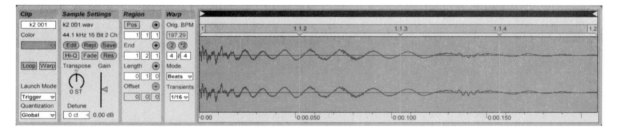

Recording your performance

Live allows every single move you make to be recorded if you're working in recording mode. This can be thought of as recording automation, in which each fader, effect, or triggered sample performance is recorded into Live for later editing or mix-down.

To quickly see how this works, press Live's Stop button (in the Transport bar) twice. Next, in Session View, arm Live's recording by pressing the Automation Record button. You can commence recording by clicking on Live's Start button, pressing Live's Spacebar, or triggering any cell/loop. From now, until you again press the Stop button (or Spacebar), Live will record every sample trigger, fader

Figure 6.14
Short one-shot loops are a quick way to add steady dance rhythms or sonic effects.

move, or effect tweak. The beauty of recording in Live is that it does not record this data as audio, but as MIDI information. Because of this, each recorded Live song takes up much less hard drive space and system resources than a traditional two-track recording. Even better, you can edit any single portion of your performance by either overdubbing a fix or redrawing the automation in Arranger View. You can also add a fresh track, delete a stale moment, splice your performance, or change (or draw in) your song's tempo.

While the possibilities are truly endless for editing Live recordings, don't get mired in minutia. Instead, experience the freedom (and comfort) of knowing that you can simply record all Live's audio output and fix it later if need be. You can also record audio straight into Live's Arranger View. We will cover that in Chapter 12, 'Recording in Live', and keep this chapter focused squarely on live performance.

What do I do between songs?

One of the tricks to pulling off a successful live set with Ableton Live is to create smooth song transitions. As with many things in Live, DJs may approach this differently than electronic musicians or bands would. Some musicians have the luxury of time when loading up a new song set, while band members or other instruments cover for them. Other Live musicians will need to play seamlessly, without ever stopping their set. Since Live streams your sample media directly from your hard disc (as opposed to taking up your RAM), Live has the distinct ability to house as many samples as needed for your set. In this case, one Live song can house an entire set's worth of music. Since this is an important and challenging task, let's explore a few ideas on how to make 'song to song' transitions work within the same Live song file.

- **Handoff.** Song to song handoffs can be the sign of a weak DJ, or they can be the perfect musical decision. The idea is simple but can take a little practice in Live. A typical DJ handoff is when you stop one track at the same time you start another. One hint for accomplishing this in Live is to turn the Warp and Loop Clip View settings off (not highlighted) for the new track you want to start. This way, Live will simply play the new track at its original tempo (with no warping). Then, after the successful hand off (the new song is playing), you can use Live's Tap Tempo button (four times) to force Live's project tempo to the new track's tempo. Once the song tempo is right, you can begin adding clips or new songs. You may then want to engage the latest clip's Warp and Loop settings (particularly if you want to do some looping of the song).
- **Use effects.** Another way Live musicians move from song to song is to use effects as a sort of distracting, and, hopefully, musical transitional sound. Delays and reverbs are the obvious choices for this, since they actually create sound reflections of the original piece of music. However, EQs can also help mask the harshness of bringing in a new song or exiting the current track by cutting certain frequencies. Taste and restraint are important when using effects in this manner. In the Countoff tip, Robert Henke (of Monolake) gives us some insights on how to practice.
- **Sound/sample/ambient sound.** By creating a diversion or rhythm-less (ambient) sound, drone, or pad between songs, you may escape detection or, better

yet, be musical. I find that this technique can work exceptionally well in some instances, such as theatre or stage settings. But in a club, you may not want to stop the beat. To make a sonic diversion work, I recommend playing it once or twice (or more) as the original track is ending. This way the audience has the sound in its ears.

In Figure 6.15, I have summarized Robert Henke's (Live conceptualist and mastermind behind the ambient electronic group Monolake), basic working strategy for song-to-song migration.

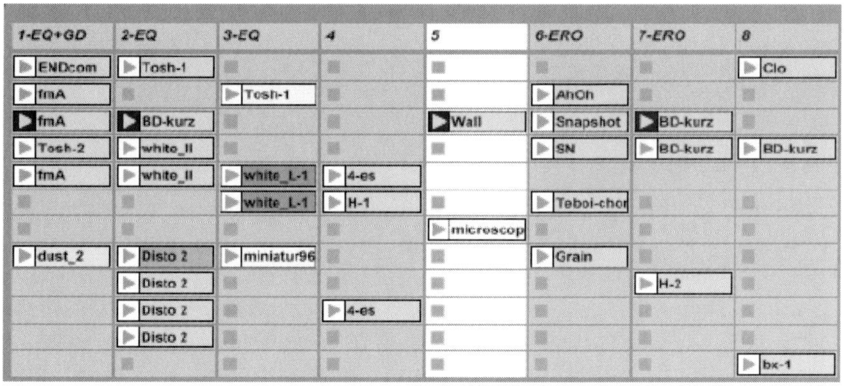

1-EQ+GD	2-EQ	3-EQ	4	5	6-ERO	7-ERO	8
ENDcom	Tosh-1						Clo
fmA		Tosh-1			AnCh		
fmA	BD-kurz			Wall	Snapshot	BD-kurz	
Tosh-2	white_ll				SN	BD-kurz	BD-kurz
fmA	white_ll	white_L-1	4-es				
		white_L-1	H-1		Teboi-chor		
				microscop			
dust_2	Disto 2	miniatur96			Grain		
	Disto 2					H-2	
	Disto 2		4-es				
	Disto 2						
							bx-1

When Robert plays Live, his Session View may look messy. He likes to improvise his sets by loading fully pre-conceived tracks as well as self-produced loops. Robert will usually loop sections of his songs, make copies of these sub-sections, and then run them through an adventurous effect scheme. He recommends using many mono loops and few tracks at a time to maximize processor power. He is also a wizard with Live's effects and here are a few of his choice methods:

1 Use an EQ Four in each track (turn off all unneeded filters to minimize CPU load).
2 In your song's first Send Track, load a Ping Pong Delay (make sure dry wet is set to 100% wet).
3 In you song's second Send Track load one EQ Four, and then a Grain Delay (make sure Grain Delay's dry wet is set to 100% wet).
4 For added phasing effects or thicker sounds, use Live's Chorus effect on the master track.
5 Robert's other favourite effects are Gate, Redux, Erosion, and the Compressor.

We will dive deeper into what is possible with Live's effects in Chapter 8, 'Live's Effects', but for those who are experienced enough with EQs, Delays, Gates, etc., you now have a basic starting point when attempting your first couple of Live sets. Remember that each of the above mentioned effects can be controlled via MIDI-controller for a broader range of possibilities. You will notice also that I didn't mention any VST effect plug-ins in this chapter, in an effort to ensure your system stability. After all, some VST plug-ins will not run smoothly on every system or in Ableton Live 2. This shouldn't discourage you from trying out new plug-ins at home, and even using them in your live set. But as we'll discuss later, Ableton's

Countoff

Another method for song-to-song transitions within Live is to 'count off' the next song's tempo by triggering Live's Tap Tempo button. Since I am a drummer, I map one electronic drum pad from my Drumkat triggering interface to Live's Tap Tempo button (you could also use a keyboard or QWERTY key). I then strike that trigger four times in succession to set the tempo of the next piece I will perform. Live will then commence playback on 'one,' so it is important that you have selected the next scene you would like to play. I have also found it handy to change my set's time signature to 8/4, which will then allow for a two-bar countoff with Live's Tap Tempo function. A longer countoff is often more accurate.

Figure 6.15

In the above screenshot, you will see that while organization is extremely important, symmetry is not. This set may look scattered, but there is a method to its madness.

plug-ins are flawless workhorses that can handle most common audio effects (and then some). Even more exciting is that future versions of Live will undoubtedly feature upgrades and additional effects.

Backup

In wrapping up this chapter, I want to return to the subject of making reliable and frequent backups of your work. Whether you are touring, borrowing a computer, or merely playing your first gig, it is imperative to make a backup of all of your song files and sounds. How often you do this is up to you, but I like to do so about once a week. If you are limited on time or resources, you really only need to back up any files modified since the last backup. Full system backups are best done in the middle of the night (when no one is working on the machine), or to a fast storage medium such as a FireWire or USB 2 hard drive.

You never know when you may have to rebuild your system as a result of a hard drive crash, or merely want to use your own material on a different system. Usually, I can fit a whole night's worth of music on a couple of CDs, but this will depend upon how much material you are archiving. Most CDs can hold up to 700 MB of data. Many musicians are now resorting to writable DVDs (DVD-Rs), which can store up to 4.5 GB per disc. Remember to keep both your song file and the corresponding folder of sounds (that we learned how to create back in Chapter 3 using Live's Save As Self-Contained settings) in a safe and easy to locate folder on your hard drive. It is a disheartening and discouraging experience to lose even a single song or part of a song.

Monolake – Live Co-Inventor/Producer/Performer

The future of music may just rely on artists like Robert Henke (a.k.a. Monolake). Robert's DIY approach includes scripting his own software and effects with MAX/MSP, running his own label, producing his own records, and touring the globe to perform with the very software he helped design: Ableton Live. For more on Robert and his latest happenings, see www.monolake.de.

To set up his Live performance, Henke takes pre-produced recordings and segments them into smaller loops. Each looped subsection of a song is then copied to various clips in Live's Session View. Each Monolake performance is a live improvisation (done in Live) on this material as well as any loops Robert has cooked up on the road. Robert explains, 'My track layout is not a rigid linear progression of files, but a collection of possibilities. When performing, I am mixing existing Monolake pieces with additional sound files (like beat loops or chords). Most of the pieces are sliced into parts, which allows me to change the order and duration. In almost every piece I have parts which serve as starting points for improvisation. The most exciting moments in my music occur during these manipulations.'

Henke often relies on Doepfer's Pocket Control and Pocket Fader MIDI-controllers (www.doepfer.de) to manipulate the mix by adjusting track levels, panning, and various effects' parameters. 'In order

to use Live as an instrument, I have assigned lots of functions like FX bypass or firing special clips to computer keys.' He also uses an RME Hammerfall (www.rme-audio.com) audio interface or even the built in sound card on a G4 powerbook.

A master performer with Live, Henke divulges, 'when I am producing new pieces, I always cut footage out of them for later usage on stage. During my performances I jump through my collection of files

so that the order is created on-the-fly. I am constantly adding and deleting files right before the concert. If the event is focused on dancing, I put in more appropriate rhythmical material (and dance-oriented effects) and throw out the experimental soundscape stuff. For an ambient set, I would have more sends with delays and less tracks with clips. Sometimes, I use my own self-written Pluggo plug-ins for special tasks or run MAX/MSP via ReWire in sync with Live.'

Referring to Figure 6.15, Robert tells us, 'The set seen earlier in this chapter (Figure 6.15) shows a small part of a set I made in Porto (Spain) in 2002. It's a pretty unorganized one (but that is the point). Track 1 plays a bassline loop, fmA; track 2, a bass drum pattern, BD-kurz; track 5, a long progression of chords, Wall; and track 7, a completely deconstructed version of the BD pattern. If I prepared the set in advance, I would have used different colors and names to indicate that it does not sound like a bass drum pattern at all[– it is pitched up 27 semitones and time-stretched to sound more like a lead synth.' Of course, Robert can always go back and fix these sorts of details, fine tune the mix and effects settings, and rename/color files. Instead, Henke shows us by example that a little right-brained chaos is good for the music, and good for the soul.

Editing your performance

I n Chapter 6, 'Playing Live...live', we talked about how to record a song sequence, or live loop performance, by arming Live's recording. We also pointed out that virtually every performance parameter (volume, panning, effects, and so forth) in Live can be edited, automated, or otherwise modified at a later time. In this chapter, we are going to look at how to make these edits happen and discuss some of the basics of making a sensible musical arrangement, as well as befriend mix-automation.

What is a musical arrangement?

Before we dive into tips and tricks for working with your musical arrangement, it is important to understand exactly what it is we are referring to when we say *arrangement*. Any song, be it an 8-minute jazz odyssey, a 9-minute movement of a Mozart concerto, or a 20-minute techno mix has some kind of linear sequence or order, which is usually categorized as a musical arrangement. Just as film directors construct a film's sequence of events, composers, remixers, and even musicians themselves, arrange their music by determining the sequence of events, length of certain song sections, and choices of musical instruments. Each decision can manipulate the mood of a piece, as can other factors such as interrelated volume, tempo, harmonic movement, and lest we forget, the melody.

An arrangement can be as stylized, as original, or as generic as you like, and will depend largely on the goal of the kind of music you are making. If you are looking to create music in a particular style such as rock, pop, or blues, the arrangement should generally conform to the common arrangement formats of the given genre. For instance, a standard rock song will usually have a quick intro and then a verse before proceeding to the chorus. Typically, the song will then alternate between the verse and chorus, back to the verse and then again to a longer, and more dramatic, chorus. To add flavor, many composers set up the chorus by adding a *pre-chorus* section, a bridge, or a stylized second verse to break up the monotonous verse-chorus-verse-chorus formulaic result. Ultimately, the most musical decision is the correct one, yet this point can be highly subjective. To give you an example of what I'm talking about, here is an outline of a typical popular song arrangement.

- intro
- verse 1

- chorus
- verse 2
- chorus
- bridge
- verse 3 or chorus
- end or outro (optional)

Each section (verse, chorus, bridge) will usually consist of 8-, 16-, or 32-measure sections. Of course this is not a hard and fast rule, but it's an advisable format to follow when just starting out. In Figure 7.1, I have outlined what an arrangement might begin to look like in Live. Figure 7.1 shows a small 8-measure intro and a 16-measure verse, followed by a 16-measure chorus.

Figure 7.1
A basic arrangement in Live.

Intro   Verse selection   Chorus section

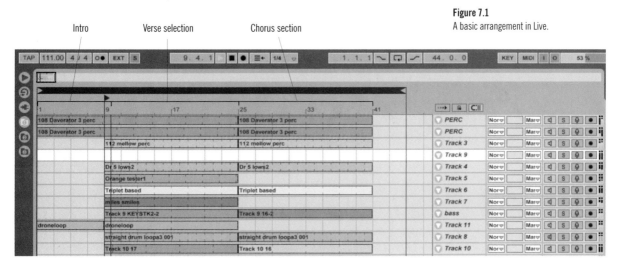

It is helpful to note that in Live's Arranger View, you can determine each cycle of a loop by the small vertical dash mark in each instance of a loop (clip), as pictured in Figure 7.2. Eight repetitions of a given loop will show six such dashes, or indentations, since the first and last bars do not link and are therefore not indented. By keeping your eye on the measure numbers at the top of Live's Arranger View (in the Beat Time Ruler), as well as the notch markers in the loop, you will be able to keep track of the number of bars passing by, and therefore monitor your overall song arrangement.

Figure 7.2
Several cycles of a loop in Live's Arranger View.

Make sure your song and clip time signatures are in alignment when relying on Live's measure numbers. For instance, if you are working in 4/4 time at 120 beats-per-minute, and you have a 5/4 or 7/8 clip in the project, you will not be able to rely on Live's measure numbers to give you an accurate accounting of your arrangement.

Small vertical dash indicates each instance of a loop

Measure numbers

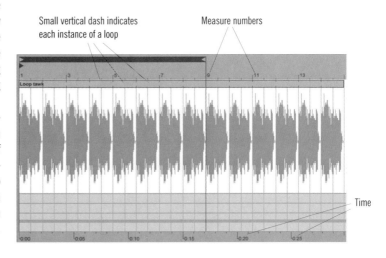

Time

Note: more experimental music will often have more unusual (experimental) arrangements, while some avant-garde or free jazz pieces may appear entirely free of arrangement.

Creating an arrangement

By now I hope you have spent a couple of hours in Live's Session window, dragging in your favourite loops, mixing them with other loops, adjusting the clip properties, and maybe even adding/tweaking a few effects. With any luck, you are starting to make some real music. Once you've developed a progression of scenes that you like, it's time to start thinking in terms of an overall arrangement, or song-form. Since this chapter is dedicated to editing your arrangement in Live, we must first know how to make or record one (we touched on this back in Chapter 5, 'Making Music in Live').

To create your first musical arrangement in Live, you must first place music into Live's Arranger View (the horizontal view without the mixer channels – for those skipping around). This can be done by two different methods, which will both be explained in the sections that follow. Method 1 is for those wanting to create a piece of music by stringing together their Session View scenes in a recorded live performance, while Method 2 will benefit composers who prefer to compose in the Arranger View in a 'paint and play' manner. Of course, both methods can be combined, and usually are, to create a song. When doing so, you would start with Method 1 and then add audio (via Method 2).

Method 1, 'The take'

To begin with, you will need to have some loops (often many) in Live's Session View clip slot grid. If you have not gotten around to doing so, load the Live 2 Demo Session song to follow the numbered steps below. Note: most of this chapter's examples will be using Live's other demo song called Live 2 Demo Arrangement, but since we need to practice creating an arrangement, we are going to use the Session demo for just this instance.

1 Load the demo song called Live 2 Demo Session from Ableton Live's Content folder. If you have downloaded an upgrade since the initial install, both of Live's demo songs will still be in the original (version 2.0.1) Content folder. If you have trouble finding the demo, try your system's search tool.
2 Press the Stop button twice (on Live's Transport bar). This resets the track to the beginning and ensures a clean beginning.
3 Next, click the Record button once to arm recording. Be sure to check that Live's Back to Arrangement button is not lit (red). If it is, click it to deactivate.
4 Click the Play arrow corresponding to the first scene (group of loops) that you want to play. Playback and arrangement recording will begin instantly and simultaneously. You can also begin recording by playing a single clip (loop or sample).
5 Now play the loops, scenes, and mixer as you would want to hear it. Every single move will be recorded. When you are finished, press the Spacebar.

Once you have begun the recording process, all audio heard through the main out-

Tip

Back and forth

To quickly toggle back and forth between Session and Arranger views, press the Tab key.

put, as well as all mixer, effect, and clip parameter changes, will be recorded. Make sure to experiment, and don't worry if you make mistakes. You will be able to clean it up later in Arranger View – or if you feel like you want to do it again, no problem. You can retake the song from the top by double clicking the stop button again (pressing Spacebar) and then using the Undo command to wipe out all remnants of the past recording.

If you decide you want to fix a certain section of the song without redoing the entire piece, follow these steps. This treatment is often referred to as an *overdub*.

1 In Session View, identify which loops or scene you would like use for the fix.
2 Move the start marker in Arranger View to the desired start position, or fix Live's arrangement position (Transport) bar by dragging or typing the location where you would like to start your recording.
3 Check to be sure that the Back to Arrangement button is not depressed–press Stop twice or the back to arrangement once to deactivate.
4 Press the Record button.
5 Launch scene, or individual loop to begin the recording at the current arrangement position. Like the original take, all scenes, loops and mix moves will be recorded into Arranger View.

Method 2, 'Paint and play'

So now you clearly see that any recordings made from Session View will end up in the Arranger View – the view from which you will complete songs. Sometimes you may want to try a different compositional approach. For instance, you may want to build your song one loop/track at a time without using the Session View at all. You may also want to simply drag a couple of extra loops/samples into an existing arrangement. This style of composing is often referred to as *paint and play*. The idea is that you place loops into the arrangement first (paint) and then listen to the results (play). This is a quite different experience from listening and recording as you play in Live's Session View. Here is how *paint and play* works.

1 To paint with audio loops, simply drag a loop from Live's Browser (on the left side of the screen), to any one of the numbered tracks in Live's Arranger View. You will now see a single occurrence of the loop or sample at the exact location you placed it.
2 To paint or duplicate, this loop in the given track, move the mouse cursor just to the right of the loop until your cursor resembles an end-bracket (])–click and then drag the loop to your desired length.
3 You can also extend the front end of any loop in the arrangement by hovering over the loop's beginning–you will see the inverse bracket ([)–you can then stretch the loop to the left so that the loop will sound before its original location.
4 Once a loop is in the arrangement, you can copy, paste, and tweak to your heart's content. Automation for all mixer settings, such as volume, panning, and aux send level, will be recorded in the form of envelopes–we will delve into this at the end of this chapter.

To sum up these two methods, Live's Arranger View is a linear representation of your recorded improvisation in Session View or your piecemeal construction of

---

Info

Do over

Sure, you can always fix your mistakes later via editing, but you can also redo the take from the top. Just be careful to delete the past take by doing a quick undo – Ctrl (Cmnd) + Z – after you have pressed the Spacebar to stop recording. By clearing the slate, you eliminate any erroneous automation or recording data that may get in the way of your new recording (see the following explanation on how to overdub).

Tip

Listen before you leap

You may also listen along to a song in record mode before you begin recording an overdub. To do this, click Record and then Play. The song will play along without recording any new information. The moment you launch a clip or move any knob/fader on the mixer, recording will begin. Any previously recorded automation, or audio data will be replaced, though you can always undo any mistakes. This *punch-in* method differs from Live's Punch-in/Punch-out feature, which I will detail in Chapter 12, 'Recording in Live'.

loops. This horizontal (linear) style is common to many professional audio applications. Much of your expertise and many of the tricks you have acquired in one DAW application can be applied to Live. The key is to remember that each row represents a separate audio track, a great contrast to Live's Session View.

Getting around in arranger view

Once you begin playing with an arrangement in Live, you will find that in order to keep a creative workflow going, it is vital to be able to quickly maneuver to various locations within a song. Back in Chapter 3, 'Live Interface Basics', we discussed Live's Overview section at the top of the Arrangement window. By mouse-clicking on certain areas within the Overview, you can quickly jump to specific areas within your musical arrangement. Also, you will want to get comfortable zooming in and out of the desired work area as well as looping certain sections of your song for more specialized editing.

Magnifying glass

Live's magnifying glass zoom-in/out tool appears in three different sections of the screen. The Beat Time Ruler, The Overview, and any active Clip View Sample Display section. Basic handling of the magnifying glass is straightforward enough. Click and move right to left to scroll in any of the aforementioned areas. Zooming, however, is the exact opposite of how many of us might intuitively think to use it. For instance to zoom in, you want to click on the target (while the magnifying glass is showing as your mouse icon) and then drag the mouse downward (toward you). To zoom out, click and drag up (away from you) and toward the computer. After some practice this does become natural, so keep at it if this is tricky to get a handle on.

Looping

You may find it helpful to repeatedly loop a segment of the song that you are working on in order to zero in on problem spots, automate mix settings, or merely give it a good listen. To do this, press the Live Loop Switch button seen in Figure 7.3. You will also want to set the Loop's length, and start and stop points by either dragging the Start/Stop Bracket in Live or manually selecting the numerical values in Live's transport area.

Tip

Zoom shortcut

To zoom in/out without using the magnifying glass, click once on any of the three zoomable areas (Beat Time Ruler, The Overview, or Clip's Sample Display), and then press the +/- keys, respectively.

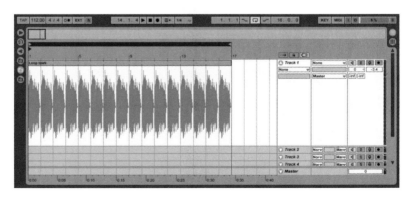

Figure 7.3
Here, I have set Live to continuously loop playback in a 16-measure phrase (Loop/Punch Length set to 16.0.0) at the song position 33.1.1 (loop start position).

Another use for Loop Switch is for punch-in/punch-out style recording. Say you want to get a couple of practice attempts before actually laying down the take. We will talk about how to achieve this in Chapter 12, 'Recording in Live'.

Working with your arrangement

If you are new to digital audio recording/remixing software, mastering Live's Arranger View can take some time. Be patient with yourself as you learn to see and work with audio in such a linear fashion. One of the revolutionary aspects of digital audio is its ability to be cut, copied, and pasted in similar fashion to text in a word processing program. Any loop, sample, or recording in Live's Arranger can be dragged to any other location. The only rule is that you cannot place one loop on top of another loop on the same track. Otherwise, any sort of cutting, pasting, and recombining is fair game. Let's explore how this works by again loading the Live 2 Demo Arrangement file.

1 Load the Live 2 Demo Arrangement file (and stay in Arranger View).
2 Select the loop on track 3 called *flirr* and make a copy by pressing Ctrl (Cmnd) + C.
3 Now paste the loop to track 4 by clicking on the track's second measure marker and pressing Ctrl (Cmnd) + V. The new track should be directly beneath the original and look like Figure 7.4. If you have accidentally pasted the loop elsewhere, try dragging it to the location shown in Figure 7.4.

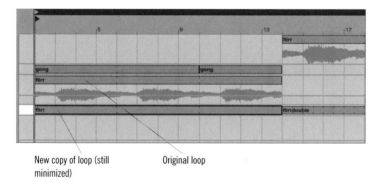

New copy of loop (still   Original loop
minimized)

Live also allows for insertion and deletion of sections in the middle of an arrangement. This may not sound like a big deal, but when you see this in action, light bulbs may begin to glow. Here are the steps for inserting a new eight measures of silence so that you can then add a new piece of audio (in the middle of a track).

1 Load the Live 2 Demo Arrangement song if you have not already done so.
2 With Snap to Grid active, click on measure 14 and drag to measure 22 on an Arranger View Track. This can be done on any track anywhere on the arrangement. Also, you may need to zoom in on your arrangement if you are unable to grab exactly measure 14 and 22.

Figure 7.4
Here is what the altered Live 2 Demo Arrangement song should look like after your copy and paste.

Info

Isn't it harmonic?

For an added trick, double-click on the new copy of the loop flirr used in the above instructions, and adjust its Transpose to − 4 in Clip View's Sample Settings. You might want to also reduce the gain a bit (right next to the Transpose button) because you have doubled the sound of the flirr loop. Now press play (Spacebar) and listen to your new harmony. The second flirr is a major third below the first, giving it a sort of moody quality. Experiment with different pitches to see what kinds of results you get.

3 Insert 8 measures (the eight measures you have selected) of silence by pressing Ctrl (Cmnd) + I, or going to Edit > Insert Silence. Your modified arrangement should resemble the arrangement pictured in Figure 7.5.

Inserted 8 bars of silence

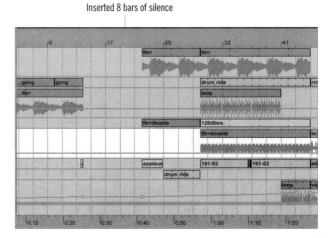

Figure 7.5
The Insert Silence command is a great ally when adding or extending sections of an arrangement.

Take notice of how the Insert Silence command has kept the arrangement intact (including all automation!) and simply moved it eight measures back. The song prior to the insertion remains untouched, and you now have eight blank measures to work with.

To delete a segment of a song, and to compact the arrangement (omitting the silence), highlight the section you would like to delete by click-dragging on it. Then use the Delete Time command by pressing Ctrl (Cmnd) + Shift + Delete. The highlighted section will be deleted and all of the arrangement after your deletion point will be moved towards the beginning of the song, while staying completely intact.

If you are an experienced musician and/or composer, you will immediately see the relevance and power of commands such as Delete Time and Insert Silence. It is common for composers to elongate or truncate sections of a song, or even add a bridge after the fact.

The speed and ease of working with audio in such a way can take getting used to. After playing around with the preceding example and practicing some moves of your own, you'll find the Arranger View is the perfect place for making edits.

Editing tips in Live

For many, editing audio is where the bulk of their time in Live is spent. In fact, editing has become an art unto itself and is frequently an even more creative endeavor than adding loops or recording. Whether you are putting the final touches on a project or starting anew, the editing techniques discussed in this section are aimed at making audio editing in Live a creatively inspiring breeze.

Split

To dissect or split a Clip at any given gridline in Live's Arranger View, expand the loop by pressing the Track Fold-In downward pointing arrow. Then left-click on the point at which you would like to create a division, and press Ctrl (Cmnd) + E. There is virtually no limit to how many times you can split a clip, so long as there is a visible gridline marker to click on (in the clip in Arranger View). Once the section is split from the original, each half of the former clip is treated as an individual clip, complete with its own properties, clip view, and settings. You can then take it a step further by changing one of the newly created clip halves, shuffle the clips to rearrange their order of appearance, or move one of the new clips to another track (with different effect and mix settings). We will explore these possibilities in detail in Chapter 14, 'Power Tips, The Magic of Live!', but for now this should tide you over.

One popular trick is to change the Loop Offset in one of the new clips. To do this, split a loop. Then double-click on the second clip and change the Loop Offset just above the Clip's sample display region. This can be a powerful tool for creating drum fills, bass turnarounds, or other embellishments that break up stagnant loops. Of course, you can change other settings too, such as the second clip's transient setting or warp markers. Practice these suggestions on several types of loops until you get it down. After a short while, you will begin to anticipate what a split/embellishment might sound like, and give your mixes some new interesting twists.

If you want to apply the same treatment to a one-shot or non-looped selection of audio, you will need to use Live's Clip Loop/Region bar above the Sample Display window. Simply grab the right or left side of the bar, and constrain the loop.

Tip

Copy cat

Did you realize you can copy loops or samples from your Session View into your Arranger View (and vice-versa)? To do so, simply click once on the clip while you are in Session View, and then press Ctrl (Cmnd) + C. Next hit the TAB button to swap views, and then paste the sample / loop where you like by using the shortcut key Ctrl (Cmnd) + V.

Why would you want to do this? Say you spent a good amount of time adjusting a clip's parameters or tuning and don't want to have to repeat the work. Or you just recorded a long vocal take and want to have the sample available in your Session View for the live show. There are many more reasons, but take my word for it, this comes in handy. Give it a try!

Adding audio

We have already touched upon a couple of methods for getting audio into your arrangement. In Chapter 6, 'Playing Live…live', we talked about recording a loop performance as a Live sequence to add audio to an arrangement. Later, in Chapter 12, we will learn how to add audio the old fashioned way, by recording it. In that chapter we will also take recording a step further by learning how to do punch-in/punch-out-style overdubbing. However, until then, let's look at a newer method of composing/creating music, adding audio the digital way, using good old drag-and-drop. If you are familiar with programs such as Sonic Foundry's Acid Pro or Cakewalk's Sonar, you are used to the idea of browsing for loops, auditioning what they sound like, and then dragging them into your song. As we discussed in Chapter 3, 'Live Interface Basics', Live's Browser can be accessed in either Arranger or Session View. This simple-looking browser will soon become your good friend, collaborator and composition partner.

Tip

Snap to it

In the Arranger View, Live's Snap To feature can help you line up your incoming loop or sample so that it snaps to the visible gridline, at whatever level you are currently zoomed in to. To turn off the Snap To, click on the small, sideways shaped, magnet-shaped icon just above the tracks in Arranger View.

Any loop that has been dragged into a track in Live's Arranger View can be extended or contracted by hovering the mouse cursor over the loop's endpoints and then click-dragging in the direction you would like to go. As we pointed out in the Paint and Play section above, you will notice small vertical marks on the bar representing each instance (repetition) of the loop.

Auditioning loops

Live's Pre-Listening feature can come in handy when composing via the Arranger View. This can be especially powerful if you have a lot of loops and samples on your hard drive(s) from which to choose. While each composer or remix artist will develop his or her own methods, many find it helpful to start with drum loops and work up from there. Auditioning loops can be an indispensable tool for this kind of building-block method. What follows are some suggestions for making the most of Live's Pre-Listening feature.

- Organize your audio content: By grouping like loops in the same folder, you will be able to quickly choose the best option for the job at hand. Some loopists prefer to group loops by tempo, timbre, content, or style. Experiment a bit to find a method that works best for you and stick to it.
- Volume (of pre-listening): Adjust your pre-listening volume to a reasonable level when auditioning new loops (by using Live's Pre-Listening (Solo) dial on the session mixer interface). If playback is too loud or soft, you will not really be previewing the loop as it will sound in the track.

Info

Comping a vocal/solo

Comping a vocal, or solo, is a term, used by producers, that is derived from the act of COMPiling or COMParing several different takes from several different tracks onto one single track. For instance, a singer may do three or more takes of a song, and each version may have its strengths and weaknesses. A producer who wants to comp that vocal will then take the best parts from each track and compile them into one pristine, heartfelt vocal take. It used to be that tracks were so limited that once a track was comped, the other tracks would be erased to be ready for additional overdubs. In a software studio such as Live, the number of tracks is limitless – so automating the comping procedure makes sense. That way you will have all of the original tracks available in case you change your mind.

What is automation?

One of the greatest advances in audio recording has been the development of automated mixdown (also called automated mixing or mix-automation). Automation is the technology that allows mix settings such as volume, panning, and effect levels to be written or recorded as data, and then later recalled or edited within a given song. When used correctly, automation enables you to achieve complex or professional-sounding results, such as smooth fades and lightning quick effects routing. Due to subtleties of timing, the limits of human dexterity, and the finite number of human limbs, some mix moves are simply impossible to achieve manually and can be achieved only via automation.

Typical uses of mix-automation can include things as simple as fade ins and fade outs, comping a vocal (see the Comping a Vocal/Solo note), and panning and other effects. You may have witnessed analog mix-automation years ago when it was usually done on expensive mixing boards with motorized faders. New hardware controllers such as the Mackie Control (www.mackie.com), and Emagic's Logic Control (www.emagic.de), also contain movable faders. But these newer boards, and all audio mixing software applications, now employ MIDI to achieve automated mixing.

Even if you have no prior experience, or if you have limited firsthand knowledge of software-driven automation, Live's Breakpoint and Breakpoint Envelope automation editing method is as easy to learn as it is flexible. First of all, any effect, mix-setting, or parameter can be automated in either real-time (while the song is in playback mode) or from a dead stop–in other words, any mix-related setting in a

Live song can be modified at any time. This means that any changes to your mix in record mode will be recorded as new automation. Also, you can stop the track to delete, modify, or add new changes.

In the next section we will look at some of the most practical and popular ways of editing your mix's automation, one parameter at a time. The following steps teach you how to automate any parameter in a mix (song), while in record mode (either for the first time or as an overdub).

Editing breakpoint envelopes

There are several different ways you can edit or shape the parameters affecting your music in Arranger View. The following sections will give you a few of the most commonly automated parameters and some ideas on how to use them.

Volume fade-ins/fade-outs

Volume adjustments are the most common automatable task. Fade-ins and fade-outs, as well as minor volume tweaks throughout your track, can help you achieve a more musical and professional-sounding final mix. To create an adjustable volume envelope, click on the track's volume level (in Arranger View), which will create a red horizontal line though the track (Device Chooser should say Master, Control Chooser should read Track Volume). You can then make individual edit points, to customize fade-ins and fade-outs, along the envelope by double-clicking, and then dragging the edit point up and down to either raise or lower the volume. The default location, or the unaltered breakpoint envelope, will automatically remain at the level of Live's session mixer for that track. For instance, if a given track is set to −2 dB in the session mixer, it will start there in Arranger View as well. Also, you can delete an existing edit point by double-clicking on it. Figure 7.6 demonstrates a Fade Out in Live. Note the position of the breakpoints and the gradually sloped line.

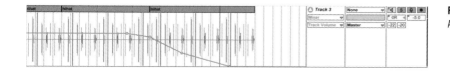

Figure 7.6
A fade-out drawn in via breakpoints.

Panning

Panning automation can wear out a listener in a hurry, but for special musical effects, or Leslie speaker cabinet emulation, you may want to try automating a track's panning envelope. To do this, click on the track's pan settings in Arranger View (Device Chooser will read Master; Control Chooser will say Track Panning). A track's default panning setting will typically be in the exact centre of your stereo field (between your speakers), but if you have changed this for a given track in Live's session mixer, you will see those settings here. For panning automation ideas, you might try quickly panning a track back and forth for a special effect or try more gradual, slight panning for adding complexity to your sound. To do this, create several Breakpoints by double-clicking on the red breakpoint envelope as seen in Figure 7.7. Then drag the breakpoints up to pan right, down to pan left, to distribute your audio to the desired stereo position.

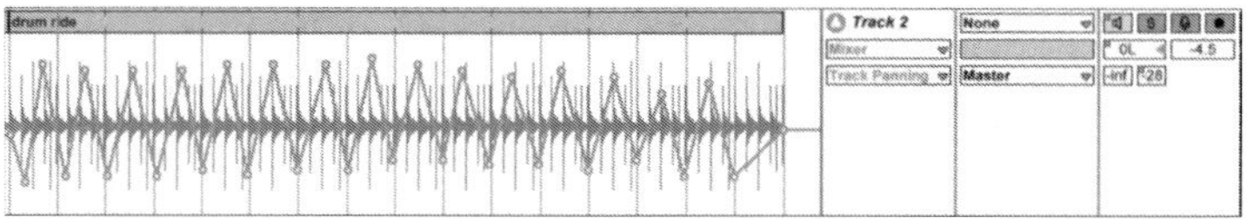

Figure 7.7
Here I have automated a track's panning parameters to make the track move back and forth, from left to right, across the stereo field.

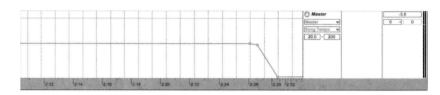

Tempo

Occasionally, you may want to adjust a song's tempo. New to Live 2, this change can be written right into your mix via automation. Tempo changes can be automated via Live's Master Track (see Figure 7.8). Device Chooser = Master, Control Chooser = Song Tempo.

Figure 7.8
I have slowed this song down to a crawl for demonstration purposes. You can also increase a song's tempo.

Effects

All Ableton or VST effect parameters, including the on/off switch, can be controlled through Live's mix-automation. This is an incredibly powerful, not to mention fun, way to spruce up your mix. Each effect will behave relatively similarly, though the number and types of parameters available will vary drastically. For more involved information on Ableton Live's effects, see Chapter 8, 'Live's Effects'. VST effect information will have to come from their manufacturers. What follows are examples of some common effect automation practices.

Punching-in effects

Try punching in (activating) a delay plug-in during the last couple of notes of a drum loop or fill. Or try this with a vocal, as seen in Figure 7.9.

Figure 7.9
Here I have turned on one of Live's delay effects on the last couple of notes of a sample. Notice that the On/Off effect switch is a binary value, so there will be no gradual slope to the envelope. Simply, the effect is either on or off. There is no in-between.

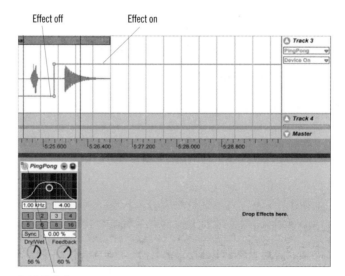

Red dot indicates automation is set

Effect level (mix)

Another common trick is to bring in and out the effect on a track or send – this is a notably more gradual effect than the punch-in idea described above and can be done in at least two ways – by automating the wet/dry level, or by automating a track's send level. The second method is technically not an effect automation, but is most often used with effects.

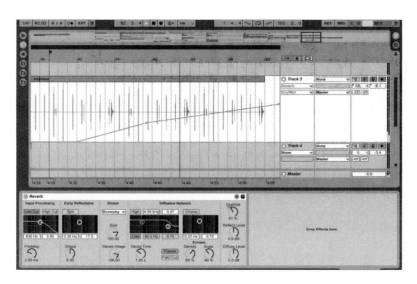

Figure 7.10
Here I have automated the Wet/Dry value of a reverb to gradually fade in the effect and fade out the dry sound.

Filter/frequency sweeps

Filter and Frequency sweeps can be a fun way of adding life to a stagnant mix or loop. They are also a very popular tool in dance and electronic styles. To automate a sweep, you will want to load either an EQ Four or an Auto Filter Plug-in and then follow these steps:

1 Load the Live 2 Demo Arrangement.
2 In Arranger View, add an EQ Four or Auto Filter to track 2. To do this, select track 2 (so that the track is highlighted), and double-click on the EQ Four or Auto Filter plug-in.
3 Move the song's Start Marker to measure 22 (where the drum loop comes in).
4 You now have two choices. Record the automation Live or draw it in via automation. To be precise, let's draw it in.
5 Click on the Freq (Frequency) parameter of the Auto Filter or one of the Bands on the Four EQ and then click on the Freq knob. The Device Chooser on track 2 should indicate which effect you have chosen (in this instance Auto Filter or EQ Four), while the Control chooser should say Frequency (for Auto Filter) or 1 Frequency, 2 Frequency, (and so on) for EQ Four.
6 Crank both the Gain and Q for the EQ, or the Freq and Q for the Auto Filter, so that you will easily be able to hear the effect.
7 Double-click three separate times on the track 2's red breakpoint envelope (to create three breakpoints).
8 Drag each break point to the top and bottom alternately up until measure 32 as shown in Figure 7.11.

Info

Wet/dry

When talking about effects, audio engineers and producers commonly refer to wet sounds as those drenched with effects and dry sounds as those without any effects. In other words, a completely *dry* sound has no effects applied to it, while the scientific term *pretty dry* means that a small amount of the effect has been applied to the sound, leaving the larger portion of the sound natural (unaffected). *Really Wet* or *Too Wet* are the descriptive terms used when too much reverb has been applied to a sound, but they can also refer to any other effect level that has overstepped its bounds.

Figure 7.11
Place the breakpoint where you like. Here is one example that will work for this exercise.

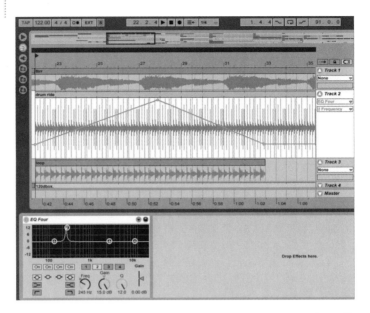

9   Before you hit play, change the Q setting to 3 on the Auto Filter, or 6 on the EQ Four.

10 Now hit Play and watch the sweeps move. For more fun, try automating the Q or other parameters on the effects.

Deleting envelopes

Hopefully the preceding examples will get you excited about the automation possibilities in Live. Before we move on, there is one other important command I have found to be helpful. Sometimes after recording automation, you change your mind. Rather than deleting each breakpoint by double-clicking, you can delete them all in one fell swoop. Here is how to do this:

1   Make sure the Device Chooser and Control Chooser are configured to the parameter whose automation you want to delete. For instance, if you want to delete the above example's frequency sweep, set the Device Chooser to Auto Filter (or Four EQ), and the Control Chooser to Frequency (or Frequency # if you used Four EQ).

2   Highlight with the mouse the section of automation to be deleted.

3   Press Ctrl (Cmnd) + Delete to delete all breakpoints in the highlighted section. Note: you may still need to adjust the two end breakpoints (outside the deleted region) to make it sound musical.

Finalizing your Live song

Once you have completed all recording, editing, mixing, tweaking effects, and the like, you may decide that you like your final creation well enough to play it for your friends, burn a CD, or take the track to market. But before you rush out and buy a spindle of blank CDs, there is, alas, one more link in the production chain. Mastering, or finalizing, your song is often the final creative step in preparing your music for reproduction, or at the very least, for playback on the world's gamut of stereo systems. Mastering, like recording, may or may not involve hiring a professional (and hopefully an experienced) mastering engineer with his or her own acoustically sound mastering studio and equipment. The advantages of hiring a pro are many at this critical stage, but it can easily cost you £100 per song or more. Mastering an entire album is especially difficult in terms of matching tonalities and treatment from song to song and requires a great deal of skill and carefully handled audio processing.

Regardless of who masters your music, the mastering process itself typically involves running your audio file (completed song) through various hardware components and software plug-ins in an effort to analyze, maximize, and standardize your music to align with current industry standards. A seasoned pro will ensure your music's volume level is adequate, assist with more advanced audio editing (such as splicing songs or fixing noises), and improve the album's overall frequency range for the best speaker response. In short, completing a song in Live can sometimes involve more than recording and arranging all of the necessary parts–mastering will give your music a more professional, standardized, and acceptable-sounding final mix.

Tips on mastering your song

The gear arsenal of a professional mastering engineer begins with the monitoring environment (room shape, acoustics, monitors, cabling, and more). Other important pieces of equipment can include expensive software and hardware limiters, compressors, equalizers, spectral analyzers, stereo simulators, and on and on. While Ableton does not tout Live as a full-fledged mastering application, some Live users have found that inserting effects such as Ableton's EQ Four and Compressor plug-ins on the Master Track can serve as a decent substitute. In the next two sections, I will point out a couple of quick methods for getting the most out of your Live song once the final mix is complete. If you are new to effect plug-ins, or have yet to experiment with Ableton's plug-ins, Chapter 8, 'Live's Effects', will feature a more in-depth exploration of what these two effects are truly capable of.

EQ

Simply stated, the goals of EQing your final mix are to both accentuate the good frequencies, and to diminish any undesirable ones. How you achieve this is highly subjective–though there are some guidelines that are generally agreed upon. Here are a few hints for you to use as a guide.

- Each mix is different and requires some experimentation.
- A little EQ goes a long way.
- Trimming is usually better than boosting.
- If a little isn't cutting it, try isolating the problem track and inserting an EQ.
- Try comparing and contrasting your mix with one of your favourite-sounding records.
- Above all, use your ears.

If you can afford a more specialized third-party VST plug-in EQ, such as TC Works Mastering EQ (www.tcworks.com) or Waves Mastering Bundle (www.waves.com), your mixes will be better for it.

Compression

If you are looking to raise the overall level of your mix – and let's face it, most of us are – Live's compressor serves as a quick sonic band-aid. The basic methodology behind using a compressor in a mastering situation is to eliminate volume spikes or peaks, and elevate some of the quieter parts of the music to add greater sonic detail. The result is a maximized overall song volume that can be raised without quashing all dynamic ingenuity of the music at hand. Sound like too much to ask? It can be. Similar to EQing, compression takes a fair amount of know-how and is often best when subtle.

If you are just getting familiar with compression, I recommend using Ableton's factory setting aptly titled Compression on your master track directly after the EQ Four. While you are monitoring your mix playback, gradually adjust both the compressor's output and ratio, until your master output approaches (but does not exceed) the peak level.

Future versions of Live may contain a more professional-level compressor or even a specific limiter plug-in, but for now Live's Compressor will have to do.

Rendering options explained

Once you have mastered or finished mixing your Live song – and you are liking the way it sounds – it is time to get it out of your computer, burned to CD, and onto the street. Though Live cannot burn CDs, it can help you prepare your song with an intermediary step called rendering – this was outlined in Chapter 4, 'Digital Audio Basics'. However, since we have just learned a few basic tips for mastering in Live, it is a good time to take a more detailed look into how rendering works. Figure 7.12a shows the Render to Disk menu that appears any time you press the render command Ctrl (Cmnd) + R. Note Figure 7.12b is the same menu in Arranger View with one exception. Since you manually select the length of the section to be rendered, you will not see the top Length [Bars.Beats.16th] settings.

Figure 7.12a (left)
The Render to Disk Menu in Session View.

Figure 7.12b (right)
The Render to Disk Menu in Arranger View.

In both the Session and Arranger View Render to Disk Menus, you have several important decisions to make. To begin with, you will need to know the exact length of the section of audio you are rendering. If you are rendering from Session View, than you are likely only rendering a 4-, 8-, or 16-bar section, whereas in Arranger View, you may well be rendering an entire song and can select the amount of desired rendering time by click-dragging on any track to highlight the desired length of your render. For instance if you want to render a four-minute song, simply drag (highlight) the entire length of the song on any track. Explicit directions for rendering are found in the following 'Rendering Techniques' section later in this chapter.

Normalize

When the Normalize setting is set to On, Live will raise the level of audio to the maximum level possible without distortion. I recommend leaving this setting Off for full songs and relegating all mastering/normalizing tasks to your wave editor. Most wave editors, such as Sonic Foundry's Sound Forge, Bias' Peak Audio, and Steinberg's Wavelab (to name a few) have a good deal more flexibility than Live in the matter of normalizing. However, if I am merely rendering a quick loop, or small selection of audio, I may switch Live's normalization setting to on (when rendering) to save time.

Render as loop

Upon first glance, Render as Loop, may seem like an insignificant option. However, this is a very important box if you have used any reverbs or delays in your soon-to-be-rendered loop, or selection of audio. Normally, any loop with delay or reverb will have a tail, or specified amount of decay, until the sound completely dissipates. The problem arises in the first few notes of a given loop, where the delay or reverb has not had time to kick in–those early notes are dry in comparison to the rest of the loop. Each time the loop cycles, you will hear the dry notes at the beginning and then a gradual swell in the effects. By activating the Render As Loop option, Live will actually render the file twice–once placing in all the reverb, delay, and effect tails, and twice to actually render the sample(s). You should be aware that this option is not desirable for complete songs. It's doubtful that you would want any sort of tail at the beginning of your compositions.

File type

When rendering, you have a choice between saving your audio in either AIFF or WAV file formats – either of which are capable of being burned to CD. If this sounds familiar, we touched on this in Chapter 4, 'Digital Audio Basics'. AIFF is usually the preferred format for Apple Macintosh computers, while WAV is the Windows audio standard. I'll leave this choice up to you. When it comes time to actually burn your music onto a CD, you will need to use either Apple's iTunes, or Microsoft's Windows XP burning utility. If you have a prior version of Windows, you may need a third-party CD burning utility such as Ahead Software's Nero (www.nero.com), Roxio's EZ CD Creator (www.roxio.com), or Cakewalk's Pyro (www.cakewalk.com/products/pyro).

Bit depth

The Bit Depth dropdown menu gives you two choices: 16- or 24-bit. This too, was touched on in Chapter 4, but I want to reiterate that unless you are short on hard drive space, you should usually render to 24-bit. Why not have a little extra detail to scrape away later if you so choose? Since Live can work with 24-bit files, loops, and samples, any loop you render can be re-imported into Live at a later time. I will point out that if you are without a professional CD burning application, you may want to render 16-bit, since this will be the final destination bit depth.

Sample rate

Typically, you will only use sample rates of 44100 (44.1K) and up. 48000 and 96000 will provide more accurate sampling at the expense of hard disk space in similar fashion to Bit Depth selection. The lower sample rates (22050 and 32000) will most often be used for creating lo-fi special effects popularized by older first- and second-generation hardware samplers.

Create analysis file

Each time Live sees a WAV or AIFF file, it has to draw a visual waveform, determine the positioning of the Warp Markers, and analyze the pitch and tempo. To do all this, Live uses a small pertinent secondary file called an Analysis File that will retain the master sample or loop's file name with the added file-extension .asd. When this setting is activated, Live will also create an ASD file in addition to the rendered audio file. This is helpful when creating loops that will be re-imported back into Live. Otherwise it is really not necessary to create the added file.

Convert to mono

Though this heading is fairly self-descriptive, I want to point out its usefulness. Many Live musicians have found that Mono loops/samples are preferable when working in a limited environment such as a laptop computer set up. The reason is that stereo loops are actually two channels of audio running on a single track. Therefore, they require roughly twice the system resources of a mono file – I say roughly because Live can forego all warp marker and file analysis since it has already been done for one side/channel of the file.

Mono loops can also be a great way to render loops or samples that you are planning to use again in an Ableton Live song. They will often have more presence than their stereo counterparts. If need be, you can always pan or use some kind of stereo simulation effect to widen the stereo field of the sample.

Rendering summary

OK, this is not an official control, but I do find it helpful to look at the summary provided by Live at the bottom of the Render To Disk menu. Here you will see a description of what you are about to print. For instance you might see, Live will render the Master output over the chosen length or Live will render the Master output over the selected time range [1.1.1-9.1.1]. If you get in the habit of watching this splash of text, you may cut down on mistakes in the rendering process.

Info

Watch the levels

As you are adjusting and automating your mix, pay close attention to Live's level meters. They will tell you when your overall or individual track levels are peaking. Any peaking tracks will result in a nasty digital glitch. To remedy the problem, you either adjust (decrease) the peaking track's volume, or, if the track has already been fully (and intricately) automated, you can employ the following tip. Add an EQ Four Ableton Live effect, deselect all four bands to conserve processing power, and then lower the gain setting on the effect until you see the levels on the track registering comfortably below the line/ceiling.

Rendering techniques

It is worth pointing out that rendering can be done with any portion of the song, at any time you are working with Live. In other words, if you want to render a loop or section of a song, you can do this from either Session or Arranger Views. Why would you do this? Listed here are some common reasons for rendering a portion of or a complete song. What follows is an explanation of how to complete the process.

• Grab a loop. I often render small loops for later use with a different piece of music, or make a complete file out of several edited clips.
• Submix a section. Occasionally, you might have added so many effects to a particular section or track of a song that the song can no longer run smoothly in Live. At this point you may want to consider rendering a single track or a sub-section of the song (such as a verse or chorus), in order to lighten the processing load on your computer.
• Export a completed song. By far, the best feeling is rendering a completed song. This is nearly always done from the Arranger View.

Grab a loop

Follow these steps to Render/Save a loop.

1 Determine how long you want your loop or rendered audio section to be. There is no need to render more than one repetition of the audio segment; however, you can often make your music more interesting by embellishing the repeated loop, and then rendering both the original and the varied loop as two loops.
2 Determine whether you are going to render in Session or Arranger View, and go to that View.
3 Highlight the loop/clip(s) to be rendered. In Session View, highlight the clips or scenes that you would like to render with the mouse. In Arranger View, highlight the desired length (on any track), at the appropriate location. Note: Live will render whatever is coming through on the master output. If you want to render the loop on track three only, you will need to either mute the other tracks (by turning of the speaker-shaped Track Activator icon), or solo all pertinent tracks, such as aux sends and the track(s) you want to render.
4 Press Ctrl (Cmnd) + R to call up the Render Options menu. Or, you can select File > Render to Disk. Note that in Session View, you will need to type in the length of the file to be rendered determined in step 1.
5 Here your choices may vary, but I will recommend for small samples that you do the following: Normalize=ON, Render as Loop=On, File Type=AIFF for Mac, WAV for PC, Bit Depth=24, Sample Rate=44100, Create Analysis File=ON, Convert to Mono=OFF (usually).
6 Click OK or press Enter and select the drive/folder where you want to save your new loop.

Submix a section

When creating a sub-mix of several tracks, or one effect-laden track that is too processor-intensive to continually keep playing, there are some slightly different options to select in the Render to Disk Menu. Follow these steps to create a track to be re-imported into Live.

1 In Arranger View, select and highlight the entire track or tracks that you would like to render. This may include several drum and percussion tracks, multiple vocal takes, or the compiled genius of your guitarist pal's efforts.

2 Solo all tracks and sends you are planning to render by activating the Solo/Pre-Listening button labelled S in Arranger View. You may also mute all other tracks (by turning off the speaker-shaped Track Activator icon). Remember: Live will render whatever is routed through the master output.

3 Press Ctrl (Cmnd) + R to call up the Render Options menu. Or, you can select File > Render to Disk.
4.Select these settings: Normalize=OFF, Render as Loop=OFF, File Type=AIFF for Mac, =WAV for PC, Bit Depth=24, Sample Rate=44100 (or the setting you are accustomed to), Create Analysis File=ON, Convert to Mono=OFF.

5 Click OK, or press Enter, and save the rendered file (and analysis file) some-where that makes sense with your current song. I suggest saving it in the same sounds folder as the other loops from your song. When you add the sub-mixed track to your mix, don't forget to mute all of the original tracks, or else you will hear an intense phasing effect.

Export a completed song

Finally the time has come to render your completed song. Don't expect this to be a one-time process. You may find that there are subtle tweaks you'd like to make to the mix after burning your song to a CD, and listening to it on different stereo systems.

1 On the master track in Arranger View, highlight the entire length of the song.

2 You may wish to place a bit of leader, or space, at the beginning of your track. To do this, use the mouse to highlight the first couple of seconds of your track, and then add the leader by selecting Edit > Insert Silence. Remember that you can always clean up the beginning and end spaces on your track in a wave edi-tor.

3 Press Ctrl (Cmnd) + R to call up the render options menu. Or, you can select File > Render to Disk.

4 For a final mix, I recommend setting Normalize=ON (OFF if you have a wave editing application), Render as Loop=OFF, File Type=AIFF for Mac, =WAV for PC, Bit Depth=24, Sample Rate=44100 (or the setting you are accustomed to), Create Analysis File=OFF, Convert to Mono=OFF.

5 Click on OK, or press Enter, and carefully save the file to a location where it is safe for final mixes.

Closing shop

In this chapter, we have discussed a number of different techniques for fine-tuning your song's arrangement and finalizing your mix. By now it should be clear that Live's rendering options can help you to get the most out of your final mix. And that each step in the audio editing process involves a number of choices right up until you burn your final mix to plastic. Although it can be a little overwhelming, the power Live gives you to edit and arrange audio and samples within your songs is truly incredible. When trying to master some of the above techniques, I find it helpful to repeatedly practice common commands, edits, automation, and rendering tactics. Sometimes I will create a song with the express purpose of making loops for other songs, future songs, or just for fun. Experiment with mixing and combining loops, cutting and pasting segments, and constantly rearranging your song. Try playing your latest mixes through a variety of speaker (monitor) combinations and stereo systems. Through this kind of focused experimentation, you will unlock your own favourite tricks and methods and become a master at producing music with Live.

Live's effects

N ow that you are making and producing music in Live, it's time to dive head-long into Live's effects. Whether you are looking to add a little spice or 'fix it in the mix', Live offers a number of (actually 13) cleverly constructed plug-in style effects. In the next sections, we will explore each effect, grouped by type, as well as some tips and tricks for tapping into the real power of these plug-ins. I will warn you that effects are often overused, seldom fully understood, and a darn good time.

Each effect is specialized to provide specific results. The right amount of delay or reverb adds an ethereal, ambient, professional quality. Too much, and you're just swimming in 'sauce'. If you haven't already, you will soon discover the power of equalization and filtering specific frequencies either to help cut through, or clash less with, the mix. At the same time, an excess of audio effects can easily make your mix muddy, cluttered, or just plain terrible. The key is to use your ears and become used to comparing (A/B–ing) your mix with and without effects. In the fol-lowing sections we will look at the particulars of Live's own brand of effects and a few select VST effects, and we'll learn how to search out new sounds for your Live compositions.

Using audio effects

In Live, audio effects come in two flavours: Ableton's own integrated effects, and any VST plug-ins that you have installed on your computer (see the 'VST Effects' section later in this chapter). Upon installing Live on your hard drive, the only effects you will be able to use initially are Ableton's included 13 effects. If you have already downloaded some VST plug-ins for use in other applications such as Steinberg's Cubase, or Emagic's Logic Audio, you will need to tell Live. The fol-lowing steps cover the basic working methods for adding, moving, and deleting effects in your Ableton Live Set (Song).

1 Determine which audio channel or send track that you want to add the effect to, and click (highlight) that track/send. This can be done in either Session or Arranger View.
2 Insert the effect you would like to add by either dragging the effect from the Live Effects Chooser tab of Live's Browser (shown in Figure 8.1) to the Track Title Bar of the desired track/send or by simply double-clicking on the effect once you have highlighted the track.

3 If you are adding more than one effect, repeat. You can add as many effects as you like to any track so long as your computer can withstand the processor demands of the sum of plug-ins.

4 The order in which the effects are applied – the signal chain – which appears in Live's title bar, shown in Figure 8.2, can be reconfigured any time by simply click-dragging the effect to a new position. All parameter settings on the newly positioned effect will remain the same.

5 To delete a plug-in, click on (highlight) the plug-in you would like to discard and press the Delete key. If you accidentally delete an effect, you can always Undo by selecting Edit > Undo or keyboard shortcut Ctrl (Cmnd) + Z.

Figure 8.1
The Ableton Live Effects Chooser section of the Browser.

Figure 8.2
Effects can be reordered in any way you like. Simply click and drag to the new position.

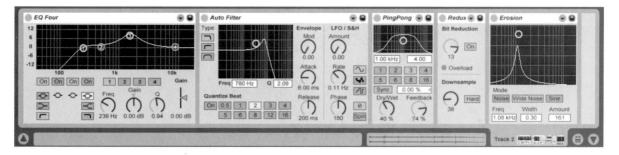

Once you have added an effect, you are free to begin working with each effect's unique set of parameters. Notice that topping each effect is the Effect Title Bar pictured in the Figure 8.3.

Each effect, including VST effects discussed later in the chapter, will have roughly the same controls. The green on-style button, dubbed the Effect Activator, is the on/off button for the effect. This can also be thought of as a traditional 'bypass' switch found on most analog and software effects. Moving to the right, you will also see the effect's title, such as EQ Four or Compressor, and then the Recall Preset, and Save/Delete Preset buttons on the far right side of the bar. For more on recalling, saving, and deleting presets, see the next section.

Figure 8.3
The Effect Title Bar.

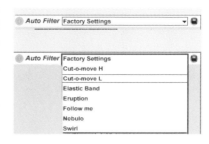

Using effects presets

Since each effect in Live can be tweaked in a number of different ways, with several separate virtual knobs, sliders, and parameters, you will find it helpful to know that Live 2 now allows you to save and retrieve effects settings (called presets). As you manipulate a given effect, you may discover a particularly useful configuration or sound that you want to use in another song or even in the same song on

Info

Effects presets

An effect preset is a defined set of parameters for a given audio effect. To view/select a preset, press the triangle on the Effect Title Bar and select the desired preset. Presets can be modified and saved using the Save/Delete Presets disc icon. Live's included presets are *called factory settings*, and are found in the top half of the Recall Presets menu. All user presets will be seen in the lower half.

Tip

On a scroll

Try quickly scrolling between presets by selecting the preset and then scrolling via the up and down arrows on your keyboard. This can be a quick time-saving tip or creative trick when in playback mode – and is quite powerful if you have a nice cache of presets from which to choose.

another track; the ability to save and recall effects settings makes such re-use of favourite effects simple. What's more, Ableton has supplied you with several practical and very usable factory presets.

To use a preset on a given effect, simply click on the Recall Preset downward-pointing arrow/triangle. The number of available options will vary with each effect, but there is no consequence to clicking around and trying them all. These factory presets serve as a template or guide to getting a specific type of sound out of an effect.

To save the current preset you are working with, click on the Save/Delete preset (disc-shaped icon) and you will see the menu shown in Figure 8.4. Give the preset a name that will remind you what sort of sound and application the preset was designed for. Then press Save, and Close. You can also save over a pre-existing preset if you choose.

Figure 8.4
The Save Preset menu.

Info

The name game

Non-descriptive names will simply waste your time. Some examples of more useful, descriptive names might be Squashed Drums for a tough quick compressor, Bass Erase for a hi-pass EQ Four, or Long Large Room for a washy and gradually decaying reverb.

Any saved presets can be recalled in any Ableton Live Set/Song file (ALS) on the same machine. The default file folders that the presets are saved to are as follows:

- Mac OS 9 – System folder: Application Support > Ableton > Live X.X (version number)
- Mac OS X – Home > Library > Application Support > Ableton > Live X.X (version number)
- Windows – Programs / Ableton / Live X.X (version number)

If you are backing up your system or migrating to another machine, it is a good idea to copy the folder that contains all of your presets. Or if you decide you would like to start fresh, you can delete this folder with no consequences.

To delete an individual user-created preset, click on the Save/Delete preset (disc-shaped icon) in the Effect title bar, choose the preset you would like to delete, and press the Delete button – then press Close.

Effects sends

As we discussed in Chapter 3, 'Live Interface Basics', effects sends are an excellent way to apply the same effects across several channels. In case you're skipping around, and you haven't seen Chapter 3 yet, I should inform you that Sends, or Aux Sends, function as separate, concealable, tracks/channels in Live that cannot house audio, but can contain effects. In Live, you can have up to four effects or aux sends in any given project. To add one, press Ctrl (Cmnd) + Alt (Option) + T – or select Edit > Insert Send Track.

Routing can work in a few different ways depending on what kind of sound and configuration you are going for. Each of the following methods has its benefits.

- Track Send: By click dragging (vertically) on any track's Send knob, you can adjust the amount of that track's contribution to the send. You will still hear the original track with the same volume and panning settings applied; however, you will also hear more of the track because you have additionally routed it to one or more send channels (one in this instance). This is a good method for adding and sharing gradual (some may say tasteful) portions of a plug-ins sonic modification.
- Pre- or Post-fader: To route audio directly to the sends, regardless of the individual track's volume fader settings, click on the Master Channel buttons labelled Post so that they read Pre (as shown in Figure 8.5). Pre-fader means that all audio sending to this aux send will be heard immediately at the designated volume, and is done when you do not want to hear any of the original (unaffected) sound, but still want to use the Send (to share effects). For instance, you might run both tracks of a 'doubled vocal' to a Send Pre-fader to take advantage of the same (and single) instance of a group of effects.

Figure 8.5
The Pre-/Post-fader switch.

In Figure 8.6a, notice that the volume (fader) on the channel is all the way down, yet the Send to the Auxiliary Channel is at 3 o'clock. By contrast, setting your aux send to Post-fader will make all audio heard on the sends proportionate to the fader level and the aux send level. To compare, the screenshot in Figure 8.6b shows the volume fader *and* the send level must be at a positive level.

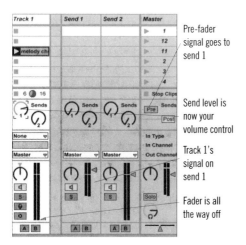

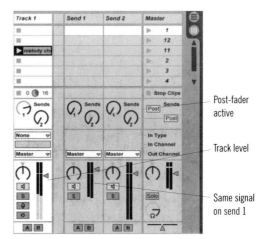

Figure 8.6a (left)
All sound heard on this channel will be heard in the aux send even though the fader is all the way off.

Figure 8.6b (right)
Sound on this channel will be heard twice. Once unaffected on the channel, and a second time with effects (on the aux send).

- **Route to sends only**: You can route any track directly to the sends by selecting Sends Only in the track's Output dropdown menu. This option forces the original track's output to be relegated directly to the sends (at whatever level is designated by the track's sends settings). This is a good option for those looking for a 'wetter' sound and still wanting to take advantage of the benefits of

Info

Auxiliary power

Aux Sends are great for conserving processor power or using the same effect across multiple samples, loops, and tracks; however, if you are looking for a more extreme or specifically applied effect sound, you may be better off reverting to Plan A and inserting the plug-in into the track. For instance, if you want to hear the sound 100 percent wet (without any of the original dry sound), insert the plug-in onto the track and crank the dial to wet.

using a send. Note: if you have not routed any audio to the sends (via the track's Send Level knobs), you will not hear the track.

Channel effects

Up to now we have examined how effects may be managed and routed in Live. The remainder of this chapter will be devoted to the actual ins and outs of the Live 2 effects (and plug-ins), which have been grouped into four separate categories: Channel Effects, Delay Effects, Filter & Distortion Effects, and VST Effects.

The first three effects, EQ Four, Compressor, and Gate are classified as channel effects, since they are nearly always applied at the track level as channel inserts typified by professional audio recording studios.

EQ four

A parametric EQ is a powerful frequency filtering and timbre-shaping tool. While most hardware and software mixers usually have some kind of equalization located separately on each track (channel), in Live you will need to add an EQ Four plug-in to either the track or an Aux Send.

Live's EQ Four features four adjustable bands of EQ represented by the green-illuminated 1, 2, 3, and 4 buttons in the middle region of the plug-in pictured in Figure 8.7. The goal when using an EQ is to either boost or diminish certain audio frequencies, or a range (bandwidth) of frequencies, within a given sound. These are often referred to as lows, mids, and highs or other subdivisions such as low-mids or high-mids, for example. High frequencies are found in the register we call treble, while low frequencies relate to the bass. Low-mids, mids, or high-mids make up the middle section (from left to right) of the sonic spectrum. With EQ Four's separate and selectable multiple bands, you will be able to adjust each of the frequencies in the audio spectrum.

Figure 8.7
Here is Live's powerful if unassuming EQ Four.

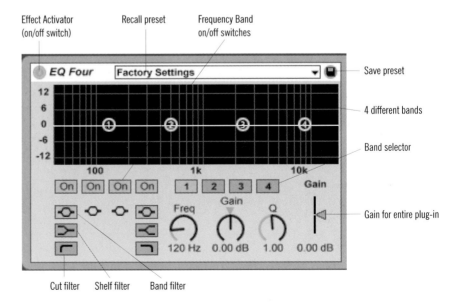

Many engineers like to *shape* or *carve* a sound's frequencies in a particular way for each song (or mix of a song). For instance, if the meat of a sound is in the bass, such as a bass guitar/synth, the track's highs and even high-mids may be uncomplimentary to the track. In other words, you may want to save the tracks high frequency for your singer's lovely voice, or your drummer's hi-hat.

Another frequency-shaping example would be to *shave* the mids and lows off of a crash cymbal sample (primarily a high frequency sound), so that no extraneous noise, such as mic rumble, is heard. Therefore, some engineers may choose to *roll off* (eliminate) the lower frequencies. While Live's EQ may not be perfect for all jobs, it will cover most basic functions.

With EQ Four, each band specializes in treating certain audio frequencies by applying particular grades of slope (called curves). Bands one and four provide the option of using one of three different curves: bell, shelf, or cut. Filter bands two and three are simpler in that they can only be bell curves.

A *bell curve* is a parabolic-shaped boost or cut of a given range of frequencies (see Figure 8.8). To change the grade of the slope, use the Q setting. To change the height or depth (the boost or the cut) alter EQ Four's gain setting.

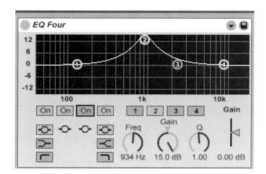

Figure 8.8
This bell curve demonstrates a swell of the high-mid frequencies.

A low-shelf or high-shelf, possible with bands 1 and 4, respectively, will cut or boost lower or higher frequency ranges. Figures 8.9a and 8.9b show an example of a low- and high-shelf curve.

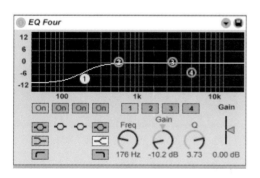
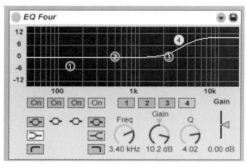

Figure 8.9a (left)
A low-shelf curve.

Figure 8.9b (right)
A high-shelf curve.

As mentioned, you can zero in on specific frequencies by altering Four EQ's Q setting. Figure 8.10 shows a steeper, more acute frequency cut, accomplished by increasing the Q.

Figure 8.10
Notice the steep V-shaped cut in this
instance of EQ Four.

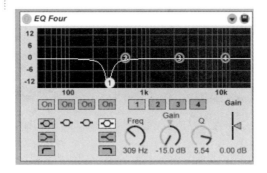

Now, in Figure 8.11, we will try a softer, more mellow/subtle bell curve by selecting a lower Q setting.

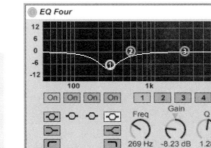

Figure 8.11
A more gradual, and therefore smaller, curve
due to a lower Q setting.

Tip

Gain

While boosting and cutting various frequencies, you may notice that the overall volume has changed. Try raising or lowering the Gain slider on the right side of EQ Four. Be careful to make sure there is no distortion.

Info

Double time

For more drastic cuts, boosts, and effects, try assigning the same parameters to two or more filters, or use more than one EQ Four on the same effect.

Tip

Power miser

Ableton suggests that you turn off any unused EQ bands to save CPU (processing) power. To do this, simply disengage (click) the On/Off button corresponding to the band not in use. For example, the first band is the first On button, the second band the second, and so on.

Filters two and three are always bell curves. Filter four can switch among bell curve, high-shelf (boosts or cuts frequencies higher than the specified frequency), or modes. Each filter band can be turned on or off independently.

To edit the filter curve, click and drag on one of the filter dots in the XY view. Horizontal movement changes the filter frequency, while vertical movement adjusts the filter band's gain. To adjust the filter Q (also called resonance or bandwidth), hold down the Alt (PC)/Option (Mac) modifier while dragging the mouse. You can also use the numbered filter selector buttons to select a band for editing, then edit parameter values with the Freq, Gain, and Q dials (and/or type values into the number fields below each dial).

Compression

One of the most popular methods for mix-boosting is to add compression. A compressor allows you to reduce (squeeze) the gain of an audio signal by a user-configurable amount, beyond a certain cutoff point (again, user-configurable) called the threshold. If this sounds familiar, it's because we touched on using Live's compressor as a mastering tool in the last chapter. Mastering engineers often apply a compressor to the whole mix (on the master track/outputs). Compression can also work wonders on individual tracks, especially if you are looking to add volume, punch, and clarity to your mix. Skillfully tweaked compression can help quell spikes, or sudden peaks, in a sample so that the quieter portion of the sound can be comfortably elevated. Acoustic drum tracks are one of the most popular applications for compression, as are vocals and solo instruments such as guitars and horns. Figure 8.12 shows Live 2's compressor.

To apply compression to your mix, you will want to determine at what gain level (threshold) you would like the compressor to start working. The Threshold slider, Gain Reduction (G.R.) meter, and plug-in Output are the three meters that respectively help you to configure the gain level at which the compression will begin, how much gain is being lopped off of your original audio, and the overall output of the plug-in. Before we talk about how to use these three controls/meters, let's take a look at the ratio control.

The compressor's Ratio control determines the amount of compression. For instance, 2 to 1 compression means that for every dB over the threshold, only $^1/_2$ dB will actually be output. 4 to 1 would mean that for each dB, only $^1/_4$ of a dB would be output. In summary, the larger the numerator, the smaller the output per dB. You may also notice that for larger ratio settings, the sound may become muffled or muted-sounding as a result of the volume-squashing that is going on. As you dial in your compression for a given track, you will want to watch the downward-spiking red indicator on the Gain Reduction meter. Extreme gain reduction, such as –12 dB and below, will often cut the life out of your sample – although you may occasionally want to over-compress an instrument as a special effect.

The compressor's other two controls, attack and release, determine how soon after a sound crosses the threshold the plug-in begins to work, and how long the compression remains active after it has been engaged. Ableton's manual recommends that using a small amount of attack time (5-10 milliseconds) is best for retaining some sense of dynamics (varying degrees of loud and soft in the music). Short attacks are great for instruments like drums and percussion, as well as vocals. Longer attacks are most often used with horns, bass, and longer sorts of sounds where the volume increase (crescendo) is also slower.

In contrast, a compressor's release settings are often better (less noticeable) when long. Basically, a long release time means that the compression continues to work for a given length of time (in milliseconds) after it has been engaged and the signal level has dipped back below the threshold. Typically, a short release time will force the compressor to repeatedly engage and disengage (start and stop), and a listener would be more apt to hear the repeated contrast. I will add that short release times can be a cool sounding effect on drums and diced up pieces of audio (where the signal repeatedly crosses the threshold).

Gate

Gates work complementarily (and often alongside) with compression, and therefore the two are often discussed together. Where compressors focus on reducing volume spikes above a certain threshold, Gates help weed out low-level noise beneath a certain threshold. The result of using a Gate is usually a cleaner, less cluttered, and overall more pleasing audio signal. Gates are a natural for reducing quiet hums, microphone bleed, and background noise (like your singer yelling for you to turn up his headphones). That said, Live 2.0's newly added Gate plug-in is an excellent utility for this kind of work.

Specifically, a Gate operates just like it sounds. Certain audio can make it through the Gate while other audio cannot. The threshold, or minimum requirement, to get through an audio gating effect is set by volume. Any sound quieter

Figure 8.12
Live 2's compressor plug-in.

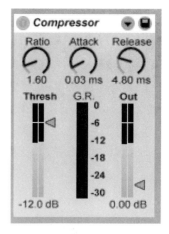

Figure
8.13
Live's Gate
effect.

Info

Noise floor

Often, when microphones record an instrument or an amplifier, there can be a sound beneath the sound, which audio engineers often refer to as a *noise floor*. This may be a rumble or amp buzz, or even a singer taking shallow breaths in between phrases. Gating out this low level, but annoying noise can add clarity and presence to your mix. To lower the Gate's floor setting, drag up or down on the little white box (default setting is −40.0dB) above the threshold setting. By reducing the Gate's noise floor, you can maximize the Gate's effectiveness. By raising the floor towards 0dB, you will allow more of the low-level noise to seep into your mix. Floor can range from 0dB to negative infinity (−INF).

than the threshold won't be heard at all. Gating can be an excellent effect to apply when attempting to eliminate excess noise, hiss, hum, or undesirable reverb decay. You may find that a slight Gate can really clean up your drum loops. Many producers use Gate on drums like toms or snares so that they can capture the essence of the instrument at its highest volume point (and eliminate all weaker background sounds). Other producers will use just a touch of Gate to clean up a noisy track. Figure 8.13 shows Live's Gate effect.

The small triangle next to the Threshold bar can be dragged with the mouse to set the minimum level of output (required to pass through the Gate). The lower the threshold, the more sound gets through the Gate. As sound passes through the Gate, you will see the small circular LED light flicker.

The Attack, Hold, and Release settings determine how the Gate is applied. For instance, a sharp/short attack will make for a harsher Gate effect, sometimes resulting in harsh audible clicks. The shorter the Gate, the quicker it will be applied once the level exceeds the threshold. A longer attack will sound more relaxed, as the Gate takes longer to close on sound crossing the volume threshold.

Similarly, the Hold and Release functions affect how long the Gate remains open. Think of Attack as how quickly the Gate will open and Release and Hold as relating to how quickly the Gate will close. A common Live trick is to tamper with the Hold and Release settings once a Gate is activating most of the time. Here is how to do this.

1 Load a loop into a Clip or Track, and then play to create audio.
2 Add a Gate by click-dragging Gate from Live's Effects to the Track/Clip you are working on.
3 Hit Spacebar or launch the loop via the Clip Launch Button.
4 Adjust Gate's Threshold to just above the loop's average volume registered in the vertical signal level section. Leave the floor at −40.0dB.
5 Turn the Attack down to .04 for a quick acting Gate.
6 Turn the Hold down to 1.00 ms (millisecond).
7 Turn the Release down to 10ms.
8 You should hear a choppy loop. Audio should be cutting in and out. If it is still playing all the way through, raise the threshold. If you are hearing no sound or not enough sound, lower the threshold just a bit.
9 Gradually increase the Hold or Attack.
10 Bonus Step: Map the Hold to a MIDI-Control Knob and try adding various amounts of sustain to the Gate.

Delay effects

Ableton's delay effects group may just be their most creative. Each effect features solid tools for both assembling new rhythmic variations and creating innovative textures with repeated long sounds. While many of the delays have similar Feedback, Lowpass/Highpass filtering, and Dry/Wet controls, each delay is also somewhat of a specialist that features one or two particular kinds of controls. As we explore them one by one, don't be afraid to do lots of experimenting and get lost in your own creativity.

Simple delay

While you may think we are starting simple, Live's Simple Delay (seen in Figure 8.14) is still a formidable stereo, tempo synch-able delay, with a rhythmic beat division chooser.

Looking at the plug-in, we see two separate beat division choosers – one for the left channel and one for the right. If you are in Sync mode – where the small synch box is illuminated in green – each boxed number represents a multiple of the six-teenth-note delay time. For instance, choosing a 4 would mean a four sixteenth-note delay, or a full 1/4-note hold before you would hear the delayed note sound. An 8 would be two beats, and 16 would be four beats – typically an entire measure. In either of the beat-division-choosers, you can choose from 1, 2, 3, 4, 5, 6, 8, and 16 times sixteenth-note delay times.

As mentioned, this beat dividing works only if the green Sync button is depressed for that channel (R or L). Sync means that the delay is set to synchronize with the song tempo (beats per minute). If you disengage the Sync, you can manually set up the delay time up to $1/100$ of a second by click-dragging (up or down) on the time field box. Note: you may also click-drag the time field box with sync engaged, but note the percentage (%) indicator. This means that you are slowing or speeding up the delay below or above the current project tempo (that you are synchronized to). In other words, you can add a little slop, or even approximate a triplet, if your delays are sounding too strict.

The Dry/Wet knob determines how much of the effect versus original sound you hear. *Dry* is the term audio engineers use to refer to the original sound, while *Wet* is the delayed or affected sound. A setting of 12 o'clock (or 50 percent) for Dry/Wet will create a delay signal that is at the same volume as the original. A 100 percent Wet setting means that you will no longer hear the original sound, and will hear only the delay effect.

If Dry/Wet controls the volume of the delay, Feedback controls the intensity. By increasing the percentage of Feedback, you raise the effect's signal output to its own input, in sort of a rerouting to continue the delay's effect. The circular signal created by feedback will radically shape the delay, from flanging disharmonic swells (small percentage of feedback) to a wild echo chamber potentially spiraling out of control (with large amounts of feedback). If your delay does get out of control, reduce the feedback below 80 percent or less. For example, 100 percent feedback will deliver an unbelievable noise – or perhaps a cool effect?

Ping pong delay

Like a game of Ping Pong, Ableton's Ping Pong Delay (pictured in Figure 8.15) plays a game of stereo tennis with your sound by serving it up from left to right. In looking at this plug-in, you may notice that many of the controls are similar to the Simple Delay covered earlier. Like Simple Delay, Ping Pong Delay is a stereo delay with built-in tempo synchronizing ability and sports the same delay-time beat-division chooser boxes, as well as the same Dry/Wet and Feedback controls. However, Ping Pong Delay is a little more creative in terms of what frequencies actually get delayed (repeated). You will find both a low- and a highpass filter, complete with an adjustable XY controller axis to adjust both the frequencies and the width of the frequency band (the Q). You can select between 50 Hz and 18 kHz and a selectable Q of .5 to 9 dB.

Figure 8.14
Live's Simple Delay plug-in.

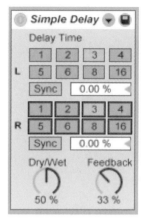

Info

Delay relay

By setting extremely short delay times (less than 30 milliseconds with the sync off), you can create some wild thickening, phasing, and metallic-sounding results. Try setting both times to 1, 10, and then 30 milliseconds, with the Dry/Wet set 30 percent and Feedback set to 70 percent, to hear what I am talking about. Although these effects may not result in a lingering discernable delay, these flaming, buzzing, and biting sounds can be a creative playground.

Tip

All wet

When effects plug-ins are located in one of the sends channels, it is generally a good idea to set the effect Wet/Dry setting to 100 percent wet. Since the original source sound is likely still being heard through Live's mixer, there is no need to route this signal again through a send.

Figure 8.15
Live's Ping Pong Delay bounces signal from
left to right.

Notice that the same Sync and delay time boxes are also present in Ping Pong Delay. When Sync is activated, Ping Pong Delay will rhythmically synchronize your audio delays, from left to right, according to your beat-division chooser. Once you deactivate the Sync, you can set the delay time manually from 1 to 200 milliseconds.

Grain delay

Grain Delay is among Live's more complex, and therefore more creative, plug-ins. The basic concept is that Grain Delay dissects audio by frequency into tiny grains, staggers the delay timing of these grains, and then opens up a toolbox full of pitch, randomized pitch, and spread (called spray) controls for some far out sound design results. While you will again see several of the same controls, like Wet/Dry, Sync, and the beat-division chooser, the lion's share of the Grain Delay interface (seen in Figure 8.16) also boasts a large parameter-assignable XY controller.

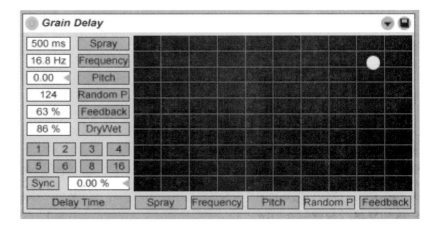

Figure 8.16
Live's Grain Delay takes audio apart, and
randomly reassigns the pitch, before
replaying the sound.

With Grain Delay's XY interface, you can quickly control two parameters of your choosing (one for X and one for Y), to allow for some wild interaction. Make sure you choose two different modifiers to achieve the maximum tweak factor. Hint: I like to use Feedback on one axis, and then choose either Random P(itch), Pitch, or Frequency on the other.

Spray

The spray parameter roughs up the average delay (like those in Ping Pong and Simple Delay plug-ins) and adds noise and garble to your signal. How the actual granular redistribution works is a little foggy, but the creative impact can be delightful. The delay time range for spray can range from 0 to 500 milliseconds. Small values tend to create a more muddy sounding delay effect, while a larger spray delay completely takes apart the original signal. The Live manual jokes that, 'this (higher setting) is the recommended setting for anarchists'.

Frequency

In Ableton's Grain Delay, small granules of sound are quickly dispersed. The frequency setting determines the size and duration of each granule that will be subsequently delayed, and can range from 1 to 150 Hz. While Ableton has yet to divulge their secret method behind the frequency setting, I can tell you that the closer this number is to 150, the more genuine the delay. Low settings sound like drunk approximations of the original sound if they resemble it at all. If you are having trouble getting a desirable setting out of the Grain Delay, set the frequency to 150 and work backwards from there.

Pitch vs. random pitch

Like the spray parameter, random pitch tends to throw sound around. The amount of randomness can range from 0 to 161 in terms of intensity (0 being none). The plain old Pitch parameter ranges from 12 to −36 half steps, while allowing for two-decimal point interim values. In other words, fine tuning a delayed signal's pitch to an actual, discernable tone would be best suited for the Pitch control, and trying to eliminate, destroy, or add movement to a pitched signal is the strength of high Random Pitch values. You can use both Pitch and Random Pitch in tandem for some robotic and wild pitch modifications.

Putting grain delay to use

Now that you get some idea of just what kind of mischief the Grain Delay is up to, let's get familiar with using Grain Delay's XY interface.

Along the X (horizontal) interface, lining the bottom portion of the plug-in, you will see the boxes for Delay Time, Spray, Frequency, Pitch, Random Pitch, and Feedback. The vertical Y-axis can be set to control Spray, Frequency, Pitch, Random Pitch, Feedback, and Dry/Wet controls. Each parameter's current value will be displayed in the respective boxes on the left hand side of the plug-in irregardless of which axis is set to adjust them.

Any parameters set to correspond to X or Y can be controlled by moving the yellow circle. Vertical moves affect the Y-axis, while horizontal moves alter the X-axis. Exactly which parameters you control are up to you. To set Feedback to be controlled by the Y-axis, simply click on the vertically aligned box labelled Feedback just above the Dry/Wet setting. To enable the X-axis to control the Delay Time (in terms of beat-division), click on the delay time box while Sync is activated. To control actual delay time, disengage (click on) the Sync button and you can set the delay from 1 to 128 milliseconds.

Filter delay

Last but not least of Live's delay group of effects is the powerful Filter Delay. This effect is actually three delays in one, one stereo delay and two mono delays – one on each stereo channel. Individual delays can be toggled on/off via the L, L+R, and R boxes on the far left, seen in Figure 8.17. Similarly, each high and lowpass filter can also be switched on/off via the green box labelled on (default setting) in the upper left-hand corner next to the XY-controllers.

Filter Delay's XY-controllers work in the exact same way as the Ping Pong Delay described earlier. The Y-axis determines the bandwidth (Q), while the X-axis shifts the frequency. Each delay also features its own beat-division chooser with tempo-synch-able delay times.

On the right-hand side of the plug-in you will see Feedback, Pan, and Volume controls specific to each delay. Each feedback control will reroute the delayed signal back though that delay's input (just like all Live Delays). Interestingly, each

Figure 8.17
Live's Filter Delay.

Frequency
Bandwidth

Three XY-controllers for filtering your
delayed sound

Dry level for
entire plug-in

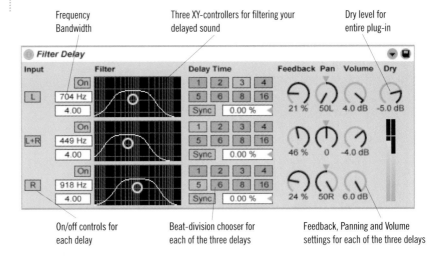

On/off controls for
each delay

Beat-division chooser for
each of the three delays

Feedback, Panning and Volume
settings for each of the three delays

Tip

Delay relay

By automating any of the delay
effects XY-controllers to move over
time, you can create some incredible
sounding delay effects. For more on
this, see the section called 'Automating
Effects' at the end of this Chapter.

delay's panning settings will override their original predisposed location. For
instance, if you pan the L delay (top delay) to the right side (with the top panning
knob), you will hear it on the right. Volume controls the wet signal or delayed signal for each delay. And finally, a lone Dry control knob is located in the upper right-
hand corner. For a 100 percent wet signal, turn the dry setting to zero.

Reverb

Reverberation occurs when sound bounces off of a surface, usually many surfaces,
several times. In the process of reflecting, the original sound dissipates, becoming
diffuse and muddy and eventually disappearing altogether. Depending upon the
shape and reflective qualities of the room, various frequencies will be more pronounced than others in the reverberated sound or, *tail*.

While Ableton's Reverb plug-in, added in version 1.5, may not be a full-fledged
delay, it is certainly from the same echo-related family. The number of controls may
seem daunting, but as we step carefully through the signal path, you will see that
each knob and XY controller is there only for your benefit. Before we get too deep,
take a quick look at Figure 8.18.

Figure 8.18
Live's feature-laden
Reverb plug-in.

Low and High Cut filtering for
your original sound

Five separate sections in Reverb's signal chain

Controls mix of dry and
wet source sound

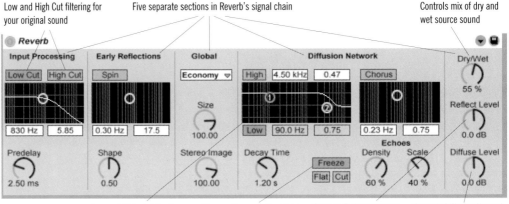

Low and High shelving for
your diffused sound

Freeze allows you to analyze
your reverberated sound

Controls Early Reflections
level in main output

Controls Diffusion Network
level in main output

Input processing

The first link in Reverb's signal chain is the Input Processing section. Here you have on/off selectable Low and High Cut filtering as well as a Predelay control. The Low Cut and High Cut XY interface allows you to trim your input's frequencies before they are reverberated. Similar to Live's other delays, the horizontal X-axis shifts the frequency of the cut (50 Hz to 18 kHz), while the vertical Y-axis changes the bandwidth (.50 to 9.0). You can also turn each filter off by deselecting its green illuminated box. I recommend spending some time playing with this filter each time you use this plug-in. Think of these filters as altering the acoustic characteristics of a room. For instance, a concrete room may not reproduce low frequencies as well as an acoustically engineered studio room. Each room will favor completely different frequencies.

Also, check out the Predelay control for adding milliseconds of time before you hear the first *early reflections*, or delayed sound, of the forthcoming reverberation. While the predelay can range from .50 to 250 milliseconds, to simulate a normal sounding room, it is best below 25 milliseconds. For large cannons, go long, baby.

Early reflections

Early reflections are the first reverberations heard after the initial sound bounces off the walls, floor, or ceiling of the room – yet they arrive ahead of the full reflection, or tail. At times, they sound like slapback delays, or mushy portions of the whole reverberated (diffused) sound. The Reverb plug-in houses two early reflection controls: Shape and Spin. Spin's XY interface controls, depth (y-axis) and frequency (x-axis), apply a subtle modulation to early reflections. Results may range from shimmering highs to whirligig panning flourishes. For quicker decay of early reflections, try increasing the Shape control gradually towards 1.00. Lower values will blend more smoothly with the normal reverb diffusion.

Global settings

In Reverb's global settings section, you can select the quality level of the Reverb: Economy(default), Comfort, or First Class. The three settings will demand small, moderate, and large processor power, respectively. You may also determine the apparent volume of the room via the Size (of the imaginary room) control, which ranges from .22 (small/quiet) to 500 (large/loud). A Stereo Image control allows you to select from 0 to 120 degrees of stereo spread in the reverberation. Higher values will be more spread out, while lower ones approach a mono sound.

Diffusion network

The Diffusion Network is by far the most complex-looking area of the Reverb plug-in. These controls help put the final touches on the actual reverberation that follows closely behind the early reflections. From here you will be able to decorate and control the finer points of the reverberated sound. To begin with, high and low shelving filters can further define your imaginary room's sound. By shaving off the highs, for instance, your room may sound more like a concert hall or large auditorium, while brightening up the diffusion (raising the high shelf) will approximate a 'bathroom' reverb. Similar to XY interface controlled filters, each filter's X-axis determines frequency, while Y-axis controls bandwidth. Turning these filters off will conserve some system resources.

Beneath the high and low shelving controls, you will find the Reverb's Decay Time settings, which range from an extremely short 200 milliseconds to a cavernous 60-second – long tail. Long reverbs can make audio sound muddy and jumbled, so use with care.

To test the colouring and sonic quality of your reverb, you can use the Freeze control. Any time you press Freeze, Reverb will indefinitely hold and reproduce the diffusion tail. This held reverb can be a handy diagnostic tool for shaping your overall sound or a creative trick to make new sounds from a piece of reverb. Typically I will freeze the reverb when I am first setting it up and then stop all other loops and sounds. After analyzing the reverberated sound for a moment, I often tweak parameters to weed out extreme or obnoxious low or high frequencies, or change the Reverb's modulation.

When Flat is activated, the low- and highpass shelving filters will be ignored. In other words, your frozen reverb tail will contain all frequencies. An active Cut command prevents further audio from being frozen even if it is passing through the reverb. For instance, you may wish to analyze the tonality of your reverb tail. To do this, you play your audio through the reverb, then press Freeze, and then press Cut (to cut off future audio from snowballing into a wall of useless noise). Even if you stop playback, the frozen reverb sample will continue to play. While frozen, you can make adjustments to the diffusion network settings and more acutely decipher their impact. Try starting and stopping audio a few times to analyze the differences between your project's audio, and the reverberating audio. Is the reverb tail adding unwanted mud?

The second XY-interface in the Diffusion Network, labelled Chorus, can add subtle motion or wobbly effect to the overall reverb tail diffusion. When not in use, deactivate the Chorus button to save system resources and turn the Reverb's Chorus effect off.

The final section in Diffusion Network controls the density (thickness) and scale (coarseness) of the diffusion's echo. The Density control ranges from .1 percent (a lighter sounding reverb), to a 96 percent rich and chewy reverb, while Scale can run from 5 to 100 percent, gradually adding a darker and murkier quality to the diffusion. A high Density setting will diminish the amount of audible change made by Scale controls.

Output

The Output section is the final link in the Reverb signal chain. At this stage, just three knobs: Dry/Wet, Reflect Level, and Diffuse Level, put the finishing touches on your reverb preset masterpiece. Dry/Wet controls the ratio of original unaffected sound to affected reverberated sound that you hear coming from the plug-in's output. When using Reverb in one of Live's Aux Sends, I recommend using a 100 percent wet setting, as opposed to using Reverb on a track, where settings between 10 and 45 percent sound more natural.

The Reflect Level control knob adjusts the amplitude (level) of the early reflections specified in the Early Reflections box from –30 to +6 dB. The louder you make the early reflections, the more you will hear an echo of the true sound (which will sound even more like a slapback delay as opposed to a reverb.

In similar fashion, the Diffuse Level controls the amount of diffusion network level in the final Reverb output. A low diffusion level will diminish the tail of the reverb, while a high amplitude of diffusion network will increase the presence of reverb in your mix.

Filter and distortion effects

This brings us to the third and final group of Ableton's effect plug-ins: the filter and distortion effects. I should point out that the Chorus effect is actually a super fast delay, but is often used as a special, tone enhancing effect, so it landed here. The next two plug-ins, Erosion and Auto Filter, are (in my opinion) the Live effects best suited for live performance. The last two plug-ins, Vinyl Distortion and Redux are designed to take apart your sound in some interesting ways. While each of these effects can quickly and drastically alter your audio content, taking time to learn the ins and outs of these babies can take your mix to a whole new level.

Chorus

The idea behind using a chorus effect is to create a phasing, flanging, or out of tune sonic-blurriness that results in a thicker and richer overall sound. In other words, chorus effects assume that two sounds are better than one. It is common to run synthesizers, guitars, vocals, and strings through a chorus. The doubling, or even tripling, effect of a chorus makes solo voices sound more powerful, take up more space in a mix, and therefore sound more present.

Live's Chorus (Figure 8.19) features two parallel delays that can be set for .01 to 20 millisecond delays or linked by activating a teeny tiny equal sign (=) shown in Figure 8.19.

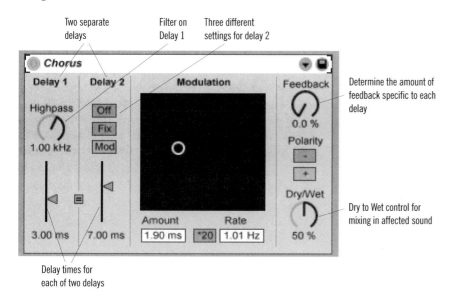

Figure 8.19
Live's Chorus effect. Note the tiny equal sign (=) sign between the two delays. This button syncs the two delays.

Delay 1

Ableton Live's first delay will always be active when the chorus is on, and really sets the tone for the rest of the Chorus' parameters. To adjust the delay's timing, vertically slide the fader. The adjustable Highpass-filter knob allows you to bypass chorusing low frequencies, which can often become muddier and less defined when doubled. The definable range is 20 Hz to 15 kHz. Delay 1 can be used on its own, in conjunction with Delay 2, or in parallel with Delay 2. If you want to link the delay time for Delay 1 and Delay 2, simply click on the equal sign (=) on the thin vertical line between the two delay faders.

Delay 2

Chorus' Delay 2 can add even more thickness and intensity to your sounds. Delay 2 can run in two separate modes, Fix and Mod, and can be bypassed by selecting the top visible button labelled Off. Fix mode will force Delay 2 to act only as a delay, while letting Delay 1's signal be modulated. In other words, Delay 2 will affect only the primary signal so that if Delay 1's signal is heavily modulated, you will still have some sense of the original sound's characteristic. The Mod (modulation) mode will route Delay 2 through the same modulation as Delay 1.

Modulation

The most creative aspect of Live's Chorus plug-in is its modulation. Whether you are going for completely unrecognizable new sounds, or just looking for a little more stereo-spread, you will want to spend some time fiddling (click-dragging) with the Modulation XY-axis. Horizontal moves the modulation rate from .03 to 10 Hz, while the vertical axis shifts the amount of modulation from zero to 6.5 milliseconds. You also have the option of typing in values by simply clicking on the box, typing a number within the allotted range, and pressing the Enter key.

If you are looking for radical sonic redesign, the *20 button multiplies the chorus' modulation effect by 20. While this may not sound great all of the time, the *20 multiplier will push the envelope of the dullest of sounds.

Feedback, polarity, and dry/wet

For increased intensity, the Feedback control will re-route the signal through the delays. The more feedback you elect to add, the more robotic and metallic your sounds will become. The positive and negative polarity switch affects the direction of sound moving through the Chorus effect. To hear the greatest contrast between the two polarities, you should use short delay times, and increase the Chorus Feedback. The results are often frequency and pitch related; a low frequency sound becomes a high frequency sound, a pitch may shift by as much as an octave, and so forth. Finally, the Dry/Wet control determines the amount of original versus chorused signal going to output.

Erosion

Similar to the concepts of subtractive-synthesis and frequency filtering, deconstructing a sound can also be a creative endeavour. Live's Erosion effect is Ableton's most unique plug-in in this regard. Erosion gives you three possible methods for sonic degradation. You can choose from Noise, Wide Noise, and Sine by selecting one of the three buttons beneath the XY field interface as pictured in Figure 8.20.

Depending upon which mode you currently have active, Erosion will use one of three different sounds (one of two filtered noises or a sine wave) to modulate the sound. Noise, Wide Noise, and Sine all have different characteristics, so you will want to experiment switching between the three.

To control the degree of Erosion's effect on a sound, move the Y-axis (vertically) to change the amount or level of additional sound. Horizontal moves along the X-axis allow you to control the frequency that you are affecting. To change the Width with the XY interface, click Alt + (option), click on the yellow dot,

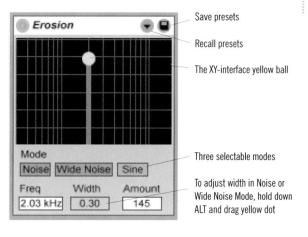

Save presets

Recall presets

The XY-interface yellow ball

Three selectable modes

To adjust width in Noise or Wide Noise Mode, hold down ALT and drag yellow dot

Figure 8.20
Live's Erosion Plug-in. Erosion's screen is primarily taken up by its unusual XY field.

and move the mouse forward and backward. You can also drag any control vertically, or manually type in a value in Freq, Width, and Amount.

Auto filter

Quite possibly Live's greatest live performance effect, Auto Filter (seen in Figure 8.21) is a virtual analog-style filter with three selectable classic filter-types (highpass, lowpass, and bandpass). Each of these can be controlled via the effect's XY-controller and modulated by either envelope, rhythmic quantization, and any of three different LFOs. As you may have gleaned from the EQ Four explanation, suppressing certain frequencies allows you to carve out specific problem or overdone frequencies – so your mixes sound more professional.

Three Filter types (top to bottom)
Low Pass, High Pass, Band Pass

LFO or Sample and
Hold amount

Figure 8.21
Live's Auto Filter Plug-in in version 2.0.3. A band reject/notch filter may be coming in a future Live update.

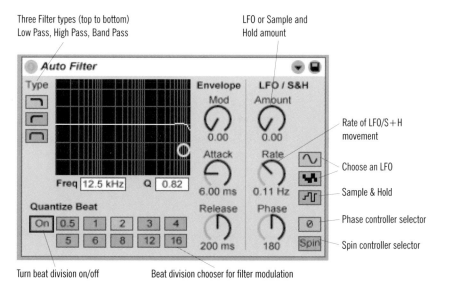

Rate of LFO/S + H movement

Choose an LFO

Sample & Hold

Phase controller selector

Spin controller selector

Turn beat division on/off   Beat division chooser for filter modulation

A common DJ trick is to mix two beat-matched songs, one with a lowpass filter, and the second with highpass filter (one on each turntable). The result is more than simply mixing two songs, but the creation of an entirely new song made from the

Tip

Filter frenzy

Lowpass, highpass, bandpass...
what does it all mean?

Lowpass simply means that the low
frequencies pass through the filter, but
nothing else. For instance, your bass
guitar and kick drums will be heard, if
a little dulled out from the lack of
highs. Some sounds will be gone
completely. Conversely, a highpass
filter will allow shimmering cymbals
and sparkly guitars and synths, but
will suppress basses and any other
instruments in the lower frequency
range. How low is up to you. This is the
point of the effect. In fact, bandpass
was designed for specific frequency
selection. In other words, a bandpass
allows a certain frequency band to
pass through the filter. For even more
filter fun, see the section called
'Automating Effects' at the end of this
chapter.

combined frequencies (highs from one, lows from another) of the two. Without cutting the frequencies, the two songs would sound like a jumbled mush. Cutting the best frequencies does require some practice and will vary depending upon the musical content. If you are new to this concept, it can be a huge ear opener. See the following note called Filter Frenzy.

To get going with Live's Auto Filter, you will want to select a filter and then use the XY axis to dial in Frequency (X-axis), gain cut/boost, and Q (Y-axis). The frequency range for Auto Filter is strangely locked between 46.2 Hz and 15.5 kHz. The Q control (also called resonance) can range from .20 to 3.0 and will affect the volume of the filtered sound. I like to think of Q as the pitch of the curve, where low Q values will generate broader, less dynamic curves, and higher Q values will usually be a more narrow, direct, and in-your-face kind of sound.

To the right of the XY controller are two strips of controls: Envelope Mod and LFO/S&H. The Envelope Modulation section determines how Auto Filter's envelope changes affect the filter frequency. In other words, it directs how much of the filter's variance or movement is audible, and how the changes are applied. Attack and Release work in tandem to determine the speed of the modulation. The shorter the attack, the quicker the modulation will be heard once the signal is present. Longer attack times will be slower to shift the filter. Similarly, small (quick) release parameters will tend to cut the modulation in and out more often. Long release will hold the modulation more steadily.

Hint: start out with quick Attack (5 ms) and a medium amount of Release (200 ms). Then gradually increase the modulation effect (Mod) to your liking. You will hear the sound get steadily brighter and louder.

Info

Filter definitions

Envelope   A signal (used to be electric) that evolves over time to shape the timbre and amplitude of a sound.

LFO   Low Frequency Oscillator generates a periodic waveform that affects – usually adding vibrato-type movement to – the envelope filter.

Modulation (oversimplified)   The act of changing a sound with a signal. An example of modulating the amplitude would be turning up the volume of an amplifier with your hand (the control signal). More common modulations, as in Live's Auto Filter, involve using vibrato (periodic waveform or LFO) to modulate

oscillator pitch. Frequency Modulation is the use of a control device to change the frequency of a sound.

S&H   Sample & Hold uses randomly generated pulse waves (on/off square waves of varying values) as modulators. The middle wave (on the right side of Live's Auto Filter) looks like a filled-in random pulse wave and is actually two independent (left and right) channels) non-synced random pulse modulators. The third (lowest) button is a single (L/R-synced) random pulse modulator. When using the S&H modulators the Spin and Phase functions are not relevant; thus, they have no effect.

You will also want to check out the Quantize Beat section at the bottom of the Auto Filter effect. The default position is off, so you will need to click the switch on to hear Auto Filter modulate your filter to the sixteenth note of your choice. Depending upon the rhythmic quality of your sample, you may or may not want to use the Quantize Beat settings. Short times can sound very choppy, while longer times can have strange shifts that may or may not make musical sense. Each loop will react differently, so try to listen closely to how the filter moves.

LFO stands for Low Frequency Oscillator (see the Filter Definitions note) and can help add further expression and movement to your original filter in an imprecise but rhythmic fashion. The Amount knob controls LFO's effect, while the Rate control designates the speed of the oscillation (movement) – the range is .01 (slow) to 10.0 (fast). Next to the Rate knob are three separate waveforms from which to choose. The top two are Sine wave shapes and will dictate fairly smooth sailing in terms of frequency modulation. The third wave tells Auto Filter to Sample and Hold to create random (both positive and negative modulation values) filter shifts.

To help rein in the wild waves created thus far, the selectable Phase/Spin knob (located at the bottom right half of the plug-in) will add stereo dimensions to your frequency modulation. Phase will keep both right and left side LFOs at the same frequency. Of course, you can then gradually knock them out of phase by turning the knob to 180 degrees. The Spin setting, which trades places with the Phase knob when activated, detunes the right and left channel LFOs, so that each channel is modulated at a different frequency.

Vinyl distortion

The imperfections of vinyl have actually become quite lovable these days. Whether you are missing the dust pops and crackles of an old record or the warped vinyl sound of a record left out in the sun, vinyl has a certain retro charm. Though CDs and digital recordings are great, they are hopelessly clean and free of these impurities (which is also their strength). Of course, Ableton thought about this too, and as a result, I happily introduce: Vinyl Distortion (Figure 8.22).

Figure 8.22
Live's Vinyl Distortion effect hopes to make you miss your turntable just a little bit less.

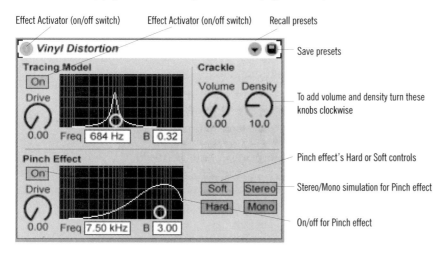

Effect Activator (on/off switch)   Effect Activator (on/off switch)   Recall presets

Save presets

To add volume and density turn these knobs clockwise

Pinch effect's Hard or Soft controls

Stereo/Mono simulation for Pinch effect

On/off for Pinch effect

Vinyl Distortion is divided into three separate sections: Tracing Model, Crackle, and Pinch Effect. While the controls for Tracing Model and Pinch Effect look identical, each section generates a totally different sound. Also note the Soft/Hard, as well as Stereo/Mono switches are also a part of the Pinch Effect. If Pinch Effect is off, these controls will remain greyed out (inactive).

Tracing Model adds a subtle amount of harmonic distortion to your audio as a means of simulating wear and tear on vinyl or an old stylus. To adjust the intensity of the distortion, increase the drive by turning the knob clockwise, or moving the yellow circle along the Y-axis (range from 0.00 to 1.00). Frequency of the harmonic can be altered via the X-axis (range of 50 Hz to 18 kHz), and can also be input manually by typing in the box. To adjust the size of the bandwidth you are affecting, hold down ALT $_+$ (Option) and click-drag forward or backward on the yellow circle.

The Pinch Effect section of Vinyl Distortion is a more drastic and wild-sounding distortion at the input level. The resulting richer stereo image is from Pinch Effect's 180 degrees out of phase harmonic distortions. Like the Tracing Model, you can increase the intensity of the distortion through the drive knob or Y-axis. The X-axis will configure the Frequency range. You will want to pay special attention to the Soft/Hard boxes to the right of the XY interface on the Pinch Effect. Soft mode is engineered to sound like an actual dub plate (acetate), while Hard mode will sound more like a standard vinyl record. Also, the Stereo/Mono switch correlates with Pinch Effect only.

Of course no vinyl simulation plug-in would be complete without a vinyl pop and crackle simulator. Crackle provides two simple controls: Volume and Density. Volume is obviously the level of the hiss and crackle in the mix. Density adds a thicker amount of noise to the output. Note: you will hear the crackle and hiss whether Live is in playback mode or not. If you forget this, you might just take a screwdriver to your audio interface!

Figure 8.23
Live's Redux Plug-in is a talented sample-rate and bit-depth reducer.

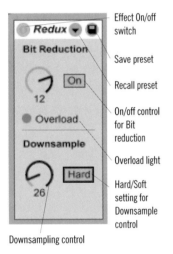

Effect On/off switch

Save preset

Recall preset

On/off control for Bit reduction

Overload light

Hard/Soft setting for Downsample control

Downsampling control

Redux

While we're digging into new tools for sonic decimation, you will definitely want to check out Live 2's Redux plug-in. Redux (Figure 8.23) is a bit-depth and sample-rate reducer that can make even the prettiest of guitars, or anything else for that matter, saw your head off. Of course, results need not be this drastic if you are capable of restraint. In fact, reducing the fidelity of a sample is like a tip of the hat to old Roland, Emu, and Akai 8- and 12-bit samplers – or even old 2- and 4-bit computer-based samples (Commodore 64, anyone?).

The controls for Redux are split into two tidy sections, with a Bit Reduction knob and on/off switch on top, and a Downsample knob and hard/soft switch on the bottom. The default position for Bit reduction is 16 bit (off). As you reduce the bit, you will hear an increasing amount of noisy grit infect the sample. The numerical setting will indicate the bit-depth (i.e., 8=8 bit, 4=4 bit). For extremists, try trimming it down to 1-bit – ouch, that hurts!

When it comes to sample rate reduction, the settings are a little more inexact. In Hard mode, Downsampling will stick with whole integers such as 1, 2, 3, up to 200, while in Soft mode, you can adjust from 1 to 20 to the nearest hundredth of a point (1.00 or 19.99). A setting of 1 means you are not hearing any sample rate reduction – oddly, the higher the number, the lower the rate.

For a quick course, spend a minute perusing the Ableton factory presets such as Old Sampler and Mirage. This will give you a basic template to work from. Also, try toggling back and forth from Hard to Soft Downsampling with different settings (while you are in playback mode) for a cool effect.

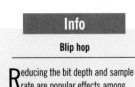

Blip hop

Reducing the bit depth and sample rate are popular effects among many laptop performers exemplified by such artists as Kid606, Pole, Mille Plateaux and their fellow glitch and blip hop scenesters.

VST effects

Of course, you could spend hours with Ableton's original 13 plug-ins and never need another effect. Or you could jump onto the Internet and download a few hundred more. What? Are you serious? Yes. But before we get carried away, I want to warn you that with each VST plug-in you install, there is an additional degree of risk (see the I want my VST note). Still the possibilities are just too enticing. All of those effects plug-ins just waiting to be downloaded (many of them for free). And just what is VST, anyway?

VST, an acronym for Virtual Studio Technology, was conceived by Steinberg (www.steinberg.net) – the same innovative German software company that makes Cubase, Wavelab, Nuendo, Halion, and many other industry leading products. As VST has gained popularity over the last few years, Steinberg has licensed the technology to third-party vendors. Ableton Live, for instance, was written to be a VST plug-in host – or as they say in the biz, 'Supports VST'. In fact, VST is not really a product at all, but a piece of software technology. A VST host can house nearly all VST-type effect plug-ins. I say nearly all because this is the software world after all, and rarely do universal truths apply. I should also point out that there is a related bit of technology called VSTi – where the i stands for instrument – that cannot run in Ableton Live (at least not yet).

To understand what VST actually does, imagine a software studio patch-bay, where you can plug in any effect with a $1/4$-inch patch cable (or a double-click of the mouse). This may seem insignificant, but hosting an application inside another previously launched and running application is not to be taken for granted. How it does this is more than you or I need to know, but I will say that there are a couple necessary steps to make sure your host application (that would be Ableton Live) and your newly found friends (this would be new VST plug-ins) cohabit harmoniously within Live. In the next sections, I will talk about how to find and install VST plug-ins for your Live software.

List of Live-supported effects

If you are looking for a few good plug-ins that will run in Live, the Internet is a huge, if daunting, resource. The list in the next section contains a few of my favourite stops for commercial plug-ins – yeah, the ones that cost money. Before you buy a plug-in, it is a good idea to download the demo and stress test it on your machine running Live. It would be impossible for me or Ableton to guarantee that a plug-in will work. Unforeseen problems with your system configuration, audio interface, computer hardware, and the kind of audio you are running in Live (i.e., 16- or 24-bit), can affect the way a plug-in will work.

Commercial plug-in developers

- **www.cycling74.com**   With over 100 plug-ins for $199, Cycling 74's Pluggo VST effect pack is the perfect example of 'bang for the buck'. Uh, sorry PC people – Mac only!
- **www.pspaudioware.com**   Poland's first software company, but one of the world's finest audio developers. For cool 'tube' simulation, check out Vintage Warmer, or for crazy delay effects (quite unlike Ableton's own brand) try out the Lexicon PSP 42 (or 84).

- **www.steinberg.net**   The inventors of VST technology offer several effects plug-ins.
- **www.tcworks.com**   Excellent, professional, and typically work well in Live.
- **www.waves.com**   Recognized the world over for premium quality (and priced) plug-ins. Their mastering and restoration plug-ins are amazing. Quite possibly overkill for rocking a club with Live.
- **www.ohmforce.com**   If aesthetics alone determined the quality of their plug-ins, Ohmforce would be the kings of cool. Maybe not for everybody, but some wildly interesting effects can be found here.

Free plug-in developers

Though the saying 'you get what you pay for' certainly holds merit, the Internet was built on freeware, shareware, and try-before-you-buy business models. If you are pinching pennies or just looking for a quick batch of new sounds, the following list should keep you busy for a while.

- **www.db-audioware.com**   Dave Brown is the self proclaimed first third-party developer to post VST effect freeware plug-ins on the Internet. He still provides the original four.
- **www.mda-vst.com**   MDA generously provides 23 (at the time of this writing) plug-ins, which, I might add, aren't too shabby. Let's see, 23 times zero is still zero! What a bargain.
- **www.funk-station.co.uk/effect.htm**   A funky, and a little clunky, filter effect.
- **www.smartelectronix.com**   DestroyFX, Magnus, and other plug-in makers live here. You'll find some stable, interesting, and experimental effects.

Staying informed

Since the Internet changes every second, staying current can be a full-time job. Here are a couple of pit stops that I have found helpful over the last couple of years for keeping up to date on the latest happenings.

- **www.ableton.com**   For any serious Live user, the Ableton Forum is not to be missed.
- **www.kvr-vst.com**   This site is updated daily with new VST instrument and effect plug-in information. Just follow the links.
- **www.hitsquad.com**   Hit Squad can be difficult to surf, but is informative.
- **www.harmonycentral.com**   This site is packed with music news of all shapes and sizes. Still, I recommend it for VST and software development news.

Installing VST plug-ins

If you are ready to try installing your first VST plug-in(s), the following steps will outline a successful VST installation. If you are not quite ready, jump back to Ableton's original 13 and get to work. There is a wealth of inspiring sounds to be discovered either way. For the following example, we are going to install four plug-ins from Dave Brown's free VST plug-in download page.

1 Sign on to the Internet and go to http://www.db-audioware.com/download.htm.
2 Scroll to the bottom of the page to the free download section .
3 Click on the plug-in format you need (Mac or PC) and download the plug-ins.

The file is fairly small even for dialup users (about 150k).

4 Once the file is downloaded, click on the Winzip or Stuffit self-extracting file and follow the directions. Note: you will be asked to save the four DLL files in your VST folder. If you are using another VST host such as Cubase or Fruityloops, then you may want to compile all VST plug-ins into the same folder. Typical locations are C:\Program Files\ableton\Vstplugins or C:\Program Files\Steinberg\Cubase\Vstplugins.

5 After you have extracted all of the downloaded files (contained in the self-extracting zip), close the installation window, and re-launch Live.

6 Live's VST Plug-in Chooser (in the browser) will now contain four new plug-ins as seen in Figure 8.24.

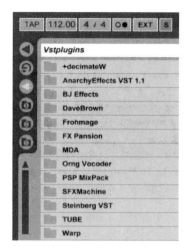

Figure 8.24
A healthy happy new family of VST effects.

Controlling VST plug-ins

Once your new VST effects are working in Live, you have up to four different options for controlling their parameters (depending upon the plug-in). Here is an outline of the four methods along with directions for using them in your Live song.

- Expand the Plug-in. By clicking on the Unfold Effects Parameters triangle, you can open up any VST effect (in Live's Track View), so that you can individually adjust the plug-in's settings. Once you see all of the parameters, simply click-drag on the slider of choice to adjust the plug-in. In Figure 8.25 I have expanded one of my favourite PSP plug-ins.

Figure 8.25
A PSP-made plug-in expanded for improved accessibility and control.

Fold/unfold effects parameters

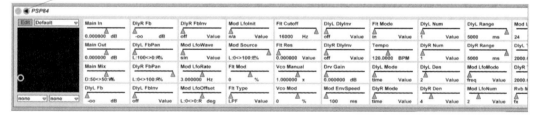

- Use the plug-in's interface. Many plug-ins have a GUI (Graphical User Interface) that can be accessed inside Live. If this is possible for the plug-in you are working with, you will know by seeing a small Edit button next to a dropdown menu toward the top of the plug-in. Click on this to use the effect's graphical interface. In Figure 8.26, I have pressed Edit on the same PSP plug-in (the PSP 84) from the previous Figure 8.25.
- Assign the XY Control. You will notice that Ableton has continued their XY grid motif with VST plug-ins. At the bottom of any VST plug-in inserted in Live, you will see two parameter chooser dropdown menus (side by side). These are the

Figure 8.26
Editing the plug-in's actual interface (shown here with PSP 84) always seems like more fun to me.

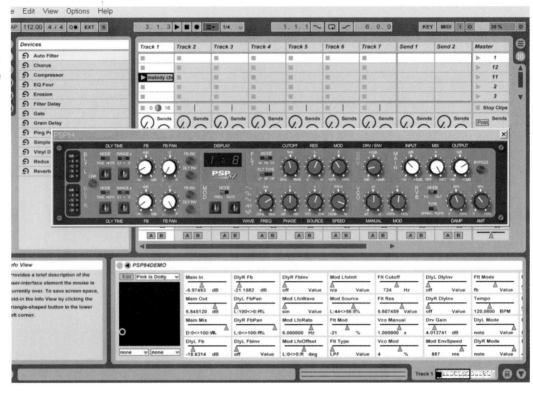

Y and X axis parameters, respectively. For instance if you wanted to use the Y-axis to control the Threshold of Dave Brown's compressor (installed in the Installing VST Effects example), simply open the left-hand dropdown menu on the VST plug-in, and choose Threshold. You can also choose an X-axis parameter and then adjust any two parameters with the now familiar yellow XY-interface dot. In Figure 8.27, I have assigned the Filter Modulation to the X-axis and Filter Cutoff to the Y-axis.

Figure 8.27
By click-dragging the assigned XY values, you can play with the effect in a more musical way.

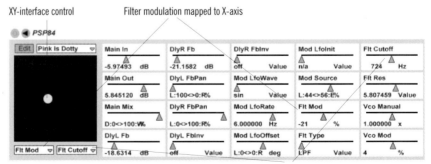

- Assign MIDI-controller. You can also control any VST effect parameter with a MIDI-controller by pressing the MIDI button on Live's Control Bar, clicking on the parameter you wish to control, and then moving the hardware knob you would like to correspond with that control. If you need help setting up MIDI, refer to either Chapter 9, 'Using MIDI', or Chapter 6, 'Playing Live...Live'. In Figure 8.28, I have mapped a couple of my favourite PSP84 live controls.

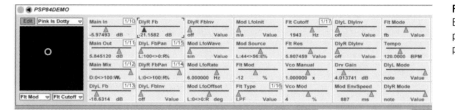

Figure 8.28
By assigning MIDI values to a VST plug-in's parameters, you can crank up the jamming potential.

Automating effects

While we have covered many aspects of mix and effect automation in Chapter 7, 'Editing Your Performance', it makes sense to touch on it again here before moving on. The most important thing to remember about automating effects is that any effect parameter can be automated in Live. If you can imagine it, it can be automated. Even the on/off (Effect Activator) button changes can be recorded as automation and then cleaned up at a later time. Here is how to do it.

1 Insert an effect into a Live track or Aux Send by double-clicking on it in the Live Effects Plug-in Chooser. For the sake of my example, double-click on Auto Filter – the top plug-in.
2 Make sure you have audio going through the plug-in. If it is on a track, load a clip into a clip slot on that track. If Auto Filter is on an Aux Send, make sure you have audio playing on a track and a fair amount of send level set up (increase the Send knob to 3 o'clock position).
3 Press the Automation Record Button at the top of Live's screen (on Live's Control Bar).
4 Hit the Clip Launch button on the loop (going to the effect) to begin your performance.
5 Move the Auto Filter XY-interface yellow dot as you like. Try playing the filter to the music to create swells and drop-offs in time with the loop.
6 When finished, press Stop (Spacebar).
7 Now hit Stop twice and press Play to listen to your performance. Make sure you have the effect active so you can watch the automation you created.
8 If you want to make a correction, insert more automation (like other parameters), or just have another chance, simply arm recording and get back to it! You can do an unlimited number of automation takes.

Of course VST plug-ins can also be automated in the very same way. Any parameter, be it fader, knob, switch or XY-interface dot, can be automated while in record mode in either Session or Arranger View. As we pointed out in the last chapter, this automation can be edited via breakpoint envelopes (either in playback or stop mode).

After a Live effect is automated, you will notice a small red dot on the plug-in next to the parameter you adjusted. In going through the steps described in this section, you will see this dot in the upper left corner of the white Freq (frequency setting) box and the white Q setting box. To delete an unwanted take of automation for a single parameter, simply click on the parameter and press Ctrl (Cmnd) + Backspace (Delete). This way you can keep all other automation.

While this chapter has touched on all of Live's effects and how to use them, there is no substitute for practice and experimentation. Each sound will have different characteristics and therefore behave differently when run through an effect. You should also experiment with how you order your effects (how your signal is routed). Delays and reverbs typically come later in the chain than EQs or Choruses, or even special FX plug-ins like Vinyl Distortion. However, as a rule, don't be held fast by the laws of conformity! In other words, once you understand how an effect works, have fun making your own rules.

Using MIDI

B efore you assume that MIDI is only for sequencer-happy techno-producers, and you decide to turn the page, give me a chance to dispel the myth. Using MIDI is a breeze (at least in Live), and it is also the key to controlling your Live (computer) instrument. If you enjoy the feel of knobs and faders, as opposed to keyboards and a mouse, setting up Live's MIDI is for you. By taking just a few moments to set up Live's MIDI control (and/or MIDI sync) you will begin to feel like you are 'making' the music, as opposed to programming it. And if you are one of those sequencer-sporting techno or hip hop producers who needs Live to run alongside your drum machines, synthesizers, and/or other computers, we will cover that too (see MIDI Synchronization).

Whether you are a MIDI novice, or born from your mother's MIDI Out port, you will need to achieve only two MIDI functions in Live:

- MIDI synchronization with outside MIDI-sequencer, drum machine, or software.
- MIDI control over Live with your hardware (knob or fader sportin') MIDI-controller.

The rest of the garble (such as recording MIDI performances, quantizing MIDI, and MIDI-controller changes) that you hear in MIDI seminars, hardware and software sequencer manuals, musical equipment magazines, and the like, are primarily geared for applications with true MIDI sequencers, piano roll step editors, and multiple MIDI Input buses. Live (at least for now) has none of these, so we will skip them, making your introduction to Live's MIDI features as painless as possible.

What is MIDI?

MIDI stands for Musical Instrument Digital Interface, and is a language or communications protocol used by computers to talk in musical, if a little keyboard-centric, terms. To use MIDI in Live, you will need one to three MIDI cables, and at least one other MIDI-capable piece of equipment besides your computer (it takes two, baby). Most keyboards, samplers, drum machines, and audio interfaces (for computers) sport both MIDI In and MIDI Out/Thru ports. These are so your computer, or any other MIDI device can talk, relay, and listen to MIDI information. This information can contain note, volume, panning, and effects handling instructions, as well as hundreds of other important (and okay, yes, a little bit boring, other kinds of parameters). But before I lose you to the land of 'how does this pertain to me?' we need to understand a couple of basic fundamentals for what you can and cannot expect MIDI to do in Ableton Live 2.

- MIDI is not music, but musical information – a set of numbers telling Live to play loop X or sample Y, raise the volume on track X, pan track Y, or simply direct Live to follow a tempo by sending it regular updates and start and stop instructions.
- MIDI-In ports always connect to MIDI Out ports, and vice-versa. In other words, opposites attract. MIDI information can only transmit from sender to receiver; you will never have like ports connected. The most common connection for the Live musician is a MIDI In signal from your MIDI-controller's MIDI Out. If you are foggy about what a MIDI-controller is, we talked about a few different options way back in Chapter 2, Getting Started'.
- A single MIDI cable can carry 16 channels of MIDI information. Each channel can contain hundreds of different instructions, which gives you thousands of options. For instance, if you have a multi-channel MIDI-controller, you could easily send volume and panning instructions on one channel, and note-on and note-off information on another.
- MIDI cables may not carry audio, but they can still go bad. Most often, MIDI cables will go bad only if they are packed and unpacked repeatedly – as occurs, for instance, if you are using them for live performance. In short, always carry a spare.

There are several outstanding MIDI resources on the Internet for those looking to bone up. Here are a few to get you started.

- **www.midi.org**   This is the MIDI Manufacturer's Association and contains a brief history and detailed guidelines for developers.
- **www.harmony-central.com/MIDI**   A highly informative site with lots of MIDI links and recent, relevant music-making news coverage.
- **www.midiworld.com**   MIDIworld is one of the many sites out there that distributes MIDI files. MIDI files are irrelevant in Live, but the 1989 article under the MIDI Basics tab is a solid history of MIDI.

Preferences and settings

In Chapter 3, 'Live Interface Basics', we learned to open Live's preferences by going to Options > Preferences (or simply Live > Preferences on a Mac running OS X). To set up for MIDI, select the MIDI/Sync tab. If this seems fuzzy, you may want to reread the guidelines for getting started using MIDI with Live. Next, we are going to learn about some more advanced concepts such as handling latency, multiple MIDI input, and preliminary setup of MIDI/Sync in Live. Live's MIDI/Sync Preferences tab is shown in Figure 9.1.

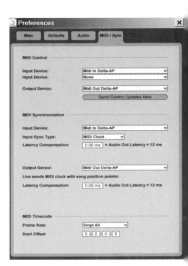

Figure 9.1
Live's MIDI/Sync Preferences tab.

MIDI-controller setup

If you have a MIDI keyboard or MIDI-controller, you will need to configure Live's Preferences so that Live will know where to look for commands coming from those devices. Any properly installed MIDI devices will appear in the dropdown menus seen in Figure 9.2. Once you select your device, try

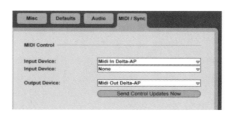

Figure 9.2
Preference's MIDI Control section.

pressing a key or moving a knob while watching Live's MIDI In Indicator on Live's Control Bar (small I in the upper right corner of your screen). You can do this while Live's Preferences are still open.

Live can accept up to two separate MIDI inputs, as well as send MIDI control updates via the selected MIDI output device. Output controller data is only relevant for MIDI-controllers with endless knobs (also called continuous controller knobs) or faders. This way, if you adjust a mapped value in Live with your mouse or computer keyboard, your controller will realize the update. Any time you add a new controller, click on the Send Control Updates Now bar (beneath MIDI Output Device) to make sure your controller data is current.

MIDI synchronization setup

MIDI Synchronization is the act of running two or more sequencers, drum machines, samplers, computers, digital medium (video, tape, ADAT) at the same clock speed (tempo). Reasons you might want to do this with Live vary from running some of your loops and/or more fully developed Live compositions alongside your hardware or software sequencer (located on another machine) to scoring for video. For instance, you may want to have Live handle the audio sampled loops, and let your drum machine or sequencer play the rest of the song via a MIDI file at the same time. In Chapter 13, 'ReWire – Synchronizing Your Software', we will explore how Live's integrated ReWire software component can drive or slave to another application's tempo (on the same machine).

Until then, let's take a look at good old-fashioned MIDI syncing. To synchronize Live to an outside sequencer, drum machine, or external computer, you will need to first decide which device is driving. This is called setting up the master and slave direction in the MIDI sync chain. Live can slave to MIDI clock or MIDI time-code source. This means that when the drum machine slows down, Live also plays audio files slower. It does this without altering the pitch or the groove. Alternately, Live itself can be a MIDI clock source. In the next sections, we will run through several scenarios for applying MIDI synchronization. For now, let's get started by zeroing in on Live's sync preferences on the MIDI/Sync tab (Figure 9.3).

Figure 9.3
Preference's MIDI Synchronization section (on the MIDI/Sync tab).

Setting Live as slave

To set up Live as a slave you will focus on the MIDI input portion of the MIDI/Sync tab. Next you will need to decide between sending Live MIDI clock or MIDI timecode. MIDI Clock, which is easily the most common method for Live users, is actual metronome BPM information that streams quickly and constantly from the source machine to the slave – in this case from any MIDI master sequencer to Live. Any tempo changes made in your master sequencer will be relayed immediately to Live (slave). If you are new to MIDI sync, here are a couple of instances in which you might use MIDI Clock with Live:

- Playing your arrangement or scenes in Live alongside a hardware sequencer. This may be a drum machine, or instrument sequencer, such as an Akai MPC 2000/3000.
- Driving an outside sequencer or MIDI sound module (such as a drum machine) via Live.
- Playing your Live arrangement or scenes along with an outside hard disc recording unit such as a Roland VS-series (VS-1880 or VS-2480), ADAT, Tascam, or other such device.

Info

Update mate

If you are using a hardware sequencer with Live, make sure you are using the latest hardware or firmware operating system. Many people do not realize that sequencers, hard disc recorders, digital mixers, drum machines and samplers, may need to be updated. Visit your manufacturer's website for details. Click on support or updates as a good starting point.

The following steps will guide you through setting up Live to run alongside MIDI Clock.

1. Connect a MIDI cable from your master sequencer's MIDI Out to your computer's (Live's) MIDI In.
2. Configure your sequencer so that it is indeed the master, and check to see that its clock is geared to internal (often abbreviated to INT). You may need to consult the manual for that device.
3. Open Live's Preferences menu, and click on the MIDI/Sync tab as we did before.
4. In the Midi Synchronization section, select Live's MIDI Input Device from your dropdown choices.
5. Select MIDI Clock for Live's MIDI Sync Type.
6. Close Preferences.
7. To make Live run in sync, you will need to activate the EXT button (officially called the External Sync Switch) atop Live's Control Bar.
8. Press Play on your master device and you will see the S (officially called the External Sync Indicator) blink at the project tempo.

If you are working with film or television data and would rather slave Live to MIDI Timecode (often referred to as MTC), you need only swap out steps two and five. In other words, make sure your master sequencer is sending MIDI Timecode, and then tell Live to look for that Timecode via the MIDI Sync Type dropdown in step five. Simply set Live's Output Device to send to your slave device in the Preferences dialog box.

Figure 9.4
My Output Device is set to an M-Audio 2496 audio interface MIDI Out Delta A-P.

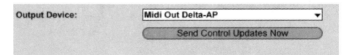

The Ableton Live manual aptly describes MIDI Timecode as 'the MIDI version of the SMPTE (Society of Motion Picture and Television Engineers) protocol, the standard means to synchronize tape machines and computers in the audio and film industry'. MIDI Timecode information is conveyed from the master to the slave in the form of actual time in frames (subdivisions of a second), and while this may sound like a good idea, it can be a devil to work with. Since internal clocks may operate at slightly different speeds, within the course of a four- or five-minute song, things can really start to drift. Also, since there is no continual tempo update information, you will have to manually set and change Live's tempo (particularly tricky if there are tempo changes within a given piece of music). However, some machines (such as my Roland VS-1680) will send a project tempo (one time only) once the sync is established, though getting the machines (the sequencer and the computer) to line up exactly can take some finagling. For instance, my Roland hard disc recorder will send the slightly wrong tempo unless it is perfectly rounded to the nearest second.

Setting Live as master

If you are feeling a little overwhelmed with running Live as a slave, you will be pleased to hear that running Live as the master clock is a good deal easier. For one, there is no Timecode option when sending MIDI sync from Live. In the section below, we will go through the steps to running Live as the Master in the MIDI sync chain.

1 Connect a MIDI cable from Live's MIDI output to your master sequencer, drum machine, or alternate machine's MIDI input.
2 Configure your sequencer, drum machine, or alternate computer so that it is looking for an external clock (usually indicated by an EXT setting in the MIDI settings). Check your device's manual if you are having trouble locating these settings.
3 Open Live's Preferences and click on the MIDI/Sync tab as we did before.
4 In Live's MIDI output, make sure that Live is set to send MIDI information to an outside source by selecting a MIDI out device that is connected with your computer's MIDI cabling.
5 In the Preference's MIDI Synchronization section, again select Live's MIDI Output Device from your dropdown choices.
6 Close Preferences.
7 Press Play in Live, and you will notice the MIDI output indicator (the O in Live's control bar) blink to show MIDI transmission.

Latency

When people speak of *latency* in regards to audio software, they are usually referring to the time lag between the playing of a note (into your computer from an outside source) to actually hearing it come through your speakers, or the time that passes between applying audio processing and hearing it. Both latency issues are undesirable and can be caused in a couple of different ways, which we will cover in detail in Chapter 12, 'Recording in Live'. For our immediate purposes, we are only going to adjust Live's Latency Compensation (seen in Figure 9.5) to compensate for any audible MIDI-synchronization lag in your audio interface (or sound card). This can be done for Live's MIDI input or output synchronization.

Figure 9.5
Latency Compensation can be adjusted for
either MIDI input or output.

Figure 9.5
Latency Compensation can be adjusted for
either MIDI input or output.

MIDI synchronization latency is best adjusted by ear. To do this, simply play the
master device or Live, while Preferences is open, and adjust the control until you
can no longer hear the one source falling behind (or racing ahead of) the other. You
should have to do this only one time for each studio setup. Also, it will be easier
to synchronize if you put the same loop on each source. For instance, you could
have your sequencer repeatedly trigger a non-looping clip on the one, while that
same loop is copied and playing from another clip.

MIDI triggering in Live

Once you have configured Live's MIDI/Sync Preferences tab for use with your
respective MIDI Input and Output devices, it is time to start playing Live for the
instrument it is. To do this, we will make a custom MIDI map for you to control Live
with a MIDI keyboard, or MIDI-controller. After doing so, you will be able to trigger
(play) any clip from Live's clip slot grid, as well as tweak all VST/Ableton effects or
Live session mixer parameters with virtually any MIDI-controller or keyboard.

Setting up a MIDI map

Follow the steps below to map some MIDI.

1 Make sure your MIDI-controller is connected correctly (MIDI cables running from
MIDI output on the controller to MIDI input on your computer and MIDI output
on your computer to your controller's MIDI input). If your audio interface does
not support MIDI, you should refer to Chapter 2, 'Getting Started'.

2 Check to see that Live's
Preferences menu (MIDI/Sync tab)
is set up to receive MIDI input
from your desired source. Figure
9.6 will give you an example of
what my configuration looks like.
For this example we are concerned only with the uppermost
portion of the MIDI/Sync tab:
MIDI Control.

3 Depress Live's MIDI Map Mode
Switch. All assignable parameters
and clips will be highlighted.

4 Click once on the assignable clip
or parameter that you would like
to map to your controller.

5 Move the desired controller or
depress the desired key. You will
see the assignment show up in
the parameter below in the follow-

Figure 9.6
My Live Preferences MIDI/Sync Tab.

ing format MIDI channel/MIDI note or value number. Figure 9.7 shows several mappings made in my Live session.

6 Repeat as desired, and then deactivate the MIDI Map Mode Switch to try out your mapping.

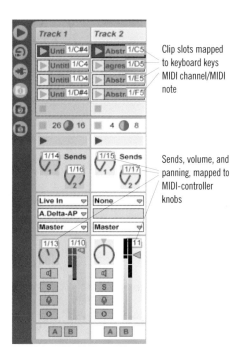

Figure 9.7
Some clips and mix parameters mapped to a MIDI-controller.

Clip slots mapped to keyboard keys MIDI channel/MIDI note

Sends, volume, and panning, mapped to MIDI-controller knobs

Tip

Map on-the-fly

Now that you know how to set up Live's MIDI-mapping, you will be delighted to know that you can do this while Live is in playback (or recording) mode. Also, so long at the MIDI Map Mode Switch is depressed, you will not hear your results. The same holds true for setting up QWERTY keyboard commands.

MIDI-controller types

While piano-style keyboards are the most common, there are several different types of MIDI-controllers. Most keyboards feature knobs and sliders, but as we saw in Chapter 2, you may purchase dedicated controllers with just sliders (faders), knobs, dials, or some combination thereof. Drummers can also send MIDI information by striking electronically wired rubber *trigger* pads, which are most often used as electronic drums. Live supports the common standards for incremental (endless) and absolute controllers and MIDI devices with motorized faders. Once you have connected a MIDI device, Live will automatically detect what kind of device it is. You can override Live's selection via the dropdown menu appearing at the bottom of the screen (when the MIDI Map Mode Switch is active and you are mapping a knob, fader, modulation wheel or other continuous controller). Almost invariably, Live will select absolute, but should you have a relative controller, Live can accommodate you. I have used Live with a variety of MIDI-controllers, triggering devices, and digital mixers and have always relied on the absolute value. The signed bit, 2's comp, and bin offset have to do with MIDI-program change values, as does absolute (14 bit).

The following list outlines a few common situations in which a Live musician might map a MIDI-controller to Live.

- MIDI mixing. There are several digital and MIDI-enabled mixing devices currently on the market – a great tool for adding a classic mixer feel or desk to your software studio.
- MIDI knobs. Most musicians and engineers are a bit disappointed when there

are no knobs to turn. Perhaps there is something psychosomatic about the process, but try mapping a couple of knobs and I think you'll be hooked.

- Mod and Pitch Wheels. Modulation wheels are great for gradually increasing/decreasing a given value. Pitch wheels are a bit different since they are usually spring-loaded with a default position of centre (as opposed to a zero value). For example, if you map a Pitch Wheel to a track volume level in Live's session mixer, your default position will be -12dB. You can increase or decrease the value (volume in this instance), but once you let go of the wheel, the volume will snap back to -12dB.
- MIDI faders. MIDI-sliders are similar to the MIDI-mixer, in that they approximate the feel of an analog mixer (desk). I point it out separately because there are several products on the market such as Doepfer's Pocket Fader (www.doepfer.com), Kenton's Control Freak Studio Edition (www.kentonuk.com), or a host of other products that are expressly designed for fading. While volume control may be the obvious use for a fader, you may also experience some creative results by mapping to Live's crossfader, effects wet/dry level, or aux send levels. For more on methods, take in the next 'MIDI Controls' section.

Tip

Reason and VST plug-ins

One of the most common questions asked by prospective users of Reason is 'Can I use VST plug-ins with it?', and VST plug-in compatibility is also one of the most-requested features by existing users. Well, this facility within Reason will not be coming any time soon, if ever, so your best bet is to run the program in conjunction with a sequencer that is VST-compatible, if you really want to use VST plug-ins.

MIDI controls

While nearly every parameter in Live can be controlled via MIDI-controller, there are four basic types of controls: slots (clips), switches, radio buttons, and continuous controllers. The reason we are making the distinction is because different types of controls will behave differently. For example, a volume slider will react differently to an effect activator (on/off switch). Or, a clip can be launched or stopped by a single MIDI note, but a gradual pan from left to right will require a MIDI-controller's knob or slider (sending a continuous stream of MIDI data). To clarify what's what, let's take a look at each type of control.

Tip

Why do I neeed input for output?

In the first part of this chapter, I instructed you to connect both MIDI input and output ports even if you are only planning on sending Live MIDI-controller data. The explanation for this extra cable (Live's output to your controller's input) is so that Live can update certain kinds of controllers with endless knobs or motorized faders with the current positioning of the parameter, and eliminate jumps or gaps in your MIDI conversation. If you have connected a new device while working in Live, open Preferences, click on the MIDI/Sync tab, and press the Send Control Updates Now button to inform your MIDI device of the position of Live's currently mapped MIDI parameters. However, in testing different MIDI-controllers for this book, there were occasional MIDI feedback problems – specifically with a Peavey PC1600x MIDI fader controller. If you notice your controller isn't working properly, try unplugging the MIDI input on the controller, and re-launching Live.

Figure 9.8a
A loaded Clip Slot with MIDI mapping.

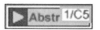

Figure 9.8b
An empty Clip Slot with MIDI mapping.

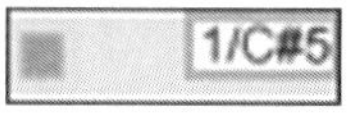

- Slots – Clips or clip slots (seen in Figures 9.8a and 9.8b) can each be mapped to any given MIDI note (called Note-on and Note-off messages). You may also map knobs and sliders to control a slot (where MIDI values above 63 turn the note on and MIDI values below 64 turn the note off), but that will likely only be done in rare instances. Once a clip slot is mapped to a value, any sample, loop, or recording placed there can be triggered. If you remove the clip or map your MIDI-controller to an empty slot, you can trigger the cell's stop button.

- Switches – A switch control is a toggle on/off device used in Live for channel mutes (Figure 9.9), effect activators (Figure 9.10), and Control Bar parameters (Figure 9.11). Similar to slots , switches can only be on or off (a loop can only be played or stopped). Therefore, you may turn on by sending a Note-on message, and turn off by sending a second Note-on message.

Figure 9.9
A mapped channel mute (switch).

Figure 9.10
Effect activators (shown as mapped) are also a type of switch.

Mapped effect activator (on/off) switch

Figure 9.11
Several switches can be found in Live's control bar.

- Radio Buttons – Radio buttons look a bit like switches, but have more than two options (on/off), yet have fewer than continuous controls. For example, the delay time subdivision section of Live's Filter Delay (see Figure 9.12) is made up of radio buttons that are best controlled by a knob or slider (absolute or incremental). Note-on messages will allow you to toggle forward through the available options – in this case 1, 2, 3, 4, 5, 6, 8, and 16 (beats).

- Continuous Controls – CCs are the most commonly mapped parameters on the planet. Mute, volume, pan, send level, and many effects parameter controls can be mapped to either absolute or incremental controls in the 0 through 127 value range. MIDI-capable mixers can add great control over your Live project – previously impossible to achieve with an ordinary mouse. Figure 9.13 shows a channel in Live's session mixer mapped and ready to control.

Figure 9.12
Live's Filter Delay's delay subdivision section is made up of so-called radio buttons.

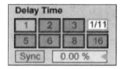

Figure 9.13
Continuous Controls such as mute, solo, volume, and pan will give Live that 'analog feel.'

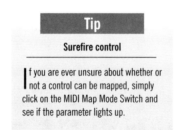

Tip

Surefire control

If you are ever unsure about whether or not a control can be mapped, simply click on the MIDI Map Mode Switch and see if the parameter lights up.

MIDI ideas

With such a wide range of possible MIDI-controller options, it might be helpful to look at a few of my favourite Live performance mappings. As always, I encourage you to explore your own options, modify my examples, and trade templates with a friend. Fun should definitely be the most important MIDI concept.

- Volume – I'm not sure who invented it, but something about the idea of a slider (or fader) as a volume control just works. Knobs too, can be a musical way of controlling your level, but make sure you try using a fader if you have one. I use a hard disk recorder at home and a digital mixer live – both have MIDI input and output ports that I connect to my laptop's out and input. To map, simply activate (click on) the MIDI Map Mode Switch, click on the volume (channel or

Tip

Template time

Once you have spent a few hours (days) customizing your MIDI configuration to your MIDI-controllers and keyboards, you may want to save this song as a template. To do this, I recommend that you delete all clips in session view by clicking on any clip slot, pressing Ctrl (Cmnd) + A to select all clips, and then press Delete. You should also delete any automation (if you have any) in the Arranger View by selecting the entire song length on any track, and then using the Delete Time command.

Now you are ready to save the template. Open Live's Preferences and go to the Default tab. Press the Save button in the Save Template section. From now on, each Live set you open will have the same MIDI setup you have so carefully created. A super time saver! For more on templates, see Appendix B at the end of this book.

Tip

Channel surfing

If you are using Live in ReWire mode (see Chapter 13, 'Rewire – Synchronizing Your Software') you may find it helpful to designate separate channels for each application. I will often run Propellerhead's Reason on one channel and Live on another. That way, if I want to change the application I am controlling, it is as simple as changing the MIDI channel on my controller, and I don't have to change a thing within Live.

master) you would like to control, and then move the MIDI-controller – deactivate the MIDI Map Mode Switch when done.

- Panning – To keep my software studio feeling as comfy as possible, I also like to assign MIDI-controller knobs to Live's panning controls. Instructions for doing so are the same as above, but I'll remind you one last time. Once the MIDI Map Mode is active, it is as easy as click (on the virtual knob) and turn (the real one).

- Effects Wet/Dry – By mapping a controller to increase or decrease the ratio of effect to dry sound, you can achieve some musical-sounding effect performances. I do this most often with delays or reverb type effects, but you can let your imagination take you other places. For instance, adding a bit more of Live's Chorus effect to a vocal (increasing the Wet), might add a lift to a chorus. Typically, I use this technique with the effect inserted on the channel level (rather than on a send track). If the effect is inserted on a send, I use the next technique.

- Send Level – Another handy MIDI-control tactic is to map a knob to the send level of a track to increase the amount of effects you hear as a composite. While increasing the send will increase the volume (especially if the send is routed pre-fader), you will also allow more of the original sound's level to be affected by whatever effects reside at the send. Another neat dynamic effect is to completely dry up the effects on a sound (track) by quickly reducing the send.

- Delay Feedback – For obnoxiously big and noisy crescendos, I will frequently map a delay's feedback to a MIDI-controller knob. By increasing the amount of feedback, the original signal will reroute itself through the delay, its volume snowballing in the process. The key is to be able to reduce the feedback in an instant if the noise begins to get out of hand. Otherwise, cover your ears and duck for cover.

- Crossfader – Since the crossfader is relatively new, I am still learning how to best apply it. Still, I find that mapping a knob or fader (preferably a horizontal one) to control Live's crossfader is approximately one million times more musical than a mouse. Try loading up two drum loops and assign each to a channel (one A and one B). Then with both loops playing, jiggle the fader mapped to the crossfader back and forth – instant breakbeats.

If any of the above examples have caught you by surprise, this is really only the tip of the iceberg for what you can uncover within Live. You should now feel inspired to experiment with your own ideas for MIDI mapping or set up a MIDI synchronization scheme. In Chapter 13, 'ReWire – Synchronizing Your Software', we will look at some more ways to synchronize your software studio.

Wave editing tips

N ow that you have a good basic working knowledge of Live, you may discover that your audio content (samples and loops) could use a little extra cleaning up, examination, and/or processing. This kind of detail work requires additional software, such as a specific audio waveform/sample editing application (see the 'Which Audio Editor to Use' section later in this chapter). Whether or not you decide to purchase specific audio editing software, Chapter 10 is designed to teach you a few more tricks and tips for getting the most out of your sounds – the fuel for your Live songs. In my experience, these techniques and concepts are some of the least talked about, yet fundamentally most important and relevant concepts for any computer-based musician or producer to understand. Specifically, I am talking about professionalizing your sound and fixing the digital audio challenges that every producer faces.

Earlier in the book, we pointed out the Launch Sample Editor button located in Live's Clip View (seen in Figure 10.1). If you have not already designated a sample editor, pressing the Launch Sample Editor (Edit) button will bring up the message: No sample editor application has been selected. Would you like to select one now? Press OK to call up the folder browser and then locate the application (or application's shortcut). Once you have done so, you can quickly open any clip in your audio editor by pressing Edit. If your wave editing application isn't already open, the Edit button will launch it and open the AIF or WAV file. Once you are done working with the file, save and close it. Live will automatically reopen the new file (with any changes) once you revisit your Live session.

Launch sample editor

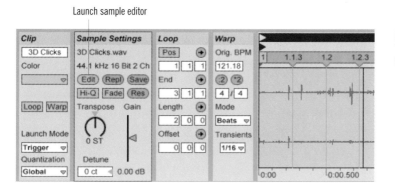

Figure 10.1
The Launch Sample Editor button found in Clip View.

Which audio editor to use?

At the time of this writing, there are several exceptional, versatile, and professional audio editor applications (also called wave or sample editors) on the market. Most pro-level audio editors are also fairly expensive (roughly £250 to £500), or as much as twice the cost of Live. With this in mind, I put together a list so you can choose your audio editor quickly and confidently. Be aware that most companies make several versions at various prices and in various configurations, ranging from limited to full feature sets. For example, make sure your audio editor can handle 24-bit audio – Peak DV, a limited version of Peak, cannot. The following list compares the professional versions of each application.

- Cool Edit Pro by Syntrillium (www.syntrillium.com) – A good deal cheaper than the competition, and an excellent value, but is, unfortunately, PC only. Cool Edit Pro is also a multi-track recorder that hosts a variety of fun and inspiring features. Recently, Adobe acquired this technology and is calling the new version Audition. See www.adobe.com/products/audition for more details and upgrade pricing.
- DSP-Quattro by DSP-Quattro (www.dsp-quattro.com) – Originally available as a shareware application called D-Sound Pro, DSP-Quattro is an inexpensive yet fully featured audio editor for both Mac OS 9 and OS X. Looks like an excellent value, but untested by this author.
- Goldwave by Goldwave (www.goldwave.com) – Inexpensive, and a little bit ugly, Goldwave will get you up and running (on a PC only) if you are saving your pennies for a more robust application.
- Peak by Bias (www.bias-inc.com) – Peak users are a loyal crew, and for good reason. The interface is slick, the features are deep, and the sound is amazing. However, if you are composing your music on a PC, you will be left wondering – Peak is for Macs only. Also, Peak's pro version is as expensive as Sound Forge or Wavelab (see next).
- Sound Forge by Sonic Foundry (www.sonicfoundry.com) – Sound Forge is an expensive, comprehensive, and widely used PC-based audio editor. You can attain a 'lite' version of this product, but keep in mind that these versions don't support higher and more professional sample rates and bit depths.
- Spark XL by TC Works (www.tcworks.de) – Comparable with Peak, Spark XL is a professional grade audio editor for Mac OS 9 and OS X. Spark includes many powerful effects and features.
- Wavelab by Steinberg (www.steinberg.net) – Steinberg's Wavelab is a favourite among DJs who choose to digitize their vinyl and is priced around the $500 mark.

Wave editor tips

Like sampling, editing audio waveforms has become both a craft and an art form. Though you will not master it in a day, I find that a basic understanding helps a great deal when working within Live. After some initial practice, working with visual audio, a.k.a. waveform (see Figure 10.2), can be a whole new way of developing, working with, and designing new sounds. If this sounds vaguely familiar, it is because we touched on the concept of visual audio back in Chapter 4, 'Digital Audio Basics'. Now would be a good time for a review if you need it.

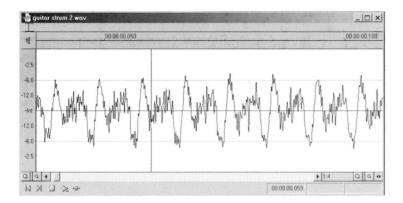

Figure 10.2
A basic waveform.

Sprucing up your loops

Wave editors are great for diving deeper into your loops and samples. Like looking under the hood of a car to check out a mysterious noise, you may be surprised to pop open an audio file and discover volume inconsistencies, clicks/pops, and other digital maladies. And similar to a car, you may not be entirely sure what you are looking at.

In this section, we will look at a couple of gain-maximizing tricks (to include normalizing), how to declick your digital audio, and a couple of musical ideas related to audio editing. Since these tips will only be a taste of what any decent wave editor is capable of, you might need to spend some extra time with that application's manual (or relevant tips/tricks book) to take your digital noise to the next level.

Normalizing

Remember, nothing exposes the lack of audio engineering professionalism quite like quirky volume levels. Too much gain during the recording process, or excessively boosting audio with a filter or EQ can cause level peaking, which in the realm of digital audio is just plain ugly. Conversely, a signal level that's too low often sounds wimpy and feeble, and can weaken an otherwise perfect mix. Other times, audio will develop a combination of the two problems, with great peaks and deep valleys providing an ultimately unsettling experience for the listener. For these reasons, audio engineers rely on a process called normalization. Live musicians (or artists using other loop-based applications), should also take great care to normalize loops and samples.

Normalization is the process of raising the level of an entire audio file so that its loudest parts are as close as possible to the maximum level possible, without peaking. In other words, the entire file is made to behave as a 'normal' file should. This is great for extended tracks, where the volume may fluctuate a great deal. However, keep in mind that when you normalize, you increase the bad along with the good, and that normalization is not the same as audio compression or limiting (discussed in the 'Volume Maximizing' section of this Chapter).

Tip

No wave editor? No problem.

Even if you haven't yet made the leap and purchased a wave editor, you can still normalize like all the cool kids. Normalizing is actually a built-in feature of Live's rendering options. So, if you are having trouble making levels match up, turn back to Chapter 7, 'Editing Your Performance,' and reread the section called 'Rendering Options Explained.'

In Figure 10.3, I have opened the Normalize dialog box in my audio editor (Sonic Foundry's Sound Forge 6.0). Like many audio editors, you can normalize in terms of percent of maximum dB, where 100 percent means that the highest peak in your waveform will be brought to the brink of the digital maximum. You can also determine more advanced settings, such as how the application looks for the highest gain values, and how peaks are handled. I typically normalize only problem loops/samples (too quiet) and all of my finished mixes, but some musicians normalize every single sample. The latter technique will provide more consistency, but may also be less urgent if your original recording levels are closely monitored. For loops to be used in Live, I usually normalize at 95 percent and up, while for finished mixes, closer to 100 (depending upon the dynamic nature of the material) – it is important for the more dance- and radio-oriented pieces to be maximized in terms of volume.

Figure 10.3
Sound Forge's Normalize dialog box

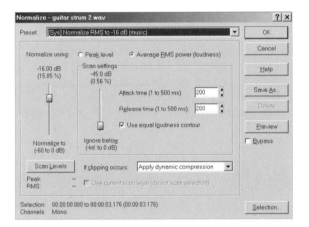

Volume maximizing

To further support your volume consistency efforts, most audio editors feature at least one compressor, one or two limiting options, and often one volume maximizing (mastering) tool. Each of these effects can help volume peaks and valleys appear less dramatic, but can also remove some of the dynamic (loud to soft) musicality of your sample's performance. You may also want to maximize your small one-shot audio samples (as well as loops). For instance, a single drum hit such as a kick or snare might sound good compressed, but a jazz drum set or guitar rhythm might become more sterile sounding with an even dynamic range.

Compression   As we discussed when learning about Live's Compressor in Chapter 8, 'Live's Effects', a compressor minimizes audio's peaks at a given threshold. This is usually done for two reasons, first to alleviate the shock of a volume spike and second to allow for the overall mix volume to be increased. Compression can help even out the dynamic range of an erratic loop, as well as add presence to a lifeless performance.

While each compressor or compressor plug-in will have a different interface, the basic ratio, threshold, attack, release, input/output level controls will remain the same. Some compressors also include other kinds of effects such as EQs or even distortion to make for some powerful and creative combo plug-ins (see the 'Combo Plug-Ins' section that follows).

Limiters   Similar to a compressor, a limiter is able to squeeze a mix (in part by reducing spikes in volume). A limiter can also add gain to quieter sounds, and therefore elevate the overall mix's presence to just shy of peaking (more standardized) gain levels. The results can sound less severe than a compressor, depending upon the dynamic nature of the music. For instance, music with a wide dynamic range will sound the most affected by compressors, and slightly less so by a limiter. Most mastering engineers will use limiting instead of normalization because of its compression-like qualities.

Combo plug-ins   Some compressors also feature adjustable frequency bands (similar to the EQ Four) that can be set to compress certain frequencies more than others. For instance, you might compress the high end of a drum loop to add crispness without adding more low-end woof. You can also achieve similar results in Live by using an EQ plug-in before your compressor. Another example might be to compress the upper mids of a drum loop in order to add a little oomph to the snare and body of the drums. For this, I would insert an EQ plug-in first (and boost 1.2 k to 2500 k) and then lightly compress (2 or 4 to 1 ratio setting).

Other combination plug-ins offer both compression and normalizing functions at the same time. In Figure 10.4, I am using Sound Forge's included Wave Hammer effect to simultaneously compress and maximize volume. This might be thought of as compressing while normalizing on-the-fly.

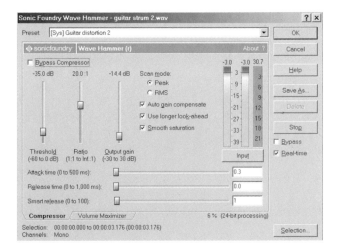

Figure 10.4
Wave Hammer is a combination Compressor and Volume Maximize plug-in for Sound Forge 6.0.

De-clicking

Clicks and pops are an unfortunate occurrence in digital audio. They occur for a variety of reasons, including cutting off a sample midway through the wave cycle, system strain (CPU, RAM, or hard drive), or inadequate audio interfaces/drivers. Manually removing these annoying little guys can range from simple to next-to-impossible. However, there are several existing click-removal applications for both PC and Mac – although most that I have tried tend to dampen, or diminish, audio clarity for the rest of the audio as well as take out the clicks. So, try the demo before you buy the plug-in/application.

Often times, manual removal is your best and only option. Let's take a look at how to do this.

1 First, you must locate the offending click. To do this, open the sample in your audio editor and loop a small section of audio to see if you can zero in on exactly where the pop is sitting inside the waveform. Occasionally, I will make a marker where I hear the pop occurring during playback (which in Sound Forge can be done by pressing the short-cut key M).
2 Zoom in on waveform to magnification that makes sense with the audio you are working on. See Figure 10.5 as an example of a pop found and zoomed in on in the waveform.

Figure 10.5
By zooming in on the click/pop, you can prepare to fix it.

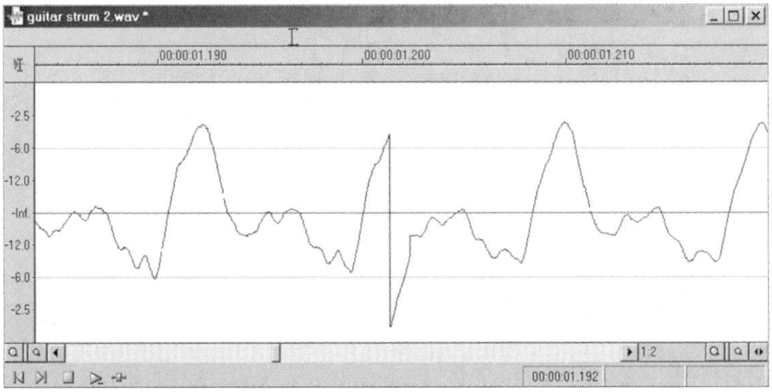

3 Activate your audio editor's Draw tool and carefully round out the harsh angle or jag that is most likely giving you the pop. If you accidentally draw too much or make some other mistake, Undo your last action. The shortcut for Undo is almost invariably Ctrl (Cmnd) + Z.
4 Check your work. Play the same looped section in step 1 to hear if the click is partially or completely gone. Listen for any other ill effects such as a muffled sound, additional clicks, or other sonic problems. Sometimes you can make things worse in a hurry by drawing on the waveform. If it does get worse, consider starting over and drawing a less severe curve or fix.

Tip

Fade in and fade out

The most common clicks in digital audio occur when slicing a sample at a point other than where the waveform crosses the middle horizontal line (often called the zero crossover). If you hear a click at the beginning or end of your sample, you will know that this is your culprit. To rid yourself of these kind of glitches, create a very small (less than 5 millisecond) fade-in at the beginning, and a fade-out at the end of your sample.

Shaving attack

So many drum and percussion loops start on the first beat of the measure that continually mixing them together often creates a sonic mud puddle. One way to sidestep this annoyance is to shave the attack of the offending sample. I do this most often when I have two drum loops that sound great together, but are still *flamming*, or sloppily doubling up on one another. How much attack you eliminate is up to you, and will vary for each loop. Figure 10.6a shows two loops that were flamming when I played them in Live. Figure 10.6b shows the same two loops (the second one with shaved attack).

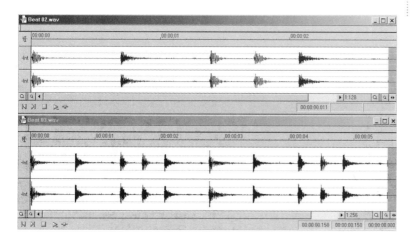

Figure 10.6a
Two drum loops in my wave editor.

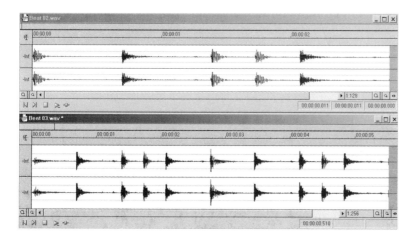

Figure 10.6b
One normal drum loop, the second one with shaved attack, for smoother playback.

Maximum punch

Many reference manuals and online tutorials tell us that samples sound best (have fewest digital glitches) when there is a gradual fade-in at the beginning of the first audio event and a similar fade-out at the end of the loop. However, some dance music producers have figured out that by cutting away a sample's long fade-in and triggering the sample at or near its peak, they increase the velocity of the attack. The severed sound now assumes massive punch and presence – a necessity for loop-based dance music. To give you an idea of what I am talking about, Figure 10.7a represents the expected gradual fade-in of a drum loop or sample, while Figure 10.7b shows this more progressive (and a little bit dangerous) method.

Figure 10.7a
A gradual fade will work fine for most samples.

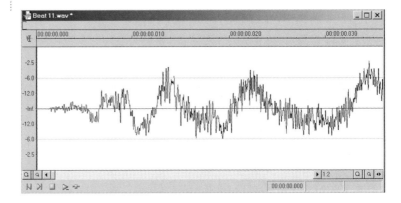

Figure 10.7b
By cutting closer to the bone (sound), you can achieve chest-smacking thump.

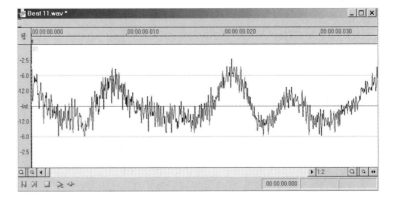

Loop variations (resampling)

One of the best things you can do to build up your loop collection is to make multiple variations of your favourite creations. In Chapter 11, Where to Get Loops', we will look at the myriad ways to attain, purchase, or uncover new loops. But I wanted to bring this up here because once you load a loop into your wave editor and begin to play with effects, you will discover that it is quite easy to save several radically contrasting loops for use in later tracks. Let's consider an example:

1 Load one of your favourite drum loops in your wave editor and save this fresh copy as drumloop1.
2 Call up an effect, let's say a compressor.
3 For some radical, creative compression, set your compressor ratio between 15 and 20 to 1. Make sure neither of the levels (input or output) is peaking; use a short attack (less than 2 milliseconds), and then play with the release until it sounds good. Rock drum loops with mashy hi-hats and cymbals will sound more normal with longer release times, while short staccato-style drums will sound elongated or tubby. Figure 10.8 shows my compressor in Sound Forge.
4 Save this loop as drumloop2(comp).
5 Let's try some radical EQ settings on this one by raising the high mid frequencies and eliminating the lows. If you try to approximate my settings, make sure that your drum loop has enough headroom, or your speakers may clip. Take a

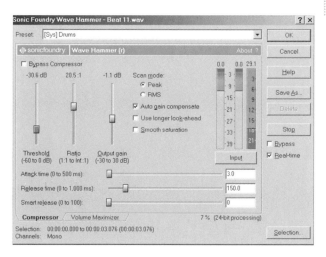

Figure 10.8
Creative compression settings in Sound Forge.

look at Figure 10.9 to see how I have configured Sound Forge's EQ effect. Kind of sounds like an old AM radio, doesn't it?

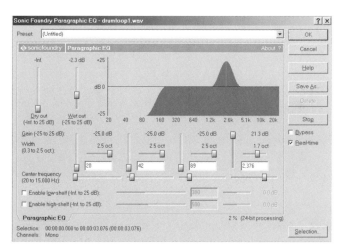

Figure 10.9
Sound Forge's EQ effect.

6 Save this as drumloop3(eq).

7 Close that loop and reopen drumloop2(comp) again.

8 Open one of your wave editor's multi-tap delay effects (Sound Forge's is seen in Figure 10.10 on page 198) and dial up something rhythmic by setting the number of taps to 1 or 3, and the delay time within the 300 millisecond range, and set the feedback between 30 and 40 percent. Some delays, such as this one in Sound Forge, will also allow you to do low-pass (or other band) filtering. This can help lessen the thuddy quality of delaying the entire signal. Remember that a low-pass filter will allow lower frequencies to pass and weed out higher more shrill sounds.

9 Save this as drumloop4(delay).

10 While you could keep going all night, let's stop and listen to our results. Go back into Live and locate the four drum loops and load them in Live. You could use these four different moods/ideas within the same song, or in concert. When mix-

Figure 10.10
A multi-tap delay effect in Sound Forge.

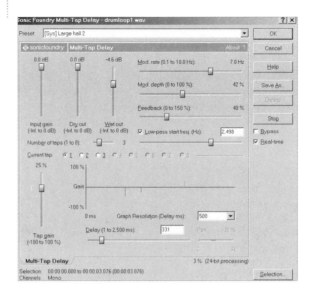

Figure 10.10
A multi-tap delay effect in Sound Forge.

ing loops that are the same frequency on top of one another, I will detune them to avoid phasing effects.

While the preceding process is not exactly resampling, which is to make a sample of a sample, it is a similar idea (making a copy of a sample, modifying it, and saving it as a new sample).

Streamlining loops for Live

Laptops are often limited versions of their desktop brethren. They may be a little short of RAM, extra hard drive space, or processor speed, but they are designed as a sleeker, more portable stand-in for your desktop (as opposed to the fully featured multi-processor computers that are common in most recording studios). Since many Live musicians will be porting their music from rehearsal to club to recording session on a laptop, here are a few tips for streamlining audio loops and samples for maximum musicality and minimum system drain in these situations.

Stereo or mono?

In a typical club, a true stereo field will be experienced by only a small percentage of listeners. Some clubs or performance halls will not even support stereo (right and left) channels. Mono files require roughly half the processing and system resources as stereo files. Also, mono audio files will tend to sound more 'present' and deliver a bit more punch (particularly in a dance music environment). To convert your files to mono, you can either render each file in Live (using the render as mono option) or in a wave editor. The following steps detail how I create a mono file from a stereo file using Sonic Foundry's Sound Forge 6.0 – most other wave editors will contain similar features.

1   Open the loop by clicking on Edit in Clip View.
2   Once the wave editor is open (Sound Forge in this case), select File > Save As and choose Mono in your Save options (see Figure 10.11). Most wave editors allow you to grab one side of the audio waveform (to make a mono loop stereo),

but be warned that this is not the true stereo image made mono. For example, if you have a stereo drum track with several different pan settings, grabbing one side only will disproportionately represent your original recording.

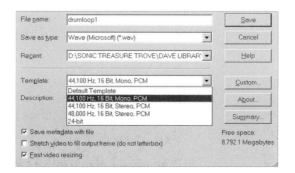

Figure 10.11
Select mono in your wave editor's Save options – note the highlighted bar in the Description dropdown menu in Sound Forge's Save As options.

3 Since you have created a new file, you need to take advantage of Live's replace (Repl in Live) command, conveniently located in Live's Clip View next to the Edit button (seen in Figure 10.12).

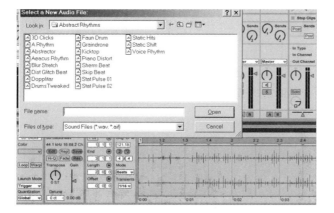

Figure 10.12
The Replace / File Locator button calls up the Chooser (Explorer on the PC) so you can swap the files.

4 Save your newly configured set as self-contained.

Once you have made your stereo loops mono, your set should demand significantly less CPU power. You will also likely need to readjust your volume, panning, and some effect settings since the new loops/samples will have changed.

Effects

When running effects within Live, you will continually put pressure on your CPU. Some Live musicians have found it helpful to apply effects from a wave editor, particularly if they are looking for a single effect applied consistently on a single loop. For example, say you want to add a bit of compression to a drum loop, but don't really need a continuous instance of a compressor plug-in loaded in Live. Simply import the drum loop into your wave editor (press Edit in Clip View), and then call up the desired compression plug-in (seen in Figure 10.13). After you apply the effect, save the file and switch back over to Live. Live will update itself with the

Info

Rocktail

Earlier in the book we talked about how Live's Render As Loop option can help save extra instances of Live's delays and reverb effects. In this instance, you will not need a third-party audio editor, but will instead use Live as a temporary one. Solo the loop that you want to render with effects in Live (using the S Solo/Pre-Listening button in Live's session mixer). Apply as many effects as you like, and then call up Live's Rendering menu either by clicking on File > Render To Disk or Ctrl (Cmnd) + R. To preserve the reverb or delay tail, make sure you have turned on Live's Render As Loop box in the render settings. Live will then play the loop internally several times and give you a rendered loop with the correct tail (inside the loop).

modified (compressed) file. Warning, this sort of modification is destructive and permanent, so, as they say, choose wisely. Simply save your set as self-contained to be sure you are working with a copy of the original loop – then be as destructive as you want to be. Also, you should take special care when using any delay-based effect (reverb, echo, chorus, or delay). These effects will carry on after the initial loop has stopped playing to create a tail (see the Rocktail note). The problem created is that you won't hear a tail until the first several notes have sounded.

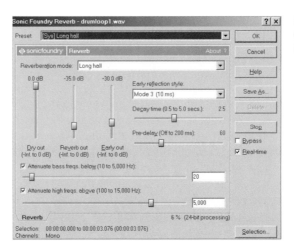

Figure 10.13
Cakewalk's Compression Direct X plug-in in Sound Forge.

If you are wondering what other kinds of effects are possible in a audio editor, you will be impressed. Most wave editors include a large and varied section of VST (Mac or PC), Direct X (PC only), as well as included mastering, audio restoration, and signal maximizing helpers. Figure 10.14 shows just a few of the effects offered in Sonic Foundry's Sound Forge 6.0.

If you have yet to purchase a wave editor you may be salivating after reading this chapter (don't say I didn't warn you). An audio editor is a powerful tool and ally in the digital recording world. Still, by knowing what is possible, and what sort of pitfalls to avoid, you will fare far better as a Live musician, producer, or DJ. In Chapter 11, 'Where to Get Loops, we are going to look at where and how to get loop fuel for your Live software. While this may seem like a left turn, the more loops you load, examine, and play in Live, the more you learn about how to make your own. Speaking of making your own, 'Recording in Live' is just around the next corner, in Chapter 12.

Figure 10.14
Sound Forge 6.0's included effects.

Where to get loops

W hile it is possible to use Live without any pre-made loops and samples, it is sure a lot more fun to grab your latest sample CD, throw (save) some loops on your hard drive, and get to work. Most producers and Live musicians spend a large part of their creative time in pursuit of the loops and samples that will define, or at least support, their 'sound'. Some feel that they must make every loop themselves in order to be authentic. Others feel that any sound in the world is fair game (called *found sounds*), and frequently sample other artists, as well as television and movie soundtracks to use in their compositions. Our goal in this chapter is to explore the options, make sure that you know the basic legalities, and get inspired to make music by building a huge and personalized library of loops. Regardless of where your sounds come from, the key is that your assembled loop library will become your personal musical palette, and ultimately inspire you to make music.

Making loops in Live

By its very nature and aptitude for handling audio, Live is a loop-making machine. Each time you record, edit, or route an outside application (such as Reason, Project5, or Max) into Live via ReWire, you suggest the possibility for creating new loops. By getting yourself in the habit of rendering loops throughout the composing and arranging process, you will quickly and easily amass a sizable library of your own loop and sample musings. These samples can later be used to remix your own work, develop new songs, or serve as a breakdown or starting point for a Live performance. If you are new to loop-based composing, it will become clearer in the next few sections as we explore how to make or select the building blocks for your next musical composition.

Recording a loop performance

When recording in Live, looping can be done automatically without ever skipping a beat by simply activating a Live track to record (click on the Arm Session Recording button), and then click on the empty clip's triangular Record button. Once you have performed your musical idea, stop the recording clip by clicking on any of the same track's Stop buttons, or the newly recorded clip's Clip Launch button (to immediately play the recorded clip). Voilà, you now have a loop. If you choose to stop the clip after recording, Live will continue grooving at the tempo of your song.

You can play this loop at any time by pressing its respective Clip Launch button. In Chapter 12, 'Recording In Live', we will look at several methods for capturing audio into Live's Session and Arranger screens, and revisit this style of recording in great detail.

ReWire loops

In Chapter 13, 'ReWire – Synchronizing Your Software', we will look closely at the different kinds of software applications that are capable of synchronizing with Live. The basic idea is that when audio software applications sync, there is one master and one slave, and only one application retains your audio interface's outputs. Depending on your setup, all audio will go through either Live or the other application – the master application. When audio is routed through Live, as in Figure 11.1, it can easily be captured (recorded) into Live, which is acting as the master in this instance. I use this trick all the time to record loops and performances from Propellerhead's Reason 2.5 software. Once the loop is recorded into Live, it will still need to be rendered, in order to be used in another song.

If you have forgotten how to render, check the 'Rendering Options Explained' section of Chapter 7, 'Editing Your Performance'.

Rendering loops

Since you can render audio in either Session or Arranger Views, virtually any sound made in Live is fair game. I will often grab (render) a small section of a song I am working on, so I can use it in some other way. Once you have compiled several loops into one, you have a more permanent and flexible file. This is similar to the idea of submixing as we discussed in Chapter 6, 'Playing Live...Live'. Each snippet you grab becomes yet another loop for your next Live set or remix.

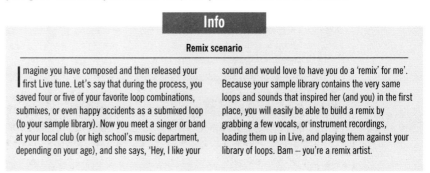

Info

Remix scenario

Imagine you have composed and then released your first Live tune. Let's say that during the process, you saved four or five of your favorite loop combinations, submixes, or even happy accidents as a submixed loop (to your sample library). Now you meet a singer or band at your local club (or high school's music department, depending on your age), and she says, 'Hey, I like your sound and would love to have you do a 'remix' for me'. Because your sample library contains the very same loops and sounds that inspired her (and you) in the first place, you will easily be able to build a remix by grabbing a few vocals, or instrument recordings, loading them up in Live, and playing them against your library of loops. Bam – you're a remix artist.

Sample CDs

Sample CDs include samples, loops, and/or instruments and come in a wide variety of formats. While the idea of sample CDs is not new, the formats are ever-changing. For working with Live, you will want to buy a CD that includes either WAV or AIFF files. You can also buy audio format sample CDs (which can be ripped via iTunes or Music Match with minimal inconvenience). The cost will vary, but you can figure on spending between £20 and £200 per CD. Each year, sample CDs become less expensive as a result of increasing competition. In the following sections, I have mentioned a few of my favourite places to shop.

Tip

Plug and play

One sure-fire way to record cool loops is to synchronize Live with your drum machine of choice, and then record the output. To do this, I set up Live to send MIDI clock to my drum machine and then reroute the inputs into my audio interface (to Live). Then I will program or modify existing preset patterns on the drum machine, and record any that I like. Remember, the best thing about a drum machine is that you can change the sounds in an instant. So, to give your newly recorded loops added dimensions, take a minute and record several different kits (or drum set sounds) playing the same patterns. Of course this method will work for more complex sequencers, such as Akai's MPC 2000/3000/4000 or EMU's XL-7 or MP-7 command stations as well.

Figure 11.1
Live is recording an input from Reason on a ReWire channel.

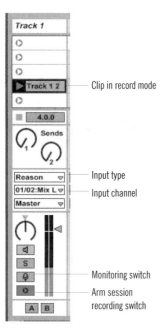

Clip in record mode

Input type
Input channel

Monitoring switch
Arm session recording switch

CD manufacturers

If you are just getting into using sample CDs, there has never been a better time in terms of the quality and variety available. Several companies, such as AMG, BigFish Audio, East West Sounds, Ilio, and Sonic Foundry have been making WAV loop/sample CDs for some time now and feature healthy-sized online catalogs full of what they call acidized loops. *Acidized* means that the loops have been trimmed correctly and contain a tiny bit of file header information for quicker reading in Sonic Foundry's Acid Pro application. These Acid-ready files also work splendidly in Live.

The following list is but a sampling (pun intended) of my favourite loop purveyors. Nearly all of their websites feature downloadable demos or even free content for you to play with. If you happen upon a collection of samples that really work for your project or sound, most sites will also recommend other titles similar to the way the Amazon.com website recommends books – if you liked this, then try that.

- AMG (www.amguk.uk.co)
- Bigfish Audio (www.bigfishaudio.com)
- East West (www.soundsonline.com)
- Electronisounds (www.electronisounds.com)
- Ilio (www.ilio.com)
- Q-UP Arts (www.quparts.com)
- Sonic Foundry (www.sonicfoundry.com)
- Sample Craze (www.samplecraze.com)
- Peace Love Productions (www.peaceloveproductions)
- PowerFX (www.powerfx.com)
- Wizoo (www.wizoo.com)
- Zero-G (www.zero-g.uk.co)

You can also purchase sample CDs at most local music retailers such as Guitar Center, Sam Ash, and Manny's Music, as well as online retailers like Sweetwater.com.

Figures 11.2, 11.3, 11.4 and 11.5, show examples of several sample CDs.

Figure 11.2
Discrete Drums Volume 1 by Sonic Foundry.

Figure 11.3
Discotech by Peace Love Productions.

Figure 11.4
Nu Directions – Phuture Sound of House by Big Fish Audio.

Figure 11.5
Ambient Realms by Kit Watkins available at Qup Arts.

Internet resources

If you just can't wait for a sample CD, or if you prefer to shop via the Internet, there are several established and professional sample houses that offer downloadable wares. You can preview the files first and download the ones you like (for approximately two or three bucks per loop). This can be a convenient and inexpensive way to shop, considering that some sample CDs will only provide you with a few loops that give you what you are looking for.

- Sonomic (www.sonomic.com) – One of the most respected pure online sample retailers on the net, Sonomic will even store your sounds for you on a secure drive in case you need to access your sounds from the road.
- Sound Dogs (www.sounddogs.com) – While Sound Dogs specializes in movie and television sound effects, their online database will turn up several quality loops of virtually every musical style. Also, you might be amazed what a little 'space ship rumble' might do for your next ambient dub jam.
- PowerFX (www.powerfx.com) – PowerFX sells both CDs and loop download packs from their website. Download packs, usually in the $10 range, provide a solid batch in a given style (for example Hip Hop, Techno, etc.).
- Platinum Loops (www.platinumloops.com) – Platinum Loops offers 9000 original loops and samples for download or in DVD and CD formats.

By doing a couple of Google searches, you will stumble across many other pros, hobbyists, and startup sample making companies. The next two caught my eye.

- Loop Kit Pro (www.loopkit.com)
- Acid Fanatic (www.acidfanatic.com)

Continuing in the tradition of doling out free stuff on the net, many sample makers have decided to provide free downloadable sounds. With some reservations, I am going to give you a few starting places, but please keep in mind that many of these sounds can raise unforeseen legal issues (see the 'Copyright Considerations' section later in this chapter). Because you are not paying for the sounds, you can hardly expect the creator, or sampler, as the case may be, to have made these sounds legally. You never can be entirely sure where the original content came from, who played what, and if the material is protected. Also, the quality of what you may discover can vary a great deal.

- Ableton's Artist pages (www.ableton.com > click on artist) – In Ableton's artist section, you can read interviews and, yes, download free loops. As I alluded to earlier, these loops are for personal use only. However, they are great to learn from and are usually of outstanding quality.
- Phatso's Place (www.phatdrumloops.com) – Some of Phatso's drum loops are available only in MP3 format, so you will need to covert them to a wave file using a wave editor or ripping application (such as iTunes). Nearly every loop on this site has been swiped from 'phat' and soulful 70s-era vinyl. So be careful about relying on them for your next Euro dance single.
- e-drummer (www.e-drummer.net) – Quite a few electronic drum loops to download and *learn* from. If you read the copyright notice, you will realize that you cannot use these in commercial releases.
- Dooley Drums (www.dooleydrums.com) – Lots of clean-sounding acoustic drums for use as you see fit, so long as you don't sell them or take credit for making them.

Making your own samples

There are literally too many ways to make loops in Live for me to cover them all here. Still, I want to give you a few ideas for using Live to make fresh and inspiring loops. You can do this from Session or Arranger Views. I typically prefer Arranger View since I can draw in automation and analyze the wave files visually, where Session View allows me to see only one clip at a time. In Figure 11.6, I have created a drum loop using three tracks in Live. Track one is the hi-hat rhythm. Tracks 2 and 3 are the respective snare and kick drum parts. To determine the rhythm of the beat I am building, I use Live's grid and usually work with 2, 4, or 8 measures at a time. Notice that I am using one-shot samples, not loops. I use this technique to make specific drum patterns, with sounds from my sample collection.

Figure 11.6

You can create drum loops one sample at a time

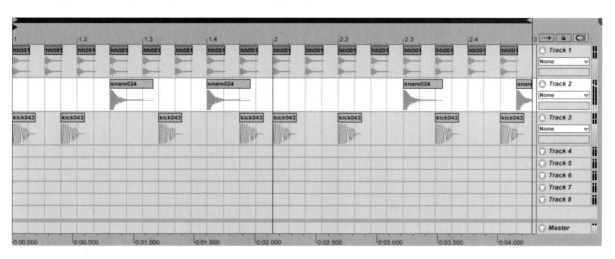

Tip

Only human

One trick to making pattern-based loops sound more musical – and some might say more *human* – is to add subtle variances in volume. By their very nature, hi-hat patterns are primed for this sort of dynamic treatment. I often vary every other hit by decreasing the volume on the up-beat or down-beat consistently. For example, if my first hi-hat sample is zero dB (in Clip View), I make the next one -3 dB. The third hi-hat will be zero dB again and then the forth one –3 or even -5 for more complex programming. Once I have a couple of measures I like, I copy the pattern and paste it throughout the piece (see the Pattern Junkie tip). If you are looking for a disco-esque dance groove, try reversing the dynamics (the first hit softer than the second). This technique also works for other instruments such as funk guitar, organ, and horns.

In Figure 11.7, I have added another kick and snare (tracks 4 and 5), in order to bolster the loop I made in Figure 11.6. In order to remove the inevitable flamming, which occurs when two percussion sounds strike at almost the exact same time, I will shave a little attack from the newly added sample by drawing an automation fade-in for each sound. This sort of editing is a little tedious, so I usually do it once and then copy and paste the edited samples to their desired location – you will need to make sure Live's Lock Envelopes button is off (deactivated). Also, you might try altering sounds by transposing, detuning, adding effects, or

Figure 11.7
You can layer sounds for added complexity and musicality.

changing Live's warp mode. It is a good idea to make several variations once you begin making loops. This way, the next time you are scrolling though your loop library, you will have several options.

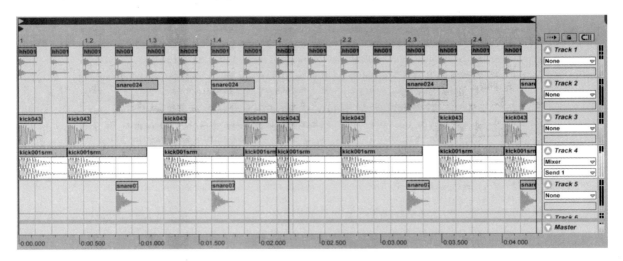

If you would prefer to play rather than program, try mapping each of the preceding hits to your computer keyboard, then place Live in record mode and pound away. You can usually fix any mistakes you made later, so I encourage you to go for it.

Sample storage

Once you begin to get the sample-making/shopping bug, you are going to want to take a look into storage options – since each minute of stereo digital audio takes roughly 10 MB of space. Many Live desktop users dedicate an entire hard drive, multiple hard drives, or hard drive partition, to their sound library. This keeps your main system drive clean and clear from the multiple gigabytes of samples that you acquire.

Laptop users may wish to opt for portable USB, USB 2, or FireWire drives. At the time of this writing, I prefer to use a FireWire drive because of their speed and relative cost savings. However, if you are going to be porting your samples all over town (or around the world), you want to make sure your FireWire drive is durable. Some drives are not meant to be repeatedly transported regardless of how they appear. Make sure you read any special warnings about the FireWire drive before you purchase it.

Recently, I have been using an Apple iPod as a portable and durable hard drive. It is an expensive way to get 20 gigabytes of storage, but the small size and solid design make it the perfect Live loop storage companion – they are built solidly for those on the go.

Organizing your samples

As we learned early on, Live's browser is capable of renaming your sound files. This is an excellent tool to use for organizing your library. The names you choose to use are up to you, but make sure you use folders to sort samples according to content, style, or other naming system. One trick I have developed is to provide the tempo and stylistic hint at the very beginning of the title. Live can always adjust the tempo, but if you are close to the original tempo, the loop will often sound better and make more musical sense. For example, I may call one loop 85_funkydrummer, to tell me the loop is 85 beats-per-minute (BPM) and is a funky drum-oriented loop. For three-digit tempos, I place an underscore at the beginning so that Live's browser will list them numerically. An example would be a strumming guitar loop, at 120 BPM, would be _120_strummyguitar, or a rock bass riff at 115 BPM would be _115_rockbassriff . The key is to be clear and consistent, so that you will easily be able to recall what loop you are going to be dragging back into Live, and be close enough to the original tempo that the loop still retains its original intent. DJs can also employ this trick by listing the tempos and styles of their songs for easier recall.

Figure 11.4 shows one of my hard drives chock full of sample CDs. As I am working on a piece of music, I pull loops and samples from various places. Typically, I rely on my own sounds made in samplers or drum machines, but I still get a lot of inspiration from loop collections. I want to remind you that once you pull a sound from the sample library (that you had better own), save the new file as self-contained so that you will have a fresh copy of the loop in the song/set's folder. This way if you do any destructive audio editing, you can recall the original sample if needed.

Figure 11.8
I have one hard drive specifically allocated for my loop and sample CDs.

Copyright considerations

If you are merely composing and playing with Live at home, you don't need to worry about the legality of your samples. However, the second you start swapping files on the Internet or selling your original compositions, you need to be aware of where the sounds come from (their source). I may not be popular for saying so, but any sound that has been protected via copyright cannot be used until it has been cleared by all proper channels. What sounds are protected? Virtually your entire CD, DVD, and movie collection, television sounds, and most radio broadcasts. Do people still sample these sources and use them in their recordings? Every day. Still, it is important to comprehend the legal ramifications of having someone else's content in your song. The laws have changed since the early hip hop and rap days, where artists such as Public Enemy, the Beastie Boys, and Grandmaster Flash could freely sample and manipulate anything they liked (as long as they gave credit). Now bands with commercial success (or even usage) are sued if caught. You may remember when the Verve was successfully sued by The Rolling Stones for sampling (and not clearing) one of the Stone's string arrangements from their song, 'The Last Time'. Similar cases have been won, like '60s rockers, The Turtles, suing De La Soul for using various samples on De La's *Transmitting Live from Mars* album – not including legal fees, the judgment for the Turtles totaled $1.7 million – a huge sum compared to the $100,000 cost for licensing De La's next album.

In short, I recommend you don't find out the hard way. Have fun, enjoy looping in Live, but just be mindful of where your final composition will end up, and where your samples come from. Besides, there are millions of rights-free loops available for sale, as well as loops you can make and record on your own. Speaking of recording, Chapter 12, Recording in Live', is just around the corner, so let the loop frenzy continue. Some Live musicians make all their own loops, and soon, you can too.

WHO'S USING LIVE?

Akufen – Musician/Producer/DJ

PHOTO BY MARYSE LARIVIERE

Known for his minimalist techno and house dance tracks, Akufen butchers his sonic bytes into oblivion. Whether he is taming sampled bits of Canadian shortwave radio or his own piano and guitar performances, his cleaver of choice is Ableton Live. 'Since Live was launched, a lot has changed for many of us who were using a pre-sequenced show', Akufen explains, 'I'm more flexible and more communicative with the audience. I have a couple of radio sounds banks loaded (in Live), which I can launch anywhere I want through my performance…But everything is loop-based basically. I'd love to eventually go on stage with an empty computer and sample in real time all my sources and sequence it live, but it'll take me a while before I can achieve that with enough confidence. I've been playing Live for only one year now, so I still have a lot to learn'.

When looking for samples, Akufen points to 'found sounds', and his trusty radio. 'Most of my new kickdrums are found sounds often made out of different layered radio noises and the Drumsynth 2.0 software. Same process for my hats and snares. I take sounds from everywhere now', says Akufen, 'the radio became more of a trademark time after time. Now I'm using the television, the telephone, and some field recordings almost as much, but there is something with the radio, which fascinates me more. It's this organic flow. I hate digital radio because there's no way to use a scrolling wheel. It's all digits now, so you lose that in between sweep, which sounds very much like the ocean to me. Radio is the biggest sound library available to everyone, it's free, and it will never be redundant'.

Interview excerpts were recorded by Thaddeus Herrmann and taken from the Ableton website.

Recording in Live

With version 2, recording in Live is now easier and more flexible than in previous versions. For starters, Ableton has made recording in Session View a reality, and they have added handy Punch-in and Punch-out features (which work in both views), for easy overdubbing and loop recording. Live 2 also features a customizable metronome, should you decide to record from scratch.

In earlier chapters, we were primarily concerned with how to make music with Live, and we worked from the assumption that you already had a few loops and samples to play with. In Chapter 11, 'Where to Get Loops', we mentioned several ways to get third-party loops. Now in Chapter 12, it gets personal. Though we have touched on recording several times throughout the book, it is now time to learn firsthand how to record digital audio in Live. That said, some Live musicians (such as DJs) never need to record in Live. They use Live as a loop and sample playback tool, but skip the recording aspect. If this is you, feel free to press on. However, you may want to peek at the various notes and tips dispersed throughout this chapter for a couple of interesting tricks for working with recorded audio.

Setup (monitoring)

Setting up Live correctly the first time will ensure many long hours of fun and pain-free recording. To begin with, you will need to make some decisions about how you plan to listen to your audio as you are recording (called monitoring). I advise routing your computer's output and your recording input to an external hardware mixer that is hooked up to your studio speaker monitors (or headphones). When doing this, you will still need to send your computer a direct signal to record, but you will be monitoring all audio through the outboard (hardware) mixer. To verify the recorded tone or sound of your instrument or vocal signal, you can record small snippets of audio and play them back to check for consistency. Or, you can temporarily turn on Live's Monitor through Live switch in the Preferences Audio tab. This same switch will need to be turned on if you are recording directly into Live without the aid of a mixer, but remember that latency may increase (see the 'Latency' section later in this Chapter).

Routing

Before you can route outside audio into Live, you will need to specify an Input Device in Live's Preferences Audio tab – a one-time setup for each hardware con-

Figure 12.1
The Input Type menu in Live's session mixer (Session View).

figuration. Once this is set up, you will see Live In in Live's session and arranger track inputs. To route input into Session View, click on the Input Type dropdown menu in Live's session mixer, shown in Figure 12.1, and select Live In to record an outside signal. You can also choose your ReWire inputs or Live's Master Output, should you wish to record it (we called this 'rendering on-the-fly' in Chapter 6, 'Playing Live...live').

In Arranger View, the Input Type menu is aligned vertically on the right side of your screen (as seen in Figure 12.2). If the view is hidden from sight you can use the shortcut keys Ctrl (Cmnd) + Alt (option) + I to toggle them in and out of view. Or you can select View > In / Out – a check mark indicates the section is in View.

Figure 12.2
The Input Type menu in Live's Arranger View.

If your audio interface (or sound card) features multiple outputs, you can assign these via the second (middle) dropdown box, called Input Channel, as shown in Figure 12.3. This is also the place to specify ReWire and mono (right or left) channels. For more on mono recording, which is the most common recording method for instruments and vocals, check out the Get on the Bus, Gus note.

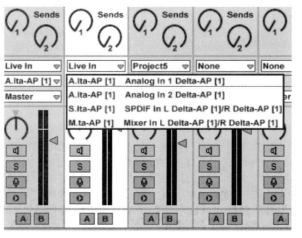

Figure 12.3
The Input Channel menu in Live's session mixer.

Latency

Latency is not only the digital audio buzzword of the decade, but also the annoying time lag present in computer-based audio. The greater the latency, the longer it takes for you to hear your audio input come through your output. This is why I suggested using an external mixer for monitoring your input (recording) source. Latency can also appear as a time lag between making an edit, applying an effect or playing a sample, and the instant you hear the change. We will look at ways to minimize output, input, and overall latency by setting up Live right the first time.

Buffer

Because digital audio data is transferred back and forth as packets from your hard drive to your audio interface, most audio software creates a *buffer* to maintain a steady delivery. If you are hearing audio dropouts, pops, or stuttering in Live's playback, it could be because your buffer is set too low. Conversely, if your buffer is set too high, additional and undesirable latency will occur. To increase your buffer size (if your current setup allows it), open the Audio tab in Live's Preferences menu. If you do not see a buffer size slider (in Live) as in Figure 12.4, it is because you are working with a Mac in OS 9 (using Sound Manager), or because you need to access your audio interface's controls separately, as seen in Figure 12.5. Keep in mind that by lowering the buffer size, you are adding to your computer's processing load, which may create noticeable audio problems.

Info

Update me

Latency can be particularly obnoxious in slow, ill-configured, and otherwise overly burdened computers. Make sure you have downloaded the most up-to-date drivers possible from your audio interface manufacturer's website. Warning, you may need to uninstall your previous drivers for the new ones to work properly. Read the fine print on the accompanying Read me file. Also, see this book's Mac and PC recommendations in Chapter 2, 'Getting Started'. You may need more RAM, a larger hard drive, or even a faster processor to eliminate intolerable latency.

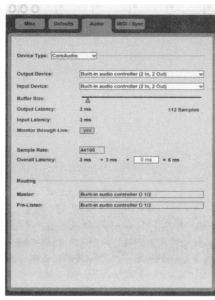

Figure 12.4
You can change your buffer setting in the Audio tab in Live's Preferences.

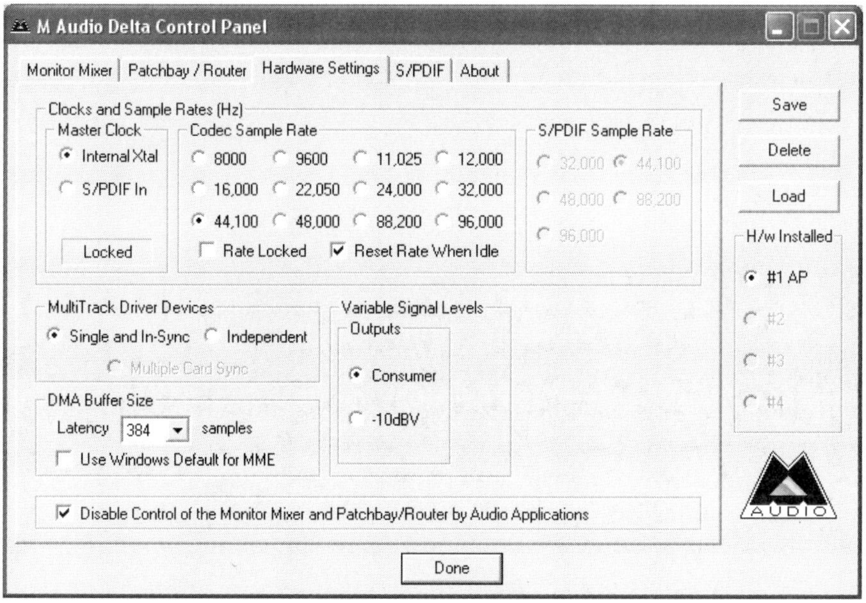

Figure 12.5
M-Audio's Audiophile 2496 interface control settings – other audio interfaces will have different controls.

Most audio interface manufacturers allow you to fine tune their performance settings, which typically include buffer size, sample rate, input/output level, and other pertinent routing and performance settings. Take time to get to know the ins and outs of these secondary interfaces. They are often the solution to problems with input, output, volume, and sample rate compatibility.

Output latency

Minimizing your setup's output latency is particularly important if you are triggering Live via MIDI or the computer keyboard in a live performance situation. The basic idea is to create a stress test for your specific hardware setup and then add a bit of buffer to ensure a crash-free performance. Here are the steps:

1 Open your system's buffer settings either in the Audio tab in Live's Preferences, or in your audio interface's control box.
2 Slide your buffer setting to its maximum (all the way to the right).
3 With Preferences still open, drag a loop from Live's browser to an empty clip slot and launch the clip. The Live manual suggests using a loop with constant audio and very little silence, such as a long keyboard pad or a busy drum pattern.
4 Gradually add effects to the track on which the loop is playing until the CPU usage meter (on the upper right corner of Live's control bar) surpasses 70 percent.
5 Click back into the Audio tab in Preferences and lower the buffer until you begin to hear dropouts, pops, or audio difficulties. Then push the buffer back up to a safer level.
6 Close Preferences, or your audio interface's control box, and see how Live behaves. This should be a one-time setup for each audio interface and computer that you run Live on. If you change your setup periodically, you may need to repeat this process.

Input latency

If you are monitoring your recording source from Live, you may have problems with input latency. *Input latency* is the time differential between the instant you trigger your recording source and the instant you hear the sound emerge from your speakers. Latency has been reduced over the last few years to lower levels, as a result of improved drivers and hardware, but it is still a problem to some degree on modern systems. Listed here are the steps to lower input latency:

1 Minimize audio output latency (as we discussed in the preceding 'Output Latency' section), and then again set your system buffer to its maximum value.
2 Create a source to monitor on the same track – like we did in the 'Output Latency' section(with all the effects loaded). To do this, you must be able to see the In /Out (input/output) tabs on Live's Session Mixer. Click on View, and make sure there is a check mark next to In/Out and then go to any mixer channel. Select Live In from the input pull down menu.
3 Now route your input signal to a track. I recommend a guitar or keyboard rather than a drum machine. You will want to be able to audition the signal to detect latency.

4 Finally, strike a key or string to get an idea of how much audible latency exists. You should hear the stress test effects processing the sound.

5.Lower your Input Buffer Size until you hear dropouts and pops. Then gradually raise the Input Buffer Size until you begin to hear clean and steady audio.

Overall latency

Any time you record into Live, there is an invisible game of compensation going on. Since no sound card or audio interface is free of latency, Live automatically advances audio along to where it should be, based on its automatic detection. Sometimes, with Direct X/MME and ASIO drivers, Live guesses wrong, and needs to be manually configured. Ableton suggests the following steps to help correct this:

1 Turn off the Monitor Input Thru Live switch in Live's Preferences (Audio tab).

2 Connect a physical cable from your audio interface's input to its output (creating a short circuit). This can be done with either an analog or digital connection, but must be done on your system's hardware.

3 Choose a short percussion sample with a sharp (easy to see) attack, and drag it to the very beginning of track 1 in Arranger View. You could also use lo dr_26.wav from Live's Demo Sounds folder – although it is a loop – it starts sharply on beat one.

4 Set up track 2's input to receive Live In, which in this case will be Live's output rerouted to itself in step 1.

5 Arm track 2 by clicking on the Arm Arrangement Recording and Automation Recording buttons, and then press Play and record a couple seconds of audio. Press Stop.

6 Track 2 will now contain a recording of track 1 delayed by the very same amount as your systems latency. Aha!

7 Double click on the new clip (in track 2) and turn off the warp switch.

8 In Clip View, move the left side of the region marker to the right until you reach the first transient of the recorded wave file. Zoom in (via the magnifying glass tool over the sample display), so that you can be exact.

9 Notice the difference in milliseconds at the bottom of the clip view display (as shown in Figure 12.6).

10 Open Live's Preferences (Audio tab) and enter the amount of milliseconds in the open box under Overall Latency. Try a second recording to see if you have fixed the discrepancy. If you have not, go back to step four and give it another try. Remember that the overall latency sum is the adjustment that Live will make when placing newly recorded audio. You do not need to compensate for it by making it zero.

Figure 12.6
Your system's overall latency.

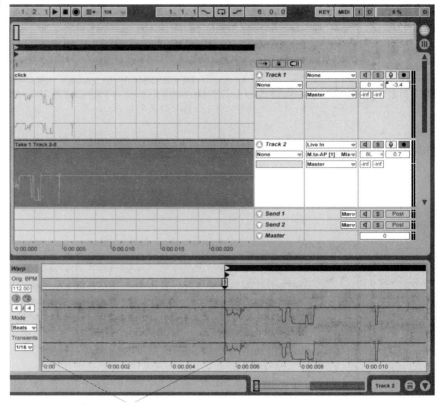

Your system's overall latency (approx 5 milliseconds)

Signal level

Figure 12.7
A peaking meter.

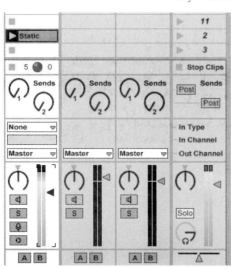

Audio Engineers are often obsessive about capturing the loudest (they will usually say 'hottest') signal level possible without crossing the line into distortion territory. Truth is, they have a point. In the analog world, the recording level directly affects the signal to noise level – the louder your musical instrument or voice is recorded, the less room there is for tape noise (hiss). Digital recording operates a little differently in that low-level recordings result in a noticeable loss of fidelity as a result of diminished sampling and lackluster signal.

When recording in Live, you will want to capture the hottest (loudest) signal you possibly can without peaking. You know you are peaking in Live when any of the level meters (seen in Figure 12.7), reach well into the red and surpass the 0 dB level. Digital distortion is nearly always an undesirable and offensive popping or glitch and should be avoided. This differs from the warmth and saturation of analog distortion caused by peaks.

To ensure that Live is receiving the loudest signal possible, you should also check your signal level to your own mixer, which may or may not have level meters. Also, you may need to again visit your audio interface's input settings, as well as Live's input bus, shown in Figure 12.8.

Figure 12.8
Live's input bus can help boost your input signal.

Metronome

New to Live 2 is the customizable metronome, which can be toggled on/off by switching on its button in Live's control bar (shown in Figure 12.9). When playing, the metronome will produce two different sounds, one higher pitched click to signal the beginning of a measure (on beat 1), and a second sound for each subdivision of the measure. A bar of 4/4 time will have four clicks, a sharp one followed by three of the second sound, while a bar of 12/8 will feature 1 and then 11. Use the signature numerator/denominator to the left of the metronome switch (also seen in Figure 12.9) to change the time signature in Live.

Tap   Tempo   Time signature   Metronome switch

Figure 12.9
The metronome switch.

In Chapter 3, 'Live Interface Basics', we discussed Live's tempo and tap tempo settings. When recording a new clip, the clip will assume the tempo and time signature settings of when it was recorded.

Info
Forgive and forget

If you are having trouble getting a hot enough signal into Live, you can take solace in the fact that there are many ways to remedy this problem after the fact. Of course, you can raise the recorded clip's volume, but you will achieve even better results by taking the time to open your audio editor and compress or normalize the results. For more information on normalizing with an audio editor, refer to Chapter 10, 'Wave Editing Tips'. For normalizing via Live's rendering options, see the 'Rendering Options Explained' section in Chapter 7, 'Editing Your Performance'.

Tip
Record in re-pitch mode

When recording audio from an outside source at the final project tempo, I recommend changing the warp mode to Re-pitch – you can also make Re-pitch your default mode in Live's Preferences if you are going to be doing a lot of recording. Re-pitch turns off Live's pitch correction and eliminates any phasing or strange artifacts resulting from Live's attempts to 'correct' your recording. You should do this only when you are recording at the exact and final tempo of the piece. If you plan on changing tempo, you should experiment with the Loop Modes as we discussed in several places earlier in the book – Beats for percussion, Tones for basses and melodies, and Textures for noise and more complex sounds. If you want refresh your memory about Live's Warp Modes (loop treatment), see Chapter 4's section called 'Warp Markers', and Chapter 5's 'Warp Mode' discussion.

Recording in Session View

Session View is generally the place to capture quick loops and performances while putting together your Live song (or set). For extended recording, most Live musicians prefer the Arranger View (see next section). Regardless of which view you record in, all recordings in Live will immediately become clips, and their audio data will be stored in your designated Audio Record folder (see the Clean-Up Time note).

To record a clip, click on the Arm Session Recording button in Live's session mixer (shown in Figure 12.10). After doing so, all of the empty clip slots on the corresponding track will display a red triangle-shaped Record button. Click on any Record button in the track to begin the clip's recording. While recording, the triangle becomes a red square Stop button. To watch your recording as it happens, double-click on the bar of the clip in Record mode to open Clip View. You can also stop the recording by clicking on any other record or clip launch buttons on the track. If you are recording multiple tracks (clips) at once, you can start and stop clips by using the Scene Launch section. This is handy for recording a group of musicians or instruments that use more than one microphone (such as drums or piano).

In Chapter 13, 'ReWire – Synchronizing Your Software', we discuss how to capture performances from ReWire-enabled applications (such as Reason, Project5, Orion, and others) in Session View.

Figure 12.10
Live's arm session record and record buttons.

Record buttons

Clip in record mode

Press to stop recording

Measures and beats recorded so far

Arm session recording

Tip

Clean-up time

All recordings, or *takes*, made in Live will be stored in the designated Audio Record Folder set via the paths section in the Preferences Misc tab). However, once you delete a newly recorded clip from the Live set or song you are working in, you can then opt to permanently delete these files from your hard drive by closing the Live song, and answering Yes to the dialog box when Live asks, Would you like to delete the temporary samples in (your audio record folder)?

Tip

Go long, Dr. John

I am not a professional keyboardist, but I play one when recording in Live. I frequently capture five-minute (or even longer) recordings into a clip and then build my solo by piecing together the best sections. To do this, I will make several copies of the very same clip and grab loops of two, four, or more measure at choice selections of the larger recording. In other DAW applications you may be used to editing each performance, eliminating excess audio data, and pasting to a new track. However, Live allows for these edits to remain non-destructive (temporary), and yet be treated as separate samples (clips). In Figure 12.11, I have edited and fixed a small keyboard lick. Notice that I am using a very small section of a much longer recording. This method works for many types of instruments, and is a natural for comping a vocal track.

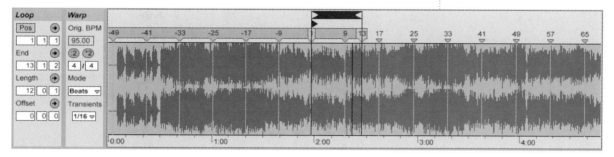

Recording in Arranger View

To record a track or tracks in Live's Arranger View, simply designate an input source, arm the tracks for recording by clicking on the Arm Arrangement Recording button, and then press Live's Arm Automation Record button in Live's control bar. Once you press Play, Live will record until you either stop the track from recording by deactivating its Arm Arrangement Recording button, or turn off the main Arm Session Recording button in the control bar. In Figure 12.12, I have grabbed a screen shot of a track that is in Record mode. Notice that the input must be set to something other than None in order to receive input.

   If you are monitoring through Live (set in Live's Preferences), you have the option of monitoring your recorded track by clicking on the monitoring box (with the microphone icon) next to the Recording button. After you record your audio, you will need to switch off monitoring your input to hear your newly recorded track's output.

Figure 12.11
Make small loops or sections out of longer recordings.

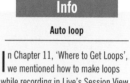

Auto loop

In Chapter 11, 'Where to Get Loops', we mentioned how to make loops while recording in Live's Session View. Any recordings made in Live can be looped, and will loop automatically if your clip's loop/warp default setting in Preferences is set to Auto.

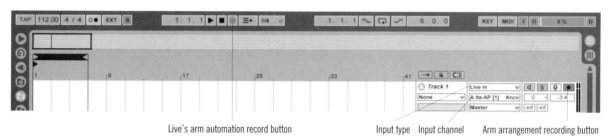

Live's arm automation record button   Input type   Input channel   Arm arrangement recording button

Punch-in/punch-out

New to Live 2 is the punch-in and punch-out feature. Punching in (or out) is a trick used by audio engineers and musicians alike to fix mistakes in small (or even medium size) sections of a recording that is otherwise in good shape. It saves having to re-record the entire piece. For example, you may love the first 64 bars of your guitar part. Then, you broke a string and played poorly for a minute or two, yet still managed somehow to play the guitar solo of your life on the last half of the song. In this instance you would *punch-in* (drop that track into Record mode) somewhere before you broke your string, and *punch-out* (take that track out of Record mode) before your beautiful solo. Live allows you to set up these points ahead of time, so that your solo and intro remain intact no matter what you play in the interim. In Figure 12.13, I have set up Live's punch-in and punch-out markers, which will also

Figure 12.12
A track set up to record in Arranger View.

be Live's master loop endpoints. This is handy since you may need to loop the punch-in section for multiple takes, or passes.

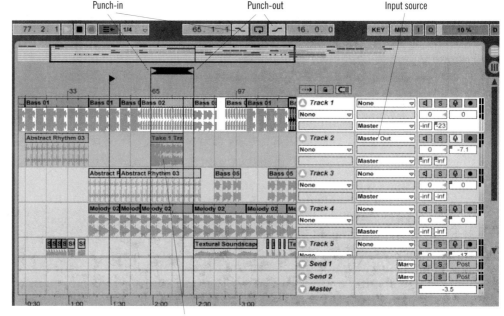

Punch-in   Punch-out   Input source

Figure 12.13
Punching in on a track.

Punch-in recording

You can also use just the punch-in or the punch-out by itself. Say you like the first part of the song, but want to redo the rest. This would be a perfect time to punch-in just after things got hairy. Or you may like your performance at the end of a song, but you flubbed the intro section. Here you would set up only the punch-out marker and begin with your track in record. There is no size limit to the section of audio that you can fix by punching in and out. You can fix mixing and effects automation, or your song sequence by punching in with a scene. Punching in/out is most often used in Arranger View, but is able to work in Session View too should you need it.

By putting what you have learned in this chapter to use, you will be well on your way to mastering recording and composing in Live. Don't be discouraged if your first few recordings need a little signal level adjustment, or even need to be replaced. The best part about digital audio may be that tape (hard drive space) is cheap. So make sure and record several takes if you are not sure you've got 'the one'. In the last few chapters of this book, we are going to get into increasingly advanced and powerful topics: Rewire, Warp Marker tips and even more examples of how artists are using Live – see the next 'Who's Using Live?' notes. If you feel like you need to refresh a concept or practice what we have just learned, please take the time to go back and review earlier chapters. After all, you already know more than enough to make amazing music with Live.

WHO'S USING LIVE?

Mogwai — Band/Musicians

PHOTO BY BERND ZHAN

Always looking for adventure, Mogwai delivers songs in the key of indie rock as freely as they dive into ambient, if angry, instrumentals walled by guitar feedback. They've been compared with Godspeed You Black Emperor, Sigur Ros, and, dare I say, Radiohead. Now for their next trek, how about a little Ableton Live loop-controlled electronica? In the summer of 2003, Ableton hooked up with Mogwai's guitarist John Cummings to discuss how his band stumbled upon Live 2.0, and how their music will be rewarded. And how references such as Vladislav Delay, Kid 606, Pita, and Cylob, attach themselves to the Mogwai aesthetic. The following interview was taken in part from the Ableton website > artists section.

Ableton: It is common knowledge that a typical mixdown these days is done in programs like Pro Tools. How much are you interested in that process, or do you let somebody else handle it? Do you generally use software when it comes to working on a Mogwai track?

John Cummings: The last three albums that we've recorded have used computers extensively for pretty much everything from tracking, mixing and editing to whatever else, along with more traditional equipment. I'd worry that we would be stupid to avoid electronic equipment. It would be to the detriment of what we do. If we're going to bother making music at all, we should try to make it the best that it can be and there are loads of things that

you can do with computers that you can't do with anything else. We've been using various keyboard sounds from Barry's PC and Supercollider from a Mac for a while. Previously, it had been in the hands of the engineers. We worked with Tony Doogan on the last couple of records and he's some kind of Pro Tools genius, while also being able to rebuild any analogue gear. So we can work with pretty much the best of both worlds.

Ableton: How and when did you discover Live?

John Cummings: Stuart has been going on about it for ages, but he didn't know anything about it really, so it took us a while to get it together. We had been using Cubase to sequence some stuff live and it just wasn't working out for us, so we finally had a go at it.

Ableton: How was Live used on the new record? What do you intend doing with it in the future?

John Cummings: We hadn't really had a look at Live until after the record was finished. We had a lot of tunes with a lot of samples and needed to make them work at gigs. We've been using a Roland sequencer with an S5000 for the last couple of years to do the stuff off the last record, but there was a song that needed lots of different loops running on different time signatures and we couldn't get it together. Then we tried to run it from Cubase, because we had been using it a lot for demos, but it's obviously not meant to be used live, so it was a bit of a worry. Live has worked out totally cool though, thankfully. We were in a bit of trouble if we couldn't play a lot of these new songs live.

It looks like we'll be using it a lot for getting demos for the next record ready over the next year or so. We will also be adding more to our live tunes to make them a bit different from how we've been playing them for the past seven years or so.

Ableton: How does Live differ from other programs you use? What's the beauty of it?

John Cummings: It's really, really, really, really simple to get stuff in and out of it and we can depend on it to not stop in the middle of a song, which would be a bit of a nightmare. Mortifying.

Mogwai's newest release, Happy Songs For Happy People was released June of 2003 on Matador.

ReWire – synchronizing your software

In this chapter, we will explore how to link your virtual studio by using a quick and easy software application called ReWire. If you have yet to experience the joy of working with ReWire-linked applications, you are in for a treat. For those who know and love ReWire, Live is your new best friend. If you do not have another ReWire-enabled application (such as Reason, Project5, or MAX/MSP), you may soon (in about two more paragraphs) be feeling the urge.

ReWire basics

'ReWire was developed and is licensed by Propellerhead (www.propellerheads.se). who intended to provide a 'realtime audio streaming between applications, sample accurate synchronization, and common transport functionality. 'It's free, basically automatic, invisible, and comes with all ReWire-capable applications. Even better, ReWire simultaneously connects your virtual studio's software by enabling audio and MIDI synchronization between two (or more) applications – a client and a host.

You can route another ReWire-enabled application through Live seamlessly, synchronize playback, and control starting and stopping from either application's transport bar – in Live, we refer to this as the control bar. You can record any ReWire slave application's output into Live while using Live or VST effects. Or, you can take advantage of Live's awesome loop synchronizing ability by routing its output through Cubase, Sonar, or Logic Audio, to name a few. In these instances, Live would be the slave and the DAW application, the master.

ReWire is quickly becoming standard issue for most audio applications. New applications such as Cycling 74's radiaL and Cakewalk's Project5 feature full ReWire (client and host) connectivity. Cementing the trend for more established applications, Digidesign recently announced plans to integrate ReWire into future Pro Tools versions. The following two lists show common slave and master applications. You will need to own at least one of these (in addition to Live) to experience the thrill of ReWire.

ReWire slaves (to be routed through Live)

• Storm by Arturia (www.arturia.com).
• Retro AS-1 and Unity DS-1 by Bitheadz Inc. (www.bitheadz.com).
• MAX/MSP and radiaL by Cycling 74 (www.cycling74.com) – Both master and slave.

- Reason and ReBirth RB 338 by propellerheads (www.propellerheads.se).
- Orion by Synapse Audio (www.synapse-audio.com).
- Girl by Yowstar (girl.yowstar.com).

ReWire masters (to route Live through)

- Sonar 2.0 and Project5 by Cakewalk (www.cakewalk.com).
- Cubase SX, SL, VST, and Nuendo 1.5+ by Steinberg (www.steinberg.de).
- Tracktion 1.2 by Raw Material Software (www.rawmaterialsoftware.com).
- MAX/MSP and radiaL by Cycling 74 (www.cycling74.com) – Both master and slave.
- Logic 6.0 by Emagic (www.emagic.de).
- Digital Performer by MOTU (www.motu.com).
- Pro Tools by Digidesign (www.digidesign.com).

Master or slave

To run two ReWire applications, you must always have one master and one (or more) slaves – these are also commonly referred to as host and clients. Master ReWire applications communicate with the audio hardware to act as the audio output hub for any connected slave applications. With Ableton's release of Live 2.1 (July 2003), Live is now capable of running as either Master or Slave in Windows, OS 9, and OS X.

To determine which application is the master, simply open it first. Once launched, all ReWire-capable applications assume they are the master, and prohibit other applications from claiming access to your system's audio hardware. So, the second (and subsequent) ReWire applications launched will become slaves. When closing ReWire applications, you will always have to close the slave first, and then the master. Though attempting to close applications in the wrong order can do no harm, you will see a warning message telling you to close the slave first.

Live as master

The following steps outline how to establish a ReWire connection in which Live is in the driver's seat (the master), and your second application will be the slave.

1 Launch Live.
2 Launch ReWire-capable slave application – you have just set up Live as the ReWire master and the second application as a slave. Now let's correctly configure the audio.
3 To hear your slave application's audio in Live, you will have to route it into the channel of your choosing by selecting the slave application's name from the Input Type dropdown menu in Live's track's inputs (Figure 13.1).
4 Then designate the channels you want to listen to in Input Channel (Figure 13.2 on page 222).
5 To hear the results of your routing, you must activate a track's Monitoring button – the microphone icon in Figure 13.3.

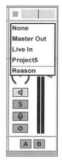

Figure 13.1
Choose the ReWire slave from Input Type.

Figure 13.2
Choose the slave's inputs from Live's Input Channel.

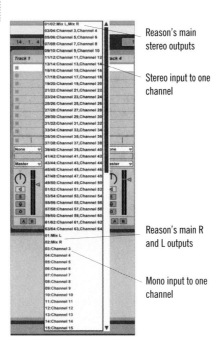

Reason's main stereo outputs

Stereo input to one channel

Reason's main R and L outputs

Mono input to one channel

Figure 13.3
A track's Monitoring must be enabled to hear ReWire slave.

Live as slave

1 Launch ReWire-capable master application.
2 Launch Live. Live's audio will now have to be redirected to the ReWire master app.
3 Follow the instructions for routing the slave's audio through your master application.

Sample rate matching

When working in ReWire mode, your master and slave sample rates must be the same to ensure recording and playback stability. Some things to consider:

• Your project's sample rate will always be determined by the master (host) application.
• Any ReWire slave will need to be capable of operating at the master's sample rate, or else the master's rate must be reduced.
• Make sure to save and close any running ReWire slave application before resetting your master application's sample rate (in that application's preferences or options settings).
• You may be required to restart both applications so that changes can take effect. In fact, it is a good idea.
• If sample rates do not match, Live's Ext (external synchronization) button in the control bar may flicker rapidly.
• For a detailed discussion of sample rates, refer to Chapter 4, 'Digital Audio Basics'. Live's Preferences explanation in Chapter 2, 'Getting Started', will explain how to set Live's sample rate.

ReWire power

Now that you have established the basic ReWire connection, you may want to explore a few of the more powerful ways to work with ReWire. For instance, you can assign multiple outputs from your slave to your master, or control both applications at the same time using multiple MIDI channels. You may also want to record a ReWire application's output into the host, for more centralized (flexible) control. In the following sections, we will outline how to take even greater advantage of ReWire's virtual studio link capabilities.

Recording ReWire audio in Live

Once you are successfully monitoring a ReWire channel in Live, you need only press the Arm Session Recording button on the channel you wish to record, and you are tracking (as we saw in Chapter 12, 'Recording in Live'). Why would you want to record if you can already play the audio through Live's output? Here are a few possible reasons:

- System strain – Running two or more applications may be too much for your system. In this instance, solo the ReWire track (to conserve system resources), and then record the loop or loops one at a time into empty clips. Then close the ReWire applications and work exclusively from Live.
- Flexibility – By recording loops or audio into Live from your ReWire app, you may be able to work with the material more easily. I find this particularly true with drums and vocals, which can often require a few extra nudges in Live to get the timing just right.
- Simplicity – ReWire is fairly straightforward; however, viewing both applications on a single monitor (even a really big one) just isn't possible. If you need to get a better idea of what is going on in a certain song or song section, consider recording the audio for at least mock-up purposes.

Multiple inputs/outputs

Once you have set up your ReWire master to receive a stereo pair of inputs from your slave application, you may begin to imagine the possibilities of routing audio to different channels. For instance, you may want to use different effects on the drums than on the bass, keyboards, or sampler output. Or you may want to record simple loops containing part of the slave's output – as opposed to the entire mix coming through on two tracks. To do this, you will have to set up your slave to send multiple outputs, and then set up your master to receive them. I've set up Propellerhead's popular Reason software (running as a ReWire slave) to send Live (master) eight outputs (Figure 13.4) by routing two instruments and one sampler sending six separate channels. For individual channel sends in Reason, always start with channel three – the first two channels are a stereo pair. Other applications work in similar fashion.

Figure 13.4
Eight channels of Reason output will go to eight separate Live tracks.

In Figure 13.5, I have set up eight separate Live inputs to correspond with the eight channels of Reason output. Theoretically, you can set up as many as 64 outputs from a single Reason session, and unlimited tracks in Live, though most systems would not be able to handle it.

Figure 13.5
Eight channels of ReWire input routed into Live.

Similarly, if you are running Live as a slave to an application such as Sonar, Logic, or Cubase, you can route multiple outputs from Live by allocating extra channels in your host (Figure 13.6).

Figure 13.6
Sonar 2.2's dialog box for choosing multiple inputs when opening a ReWire application.

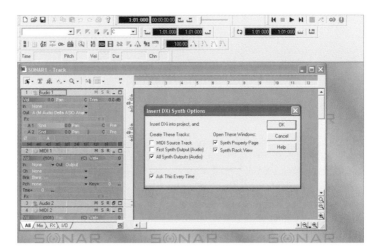

Once you do this, you will see Live's inputs inside your host (Figure 13.7) and be able to route Live's outputs via multiple Bus sends in Live's session mixer (seen in Figure 13.8).

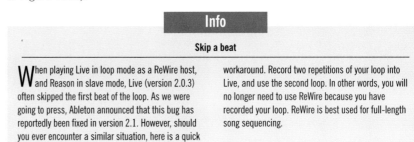

Info

Skip a beat

When playing Live in loop mode as a ReWire host, and Reason in slave mode, Live (version 2.0.3) often skipped the first beat of the loop. As we were going to press, Ableton announced that this bug has reportedly been fixed in version 2.1. However, should you ever encounter a similar situation, here is a quick workaround. Record two repetitions of your loop into Live, and use the second loop. In other words, you will no longer need to use ReWire because you have recorded your loop. ReWire is best used for full-length song sequencing.

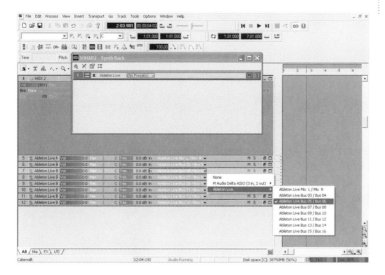

Figure 13.7
Sonar 2.2's dialog box for choosing multiple inputs when opening a ReWire application.

Figure 13.8
Choose stereo bus (tracks in ReWire master) where you would like to route Live's tracks.

MIDI-control

To send MIDI-control information to both master and slave applications, assign your ReWire slave to receive on a different MIDI channel. Since most MIDI keyboards and controllers can quickly change which MIDI channel they are sending on, this can make swapping during a live performance quick and easy. In Figure 13.9, I have set up Reason to receive on a channel 2, while my Live MIDI map contains only channel 1 mappings.

The channel you decide to use is up to you, so long as they are different. You might also decide to use one channel for loop triggering in Live, and another for channel mutes, and still another for your Reason or Project5 synths. The key is to find a workable formula, and stick to it. Then save the template. For an example, turn to Appendix B, 'Web Resources', and see my ReWire-Station Template.

In this chapter, we have looked at the most common ways to use ReWire with Live and other ReWire slave and master applications. ReWire is an incredibly exciting, creative, and fun aspect of Live. Many musicians and producers I have met come to Live because of its ability to ReWire. I assure you that, once you begin linking software applications, you will be hooked. Take time to explore your favourite ways of linking Live. As new applications become ReWire-enabled, and CPUs become increasingly faster, we may soon be linking computers via LAN, or even the Internet in similar ways to ReWire. In the next chapter, we will explore some of my favourite power tips for working with Live.

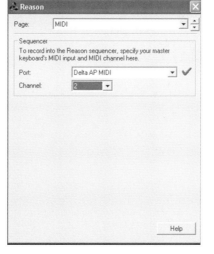

Figure 13.9
Use separate MIDI-channels for each ReWire application.

WHO'S USING LIVE?

Pat Mastelotto – Musician

Pat Mastelotto's drumming career spans the Icelandic funk of Bjork's Sugarcubes (percussion) to the definitive 80s pop-crew Mr. Mister (drums) to the artfully Beatlesque XTC (drums). Now retained by art rock luminaries King Crimson, Mastelotto remains ahead of the loop and sample-gadget curve by ReWiring Reason and Live in his Austin, Texas project studio. '(Propellerhead) Reason and (Ableton) Live can be used to write and experiment on the fly and are perfect for an ever-changing band like Crimson', Mastelotto explains. 'Live has become my frontline buddy, I'm just lovin' Live', concludes the Crimson drummer. 'There's this thing where you can go into the sample and change its Warp settings, kind of like the way you use markers in ReCycle to chop up samples. It's awesome, you just move those things randomly, or when you put beats 1, 2, and 3 all within the first 16th note and then spread all the other events between beat 4 and the downbeat of the next bar across the next

PHOTO BY BILL MUNYON

three beats. Just to move those Warp markers and flags around while it's playing, wow'.

Power tips – the magic of Live

I n this chapter, our focus will shift from the left-brained Live interface and components to the right-brained production side of working with loops, samples, and digital audio. Herein you will find several tips gleaned from my own experience working with Live and similar loop and sample manipulation software. These ideas are meant as a jumping off point for new musical ideas. Please take these concepts and run with them. And please send me a copy of your record when you're famous.

Warp Markers

The amount of groove massaging made possible by Live's Warp Markers is truly limitless. At first, you may be frustrated by how to specifically adjust a beat or loop to make it sound the way you're hearing it in your head or to get it to align properly within your audio project. But with a little practice, you will develop an intuition for how Warp Markers gradually shift a pattern's events. In the following list, I have outlined a few of my favourite techniques to get you started. After you master my examples, take time to experiment with Ableton's powerful Warp tool. There really are no rules, so go for it!

- **Feel** The trouble and triumph of loop-based music is that feel often becomes stagnant, unwavering, monotonous, and uninspired. It's why dance music is often for dancers, and not made for musicians. To combat the static element in loop-based music, it is important to add a little variety, even if the results are basically imperceptible to the untrained or unsuspecting ear. There are several methods for doing this, but the easiest I find is to subtly (not randomly!) move a few Warp Markers after several repetitions of the loop. For instance, you are working in Live's Arranger View and you have played 16 measures of a loop. On bar 16, you might try chopping the loop in half and raising the volume at the end of the measure to slightly push or rush the feel (shown in Figure 14.1). This is to simulate the excitement most drummers can't help but exude when approaching the end of a musical phrase.
- **Ahead and behind the beat** Drummers and bass players have developed a unique relationship through the years. An artist's 'feel' is often as important as what is being played. You will often hear musicians or critics say it's not what musician play, but 'how they play it'. One musical dialog common to the tradition of drummers and bassists (including organ and synth bass) is that of play-

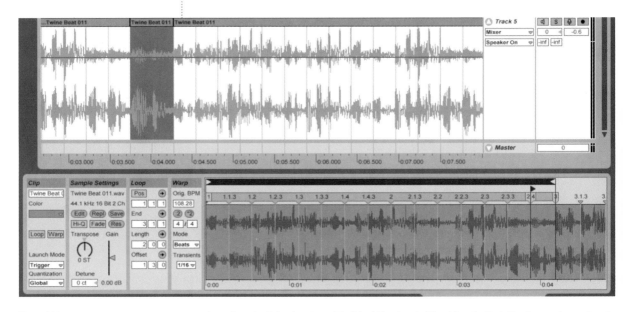

Figure 14.1
Altering the last couple of beats in a phrase can add realism.

Figure 14.2a (top)
Simple drum groove aligned with Ableton's Warp Markers.

Figure 14.2b (bottom)
Moving the Warp Markers to the left to make the beat more laid back.

ing ahead of the beat and behind the beat. The idea is that the bass player (and the rest of the band) plays on the beat, while the drummer plays slightly behind the 2 and 4 snare hits. Generally, you want your kick drum to remain in the same place, meaning squarely on the beat. To play on top or ahead of the beat, the drummer ever so slightly rushes the hit on the snare and even the hi-hats and cymbal parts. This can give the music a rushed or more energetic feel popular in many dance styles. In Figure 14.2a, I have provided a simple drum beat. Notice that the beats line up perfectly with Live's Warp Markers. In Figure 14.2b I have pushed a few Warp Markers to the left to make the snares feel sluggish or behind the beat, while in Figure 14.2c I have pushed the same Warp Markers slightly to the right of the snare for a more rushed feel – ahead of the beat.

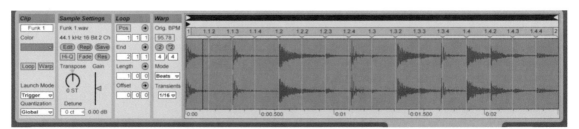

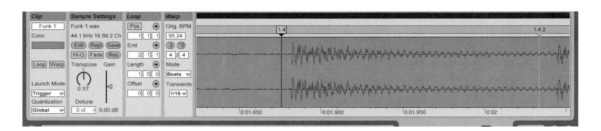

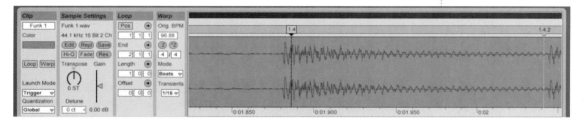

• **Extending one-shot style loops**   Sometimes a looping sample will play too often. Examples such as a single drum hit firing every eighth-note instead of every quarter, or a horn section blast on every downbeat instead of every measure come to mind. In this instance, you have two options. You can either render the small one-shot in Arranger View (best for tiny samples), or you can extend the sample region. When using the second option, I drag time (grid markers) into the clip by creating a Warp Marker close to the end of the clip and then dragging the last Warp Marker towards it. I repeat the process until I have achieved the loop duration I am looking for. Figure 14.3a is a one-shot sample that I have looped. Let's assume I want to double the length of the loop so that it occurs half as often.

Figure 14.2c
Moving the Warp Markers to the right makes the groove feel 'on top'.

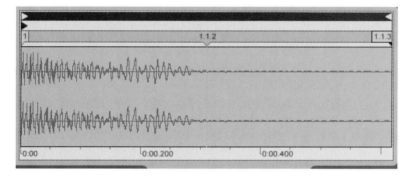

Figure 14.3a
A one-shot drum sample I have chosen to loop.

In Figure 14.3b, I created a Warp Marker at 1.1.2 and then dragged the ending Warp Marker 1.1.3 toward it until marker 1.2 is in sight – beat 1.2 is the second quarter note in the measure and makes the sample's duration a full quarter note in length.

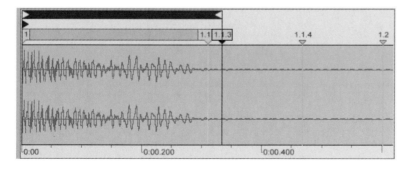

Figure 14.3b
Create an anchor, and then move the Warp Markers to the left.

Now I will create a Warp Marker on 1.2, drag to the end, and omit all Warp Markers (by double-clicking on them) between 1.1.2 and 1.2. Make sure you re-extend the loop's region to the end (1.2) when you are finished to make the sample last a full beat. With a little practice, this technique is as easy as 1.2.3, ha!

Figure 14.3c
My one-shot is now twice its original length, and will therefore occur half as often.

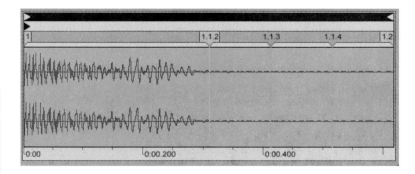

Info

Too short for tricks

In some instances, your original one-shot sample is too short to be extended and will create strange-sounding digital artifacts. For these occasions, I recommend adding space at the end of your sample in your audio editor or in Live by loading the clip into the Arranger View and then rendering it to the desired amount. Other tricks for ridding your one-shot samples of artifacts are to change the warp mode to Tones, Textures, or Repitch, or you can reduce the amount of transient detection to 1/4, 1/2, or Bar.

Beat wreckin' clinic

Making breakbeats, funky drum patterns, and fills is often best done via trial and error. Especially since so much of the music made on computers is programmed and not played. That said, here are a few ideas for making your looped drum and percussion grooves freak the beat.

- **Slice 'n' dice**   Take any drum loop in arranger view, and use Live's Split command – Ctrl (Cmnd) + E – at common rhythmic subdivisions (1/4, 1/8, and 1/16-note settings), as shown in Figure 14.4a. Then rearrange the order of the newly made clips. I like to do this in the track below the original track as shown in Figure 14.4b. Results will vary, but many a 'happy accident' will occur. As always, if you are pleased with your results, render the new loop.

Figure 14.4a
Repeatedly split any clip.

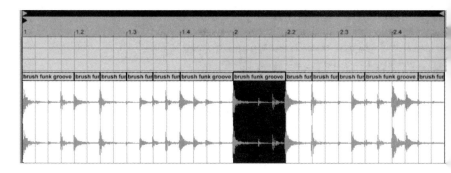

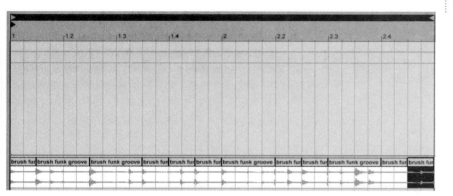

Figure 14.4b
Rearrange the components as you like.

Figure 14.5
Use these buttons to halve or double a small section of a loop.

- **Double for nothing**   Another quick trick for adding rhythmic variety to stale loops is to use Live's double and halve original tempo buttons (shown in Figure 14.5). Try sectioning off a 1/4 or 1/8-note section of a loop by using Live's Split command, and then double or halve the tempo of the smaller section.

  In Figure 14.6, I have halved the last 1/4-note section of the larger loop to give it a slight change in feel. Experiment with other subdivisions and doubling the groove as well for the best results.

Create split in loop   Then halve tempo

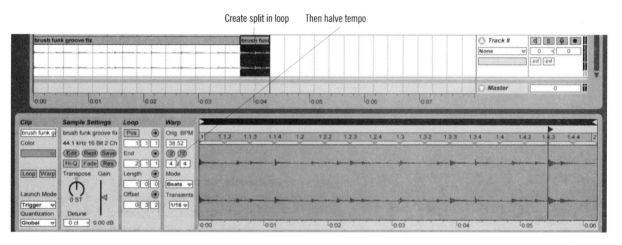

Figure 14.6
Split loop and then halve new segment to create fill.

- **From the offset**   Topping the list of Dave's fave tricks is to take any of the preceding examples and change the sample offset for a freshly made loop segment. In Figure 14.7, I have taken the section I halved in 14.6 and moved the start time to 1.2. For this particular drum groove, it creates a very realistic and normal-sounding drum fill or groove variation.
- **The rhythmic microscope**   When trying to line up a loop's feel with other loops and recordings, try working with smaller sections one at a time. I find this trick helpful when working with varying degrees of swing or unusual syncopations. In other words, I will work with the first half of the loop until it feels like it complements the feel of the song, and then move to the second half.

Move sample offset to create variety

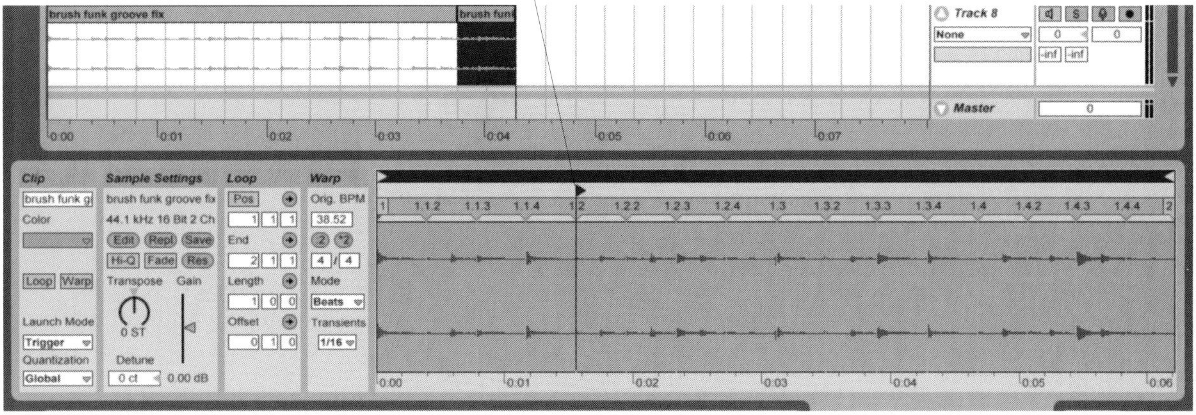

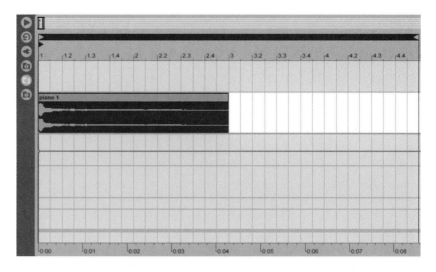

Figure 14.7
Move sample offset to create variety.

Figure 14.8
Zoom in tight to work with within the
framework of a couple of measures.

Creating melodies from samples

Single note samples can be used to make melodies and bass lines by carefully re-pitching each note. To do this, find and drag a one-shot sample of a keyboard, bass guitar, or other tonal instrument into Live. Next adjust the sample's clip properties (level, warp mode, and so on). Then copy the clip by using the shortcut keys Ctrl (Cmnd) + C and go to Live's Arranger View. Zoom in to match Figure 14.8 and paste several instances of the sample in a small two- or four-measure area (and loop Live's playback).

Now click into each instance of the sample and change a few pitches. Start with simple intervals at first to get a feeling for how it works – 12, 7, 5, 3, 2, and 1 semitone variances. Feel free to move clips for rhythmic variety (by dragging them). Also, add dynamics by changing volume levels. Once you get a melody you like, check to be sure that your overall level is not peaking in the master meter, and then render the audio. You now have a solid melody or bass loop that can be re-imported for easier sequencing. Or, you can copy and paste your melody/bass section within your current Ableton Live song. Figure 14.9 is an example of a piano melody I created while writing this section. I used a single note piano sample to make the whole line. Hint: You can use multiple tracks so that you don't eliminate a sample's sustain.

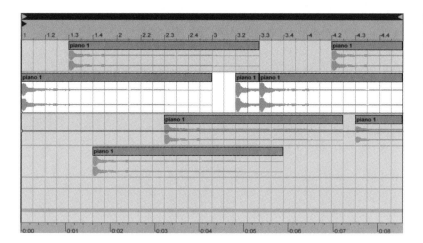

Figure 14.9
A melody made by repitching a one-shot sample.

One precaution to consider when using this technique, is that Live's repitch mode will play the sample at various lengths (and pitches). In this instance, lower pitch notes can become noticeably longer, and high-pitched notes will be shorter.

Clip View creativity

Improvising with a Clip's settings while you are in record mode can be a great way of making new samples, beats, and effects. Here is how to do this:

1 Load a drum or rhythmic synth/guitar loop into a clip slot in Session View.
2 Put Live in record mode, by clicking the Automation Record button.
3 Begin recording and play (Launch) the clip.
4 While recording and clip is playing, grab the clip's loop offset arrow and drag it back and forth. I find that gradually jogging it back and forth from left to right around the middle of the loop works best.
5 Then, try messing with the sample's Transpose setting. You can use this to make melodies or just for re-pitch effects. Either way, it can be extremely powerful.
6 Stop recording and go to Live's Arrangement window. You will now see a separate clip for each tweak made during the recording process (Figure 14.10).
7 Listen to your performance and make a mental note of sections that sound particularly good. I usually clean up and then render these subsections of the larger performance.

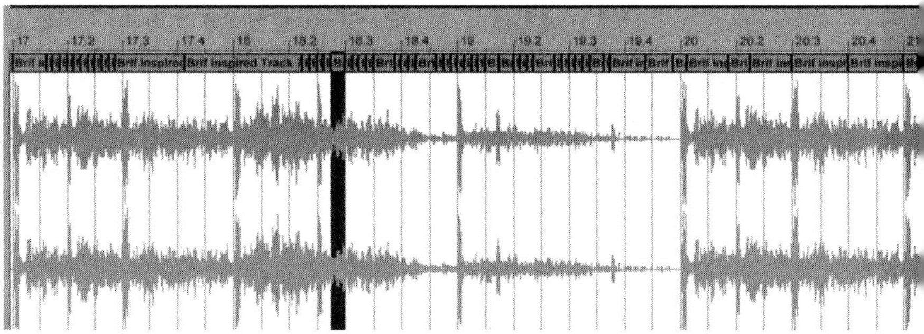

Figure 14.10
Each clip adjustment, during the recording process, becomes a new clip in Arranger View.

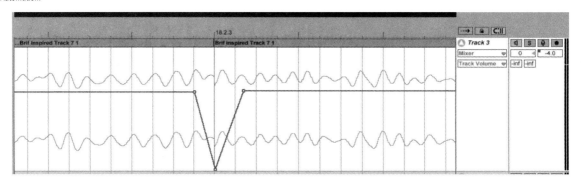

Figure 14.11
Cleaning up digital pops in Arranger View by using Automation.

Minimizing performance strain (reprise)

Effects guzzle plenty of valuable CPU juice. To combat the ill effects of, well, too many effects, I frequently rely on the following tips and workarounds (listed in order of preference).

- **Streamline effects**   Many of Live's included effects contain sections or modules that can be turned off. In the Powersave tip in Chapter 6, 'Playing Live...Live', I mentioned that by deactivating unnecessary bands of Live's EQ Four, you can shave a couple of points from your CPU meter. Live's reverb functions in three separate 'quality' modes – economy, comfort, and first class modes can be chosen under the Global tab). Other sections, or portions, of effects that will save processing power when omitted (if you don't need them) are Reverb's Filtering, Spin, Diffusion, and Chorus Activation buttons, Chorus's Delay 2 Portion, Filter Delay's L, L+R, or R delays or filters, Vinyl Distortion's tracking model or pinch effect, and/or Redux's bit reduction. In Figure 14.12, I have turned off Reverb's Spin and Diffusion options and am using Reverb's Economy setting. The difference is about five percent less CPU drain.
- **Sends**   In Chapter 8, 'Live's Effects', I recommended taking advantage of Live's sends channels. Simply take any effect that you have created on more than one track and, instead, 'share' it on a send. For example if you are using several instances of Live's Reverb on several different tracks, try consolidating by placing one reverb on a send, and then turn up the send on each track. You can then delete the multiple Reverb plug-ins for each track and save a virtual ton of processing power. If the sound changes too dramatically for you, try using

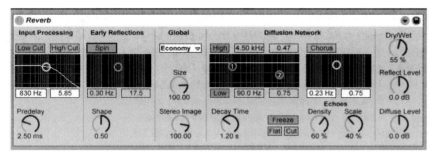

Figure 14.12
Turn off modules of an effect plug-in to save power.

the Sends Only output on the channels (as seen in Figure 14.13). You can add up to four sends in a given ALS (Ableton Live Set).

- **Render audio with effects**
Sometimes using the sends or streamlining the effects just doesn't do the trick. If this is the case, I ask myself if all the effects are absolutely necessary (often the answer is no). However, sometimes I do need all of the effects to achieve the sound I am going for. In this instance, I will render the effect-laden loop(s) (or scene(s) in Session View). In other words, I'll make a permanent copy of the loop/sample and use this file in place of the CPU-intensive effects and original dry loop(s). After doing so, I delete the original files and effects from my Live arrangement and save the set with a new name to ensure that I can

Figure 14.13
Route a track's output to Sends Only to simulate the effect at the channel level.

always view the originals. If you have forgotten how to render, see Chapter 7, 'Editing Your Performance'. In Figure 14.14a, I have selected a scene with several loops running through multiple audio effects plug-ins. In Figure 14.14b, I have rendered that scene, imported the clip, and can now play the rendered scene from a single clip with dramatically improved CPU efficiency. You could do this for each scene in a song if you are concerned about crashes or dropouts. Remember that once you have rendered a scene, you will no longer be able to adjust levels. Make a habit of saving the original mix so you can always return to the original in case you change your mind.

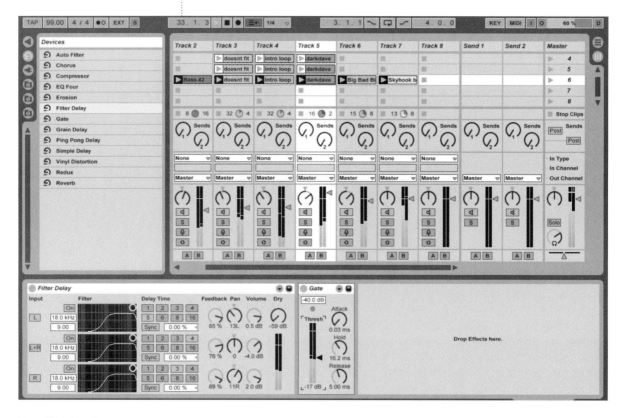

Figure 14.14a (above)
Several heavily affected clips playing in Live.

Notice the change in CPU usage

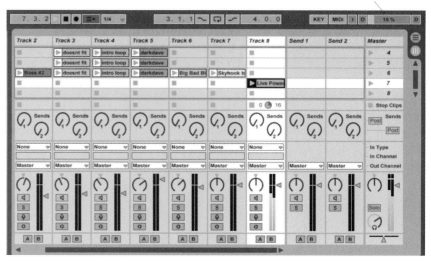

Figure 14.14b
Rendered as a single loop, you will no longer need original effects and loops.

Linking two computers

In earlier chapters, we explored several ways to synchronize Live with your software applications (using ReWire) and with your hardware (using MIDI). For my last tip, we will combine the two sync concepts by inviting your friends over to jam. Simply decide whose computer will be the master, establish a MIDI link (master computer's output to slave computer's input), set up the master to send Time Code and the slave to receive it, and go. Inexpensive MIDI splitters and multiple outputs can make the number of players limitless, though some musical orchestration (organization) is recommended. You might assign one musician to cover the drum and percussion loops, another the synths, and another sound effects. Or, you might have two Live musicians playing within the same band, or add a singer for a futuristic improv trio. The future of Live may just include two, three, or more musicians getting together, patching their laptop into the MIDI chain, firing up a ReWire application or two, and then jamming the night away. For added fun, try recording the output to some kind of multi-track recorder.

As you can imagine, there are many more tricks and tips still waiting to be discovered in Live. As you spend time experimenting with new ways of working, you will certainly discover what works for you. Also, check out Ableton's user forum that now features a section called Tips & Tricks. I encourage you to share your ideas and interact with other Live users. It's a great community to be a part of. I learn something nearly every time I go.

In closing, I'd like to sincerely thank you for your time and patience in reading my very first book, and what is presumably the world's first book on Ableton Live software. I've worked hard to make sure that it is as up-to-date as possible. But should you stumble onto a tip, trick, or scrap of info that doesn't quite do what I said it is supposed to do, there is most likely an update waiting for you at www.Ableton.com (click on downloads), or a note at my site dedicated to this book, www.brinboxing.net/abletonlive. This entire book was based on version 2.0.3, and the 2.1 beta, and was tested on both an Apple Macintosh Powerbook G4 667 with 512 MB of RAM, and a generic 800 MHz Athlon (with 256 MB of RAM) running Windows ME and XP on two separate partitions.

I can attest that Ableton Live 2 is a stable, elegant, musical, forward thinking, dynamic, and inspirational software application. I hope you find it to be the same, and enjoy many hours of making your own musical vision a reality.

Shortcut keys

S hortcut keys save time and help alleviate frustration when doing repetitive or multiple tasks in Live (or any other software application). While it is generally not a good idea to rip out pages from a book, I am going to advise you do exactly this with Appendix A. In my experience, there are two ways to learn keystroke software shortcuts: to repeatedly practice a newly discovered shortcut key combo, or to print out the manual's shortcut key list and carefully try each one. This appendix is intended to be a supplement to the Ableton Manual's shortcut key list, and to provide key (pun intended) shortcuts that I have found extra helpful while using Live and writing this book.

General shortcuts

Some shortcuts are universal – we'll call these general shortcuts because these can be used in any Live view. They also happen to be among my favourite shortcuts to use.

- Tab. This command will always toggle Session and Arranger Views.
- Spacebar. Start and stop audio playback (or recording if it is armed).
- Ctrl (Cmnd) + C copies any selected clip or selection of audio.
- Ctrl (Cmnd) + V pastes the clip on the clipboard – the last clip copied or cut.
- Ctrl (Cmnd) + X cuts any clip or selection of audio (and places it on the clipboard).
- Ctrl (Cmnd) + T inserts a track into your Ableton Live Song.
- Ctrl (Cmnd) + Alt + T inserts a Send Track into your Ableton Live Song.
- F1–F8 keys toggle mute and un-mute for tracks 1 through 8. An excellent live performance tool.
- F11 toggles Live back and forth from Full Screen mode to normal view.
- F12 toggles from Clip View, Bus, and Track (Effects on selected track) View.
- Shift + F12 hides or shows the Clip, Bus, or Track view.
- The ? key toggles Live's Info view. For this command, press Shift + ? with your right hand.

Session View shortcuts

When working in Session View, I have found several shortcuts to be invaluable during both live performance and recording sessions.

- Return. Launches selected loop or scene.
- Arrow keys move throughout Clip Slot Grid.
- Ctrl (Cmnd) + D duplicates the current clip to the scene below.
- Ctrl (Cmnd) + Shift + D copies (inserts and duplicates) an entire scene below the currently highlighted scene.
- Ctrl (Cmnd) + I inserts a new blank scene below the currently highlighted scene or clip slot.
- Ctrl (Cmnd) + M toggles MIDI Map Mode on or off. This can be done during play mode.
- Ctrl (Cmnd) + K toggles the Key Map Mode on or off. This can also be done in play mode.
- Ctrl + E (while highlighting a Clip Slot or Scene) toggles the Slot Button in and out for the selected Clip Slot or Scene. This is helpful if you want a loop to repeat while progressing to the next scene. Simply remove the Slot Button beneath the Clip you would like to continue playing.

Arranger View shortcuts

Arranger View requires a different group of tasks than Session View, though many of the same shortcuts apply. Take a few moments to practice these commands. Repeat each one several times to see if you can't form a good habit or two.

- Ctrl (Cmnd) + D copies and pastes (duplicate) the audio selection immediately after itself. This is a great command for extended repeating of a complexly edited loop or group of loops and samples.
- Ctrl (Cmnd) + Shift + D inserts a copy (duplicate) of all tracks occurring at the same time as your selection at the end of your selection. This is a great command for quickly building an arrangement.
- Ctrl (Cmnd) + I inserts the amount of silence corresponding with your selection. If you select four measures, and then use this command, you will insert four new measures of silence.
- Ctrl (Cmnd) + Delete deletes all breakpoint envelope automation for all parameters in the selected portion of the arrangement.
- F9 arms the Automation Record Button. While track is armed and Live is playing, use this shortcut to begin recording.
- Ctrl (Cmnd) + E splits any selected Clip at the Insert Mark. This is a great tool if you want to segment your clips so that changes can be made to smaller portions of the original clip.
- Ctrl (Cmnd) + F instructs Live to scroll through the arrangement as it plays. This way you can watch the events as they happen.
- Ctrl (Cmnd) + G toggles the Snap To Grid feature in Live's Arranger View.

Other handy strokes

These last few keystrokes may not revolutionize your workflow, but they are still handy to know when working in Live for extended periods of time.

- Ctrl (Cmnd) + Alt + O toggles Overview in Session View.
- Ctrl (Cmnd) + Alt + I toggles Input / Output view in both Session and Arranger Views.
- Ctrl (Cmnd) + Alt + S toggles Sends in and out of view in both Session and Arranger views.
- Ctrl (Cmnd) + Alt + M toggles Live's mixer in and out of view in both Session and Arranger views.
- + and – keys will zoom you in and out of the selected Arrangement or Clip View. You will need to hold down the Shift key for the + shortcut unless your keyboard has an additional number pad on the right hand side. Then you can simply use the + and - calculator style keypad keys.
- Ctrl (Cmnd) + E enables you to rename the selected track or scene. Press Enter to accept your new name and Esc to abandon the change. If you do this in Session View, you can press Tab (instead of Enter) to rename the very next Scene or Track.

Web resources

E arlier in this book, I mentioned that a website has been created so that you can download some starter loops and a few helpful Ableton Live 2 (ALS file) templates. I will also use this site to post any notable *Making Music with Ableton Live* updates and corrections, as well as other relevant Live news and notes. What follows are some helpful hints and general information about the website.

- The site will be hosted at www.brainboxing.net/abletonlive.
- In the event there is any problem with the above link, the templates and loop content discussed in this Appendix can be found by going to www.pc-publishing.com/support, and following the links from there.
- You will find Live templates, loops, news, and perhaps even a trick or two.
- The templates are yours to use and abuse, and can be downloaded as often as you need. Do with them what you will.
- Loop and sample content is treated a bit differently. Any sample or loop downloaded from the site is intended strictly for personal use. These loops are for your own individual learning and experimentation. If you want to use the material in a song, performance, or commercial application, you must contact the original vendor or sample/loop creator and pay them for their creation.
- From the site, you will be able to contact me, the author. Have a suggestion? Something to say? Idea about how to use Live? Please send me a note and let me know what you are doing with Live.

> ### Info
> **The horse's mouth**
>
> When it comes to getting the skinny on Ableton Live 2-related products (including both software plug-ins, helper applications, and studio/stage hardware), make sure that you visit www.ableton.com, and then click on links – located under the support tab. From there you will find a healthy assortment of links subcategorized into music software, soundcards, midi controller, magazines, research, and various.

Live templates

When working on various projects within Live, I find it helpful to have several pre-configured templates ready for different kinds of situations. For instance, you may want to quickly record a new idea, or be able to recall a previously made ReWire routed song. Or, you may be preparing to DJ somewhere and have multiple setups depending upon the kind of mix, effects, and setup you are using. The next sections describe the first three templates (available at the Web site) made in support of this book. Be sure to download the example and read along as you go.

At the time of this writing, I have three specific templates to get you started. Others may appear on the site at a later time, so do check back. Also, you will almost certainly want to further customize my templates to fit your customized machine and working methods. These templates were created in order to provide you with a good starting point and some inspiration for creating your own templates and song-starters.

Multi-tracker template

The idea of multi-tracking simple ideas in classic singer-songwriter-with–a-four-track fashion is not lost in the digital audio workstation world – just harder to get to. With Multi-Tracker (Fig. B.1), I have provided a simple four-track layout with four mono tracks, so that you can quickly start a Live project when the creative urge strikes you. Remember that you will need to Save Live Set As immediately after opening the template, since the Live templates I have created are Live Sets as well. I recommend creating a folder near where you keep your other Live songs simply called Live Templates.

Figure B.1
Multi-tracker.

With Multi-Tracker, I have made some producer-friendly modifications. In an effort to be as consistent as possible, I have maintained the following schemes for each of the four templates. Each of my key mappings are in lowercase (not capped) – remember Live is case-sensitive.

For starters, I have assigned your computer keyboard's Q key to control Tap Tempo, W to start/stop the Metronome, and E to Arm Session recording. I find these three shortcuts particularly handy when recording and overdubbing in Live. I generally use Tap Tempo to find the tempo that fits the intent of the song or piece of music I am working on by humming a few bars of the melody and tapping my left pinky on the Q. Once I feel I have dialed in the tempo (the tempo readout stops jumping all over the place), I hit W (the next custom key shortcut) to start the metronome. Since the metronome can get obnoxious when in continuous use, use the same W to turn it off.

Other shortcut keys include A for Punch In, S for Loop Switch, and D for Punch Out. Notice how I have kept all of these self-made short cuts on the left side of the keyboard. That way, if I am playing a MIDI-keyboard or synth with my right hand, I can punch in and out, loop the selection, and handle metronome functions. I have also set up each track's Arm Arrangement Recording button to coincide with a key. Z toggles the first track (called Left 1) in and out of record mode. X corresponds to track 2 (Right 1), C to Left 2, and V to Right 2.

For my final key map trick, I have set up F to be Live's Stop button (on the Control Bar). By having a QWERTY keyboard set up like this, you can record without ever having to pick up a mouse. To do this, press F twice to reset Live to play at position 1.1.1. Then activate Left 1 (track 1) to record by pressing Z. Activate the metronome and set the tempo using the W and Q keys, respectively. And then press Play (Spacebar). Live will start playing and be ready to record. When you are ready, press E and you're in. To stop, you can press Spacebar, and then F twice more to 'rewind the decks'.

Notice in Figure B.2 (the Arranger View of the Multi-Tracker Template) that I have set up Live's loop region between measures 17 and 33 so that you can practice a part for 16 bars before you punch in and out of your recording. These constraints can be changed within a single drag of the mouse, but should serve as an example of how to approach overdubs.

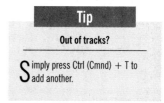

Tip

Out of tracks?

Simply press Ctrl (Cmnd) + T to add another.

Figure B.2
Punch In and Punch Out setup in the Multi-tracker Arranger View.

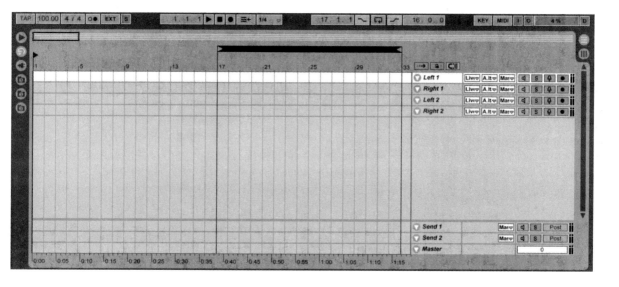

ReWire-station template

Setting up ReWire templates can take a little time – especially if you plan on routing several ReWire tracks to separate channels. In the following ReWire-Station template (Figure B.3), I have set up Live to be the ReWire master and to receive eight mono tracks from a Propellerhead's Reason project. Of course, you can easily do less by deleting tracks, or you can add tracks, so long as your computer can keep up.

Figure B.3
ReWire-Station template has eight mono ReWire channels.

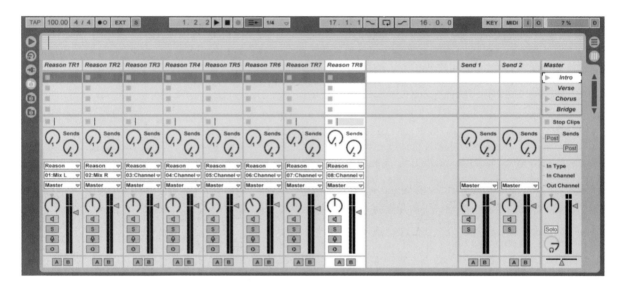

You need to set up Reason's outputs to correspond to these eight inputs (Figure B.4). I put this Reason 2.0 template on the site (called ReWire-Station Template1), but you may want to reconfigure. I recommend one synth, sampler, or sound per track for maximum separation. If you are short on resources, simply delete three or four tracks by highlighting the track and pressing your delete key.

Figure B.4
Reason's outputs must correspond to Live's eight inputs in this template.

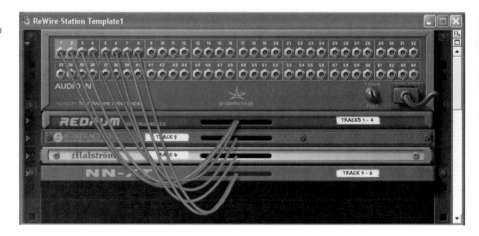

As we saw in Chapter 13, 'ReWire – Synchronizing Your Software', there are several different ReWire-capable applications, such as Project5, MAX/MSP, radiaL, and others. If you find yourself repeatedly linking Live with any one of these applications, I encourage you to spend some time developing a workable template. One time-saving idea is to take this Reason template and simply reselect your channel input source. You might also want to add ReWire-configured tracks to the Multi-Track template in the preceding section.

DJ-mix template

Another idea I find helpful is to set up an empty DJ-Mix template (Figure B.5) with two (or more) tracks that are preconfigured for your Live mixing style. Since this template will be used most often in a live situation, I have inserted an Ableton EQ Four and Compressor plug-in on the master output. Each of the four session tracks contains another EQ Four effect and is set up to work with Live's Crossfader (alternating between A and B). Depending on your mix style or preferences, you may want to set up a Ping Pong Delay, Auto Filter, or other effects on your aux sends channels. I also commonly assign a computer keyboard key to each effect's Activator Button so that I can apply quick bursts of delay or other creative effects.

Figure B.5
A DJ-Mix template should be customized to allow for quick track insertion and crossfader use.

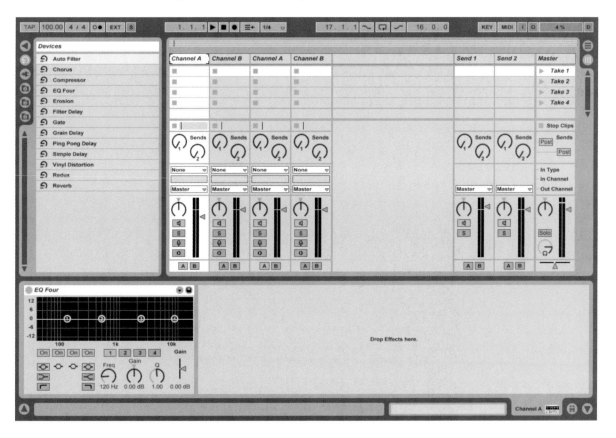

My method for using this template is to open the folder where my preconfigured songs reside, and then drag several tracks to tracks 1 and 2. When DJing, I invariably cue up the first several tracks when I get to the club, so that I can spend the first couple of minutes dialing in the compressor and EQ on the main output. I then create smaller loops of large songs and place these over on tracks 3 and 4. Hint: Once you get a group of loops or song sections working together, you may want to copy an instance of each loop to a single scene, for later recall or too use another night. When I am finished with my set (at the end of the performance) I save my set using the Save Live Set As. Warning: Don't save your DJ sets as self-contained because they will be a huge redundant file. Instead, just be careful to always put your songs in the same file on your hard drive so that Live can find them when you try to recreate moments from previous sets.

Index